The Well-Traveled Casket

To a wonderful native
Oregonian. Enjoy,
Love,
Twilo

The Well-Traveled Casket

A Collection of Oregon Folklife

By
Tom Nash and
Twilo Scofield

Illustrated by
Don Adkins

Meadowlark Press
1974 Villard
Eugene, Oregon 97403
1999

Originally printed in 1992 by University of Utah Press
1993 1994 1995 1996

∞ This symbol indicates books printed on paper that meets the minimum requirements
of American National Standard for Information Services—Permanence of Paper for
Printed Library Materials, ANSI A39.38-1984.

Library of Congress Cataloging-in-Publication Data

Nash, Tom, 1945-
    The well-traveled casket: Oregon folklore/ by
Tom Nash and Twilo Scofield; illustrated by Don Adkins.
        p. cm.
    Includes bibliographical references and index.
    ISBN 0-87480-390-X
    1. Folklore—Oregon. 2. Oregon—history. 3. Travel.
I. Scofield, Twilo. II. Title.
GR110.O7N37 1992
398.2`09795—dc20   92-53609
                                                                    CIP

To Robert and Mia Scofield, Carolyn Scofield, Cameron and
Alexis Scofield, Kelly and Paul Nash

Don Adkins, whose artistry and sense of humor brought life to many of the pages of
The Well-Traveled Casket, did not live to see the publication of his delightful illustrations.
To his memory we dedicate this book.

Contents

Preface ix

The Name *Oregon* 3

Unforgettable Moments in Oregon History 4

Oregon Impressions 5

Oregon Folks 7

Introduction 8

    The Oregon Coast 11

    The Willamette Valley 33

    Southern Oregon 71

    Central Oregon 95

    Northeastern Oregon 123

    Southeastern Oregon 145

A Folklore History 163

Works Consulted 165

Index 171

Preface

A regional identity is born when a group of people share the experiences they enjoy, as well as those they must endure. These common adventures, occupations, hopes and dreams, codes of living, and cultural values form and enrich our regional folk spirits. Eventually they become as important to the newcomer as to the descendants of Oregon's first settlers and pioneers.

The Well-Traveled Casket weaves these adventures into a folklore history; these pages narrate the Native American and pioneer experience, as told and retold through successive generations. But the book also stands as a cultural geography, a map of diversity and change as found in the far corners of the state. Telling their regional stories are Basques from the Southeast, Russian Old Believers from the upper Willamette Valley, Scandinavian fishermen at the Oregon Coast, Native Americans from mountainous Central Oregon, Scots-Irish traders in the Southern counties, and Chinese miners in the vast and wild Northeast. In this collection are songs, legends, proverbs, recipes, place-names, tall tales, superstitions, customs, beliefs, and myth tales, the pages portraying our strengths and weaknesses, our joys and sorrows, our special eccentricities and conventions.

The Cascade Mountains, dividing the "wet side" from the "dry side," are sometimes called the Sociological Alps of Oregon. Yet culturally and geographically, Oregon divides not into simple halves, but into six identifiable regions. To citizens in the Southeast, where sheep outnumber people, Oregon is a portrait of sagebrush and brown plains; the rancher in Malheur or Lake County spins legends of devastating winds and fierce drought. In the mining country of the Northeast, where history reads like a Wild West novel, the colorful tales of frontier existence make life on the "wet side" seem dull. In the soggy west, Pacific Coast Oregonians swap superstitions about fishing and commerce on the high seas; from Depoe Bay to Astoria, a good "fish story" is always welcome. In the lush Willamette Valley, "Webfooters" celebrate heavy rains and rich, dark soil; farmers in the Valley wink when they say, "Why, around here cucumbers grow so fast that, on a warm day, the vines can overtake a slow mule." Central Oregon residents treasure the etiological legends of Native

Americans, many of them telling the origins of famous landmarks, such as Crater Lake, Mt. Jefferson, or the Bridge of the Gods. And in Southern Oregon, sometimes known as the mythical "State of Jefferson," the great grandchildren of pioneer settlers entertain each other with Hathaway Jones stories or such timeless narratives as "Goldilocks on the Oregon Trail."

The Well-Traveled Casket is an anthem in many voices. From its six distinct regions, we have gathered a cultural heritage that reflects differences of geography and history, even while preserving the notion of Oregon as a place apart from all others. This collection is a sampling of Oregon life, the pages contributed by countless Oregonians willing to share their experiences and knowledge. The place-name legends derive from pioneer diaries, historical society files, centennial magazines, newspaper columns, and from early surveys, such as William Gladstone Steel's "Place

Names'' edition of *Steel Points*. The best source remains *Oregon Geographic Names*, the pioneering study written by Lewis A. McArthur. Many of the narratives come from the Depression-era files of the WPA Federal Writers' Project; others from the extensive manuscript collections in the Randall V. Mills Folklore Archives at the University of Oregon or the State of Jefferson Archives at Southern Oregon State College. Added to these narratives and folkways are items from personal interviews, library manuscripts, private collections, and other Oregon treasures.

We are grateful to several people for help in preparing this book: Barre Toelken, Director of Folklore and Folklife Studies at Utah State University; Sharon Sherman, Director of Folklore Studies at the University of Oregon; Joanne Mulcahey, Oregon State Folklorist; Kim Stafford, Lewis and Clark College; Melinda Hoder and Bill Goldsmith, archivists at the Randall V. Mills Archives of Northwest Folklore; Jerry McReal of Addison-Wesley Publishers; Kerry Lee Droesch and Cindy Ferguson of Southern Oregon State College. We also want to thank Paula von Loewenfeldt of Ashland for editing assistance and ''Gwendolyn,'' our anonymous reader from the University of Utah Press. Research for *The Well-Traveled Casket* was assisted by a grant from the Carpenter Foundation of Ashland.

The Well-Traveled Casket

No state in the Union presents greater contrasts within its borders than does Oregon. These contrasts not only include topography, but climate, architecture, customs, speech, even general way of living. Tillamook in the west may be drenched with warm soft rain on the same day the temperature hits 20 below in Baker, with a dazzling sun in the sky. The big ranch house near Burns, hedged against the weather with rows of poplar and surrounded by sagebrush, has little but shelter in common with the Spanish-type stucco home to be seen on Coos Bay and points south. The lutefisk piled high on the Astoria sidewalk at Christmastime would look queer in the wild-west Pendleton.

—Stewart H. Holbrook, *New York Times*, September 20, 1940

The Name *Oregon*

Oregon has collected many nicknames. Historians call it "The Beaver State." Long-distance drivers, dodging rabbits and prairie dogs, have sometimes referred to Oregon as "The Rodent State." Geographers write about "Oregon: Farthest West" or "Oregon: Nearest Japan." Romantics, noting Oregon's February 14th founding date, call this "The Valentine State" or "The State with a Heart." Others have proposed "The Sunset State" or "The End of the Trail State."

More interesting is the name "Oregon" itself. The first published reference to Oregon dates from 1768. Jonathan Carver set out from Boston in 1766 and traveled through the Great Lakes to the headwaters of the Mississippi. Later, while visiting England, he wrote that the Indians of the Great Lakes area knew of a great western river called the Oregon. Archbishop Blanchet, the Catholic prelate who arrived in Oregon City in 1838, had a different notion about the name. His theory was that the Spanish explorers named the region after their word *oreja*, meaning "ear." When the explorers first visited this country, said Blanchet, they found the Indians with big ears, enlarged by the loads of ornaments that dangled from earlobes.

Textbooks written in the first half of the century told schoolchildren that the name Oregon derived from the Spanish *oregano*, a plant commonly called "marjoram" today. Although the Oregon country indeed sprouts this plant, nothing in the records of eighteenth-century Spanish explorers suggests naming the region by its flowering herbs. Other guesses about the state's name have been no more convincing than the theories of Carver and Blanchet. Hall J. Kelley in 1829 wrote in one of his pamphlets that the name of the great western river is borrowed from the river *Orjun* in the Chinese Tartar country. William G. Steel, first president of the Oregon Geographic Board, said that the appellation came from *over-un-gon*, a Shoshone word meaning "a place of plenty." Joaquin Miller, the colorful frontier poet, said that the Emerald State derived its name from the Spanish *aura agua*, meaning "gently falling waters," a reference to the persistent rainfall in the region. Others have argued that the Spanish explorers, remembering the patronage of Ferdinand of Aragon, consort to Queen Isabella, named the area after the prince's homeland, pronouncing *Oregon* much the same as the Spanish pronounced *Aragon*.

These theories, while colorful and quaint, are only theories. In 1812, when John Jacob Astor petitioned Congress for assistance in settling the territory, he did not use the word Oregon in his papers. Actually, the word was not popularly employed until 1817, when William Cullen Bryant, who happened to read Carver's account of his western travels, used the name Oregon in his poem "Thanatopsis."

Unforgettable Moments in Oregon History

*The pioneers were all honest because there was nothing to steal,
sober because there was nothing to drink, no misers because there was
nothing to hoard, industrious because it was either work or starve.*
—Pioneer settler Peter J. Burnett, 1848

1810 An intrepid group of travelers, led by the Winship brothers, landed on the Columbia just east of Astoria and began construction of a fort and trading post. After eight days of incessant rain, the soggy settlers climbed back aboard the *Albatross* and returned to Boston.

1811 On March 23, the *Tonquin* arrived at the mouth of the Columbia River, bringing a load of pigs. Eight men were lost crossing the bar, but all the pigs survived the landing.

1814 The first white woman, Jane Barnes, mistress of Donald McTavish, was lured to Astoria by a promise of "a trunk full of fine clothes and a lifetime annuity." McTavish, trying to impress Barnes with a dangerous swim in the Columbia River, drowned shortly after her arrival.

1834 On July 27, Reverend Jason Lee delivered the first sermon preached west of the Rockies. The audience, French-speaking trappers and Indians conversant in Chinook jargon, nodded politely throughout the entire sermon, delivered in English.

1842 Mary Ann Smith became Oregon's first divorcee. A jury granted her divorce and awarded her "all the rights and immunities of a state of celibacy."

1844 A congressman from Kentucky rose in the House to announce that Oregon "might be a land of promise—it might be a perfect Canaan, but if so, it is contrary to all accounts I have ever received from Oregon. It invariably has been described as consisting of waste sand bogs in part, and the remainder mountains, and covered with volcanic remains."

1848 Joab Powell, opening a session of the Oregon Territorial Legislature, offered the shortest prayer in the history of that body: "Lord, forgive them, for they know not what they do."

1849 Abraham Lincoln was appointed governor of the Oregon Territory by President Zachary Taylor. Lincoln turned down the appointment, however, when wife Mary Todd Lincoln refused to move "into the wilderness." The appointment went to Joe Lane, vice-presidential candidate on the pro-slavery ticket of John C. Breckenridge in 1860.

1854 The inappropriately named Charity Lamb secured her place in Northwest history by making her husband one of Oregon's first murder victims, cleaving his head with an axe as he sat with the children at the dinner table.

1862 "The Frenchman," a notorious gambler who poisoned several men, was captured by Eastern Oregon lawmen. As a friendly gesture on the evening before his hanging, he prepared an oyster dinner for the sheriff and several deputies.

1890 In the middle of a hot July night, cowboys from Burns rode to Harney City and stole the court records, giving Burns a decided edge in the controversy over which city should be named the Harney County seat.

1905 The Crook County Sheep Shooters Association took responsibility for the slaughter of 10,000 sheep, contributing to the fervor of the Oregon range wars.

1921 The Oregon House officially seated a dead man. Representative Stannard, who died on the trip to Salem, was not disqualified because "being dead was not one of the criteria for exclusion."

1970 On November 11, the Oregon State Highway Division set a half-ton charge of dynamite under the carcass of a dead whale on the beach near Florence. Pieces of the six-ton whale rained down on gawkers and bystanders. Several half-ton chunks also landed, one flattening the roof of a parked car. The stench was noticeable for miles.

1999 In February, the *New Carissa*, an oil tanker, ran aground at Coos Bay and began spilling its cargo. Subsequently, the tanker was burned, bombed, napalmed, shelled, and torpedoed. At the mid-point of these assaults, the *New Carissa* broke in half. Soon after, on a dark and stormy night, the United States Navy towed the bow section out to sea for scuttling. By morning, the *New Carissa* was back, oozing crude oil onto the beaches at Waldport.

Oregon Impressions

Oregon has many faces. It is the Klickitat Indians meeting to barter near Oregon City, Wascos fishing from platforms at Celilo Falls, Modocs gathering *tule* reeds on Klamath Lake. It is miners lining the Illinois River, a thousand hands sifting the silt. It is a windswept clearing where wagon ruts dent the meadow floor, where names like Barlow, Chief Joseph, Applegate, and Sacajawea still whisper in the wind. It is a young girl's grave marker etched into a tree alongside the Old Oregon Trail.

Oregon is mountains so high that the snow never melts, and it is valleys etched by chilly streams. It is clear, windless skies framing a lone hawk. It is the wild and scenic Rogue River and Steens Mountain rising above the Alvord Desert like a prehistoric deity. Oregon is the first snow falling on Black Butte and aspen leaves fluttering through the blue fall sky. It is Mt. Hood, "our mountain," visible for miles in any direction. It is Pilot Rock, silent sentinel of the Northeast, and Eugene, the Willamette Valley hub, bustling with art galleries, theatres, skid roads, parks, cloverleafs, malls, and ethnic shops.

Oregon is Shakespeare under the stars, coffee at Vy's Pies on the McKenzie Highway, barbecued beef in Albina, and trout fishing near the Steamboat Inn. It is the working hands of a Dayton bean picker, a Brookings nurse, an Astoria fisherman, an Ontario farmer, a Medford mill worker, a Bandon cheese maker, and a Spray fence rider. It is the friendly smile of an Enterprise teacher, a Henley truck driver, or a West Linn housewife.

Oregon is people with fiercely independent politics, who consistently cross party lines. It's a state that elects people like Wayne Morse, Edith Green, Tom McCall, and Maureen Neuberger. It is the nation's first "bottle bill" and the Bonneville Dam. It is the homeless huddling under the Burnside Bridge and a Lake Oswego lawyer taking the kids out for a cruise. Oregon is a Chiloquin "mom and pop" grocery with one gas pump, and it's the international headquarters of Nike shoes.

Oregon is shooting the rapids on the Klamath River, wind surfing on the Columbia, fly-fishing on the Metolius, boating on the Willamette. It is camping among Hart Mountain's pronghorn and badgers; it is braving a brisk night at the nearby hot springs, looking at stars close enough to touch. Oregon is sitting by the fire listening to North Coast rains, and it is watching the wind drive snowdrifts through the Ochocos. It is a pack of coyotes yapping their way across the rimrock at night. Oregon is diamond sand sparkling in the alkali desert on an early morning, somewhere between Lakeview and Valley Falls. It is the relentless pounding surf at Cape Perpetua and pure spring waters in the Malheur Cave. It is acres of onions in Ontario, rows of iris in Brooks, fields of lilies in Brookings, and miles of wheat in Maupin.

Oregon is a prize-winning squash at the Lane County Fair or the biggest Red Delicious at the Helvetia Applefest. It is fireworks at John Day's Kam Wah Chung Days and a kaleidoscope sky over the Burns High Desert Balloon Festival. Oregon is the Merlin Buffalo Barbecue, the Keuzer Irish Festival, the Heppner St. Patrick's Day Parade, the Neskowin Kite and Sand Castle Contest. It is the Black Sheep Gathering in Cottage Grove, the Calapooia Roundup, the Siletz Pow-wow, the Paisley Mosquito Festival, the Dufur Threshing Bee, Junction City's Scandinavian Festival, Sternwheeler Days at Cascade Locks, and Rogue River's National Rooster Crowing Contest.

Oregon is Portland's Pittock Mansion, Hells Canyon Dam, the Lewis and Clark Salt Cairn, the Charles Applegate House in Scottsburg, the Chief Joseph Memorial, Wasco County Courthouse, the Newport Waxworks,

Amity's Hidden Springs Winery, the Wolf Creek Tavern, the Peter Iredale shipwreck, Hoodoo Ski Bowl, the China-town Gateway in Portland, Ukiah's Lehman Hot Springs, the Mt. Hood Railroad, Multnomah Falls, the Snake River Canyon, the Wheatland Ferry, and the Sea Lion Caves.

Oregon is a sense of place, a state of the heart. It is a recognition of warts as well as beauty marks, of saints intermingled with scoundrels. And finally—for better or worse—Oregon is a lifelong love affair with the people who call it ''home.''

Oregon Folks

Oregon's diverse population can be described in many ways, including song. "Oregon Folks" was first performed in Champoeg in August 1982 by Rusty Modrell and the "Good Ole Boys" string band:

OREGON FOLKS

Some like to live on the far eastern side
Where the skin on their bones gets as dry as rawhide;
The wind blows so hard 'cross the dry desert lands,
They tie down their buildings with big rubber bands.

They all live on clams at the coast where it's wet,
For when the tide's out, the table is set.
From belching to spouting, it never subsides
And their bladders all rise and then fall with the tides.

In the valley they get so depressed when it's dry;
They've got to stay wet or their moss starts to die.
Their webs start to crack, and they can't stand the pain;
They only feel good in the mud and the rain.

One rainy day in the east of the state
An old man passed out from a bump on his pate.
One giant raindrop had sure done him in;
It took six pails of sand to revive him again.

Just what kind of person lays claim to this state?
It might be a miner or high magistrate.
They're farmers, they're doctors, loggers and lawyers,
Fiddlers and sailors and hashers and sawyers.

They're rough and they're rugged, they're gentle and sweet.
There's no doubt about it, they're Oregon's elite.
Good-looking and friendly, there's nothing they lack;
They're a rare combination with moss on their back.

When they all get together, what a fine lot they are;
They travel by foot, bike, bus, horseback, and car.
Both sides of the mountains, from Seaside to Brothers,
They travel for miles just to see all the others.

Bunchgrassers in the East and Webfoots in the West,
They all choose the climate that they like the best.
It's only fair they should have what they oughter;
In the East they choose hell; in the West it's high water.

Introduction

In January 1975, Debra Justus, a folklore student at the University of Oregon, braved Siuslaw River rains to fish for steelhead and to interview Joel, a Cheshire fisherman. Water conditions, he said, were nearly perfect. "You know, we might just see a little action today," he said. "The water is a clear green algae color, so we'll use those stinkin' eggs for bait. The water's just about right after that heavy rain a few days ago." However, after carefully outlining the best strategies and gear, Joel frowned at Justus. "I guess I should have told you sooner," he said, "but I doubt you'll catch anything today. You aren't wearing anything green. I've never seen anyone catch a steelie that they weren't wearing green."

As Debra Justus discovered, folklore drifts on unexpected currents. Folklore is so much a part of our lives that we seldom recognize it. Perhaps that is why defining folklore—and separating it from other kinds of information—is a problem. In its most obvious sense, folklore is "folk-learning," the collected wisdom of the people. The term *folklore* suggests traditional beliefs and practices that travel by word of mouth or circulate by example, mostly with an air of anonymity. However, the word *folklore* conjures other connotations, most of them misleading. Many people believe folklore exists only in rural communities, where wizened storytellers whittle, spit, and spin Paul Bunyan yarns. That image underestimates the power and pervasiveness of folklore traditions.

As *The Well-Traveled Casket* shows, folklore is found everywhere. After spending hundreds of dollars on "okie-drifters" and Shakespeare reels, Joel pulled a superstition from his tackle box. In the suburbs of Salem, a man visits his doctor for treatment of an eye infection, but while walking home through a clearing, dips his finger into "stump water" to treat a wart. A Coos Bay business executive, planning a two-week trip to New York, leaves the details to her travel agent, but when the itinerary arrives, she calls up to say, "I'd rather not fly on a Friday." In Oregon's largest city, the manager of the Portland Beavers scans his computerized baseball charts to determine a hitter's tendencies, then, while walking to the mound, leaps awkwardly to avoid stepping on the chalked baseline.

The bearers of the folk tradition are many: story-tellers, singers, cooks and bakers, crafters and artisans. They are a diverse group, men and women of various ethnic groups and ages, many of whom originally told their stories to folklore collectors from the University of Oregon. As early as 1968, students in Barre Toelken's folklore program began to gather lore from friends, classmates, relatives, coworkers, foreign students, and total strangers, contributing their findings to the Randall V. Mills Archives of Northwest Folklore, a rich repository filled with file folders, audiotapes, photographs, and art objects. In 1985, students at Southern Oregon State College first donated manuscripts to the State of Jefferson Folklore Archives, a library patterned after the University of Oregon model.

For the most part, the collectors carefully recorded their informants' places of residence, ethnic backgrounds, native languages, occupational groups, and the circumstances of collection, providing indispensable information on the texture (literary style) and context (atmosphere and setting) associated with the text. In Creswell, Linda Lorene Miller taped several hours of oral histories from Harry Telford, a onetime Wild West buckaroo who rode with Pete French on the famous P Ranch; in Hood River, Wendy Ng contacted *issei* and *nisei*, members of the Japanese community who had endured the internment camps in the 1940s; in the high-desert community of Malin, Twilo Scofield sampled sausage and pastries while gathering recipes from Ellen Rajnus, a Czech resident; at Sumpter, Chris Grissom and Candy Anderson gathered the outrageous histories of Eastern Oregon hard-rock mining days from old-timers; in Phoenix, Pamela Jones heard *la llorona* stories from Spanish-speaking women at a migrant workers' clinic; near Roseburg, George Braddock collected a wealth of backwood tales from wandering prospector Al Renfro.

Friends, neighbors, relatives, chance acquaintances—these are the bearers of folk tradition. The stories recorded in *The Well-Traveled Casket* echo the voices of Scots immigrant housewives, Afro-American teachers, Chinese laborers, Confederate sympathizers, Finnish fishermen, German communists, Umatilla Indians, French trappers, states-rights secessionists, Spanish-speaking cowboys, and Swedish loggers, with names like Edquist,

Rubio, Davis, Longcor, Red Horse, Keil, Powell, Tsugawa, Lewis, Haataja, al-Jabir, Swenson, Pustinen, Palanuk, Feldman, Mukai, Fong, Applegate, Tabler, Schweiger, Rogers, Wodtli, D'Angelo, Martinez, and Kornik.

These women and men, of course, did not create their own stories and folk beliefs, songs and foodways, but acquired them around campfires, in political meetings, at wedding showers, and in coffee shops. Some Oregonian traditions have traveled far, such as the Basque *pelota* (jai-alai) game and the Russian Old Believers' colorful costumes. In such cases, the distance from family and the sense of isolation caused the original immigrants to grasp tightly to ethnic beliefs, leaving these settlers often more attached to older folkways than their relatives who remained in homelands. Other narratives derive directly from Oregon history, such as the stories of the Oregon Trail or the discovery of gold in Baker County; these tales usually reflect the "sense of place" that is evident throughout the six regions of Oregon.

Due to its emphasis on place, *The Well-Traveled Casket* may be called a folklore geography. The book is organized regionally (and by city) because the state's diverse climate, its mountains, its dry country, and its wetlands shape the stories that people tell. In Southeastern Oregon, a ranch hand jokes that in springtime he gets a sunburn on his face and frostbite on his butt; in the Willamette Valley, a farmer leaves his house and barn unlocked during harvest, but in town takes special pains to lock his car. "You can't be too careful in the city," he says. "Last year I left my car unlocked. When I came back, it was full of zucchini." In predictable ways, the landscape provides the surface details for a folk narrative, even though the underlying patterns may be the same. Under the haze of Albany's industrial stacks, the Conser Lake monster is an albino Sasquatch who looks like a victim of toxic waste; in pristine Northeastern Oregon, the Wallowa Lake monster is an undulating serpent, a first cousin to Scotland's "Nessie."

A good story deserves retelling, so an accomplished regional storyteller reworks, updates, and revises a narrative, giving "dry side" grit to a soggy "wet side" tale or

replacing Cumberland Gap geography with McKenzie Pass landmarks. Folklorist Barre Toelken explains this phenomenon, saying that folklore is both dynamic and conservative, meaning that a time-honored narrative retains its underlying structure as it moves from location to location, even though individual storytellers constantly update the story, fitting the characters and themes to climate, geography, folk group, and social circumstances. This process is called variation, a sure sign of the presence of folklore. Within each of Oregon's folk groups are both esoteric (insider) knowledge about the rules and patterns of acceptable behavior and exoteric (outsider) information, characterized by the tension between "us" and "them." Lakeview's "Horned Coon Hunt" and Condon's "Pig Farming, Eastern Style" make fun of easterners and sophisticates. Jordan Valley proverbs reaffirm a sense of Basque identity and provide a buffer against cultural assimilation. Canyonville's "Birds of a Feather," a narrative joke about the Northern Spotted Owl, circulates primarily among timber workers, where it functions as an act of verbal aggression against environmentalists, the owl's supporters.

In addition to serving as a cultural geography, *The Well-Traveled Casket* is also a folklore history; its pages provide an everyday link between past and present, joining the pioneer era and Native American myth-time to the present epoch. Most regional histories contain a solemn chronicle of court cases, military victories, and political maneuverings, often with an emphasis on rich men, powerful institutions, and Manifest Destiny. A folklore history, on the other hand, describes events as seen through the eyes of ordinary people; it is history without adornment. The vehicle for such a history is hundreds and hundreds of long-standing traditions, customs, and beliefs. In this way, songs, foodways, material culture, folk speech, and traditional narratives paint a lifelike portrait of Oregon's various folk groups, providing a sense of both continuity and identity. These individual brush strokes combine in a marvelously complex portrait, forming a loose chronicle of Oregon life: a folklore history.

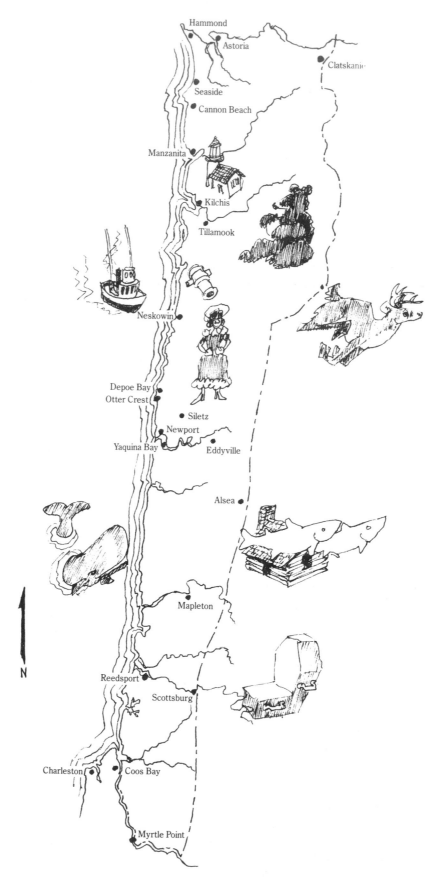

Hammond

Astoria

Clatskanie

Seaside

Cannon Beach

Manzanita

Kilchis

Tillamook

Neskowin

Depoe Bay
Otter Crest

Siletz

Newport

Yaquina Bay

Eddyville

Alsea

Mapleton

N

Reedsport

Scottsburg

Charleston

Coos Bay

Myrtle Point

The Oregon Coast

Oregon's dramatic 400-mile coastline abounds with history and legend. The Coast can be wild and rugged, peaceful and calm, depending on the location and the changeable Coast weather. Along the North Coast are steep headlands and forested hills interspersed with rocky coves and sandy beaches. Central Coast shores are wooded, with many coastal lakes, estuaries, and long, sandy beaches. Farther south the vegetation changes. Heavily forested areas give way to miles and miles of sand dunes, scattered trees, and patches of vegetation. Still farther south, white-barked alders and yellow maples yield to Oregon myrtle, a glossy-leafed evergreen that grows singly or in groves along the meadows. Nine lighthouses keep vigil along this breathtaking shore.

Highway 101, the Coast Highway, closely parallels the rocky shoreline, following, in part, the trail blazed by Coyote, or *Talapus*, when the Native American trickster-god built the bays and headlands of the Oregon Coast. Standing atop Neahkahnie Mountain, Coyote threw molten rocks into the waters below, creating the crashing surf and boiling water that remains today. Then, with his axe, *Talapus* drew a line on the shore, prohibiting the waters from rising above that mark.

According to Clatsop legend, a native woman, pulling mussels from the rocks, paused in her work to gaze at the Pacific Ocean, known to the Clatsops as "the river with only one bank." She saw a "great black-bodied bird" with strange wings swimming on the swells, its long thin beak jutting into the air. Then it disappeared. As time passed, the people saw more and more of these curious "water-birds," omens of tragedy for the native Nestuccas, Tillamooks, and Nehalems.

On the opposite "bank" of the boundless river other tales, both strange and heroic, were told. Somewhere on what is now the Oregon Coast was located the wondrous kingdom of Fu Sang, a rich country founded by mystics from Afghanistan; the people of Fu Sang flourished because of the Fu Sang tree's magical powers, stories of which brought more "water-birds" to the Coast. These ships appeared on the Pacific shores in the first half of the sixteenth century, as explorers sought a passage to the East.

In the latter part of the 1500s, men such as Sir Francis Drake and the Spaniard Martin de Aguilar were searching for the lucrative secret of the Northwest Passage. Until the late eighteenth century, however, prevailing currents generally kept explorers south of the Columbia River. In 1707, the *San Francisco Xavier*, sailing from Manila, wrecked against the sheer cliffs of Neahkahnie Mountain, spilling a load of beeswax that can still be found in gummy balls on the northern beaches.

Several worthy explorers just missed finding the legendary Great River of the Northwest. Spanish captain Bruno Heceta, arriving in 1775, knew he had found an impressive river mouth but was unable to push his scurvy-ridden crew across the Columbia bar. Two years later, Captain James Cook unknowingly sailed past the Columbia on a stormy night. In 1778, Captain John Meares decided the Columbia watershed was merely an estuary; ironically, he labeled the northern promontory Cape Disappointment. George Vancouver, commissioned by the British government to survey the Northwest, scoffed at the myth of the Northwest Passage and, ignoring the turbulent waters and crosscurrents, declared the area "not worthy of more attention." The wide Columbia River could not forever hide its existence from voyagers. In May 1792, Captain Robert Gray waited for the right convergence of tide, wind, and current, then sailed across the bar in the ship *Columbia Rediviva* and laid claim for the United States of America, setting a precedent that was to become the basis for American claims to possession of the Oregon Territory.

The natives of the coastal area were described by one of Gray's men as "straight-limbed, fine-looking fellows" and the women as "very pretty," wearing deer and other skin garments. The natives lived in small villages of plank houses along the many streams, eating the abundant bounty from the land and sea—salmon and shellfish, berries and wild game. Their lives would change drastically within a short time. The sailors of the fur trade introduced colds, rheumatism, smallpox, venereal disease, and dysentery—not to mention demon rum. As early as 1805, when Lewis and Clark began their overland trek, local Indian tribes had been reduced to about 25 percent of their original numbers—many of them sickly and vulnerable to the depredations of European settlers.

Lewis and Clark spent the miserable winter of 1805–06 in their log shelter at Fort Clatsop, plagued by fleas and incessant rains. In their long and depressing stay, the adventurers had few diversions, but Captain Clark did once take Sacajawea to the Tillamook region to see a beached whale. The men also built a salt cairn at the present site of Seaside and extracted salt from the seawater, a necessity for preserving meats on the return journey. By spring, the party was only too happy to leave for St. Louis. They brought back the important news that the Oregon Country was indeed suitable for settlement.

Astoria, named for John Jacob Astor, was the first American city to be settled in the West. Astor, who began his career in Baltimore with the profitable sale of seven flutes, quickly changed his emphasis to furs when he eyed the rich trading potential of the Pacific Coast. Astor sent two contingents of traders to the area, one by land and one by sea, but the easterners had some problems adjusting to life in the Wild West. In the space of two months, the greenhorns had cleared only one acre of land; in the process, two men had been seriously injured felling trees, one had blown off a hand with explosives, and three had fallen victim to local Indian attacks.

In 1813, Astoria was claimed by the British and renamed Fort George. For three decades, the British would dominate the Oregon Territory under the auspices of the Hudson's Bay Company, but when beaver and otter pelts began to grow scarce in 1818, the British relinquished Fort George to the Americans. By 1847 the community of Astoria housed the first United States post office west of the Rocky Mountains. By then, serious westward expansion was bringing loads of pioneers from Missouri. Folks who had angled for catfish on the Mississippi in the summer of 1847 were pulling bright red salmon from the Nehalem River a year later.

After Lewis and Clark's expedition, non-native settlement began on the Coast, but communities remained sparsely populated because most of the coastline lacked roads until 1932, when the Roosevelt Military Highway

was completed. In a way, the long isolation of communities gave each its own particular flavor. Today Tillamook is known for "cheese, trees, and ocean breeze." Newport has its canneries, Mo's clam chowder, and bay-front art galleries. Astoria and Coos Bay are log-export centers, and Bandon is famous for its cranberries and cheese. Brookings produces world-class lily bulbs, and Lincoln City dispenses wonderful saltwater taffy. Florence is known for some of the largest sand dunes in the world. The Oregon Coast also has some small wonders as well. Depoe Bay is the world's smallest ocean port; the D River, flowing from Devil's Lake to the Pacific, is the world's shortest river, at something less than 200 yards.

Oregon Coast geography is punctuated with names from the state's history and folklore. From Indian times, certain coastal areas have earned reputations for good or evil. Medicine Rock on the banks of the Siletz River was supposedly the home of a *skookum*, an evil spirit whom the Indians mollified with offerings of food. Devil's Lake, called *Neotsu* by the Indians, was known as the place of "evil waters" in Chinook Jargon and thought to conceal a water monster. Early settlers told the story of a treasure buried in the rugged terrain of Coos County, a series of ravines known as the Seven Devils, an area so overgrown that two pioneers were unable to retrace their steps to a buried fortune in gold. Twenty-five miles east of Coos Bay is an Indian burial meadow, known in pioneer times as a sacred place; today it is called Enchanted Prairie. Pioneers who discovered Gods Valley on the Nehalem River felt that a divine voice had led them to an elk herd before starvation overtook them.

Some of these landmarks are named for explorers who, for one reason or another, failed to discover the mouth of the Columbia River, one of the world's largest waterways. Midstate, just south of Cape Perpetua, is Captain Cook Point, named for the English adventurer who identified so many coastal landmarks in his voyage of 1778. Cape Meares, south of Tillamook Bay, recalls the retired British naval officer who first brought Chinese laborers to the American West on his ship *North West America*. The Spanish adventurer who attempted in vain to enter the Columbia River in 1775 left his name farther south at Heceta Head. The Lewis and Clark River flowed past the Fort Clatsop headquarters of the famous Oregon explorers, who wintered there in 1805–06; and Meriwether, near Warrenton in Clatsop County, was named for Captain Meriwether Lewis by admirers in 1896.

Other Oregon Coast sites commemorate shipwrecks and navigational blunders. Baltimore Rock near Coos Bay claimed the schooner *Baltimore* in 1889. After running aground east of Reedsport in the Umpqua River in 1850, the crew of the *Samuel Roberts* broke open a keg of spirits and christened the spot Brandy Bar. On the North Coast, the schooner *Shark* was wrecked while leaving the Columbia River in 1846, and locals reclaimed from the beach a ship's gun; thereafter, the location was known as Cannon Beach.

There are many ethnic communities on the Coast, notably those settled by fishermen from other seacoast lands. On the South Coast, the Coos County town of Norway is a near neighbor to Curry County's Denmark. And residents of Lincoln County coined the name Delake after local Finns had trouble mastering the accepted name, Devil's Lake.

Finally, there are some locations that owe their names to curious conversations or unusual events. Idiot Creek in the Tillamook Burn housed a logging operation so improbable that "only an idiot would work there." According to

Lewis A. McArthur, when a survey party in Curry County temporarily lost contact with chainman Bruce Schilling in dense underbrush, the men joked that they would find Bruce's "parched bones" next spring; consequently, the rivulet came to be called Bruces Bones Creek. Whiskey Creek is a descriptive term; one night a party of travelers stopped at this campsite in Tillamook County, and the men retired to cool the keg in the river. After several hours of urging their husbands to start the camp chores, the irate wives took the camp axe to the keg, and the waters on Netarts Spit flowed with rotgut whiskey. Snout Creek, near Agness, picked up its unusual moniker from a dogfight; old Snout won the contest but was later poisoned by the loser's owner and dumped into this creek. One can only speculate about names such as Cannibal Mountain in the Coast Range, Wake Up Rilea Creek in Curry County, and Dog Thief Point near Elsie.

Alsea

Benton County. Alsea is a version of Alsi, the name of a Yakonan tribe living at the mouth of the Alsea River in Oregon's emigration era. Because of its location in the face of the Pacific weather fronts, Alsea is one of the rainiest places in the Northwest and, according to a traditional folk song, a difficult place for pioneer brides.

"Alsea Girls" is a warning to young women not to marry the local Oregon boys. Builders made the puncheon floors mentioned in the song by splitting logs and placing the round side down, then edging the timber with a broad axe. The surface of the floor was finished with an adz; some say a well-turned puncheon surface was as smooth as a dance floor.

"Alsea Girls" describes hard times. A song popular since frontier days, it traveled across the country with the first wave of pioneers, its lyrics changing along the way to reflect the immediate landscape. Twilo Scofield learned this version from folklorist Barre Toelken in 1968. A variant for the final verse was contributed by Ralph Wirfs, whose father, Ray, heard it in 1930 while working with the Civilian Conservation Corps (CCC) on the McKenzie River.

ALSEA GIRLS

Come you Al-sea Girls and lis-ten to my

noise. Don't you mar-ry the Or-e-gon boys.

If you do, your for-tune it-'ll be, Cold

John-ny-cake and ven-i-son is all you'll see!

Chorus:
    Come, you Alsea Girls, and listen to my noise;
    Don't you marry the Or-e-gon boys.
    If you do, your fortune it'll be,
    Cold johnny-cake and venison is all you'll see.

1. They'll take you to a side-hued wall
    Without any windows in it at all,
    Sandstone chimney and a puncheon floor,
    A clapboard roof and a button door.

Chorus

2. Every night before you go to bed
    They'll build up a fire as high as your head,
    Rake away the ashes and in they'll throw
    A great big chunk of old sourdough.

Chorus

3. When they go a'milkin, they milk in a gourd,
    Strain it in a corner and hide it with a board.
    Some gets little and some gets none,
    And that's how things in Oregon run.

Chorus

Alternate Verse

4. When they go a'milkin', they milk in a gourd,
    Strain it in a corner and hide it with a board.
    When they come a'courtin', here's what they say,
    "My daddy shot a bear today."

Astoria

Clatsop County. Population 9,976. Astoria is one of the Northwest's oldest settlements. The area was visited by British Captain John Meares in 1775. Looking for the great Northwest river, Meares entered the broad mouth of the Columbia River but decided that it was a bay. Before leaving, Meares petulantly named the Astoria watershed Deception Bay and the land mass to the north Cape Disappointment. In 1856 a lighthouse was built at the cape, the scene of many shipwrecks and groundings; before construction of the lighthouse, ship captains relied primarily on tree burns and posted banners to avoid the reefs near Cape Disappointment.

In 1805 Lewis and Clark wintered at Fort Clatsop, just a few miles from the present site of Astoria. Writing in their journals, Lewis and Clark also seem to have found the area disappointing: ''We are infested with swarms of flees already in our new habitations; the presumption is therefore strong that we shall not divest ourselves of this intolerably troublsem vermin during our residence here.'' Traveling with the Lewis and Clark expedition was the first black man to reside for any length of time in Oregon Territory. York, the slave of William Clark, was an accomplished hunter and spoke some French, essential because the guide, Charbonneau, spoke no English.

In 1811, John Jacob Astor began trading in furs at the present site of the city, and the settlements of the Pacific Fur Company eventually were named after the German immigrant who did so much to develop the region. In 1926 the 125-foot Astor Column was dedicated. The spiral monument, painted with a frieze depicting Oregon history, was built in honor of Astor and Captain Robert Gray, who rejected John Meares's pessimism and sailed headlong into the Columbia River, laying claim to the waterway for the United States government.

On the Oregon side of the Columbia, where the great river meets the Pacific Ocean, lies Fort Stevens State Park. Fort Stevens, an early military outpost, was named for Isaac Ingalls Stevens, governor of Washington Territory from 1853 to 1857. Stevens was a popular leader in the Northwest Territories and a Civil War general who died in 1862 while leading Union forces at Chantilly, Virginia. The fort was named for Stevens in 1864 by George H. Elliot, its builder.

Although never a significant outpost, the strategic location of Fort Stevens at the mouth of the Columbia River made it necessary to build heavy fortifications there during World War II, and Fort Stevens has the distinction of being the only military post in the continental United States to receive fire since the War of 1812. On June 21, 1942, a Japanese submarine lobbed seventeen shells toward the shore, the explosives landing well offshore. Now abandoned, Battery Russell in Fort Stevens State Park is a dank maze of concrete turrets, storehouses, and cavelike passageways.

Battery Russell is a likely place for legend—in particular a ghost story—because the caverns have a dark, foreboding atmosphere. Furthermore, the secrecy that must have surrounded the fortress during World War II has left a fascinating aura of mystery. Probably Ben Gun, the shipwrecked Japanese sailor who prowls Battery Russell, represents a now-forgotten residue of fears about invasion

during the 1940s. But in the true spirit of the legend, the ghost story continues to circulate long after the original causes of concern have been forgotten. In 1976, an Astoria student told several ''Ben Gun'' anecdotes to Theresa Moore, who contributed differing versions to the Randall V. Mills Folklore Archives at the University of Oregon. In one of the variants, the ''Ben Gun'' legend merges with the ''Man with the Hook'' story, a popular urban legend found in collections such as *The Vanishing Hitchhiker* by Jan Harold Brunvand (see Monmouth. p. 52).

Moore's informant says, ''Now, I don't remember where I first heard it, but I think it was probably back in, like, the eighth (seventh or eighth) grade, and we heard those stories.'' While sleeping out in the backyard, the teenagers traded stories, and ''Ben Gun'' legends were among them. The following is a version compiled from the variants heard by Moore.

BEN GUN, THE BATTERY RUSSELL GHOST

Sometime near the end of World War II, a Japanese sailor was marooned on the beach near Fort Stevens State Park. He was half-crazy from floating around in the open sea for several weeks on a life raft, and he had lost an arm when his ship went down. His name was Ben Gun.

Ben Gun found a secret tunnel that goes from the middle of the South Jetty into the heart of Battery Russell, and he used this passageway as his hideout, unaware that the war had ended. For many years he lurked around the Battery Russell area, frightening locals with his long, stringy hair, rough beard, and wild-eyed look. And somehow he apparently fashioned a kind of hook from discarded metal, attaching it to his severed stump in a crude fashion.

One night, a group of kids were using their ouija board, and one of the girls asked if there was any place in the Astoria area that was dangerous. The board spelled out s-t-a-y a-w-a-y f-r-o-m B-a-t-t-e-r-y R-u-s-s-e-l-l. They all laughed, of course, and thought nothing more.

So, several nights later the kids decided to explore the caves at Battery Russell. Mary Jane Knowles and Dorothy Olson were there with three other boys. Battery Russell goes down very deep—like two stories deep. So they went down to the deepest part with their flashlights. The boys thought it would be funny to abandon Dorothy in the deepest part of the caves to scare her. So they left her there without a flashlight. They were sure Dorothy could find her way out, but she couldn't. After half an hour, they returned to find her huddled in a corner of the cave, suffering from acute shock. Next to her head, buried in the clay of the cave wall, was a crude metal hook, dripping with blood.

Dorothy couldn't talk, so they took her to a hospital, where she collapsed into a coma for three days. Finally when she came to, she said she had been chased through Battery Russell by something evil. Just when she was cornered, she heard the boys' voices coming closer. That's all she remembered, and she could not describe the creature. But everyone knows that the creature was Ben Gun.

Cannon Beach

Clatsop County. Population 1,220. In 1846 the schooner *Shark* wrecked while navigating out of the Columbia River. The debris washed ashore, leaving one of the ship's cannons on the beach five miles south of Ecola Point. The cannon lay there for several years, having been dragged above the water mark by locals. In the process, Cannon Beach took its name.

In 1971 Cannon Beach native Peter Lindsey heard a joke that was in great favor among loggers in Tillamook County. Lindsey's informant suggested that loggers, who are notoriously generous with each other, sometimes find that others lack the same sense of fair play.

THE ULTIMATE TEST

One day a logger was working up behind Cannon Beach setting chokers and complaining. Suddenly, a ferocious voice came out of the sky, asking what all the griping was about. The logger looked up and realized it was God talking, so he started to explain what a miserable life he had been leading. His only hope was that he might go to "a better place" of rest when he died.

God looked down and said, "Well, I'll tell you what I'll do. If you can accomplish a few things that need doing around here—projects that I haven't had time for—I'll make sure you get into Heaven." The logger agreed.

God said, "The first thing I want you to do is move that big mountain off there (Saddle Mountain) farther south, closer to Cannon Beach." So the logger worked for years and finally finished moving it a shovelful at a time. Then he called to God, and God spoke to him and said, "That's good, but I've got another thing for you to do. I need the south fork of Elk Creek moved about two miles farther north." So the logger slaved away for years and finally rerouted the creek and went to call on God again. God said, "That's good, but there's one more thing you've got to do, and then you can be assured of a place in Heaven."

"What's that?" asked the logger. "Go down to Stanley's Tavern in Cannon Beach," said God, "and sit there drinking 'til he buys you a beer on the house. When he does that, you can be sure of a place in Heaven." As the story goes, you can go down to that tavern to this very day, and that logger is still sitting there waitin' for a free beer.

Charleston

Coos County. Charleston was named for Charles Haskell, who settled in the area around 1853. In Charleston, where a lush, wet climate washes the South Coast much of the year, winter colds and summer rashes are commonplace. Following are traditional remedies and cures, some of them contributed by Sadie Pettinger, who remembered them from the early 1900s, when she was a girl growing up near the mouth of the Rogue River.

Even when medical science has a treatment, people rely on traditional remedies and cures. In effect, the less medical science knows about a particular ailment, the more likely that folk remedies are used. Most frequently treated with folk cures are ailments such as hiccups, warts, cancer, rheumatism, and sties. Sometimes, however, folk medicine anticipates discoveries in clinical medicine. For example, Charleston's Germans used sauerkraut as a staple and a tonic, anticipating the current popularity of vitamin C as a type of preventative cure.

COAST REGION FOLK CURES

☐ *An all-purpose liniment: Fill a container of any size with kerosene. Add camphor gum until the kerosene will dissolve no more. Then add olive oil until the container is filled. Shake the mixture thoroughly.*

☐ *The bloody flux was a diarrhea that affected young children of about two years in age, resulting often from poor sanitation during the cold, wet months of the fall, and especially during hunting season, when flies were attracted to freshly killed venison. The bloody flux often proved fatal. To cure the flux, administer grated rhubarb root.*

☐ *The chilblains was an inflammation of the feet common in wintertime on the coast. The foot would redden and* become inflamed, itching severely. To cure chilblains, soak the feet either in kerosene or in hot water with ashes dissolved in the bucket.

☐ Children often suffered cracked toes from wading in ice-cold creek water in the summertime. To cure cracked toes, get a small tuft of fresh wool, twist it into a string, and tie the string around the affected toe, rubbing the wool into the cracks.

☐ In the summertime, a child who swam often in lakes or rivers often became lethargic and sick, suffering a general weakness and bluish discoloration of the lips. This "washed out" condition was caused by the debilitating properties of fresh water and could only be cured by saltwater baths, which do not drain the vitality of a person.

☐ Every German immigrant knew the importance of sauerkraut, a rich source of vitamin C and a food that could be stored almost indefinitely. For years, German sailors had used sauerkraut to prevent scurvy, and the practice of pickling became widely used in Charleston and other coastal communities, especially those ports frequented by foreign ships.

☐ For cuts and punctures, apply a poultice of fresh cow dung.

☐ To cure impetigo, administer a mixture of sulphur and grease.

☐ For sore throats, give the sufferer a spoonful of kerosene or a spoonful of sugar and turpentine.

☐ An Indian cure for cracked nipples involved boiling the inner bark from an oak tree and applying the salve directly to the nipples.

☐ For blood poisoning, immerse the infected limb in buttermilk. If the treatment works, the buttermilk turns greenish-purple.

☐ For sties, coat a piece of cloth with the juice from a rotten apple and apply the patch at night over the affected eye.

☐ The mange on dogs could be cured by a dab of lard laced with sulphur.

☐ For severe diarrhea, drink the juice of cooked blackberries.

☐ For nail punctures and cuts, apply a poultice of raw bacon or bread and milk. These cures will draw out the poison.

☐ For congestion of the lungs, boil onions in a tiny bit of water until they are soft. Then, while the onions are warm, place them on the chest and cover the onions with a warm cloth. There will be relief by morning.

☐ Nervous prostration could be cured by walking barefoot in the soil every day. There is no therapy like getting the hands and feet into the Good Earth and feeling the warmth of the soil.

☐ For kidney disease or kidney stones, drink cranberry juice.

☐ For liver problems, boil young twig limbs of peach trees for several hours. Then administer the peach-limb tea daily until relief occurs.

☐ As a cough syrup, boil together equal amounts of horehound and mullein leaves with a small amount of liverwort. Then add enough sugar to the liquid to make a thin syrup.

☐ For spring tonic, wash and scrape burdock roots and slice them into thin pieces. Cover the mess with cold water and let it stand six hours. Then strain off the liquid and drink it. For burns, use bruised burdock leaves.

☐ The coast Indians used poison oak to burn out warts and to cure ringworm.

☐ Early coastal settlers used the bark of the Pacific dogwood tree as a quinine antidote for malarial fevers.

☐ Elderberry tea is a cure for colds, and cascara bark is a laxative.

Clatskanie

Columbia County. Population 1,629. The word *Tlat-skani* referred to a river route taken by Indians to a point in the Nehalem Valley. Clatskanie was an important settlement in the pioneer era and a prime location for sea captains to shanghai sailors. According to Mary J. Licktieg, the Mayger Store just northeast of Clatskanie had a trapdoor in the floor. Many a drunk went through that trapdoor into a boat below, only to wake the next morning under full sail on the open sea.

Clatskanie, an important trading post for the French, British, Americans, and Indians, is sometimes called the southern home of Chinook Jargon, a trade language of the Oregon frontier, and the tongue in which Lewis and Clark were first addressed when reaching the mouth of the Columbia River. According to Rena V. Grant, a functional Chinook Jargon had been in use for many years before white exploration, but was expanded by European word lists, the lexicons having been shared by traders and explorers during the earliest days of settlement. During the 1870s the Chinook language was a useful second language for nearly 100,000 people from Alaska to California. Chinook is a combination of many Native American languages, with words added later from French and English to facilitate trading. The maximum Chinook vocabulary was about 500 words, with no verb tenses, no conjugations, no plurals, no possessives, no inflections, and only one preposition (*kopa*) that meant "with," "to," "from," "for," and all the rest of the prepositions. Some words were imitations of natural sounds or borrowings from trappers. It seldom took a *cheechako* (newcomer) more than a few days to become fluent in Chinook.

Because the Chinook language was a necessary tool for the early trappers and settlers in the Columbia Coast region, full descriptions of the Native American dialect were published in several sources, including the *Alta Californian*, the *San Francisco Evening Bulletin*, and Henry

Schoolcraft's *Information Respecting the History, Condition, and Prospects of the Indian Tribes of the United States.*

A SAMPLE OF CHINOOK JARGON

The origins of the following words are coded below: Chinook (C), Chehalis (Ch), Clackamas (Cl), Calapooia (Cal), Clallum (Clal), Bellabella (BB), Nootka (N), Klickitat (K), Wasco (W), general Salishan tongues (S), English (E), French (F), and invented words (J). The examples come from Edward Harper Thomas, *Chinook: A History and Dictionary*, from Rena V. Grant, "The Chinook Jargon, Past and Present," *California Folklore Quarterly* 3 (1944): 259–276, and from the personal notes of Randall V. Mills. Other articles of interest include Chester A. Fee, "Oregon's Historical Esperanto—the Chinook Jargon," *Oregon Historical Quarterly* 42 (1941): 176–85, and F. H. Howay, "Origin of the Chinook Jargon on the Northwest Coast," *Oregon Historical Quarterly* 44 (1943): 26–55.

Boston: (E): an American
Boston Illahee—"the United States"
Mika kumtux Boston wawa?—"Do you understand English?"
chako: (N): "to approach," "to come"
Chuck chako—"The tide is rising."
Nika chako kopa Poteland—"I come from Portland."
cheechako: (F. *chee*, "new" and N. *chako*, "to come"): a newcomer, such as the ill-fated greenhorn in Jack London's "To Build a Fire"
Dutchman: (E): "any white man other than French, English, or American"
hi-yu: (N): "much," "many"
hiyu tillicums—"a crowd"
hiyu muckamuck—"plenty to eat"
hiya wawa—"much talk"
illahee: (C): "country," "land," "earth," "region," "district," "farm," "ranch"
King George Illahee—"England"
Passaiooks Illahee—"France"
Saghalie Illahee—"Heaven" (above country)
Keekwullie Illahee—"Hell" (below country)
klahowya: (Ch): "How do you do?" or "Goodbye"
klootch-man: (N): "woman," "female animal," "wife"
klootchman yaka mama—"mother-in-law"
tenas klootchman—"a small woman" or "little girl"
la-push: (F): "the mouth" or "mouth of a river"
lum: (E): "whiskey" (rum)
mem-a-loose: (C): "dead," "to die," "expire," "decay," "become rotten"
memaloose kopa chuck—"to die in the water"
Memaloose Illahee—"a graveyard"
o-lal-lie: (BB): "berries," "fruit," "the salmon berry"
klale ollalie—"blackberry"
olallie chuck—"berry juice"
shot olallie—"huckleberries"
pelton: (J): "a fool," "crazy," "insane," "an insane person" (adopted from a deranged man, Archibald Felton)
slat chuck: (F, E, and N): "the sea"
se-at-co: (Ch): "goblin" or "night demon," feared by the coast Indians

skookum: (Ch): "strong," "powerful"
skookum chuck—"rapids"
skookum house—"jail"
skookum town—"large city"
tah-mah-na-wis: (C): "guardian" or "familiar spirit"
mamook tamahnawis—"conjure," "make magic"
klale tahmahnawis—"black magic," "Devil," "dark spirit"
tillikum: (C): "people," "tribe," "nation," "relations," "kin"
hiyu tillikums—"a crowd," "many people"
ahnkuttie tillikums—"ancestors," "forefathers"
toketie: (Cal): "pretty"
hyas toketie kulla kulla—"a very pretty bird"
tumwata: (E/J): "waterfall" (as in Tumwater, Washington)
tyee: (N): "chief" or "anything of superior order"
Saghalie Tyee (God)
ul-a-lach: (K): "wild onion"
wake: (N): "no," "none," "not"
wake skookum—"not strong," "weak," "infirm"
wake kloshe—"no good"
yaka: (C): "he," "his," "him," "she," "her," "hers," "it," "its"
Yaka klatawa—"He has gone."
Nika klook yaka teahwit—"My foot it is lame."

Several Oregon place-names and geographic terms come from Chinook Jargon. For example, the Siskiyou Mountains were probably named by Southern Oregon Indians, who encountered Archibald R. McLeod, chief factor for the Hudson's Bay Company, and his "bob-tailed horse." The Canadian trader, for whom the Northern California city of McCloud is named, lost his horse in a Siskiyou snowstorm, and nearby Native Americans christened as Pass of the Siskiyou the spot where the carcass lay. Memaloose (Death) Island in the Columbia River near The Dalles is one of many Native American burial grounds. In Curry County near the ocean lies Skookumhouse (Stronghold) Butte, a former Indian fortress. Toketee (Pretty) Falls in Douglas County is a gorgeous landmark on the Umpqua River, and Olallie (Berry) Butte in the Cascades stands in pleasant spring blooms between majestic Mt. Hood and Mt. Jefferson. Lumtum (Whiskey) Butte near Crane Prairie in Deschutes County attests its pioneer-era use as a rural distillery. Hiyu (Abundant) Mountain stands prominently in the skyline of Hood River and Clackamas counties. In Crook County near the Maury Mountains is Kloochman (Woman) Creek. In Central Oregon, Crater Lake stands in the caldera of the once-majestic Mt. Mazama (Mountain Goat). Perhaps the least significant Oregon landmark for early speakers of Chinook was Wake (Nothing) Butte in Deschutes County southwest of Bend.

Coos Bay

Coos County. Population 15,020. Lewis and Clark heard the name *Cook-koo-oose* from the Clatsop Indians in reference to a south-coast tribe. A disagreement exists about the meaning of the term, as reported by Lewis A. McAr-

Hea-din' south from De-vil's Light, I heard our Cap-tain roar, "We're still a-float, so here we go, We're off to San Pe-dro!" All at once we caught hell, Smoke and wa-ter and whis-tlin' wind. In a-no-ther min-ute, boys, we star-ted ta-kin' wa-ter in.

Chorus:
Rollin', rollin' cross the bar,
Hope Coos Bay's not very far.
Rollin', rollin' cross the bar,
I'd trade this ship off for a car.

Headin' south from Devil's Light,
I heard our Captain roar,
"We're still afloat, so here we go,
We're off to San Pedro."
All at once we caught hell,
Smoke and water and whistlin' wind.
In another minute, boys,
We started takin' water in.

Chorus

No runnin' lights and one pump left,
We sailed on through the night,
But with our hardy ship and crew,
We couldn't lose that fight.
Then a big sea came, and the lifeboats went.
We sent out a hasty call,
The *Modoc* came to tow us in,
And then we crossed the bar.

Chorus:
Rollin', rollin' cross the bar,
Hope Coos Bay's not very far.
The old *Alert* may not get far,
But she got us across the Coos Bay Bar.

thur in *Oregon Geographic Names*. It may mean "place of pines" or "lake." Perry B. Marple, an 1850s settler, argued that Coos was the Kusan Indian pronunciation of the English word "coast." At any rate, the name Coos Bay is of Native American origin.

Coos Bay has one of Oregon's most active ports and has a history as a safe haven for ships in stormy weather. A popular Oregon folk song, performed by singer Barre Toelken, tells the plight of some adventurers from Seattle who set sail in the early 1960s on the *Alert*, heading for the Galapagos Islands. After leaving Seattle, the explorers put in at Astoria for refitting, then headed south. Traveling down the coast, the *Alert* hit fierce weather and limped into Coos Bay with the help of the Coast Guard. While in Coos Bay, the crew members were adopted by friendly towns-folk, who took them into their homes and fed them. As the *Alert* prepared to resume its journey, the Coos Bay folk threw a big benefit, raising money to get the Galapagos travelers under-way again. A man named Johnson from a local radio station recorded some of the songs sung at the benefit, including "Rollin', Rollin' Cross the Bar."

ROLLIN', ROLLIN' CROSS THE BAR

Rol-lin', rol-lin', 'cross the bar, Hope Coos Bay's not ve-ry far. Rol-lin', rol-lin', 'cross the bar, I'd trade this ship off for a car!

Depoe Bay

Lincoln County. Population 870. According to some sources, the harbor was named for "Old Charlie" Depoe, a Siletz Indian, who was granted 200 acres of land in the 1870s. This port, the world's smallest deep harbor, is a vibrant center for commercial fishing on the Central Coast. Every year at Memorial Day, Depoe Bay fishermen deco-rate their boats with thousands of flowers, sailing to sea through the narrow inlet in a procession known as the Fleet of Flowers. Throwing the flowers into the waves memorializes those fishermen who have died at sea.

In 1989, folklore student Carolyn S. Hill collected stories and terms from her husband and his partner, fisher-men who had sailed from Depoe Bay's small and danger-ous harbor, discovering in the process that initiation rites are common. Until a greenhorn learns the rules and codes of the sea, he must endure a predictable period of hazing, perhaps as a blunt reminder that being ill-prepared on the ocean can cost the lives of the entire crew. These observations come from Hill's collection at the State of Jefferson Folklore Archives in Ashland.

"You send 'em down to forepeak to get about fifty fathoms of *shore line*," says one of the Depoe Bay commercial fishermen. Thinking he is looking for a special kind of rope or cable, the greenhorn might look around for quite a while before getting wise. If two greenhorns have nothing to do, a salt will say, "Why don't you go paint the *waterline* on the side of the boat." Or perhaps the crew will tell a novice to "ask the captain for the key to the *sea chest*." When things get a little dull on board, the new crew member will be handed a mop and told, "Hey, go down and ask the engineer for a bucket of *propwash*." Perhaps the nastiest trick is to send the greenhorn into the wheelhouse to reveal his ignorance of the sea.

THE "NAUTICAL" SKIPPER AND THE NEW MAN

We'd send the green guy up to the wheelhouse with a grease gun, an old grody one, and the skipper was a real nautical; he didn't even like to eat up in the wheelhouse. He always thought the boat ought to be run more like a freighter than a fishing boat. So we sent John, this green guy, up to the wheelhouse with this old grody grease gun and told him, "We've got to grease the relative bearing *every day. Ask the skipper where. . . . You're there to grease the relative bearing." And he got run out of the wheelhouse.*

THE SEA-SALT'S JARGON

beatin' ice: Rain and freezing temperatures cause ice to form on the boat and equipment. The crew must beat the ice off using baseball bats.
blow: a storm
brokered: fish that are sold
bucking tide, bucking seas, bucking wind: going against something, like the tide or heavy wind
bugs: crabs
cages: crab pots
cathead: capstan (a spool)
chicken butt: undersized halibut
chickens: crabs
conking: finding a good spot and making a big catch
conked 'em: caught a lot of fish
crab slut: what fishermen call themselves because they "sell their bodies for money"
crab pots: the large (7'x 7'x 32–36'') steel cages used to catch crabs
crew share: the portion of earnings divided among the crew
fo'c'sle: the forecastle—where crews sleep on old halibut schooners. Called "sailing before the mast." In new boats, the wheelhouse is forward, but crew's quarters are up front, so the sleeping area is still called the *fo'c'sle*, though modern boats do not actually have a forecastle.
foul: bad weather
greenhorn: a novice fisherman

highliner: a boat that consistently brings in the highest catches. Can also be used to describe a person, usually the captain.
henhouse: a crab pot with too many female crabs
jogstick: the lever in the wheelhouse that steers the boat
licensed master: Every fishing boat must have a licensed master or mate, not necessarily the captain. This person is specially trained in emergency procedures and laws.
missed 'em: when the boat fails to make a good catch
mothership: the anchored fish-processing ships to which catches are brought
piss pot boat: boat in a state of disrepair
propwash: the turbulent water behind the propeller
relative bearing: the difference between True North and what is shown on the compass
sea chest: part of the piping in the engine room where the pumps draw seawater to cool the engines
shit hawks: sea gulls
shucker: someone who works in fish processing, separating the crab meat or clam meat from the shell
side bands: a long-range radio
snotty: bad weather
survival suits: insulated buoyant suits that prevent hypothermia in the ocean
tunnels: Crabs travel through slender tunnels into the crab pot, but they can't get out via these tunnels.
waterline: the place on the side of the boat to which the water rises
wheel: the propeller
wildcat: a spool on which the anchor chain is spooled

Eddyville

Lincoln County. Eddyville was originally called Little Elk, standing as it does at the mouth of Little Elk Creek. However, in 1888 the postmaster, Israel Eddy, moved the office from its location near the river and, in the process, announced he was changing the name of the town to Eddyville. A favorite story about Eddyville's famous character is "Israel Eddy and the Hay Wagon," collected from the WPA files at the State Archives in Salem.

ISRAEL EDDY AND THE HAY WAGON

Although Israel Eddy may have lacked humility and modesty in naming the small Pacific Coast town after himself, no one in the Lincoln County region complained. Israel Eddy was six-feet seven inches tall and weighed more than 260 pounds, a man of colossal strength and brawn, who rarely went through a doorway in the county without having to stoop. His favorite feat of strength was slamming an iron bar down onto an anvil until the bar molded itself into the form of his fist.

One morning in the middle of another rainy Oregon day, a fully loaded hay wagon bogged down in the middle of Eddyville's main street, right in front of the post office. The haulers were fretting and steaming about the bogged wagon, and other people who wanted to pass were equally upset. But Israel Eddy took the problem into his own hands, putting aside stamps and mail sacks for a moment.

Eddy strode across the muddy street, lifted the loaded hay wagon by its back end, and hoisted the mired wheel right out of the bog. With a quick whistle, he urged the horses forward, and they pulled the loaded wagon to firm ground. Local folks agreed with John Baggins that "Israel Eddy can call this town anything he wants. If he decides to name it Israel *and call the Little Elk the* Jordan River, *I doubt any man in these parts would have one word of complaint."*

Hammond

Clatsop County. Population 584. This fishing community near Astoria was named for Andrew B. Hammond, a lumber merchant and railroad builder. Hammond gave his name to the town while constructing the Astoria and Columbia River Railroad in the late 1890s. The Clatsop Indian name of this fishing village was once *Ne-ahk-stow*.

In earlier years, some record salmon were taken at the mouth of the Columbia River, but of course, no fish was ever as large as the ones described by old salts on the docks and piers of Hammond. In 1971 Peter Lindsey heard this story in a Cannon Beach tavern.

A FISH STORY

Just like uh, fishermen up here at Astoria—two old fishermen tellin' how big a fish they caught. This one ol' fisherman said he caught a Chinook salmon weighed a hundred and forty pounds. The other old fisherman sat there and spit out a gobbet of snoose.

He says, "I don't believe that."

"Well, I did."

He says, "That's nothin'." He says, "I was fishing here the other day, caught onto somethin'." Says, "I drug it around and brought it up, and it was an old ship's light."

"An old ship's light?"

"Yeah."

"Well's what's that? What's an old ship's light? Heck, that could have been 'ere everything."

"But," he says, "the light was still burning in it."

"Oh, the light was not burnin'."

"Well," he says, "tell you what you do. You knock about a hundred pounds off the fish, and I'll blow the light out a the lantern."

Sailing from the port at Hammond are charter boats, commercial rigs, and pleasure boats. In 1980, while taking a folklore class at the University of Oregon, John Shepherd catalogued a number of terms used by North Coast fishermen, contributing them to the Mills Archives. From port to port, fishing industry jargon changes readily, partly because ethnic populations differ and partly because "fishing" is really a number of separate skills and trades (see Newport, p. 26). Several of Shepherd's terms show up in this description of the Hammond docks and the fishing grounds.

HAMMOND DOCKSIDE "FISHSPEAK"

The commercial pilots and dockside workers refer to pleasure boats under twenty feet in length as *suicide missions*. In a small craft going over the bar, the *pukers* can often be seen hovering at the ship's rail, and the veteran sailors use the term *hospital ship* for a boat carrying a deck full of sick people.

The commercial fishing boats may be searching for fish other than salmon. A *bucket mouth* is a ling cod, and *blue eyes* are tuna. Sea bass are *brown bombers*, and *ping-pong paddles* are flounders. To catch bottom fish, such as flounder, the crew usually employs a *dipstick*, or depth-sounder. The use of radar, called *the seeing eye dog*, is also commonplace.

In the open waters of the Pacific, a bad fishing day is known as *drowning herring*, and getting *skunked* is particularly unpleasant for charter captains, who cannot afford to return often with an empty boat. On a good day, a *highliner* is ahead of other charter boats in the catch, and being *on the downhill side* means having at least half the limits caught. In the parlance of the charter fleets, *a hand* is five fish. Therefore, a captain who needs *four for three* says that four more fish will complete three hands; in short, the captain means that the charter has netted eleven fish. A *plugged boat* has complete limits for everyone on board.

After a full fishing day, the boats—commercial ships and pleasure craft—return past the Deception Bay *candlestick*, the lighthouse that marks the passage into the Columbia River. Then these boats pass *up the creek* into the mouth of the Columbia and work their way back toward *the knuckle*, or jetty, returning at dusk as the fishermen listen to each other's banter on *Mickey Mouse*, the citizen's band radio.

Kilchis

Tillamook County. In 1871 Kilchis was named for a Native American chief friendly to the settlers. According to one version of the Neahkahnie Treasure legend, Kilchis was descended from a black sailor who had been the only survivor of the Neahkahnie Treasure landing. The black man had impressed the Nehalem Indians with his skills at metalcraft, becoming the personal favorite of the Nehalem chief. Kilchis, the black sailor's son—an imposing man of 275 pounds—eventually became a chief in his own right and established the Kilchis settlement on the east side of Tillamook Bay.

The Tillamook-area Indians enjoyed a bounty from the sea. Salmon and other seafood were prepared in a fire pit, where red-hot stones were covered with seaweed and reed mats. Then the cooks poured water into the pit to steam the fish and shellfish to perfection. Around Kilchis, the settlers also had unique ways of cooking fish and game, as evidenced by this recipe from the *Kilchis Advance*, dated December 18, 1881.

HOW TO DRESS DUCKS

Mr. Editor—There seems to be a great deal of talk about dressing ducks for cooking, which seems to me to be a very simple question, anyone that is at all experienced in the culinary department ought to be versed in that art. Although everyone has their own way of doing things and of course no one else is right, I have my plan and think it is correct. It is what I call a labor-saving plan and is as follows:

First I take my gun, like all modern nimrods, and proceed to the scene of the action, pick out my game and let them have it (that is, the contents of the gun), kill a half dozen or more, gather them up and think like the old chief "Big Injun One," then proceed to the house, where I have some nails driven for the operation. I take the ducks one by one and hang them up by the eyelids, like they do in England, and let them hang there until they drop. By this process they become mellow.

Then I take and pick them, which process is simple. Just lay them on your knee and begin at the neck and stroke them towards the steerage, by doing so you will take off feathers, hair, and all together and the ducks will be found very delicious. To take the blood out I take a little soap and water and rinse them. I was asked by a little German from England how I dressed my ducks if I did not use hot water. I told him, no. When I did tell him my plan he would not believe it. He said he "had picked lots of swill from the kitchens in Hingland and he never seen it done before."

There are some fowls that have very tough eyelids, especially the old geese.

(Signed)—The King of the Kitchen

Manzanita

Tillamook County. Population 509. The manzanita bush, so prevalent in this area, bears a small fruit that has the appearance of an apple, and the Spanish word for "little apple" is *manzanita*. The town itself lies at the south end of Neahkahnie Mountain, perhaps the most famous "lost treasure" location in Oregon. Neahkahnie may mean "the place of the all-powerful god *Ekahni*," a Clatsop deity.

Having circulated for many years, the Neahkahnie Treasure legend has many versions, partly caused by the confusion of two shipwrecks in the same location. In addition to widely told tales of buried treasure, the Clatsop Indians recall a Spanish ship that wrecked in the vicinity in the 1700s, a schooner carrying no treasure, but several tons of beeswax. In 1977 Arthur Thompson, a retired writer, offered one version of the Neahkahnie Treasure story from his small apartment in downtown Manzanita. Art, as he likes to be called, agreed readily to the interview, adding, "I just love to do this." At age seventy-seven, Arthur Thompson proudly noted that his family had lived in the Nehalem area for over 100 years.

THE NEAHKAHNIE TREASURE

My maternal grandparents came to Tillamook about 1860. There were really more Indians here than white folks and, for some reason, my grandparents and their children became closely associated with the Indians. My uncles hunted and trapped with the Indians, and my mother and her sisters—they sort of traded their intellect with one another. For instance, my mother's sisters learned to make baskets from the Indians. . . . In time they all learned the Indians' language—mostly the Chinook Jargon—but two of my uncles did learn the native language.

In their relationship, why, my uncles learned many things from the Indians, and the Indians also learned many things from my uncles. The people began to get curious about this treasure and the beeswax ship and all that, but the Indians were very vague about the treasure ship. They said [the legend] had been handed down from generation to generation—for maybe 200 years. But there was a story that there was a treasure that was landed close to Neahkahnie Mountain; but that finally a Boston Man (which means any white man with long hair on their faces) came with horses around this Neahkahnie trail and took the treasure away.

This same story has been dug out of the archives of the Hudson's Bay Company, a story that was quite similar. There was a great chief, McLoughlin, [who] was employed by the Hudson's Bay Company, and anything that he discovered or found in the area, which was a terrifically [large] area— probably would take in four or five states now—anything that come under his observation, he had to turn that in to the Hudson's Bay Company.

But McLoughlin had married an Indian widow that had two sons, and he tried to bring them into the civilized life, which they couldn't stand, so they took off by themselves. It was thought that John McLoughlin . . . couldn't get his treasure without turning it in to the Hudson's Bay Company, where he wouldn't get anything out of it. But maybe one of his stepson Indians, they could do the trick. A good many people think that's the way it turned out.

Thompson's version of the Neahkahnie Treasure story seems to end with the intercession of Oregon's patriarch, Dr. John McLoughlin, but of course the legend has many other variations. Central to many Neahkanie Treasure legends are the Neahkahnie runes, supposedly left by the Spanish as clues to the burial site. These bold markings have frustrated treasure hunters throughout the twentieth century, inspiring explanations from the reasonable to the outlandish. For scores of years, treasure seekers have puzzled over the meanings of letters, dots, arrows, anchors, and crosses inscribed on rocks alongside the sloping mountainside.

According to a former Eugene postmaster, Ethan Newman, "Records in Madrid, Spain, show that the Neahkanie Treasure was part of a huge gold shipment from the Philippine Islands in 1769. One of the Spanish galleons, loaded down with bullion, was wrecked on the Neahkahnie shore, with most of the Spaniards lost at sea, but some captured and held as slaves." In pioneer times, interviews with local Indians yielded fascinating stories of shipwrecks, murder, and piracy. The Indians said that "a strange ship appeared off the coast, followed by a second, which attacked and wrecked it. Then the defeated craft was looted by the pirates who presumably buried the treasure on the mountain."

In the June 9, 1946, edition of *The Oregonian*, Virgil Smith added other details from the Indian accounts of the treasure burial.

Two ships (some versions say three) appeared one afternoon offshore and began "thundering" at each other. Toward evening one of the ships ran for the shore. It struck the beach, and still they thundered at each other, even after sundown. It was continued the next morning, but soon the distant ship sailed away.

Then strange white men with beards came ashore. There were sixty-five in all. One of them was different, all black. They spent many days carrying things from the ship to the beach. They made a camp. The black man prepared food for the others.

They went up the side of the mountain and did much labor, hard labor on the side of the mountain. It was a mystery to the Indians who watched from behind trees and shrubs. They carried beach sand in blankets up the side of the mountain.

Then one afternoon they carried things up from their camp to the spot where they had been working. Pat Smith's grandmother-in-law as a girl, kneeling fearfully with her mother in the shrubbery across a cross, saw what happened.

The thing which had been carried up the mountain was placed in the ground and covered. Then the leader spoke to the men, and when one stepped forward he was promptly killed. His body was placed in the still-unfilled hole, then the hole was entirely filled. While this was being done, the black one slipped away, then ran in terror. The two Indians, the mother and the little girl, also crept fearfully away.

In some accounts of the Neahkanie Treasure, the huge black man was admired by the coast Indians for his skill with metals, finally becoming a respected advisor to the chief of the Nehalems and fathering Kilchis, the eventual leader of a nearby tribe. In others, the black sailor was the man sacrificed at the treasure site, chosen because his uncommon color would keep the Indians from unearthing the loot.

Pat Smith, whose wife's early relatives were witnesses to the scene on Neahkahnie Mountain, spent most of his adult life and all his money searching for the treasure. Smith hewed out deep gashes on the steep hillsides. He even studied Spanish and Portuguese in the hope that these languages would provide clues to the scattered runic inscriptions. But Smith was just one of many men who devoted their lives to the search, often with disastrous results.

Even today the treasure remains undiscovered, perhaps because, as the Indian legends suggest, the sailors cursed the treasure with the blood that was spilled on the strongboxes. In 1932 two ambitious treasure hunters thought they had figured out the location of the treasure from a reading of the symbols. So they began digging into the sand of the beach, taking into their confidence a nine-year-old boy, who brought them food once a day and promised to keep their secret.

One day the boy returned, and the men were gone. He looked everywhere but could not locate anyone. So, after three days, he went into town and told everyone what he knew. The locals went to the beach and discovered that the sand walls of the diggings had collapsed, burying the treasure hunters under tons of sand.

Mapleton

Lane County. This station on the Siuslaw River was first called Seaton but later changed to Mapleton in recognition of the Oregon maple trees so much in evidence. Mapleton, one of the rainiest spots in Oregon, is also an excellent place for watching the huge salmon runs.

Kim Stafford, Oregon folklorist and singer, wrote a song about Mapleton and the persistent coastal rains after talking to an old-timer in town who had acquired a fondness for watching the salmon run up the Siuslaw. The song begins with Stafford's reflections on that meeting.

WAKE UP, IT'S RAININ'

It started out when I was talking to an old guy named Charlie Camp down in Mapleton, Oregon, on the "wet side." He told me, he said, "You can tell you're in Oregon when you step out onto the porch in a good rainfall and watch the salmon working their way up the creek, and if they hit something they can't get by, they just turn up through the rain and come right by 'em, and you can reach out and snag 'em off the porch.

WAKE UP, IT'S RAININ'

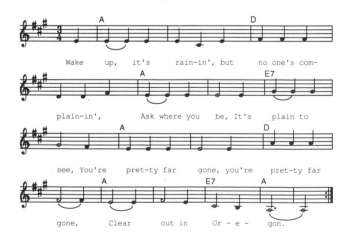

Wake up, it's rain-in', but no one's com-plain-in', Ask where you be, It's plain to see, You're pret-ty far gone, you're pret-ty far gone, Clear out in Or-e-gon.

Wake up, it's rainin', but no one's complainin',
Ask where you be, it's plain to see,
You're pretty far gone, you're pretty far gone,
Clear out in Ore-y-gone.

Now the rain makes a roar as it drips on the floor
You'd better sail, go fetch in the mail
You're pretty far gone, pretty far gone
You're clear out here in Ore-y-gone.

When a baby is born, as everyone knows,
There's moss in its fingers and webs in its toes
It's pretty far gone, pretty far gone
It's clear out here in Ore-y-gone.

But when you head south, your trouble begins
They try to shake hands, you try to shake fins
You're pretty far gone, pretty far gone
You're clear out of Ore-y-gone.

Now some raise hops, and some raise wine
Some raise hell most of the time
Pretty far gone, they're pretty far gone
Pretty far gone in Ore-y-gone.

Some works on the water, some works in the woods
Some wears flippers and others wear hoods
They're all pretty far gone, pretty far gone
They're clear out here in Ore-y-gone.

But no hardship from earthquake, no hardship from heat
It's not rainin' hard, I can still see my feet
I'm pretty far gone, pretty far gone
I'm pretty far gone in Ore-y-gone.

Out here it gets foggy, the sun seldom shines
'Fact, here it gets foggy inside people's minds
They're pretty far gone, pretty far gone
We're clear out here in Ore-y-gone.

Myrtle Point

Coos County. Population 2,705. This community, lying on a
point of land next to the Coquille River, was first called Ott.
But in 1875 Binger Hermann and Edward Bender suggested the name Myrtle Point. In this particular spot is an
abundance of myrtle trees, sometimes called California
laurel. The camphoric smell of the myrtle is one of the
tree's most recognizable characteristics, and the hard,
shiny wood is prized by both cabinetmakers and furniture
crafters. Cooks even use the myrtle like bay leaves for
seasoning meats.

Among the myrtles along the Coquille River, roving
prospectors occasionally laid sluices, hoping to find gold
strikes as rich as those in the Rogue River tributaries. As a
rule, the pioneer prospector was an independent and self-
reliant man, usually able to shift for himself in any demanding or difficult situation. City Creek prospector Al Renfro
tells one memorable story about a rugged gold miner who
managed to train a most unlikely pack animal.

THE PROSPECTOR'S BEAR CUB FORGETS
HIS TRAINING

*A prospector killed himself a bear one day, only to find
out it was a momma with a cub. So he took that cub in and
raised it as best he could. That bear grew up fast and strong,
so the prospector decided he would teach it to pack his stuff
around. He made up a harness and a big pack. That bear
took to training real well. It weren't no time until the prospector was ridin' him, just like a horse.*

*One day he set out to do a little panning. He told the bear
to stay and started out. Didn't get but a mile or so from camp
when he spotted an elk right up by the trail. He killed it and
took to guttin' it and cuttin' it up when his bear come along.*

*"This is good," he thought, " 'cause the bear can carry
all the meat back at one time." Well, that bear sure was
actin' funny. He kept pushing the man around and pawing
at the elk, so the prospector took a couple of hunks of gut and
threw it to the bear.*

*That was all right for a bit, but it weren't long til the
bear was pushin' and growlin' again. Well, that prospector
wasn't going to put up with this foolishness; he took a big
stick and whipped the hell out of that bear. That quieted the
animal down a while.*

*The man finished dressing out the elk and loaded it on
the bear's back, then jumped on himself. Well, that bear
went everywhere but where he was supposed to. He walked
into trees, tried to dump the man off, waded into the creek,
and wouldn't listen to a single command. So the prospector
cut him a good club and beat that bear without mercy. He
jumped back on, and every time the bear would make a
wrong move, he'd let him have a hit with club.*

*It took damn near an hour and a half to go that last mile
back to camp, but they finally made it. The prospector jumps
down, grabs an armload of elk meat, and goes into the cabin,
only to discover his own bear sittin' there on the floor.*

Neskowin

Tillamook County. This coastal village was once the scene of a shipwreck that deposited thousands of slabwood boards on the beach. From that time, the place was known as Slab Creek. Lewis A. McArthur says that in the late 1880s Postmaster Sarah Page overheard a local Indian pointing to Slab Creek and saying, "*Neskowin, Neskowin.*" When asked, the man said that the phrase meant "plenty fish." Mrs. Page soon after petitioned the postal service to change the name of the town to Neskowin. For a five-year period at the turn of the century, the place was known as Marx, after the German socialist who wrote *Das Kapital.* But in 1910, the Indian name for the place was restored.

In the ocean at Neskowin is a huge boulder named Proposal Rock. According to local legend, the rock was named in memory of an ill-fated love affair before the coming of the settlers. The Proposal Rock story is common to many headlands and promontories in the West, a place-name legend that enjoys great popularity. Sandy Skirving, today a noted Northwest folklorist, told the "Proposal Rock" story to Cara Gambell in 1971 while both were students at the University of Oregon.

PROPOSAL ROCK

A young girl from one of the coast tribes fell in love with a warrior from a feuding tribe. Naturally, the elders of the tribes would not let the lovers see each other. But, of course, they met at a secret place, the huge rock in the surf near where the Neskowin Creek enters the ocean.

Proposal Rock has several trees on it and a massive undergrowth. The lovers hid in the maze of underbrush and were protected from the rain by the cover of huge trees. They met on the ocean side, on a promontory overlooking the crashing waves, a very secluded and lovely place.

After the lovers had been meeting like this for a long time, one of the warriors of the maiden's tribe caught them and dragged the girl back to camp for punishment. The elders vowed that she would never again leave the encampment.

But the young girl escaped one moonlit night and ran to her secret place on the rock, where she found her grieving lover. That night, they vowed to be together forever. So, under the warmth of the full moon, they pledged an eternity of love and devotion. The next morning, when the first rays of the morning sun struck the rock, the lovers plunged together into the violent surf below.

Out on this lonely rock now stands a plaque at the place where the Indian lovers were betrothed. And that is how the place came to be called Proposal Rock.

Newport

Lincoln County. Population 8,313. The name Newport is descriptive, a new port for fishing on the Oregon Coast, a town established in 1882.

Nautical types at Newport have their own way of talking about their trade—words and phrases that represent the "in-crowd" of dock-dwellers and line-riggers. In 1978, while collecting a number of "fish stories," Springfield resident Michael O'Dell met with members of fishing crews at The Pub in Newport. One informant displayed a huge scar on the back of her leg, a reminder of the dangers of a fishing boat; the woman's shoelace had caught in the flywheel of the engine when the hatch had been left open. After accepting a bilge full of beers, the woman was willing to talk into O'Dell's cassette recorder. Another informant was Mitch, a fifty-four-year-old Norwegian ship captain, who set the tone for the evening by announcing, "I once caught an eel so long that, after filling seven barrels, I had to cut off the remaining half and throw it back."

As O'Dell discovered, Newport "fish-jargon" is a coded language, a parlance that most people need a glossary to understand. For example, *snotty weather* involves nasty or choppy seas. The whitecaps that form in bad weather are called *popcorn* or *a flock of sheep.* In such inclement weather, a captain may motor past the *Tupperware dock,* where the tourist boats tie up, and proceed to his own mooring, where the *flopper-stopper* is applied, a stabilizer that keeps the boat from rolling. The boat might remain there for a while *belly-up* if the fishing is bad.

But if the weather clears and the fishing boat leaves port, the captain will take the ship out over the rough or *lumpy* bar to do some *tripfishing,* staying out for more than a day. When at the fishing grounds, the crew members break out the *green houchie* and other plastic lures, called *junk.* If fishing with lines, the crew must watch for *whalesnot,* stringers of flayed jellyfish that tangle in the lines. On a good day, a fishing crew may hope to catch a *suitcase,* a fish so fat that a man could put his hat and coat over the belly. A *jellyfish,* however, is not what the name suggests, but an oversized fish with soft, fat meat.

Fishing, like logging, is a dangerous occupation. Nearly every year on the Oregon Coast, a fishing boat fails to return. In any such risky endeavor, there are beliefs and superstitions that form part of an unofficial work code. Although Newport fisherman may wink at these superstitions in mixed company, most of the gill-netters and purse-seiners subscribe to a healthy list of traditional beliefs. Here are a few of the most common items of fishlore from the Newport docks, most of them collected for the Mills Archives by Elizabeth Abrams in 1976.

NEWPORT SUPERSTITIONS AND BELIEFS

☐ *Never start a trip on Friday, especially the 13th.*
☐ *Never say the word "pig" on a boat.*
☐ *Never lay a keel on Friday.*
☐ *Never fill a boat completely with fish.*
☐ *Never bring a black suitcase on board. Only undertakers have black suitcases.*
☐ *Never launch a boat without first blessing it.*

☐ When you're laying the hull, hire a virgin to urinate in the bow, preferably paying her with a gold or silver coin.

☐ Never eat a banana on board.

☐ If you get St. Elmo's fire [a brush discharge of electricity] in the rigging, throw something valuable overboard.

☐ Never set the topsails before the lower sails; it shows arrogance and offends the gods.

☐ The first meal at sea is always fish. Never eat meat for your first meal.

☐ When you start out, throw your change overboard. Pay your dues early, so you won't have to pay them later.

☐ Paint the hull green for good fishing.

☐ Always eat the first salmon you catch.

☐ Never have anything to do with a woman the night before leaving port.

☐ Horns in the masthead are considered good luck.

☐ Always put a coin under the mast before stepping it [fixing the lower end of the mast in the step or supporting block].

☐ Never stick a knife in the boat, especially the mast.

☐ Never spit into the wind. It is the breath of the gods.

☐ When you arrive at the fishing ground, the captain pours the first drops of brandy or wine into the ocean.

☐ Always leave the last stitch in a sail undone, or the sail won't pull right.

☐ Never put a finished knot in a sheet.

☐ If you feed the harbor ducks and keep them fat, you'll have good luck.

☐ It is bad luck to change the name of a boat, even when it changes owners.

☐ To ensure continued good catches, put the biggest fish in the hold last.

☐ Two members of the same family fishing together is bad luck.

☐ Never whistle on board, or you will call up a storm.

☐ If you turn the hatch over on the deck, you will turn the boat over in the sea.

The following story, ''The Newport Mermaid,'' is a good example of folklore collection, capturing what Alan Dundes identifies as the text (story), the texture (narrative style), and the context (surroundings). O'Dell sets the scene carefully, noting in the ''collector's comments'' the woman's appearance (jeans and a jacket), her storytelling style (moderate drunkenness), and the surroundings (a group of old salts trading yarns late at night). However, the transcript also shows the unevenness of many folk narratives. The script contains the verbal glitches, grammatical lapses, and confused statements that one might expect in a storytelling session. Nonetheless, such a broken account has value for folklorists, who recognize the varying skills of narrators and the dynamics of folklore transmission.

THE NEWPORT MERMAID

In the 1920s—there is a recording, believe it or not. . . . You can believe what you want—there is a recording of a real mermaid that they had brought up. She was half woman and half fish. The captain of the boat, he was so infatuated with her . . . [that] he kept it down in his hold when they first brought it up. They thought it was a demon. They wanted to throw it back, a bad omen, you know. And they decided, ''Oh, no, we'd take it to an institute, we'll have it recorded, we'll have it pickled.'' Do you realize how much money you can have from a pickled mermaid?

So anyway, he went on for maybe four or five days. He didn't know how to keep this half woman alive, so he worked with her. He used to come out every morning, and he'd get the ocean water, and he'd pour it over her. The only communication he had with the mermaid was the actual human touch. You know, she gave him human reactions like touching, wanting, trying to communicate with this man: ''You know, I want to be back with the ocean. You know I want to be back, I want to feel free, I want to be back in my home environment.''

But the man was so obsessed with the ability to just have companionship that he tried taking care of her on the boat. He used to wash her down and take care of her. Well, during those times they used to not have medicine—just herbs—and they used to have things they thought would bring different changes in your chemistry in your body. So this one guy that was a crewman decided that he would make up one of his home remedies, and he'd give it to the mermaid. And he promised the captain it would give legs to the being (or half fish, half woman). And he worked and he worked for (God-knows) six months on a new solution. Meanwhile, here is the man pouring water, trying to keep her alive [but he] could never really make actually any communication at all.

Finally he figured out a solution, or whatever, that the mermaid would have to drink. So anyway the captain was desperate by then. He had to give it to her. So he washed her down and washed her down, hoped and hoped that eventually she would become with legs. . . . Right? Instead of half a woman, half a fish. So anyway, he's [the crewman] up on deck screaming ''I found it! I found it! I've gone down into the hold, and she has legs!'' And he [the captain] went down

into the hold, and all you could hear was the captain screaming and yelling, and he was mad by the time he got back onto
the deck. ''I can't believe it! I can't believe it, what happened.'' And the crewmen were just stunned when the
human being finally came out of the hold. . . . And then
finally she comes up, and she's just so grotesque. Her head is
like a fish and her feet are like legs, and she jumped overboard like she'd always wanted to be, and the captain did,
too. And there was never no sign of the captain ever again.

Otter Crest

Lincoln County. Otter Crest, named for the sporting sea
mammal, lies in the heart of Siletz Indian land. Standing in
the surf below Otter Crest is Elephant Rock, a once-
majestic rock formation that began to lose its distinctive
shape in the mid-1920s. Among the Siletz Indians is the
story of the origins of Elephant Rock and its sad decline.
This traditional narrative serves as an etiological legend for
the Siletz, an explanation of the origins of a famous landmark, as well as a rationale for its crumbling destruction.
Another ''Elephant Rock'' stands in Umatilla County (see
Bingham Springs, p. 127). ''The Great Mammoth and the
Fire Demon'' is adapted from materials collected by the
Federal Writers' Project in 1938.

THE GREAT MAMMOTH AND THE FIRE DEMON

*Many years ago, when the animals had dominion over
the Earth, the ancient Fire Demon threatened the living
beasts, driving them by heat and flames toward the shoreline
of the Pacific, and at the same time destroying the forest
lands ashore.*

*One of the noblest animals in this battle was the ancient
mammoth, largest and most proud of the beasts. When the
mammoth was driven from his home in the timbers, he took
a final stand against the Fire Demon on the coast near Otter*

Crest. There he dipped his mighty trunk into the ocean and
battled the Demon with countless blasts of cold seawater.

*In this way the Great Spirit, with the aid of the brave
mammoth, subdued the Fire Demon. In gratitude, the Great
Spirit changed the heroic mammoth to stone, leaving his
gigantic form there in the shoreline, etched against the pale
rays of the dying sun, as a symbol to the Siletz Indians, those
peoples chosen by the Great Spirit to guard forever his land.*

*Elephant Rock remained ever watchful for the return of
the Fire Demon, his long trunk dangling purposefully in the
surf, his form etched majestically against the western sky.*

*Sadly, in 1925 the United States Congress revoked the
reservation status of the Siletz tribe. As though broken by the
fate of the Great Spirit's people, the Elephant Rock began to
crumble, leaving only a shapeless form behind. And within a
few short years, fires once again raged in the forests of the
Siletz land.*

Reedsport

Douglas County. Population 4,777. Reedsport bears the
name of Alfred W. Reed, an early settler in this coastal
region.

The fishing industry thrives at Reedsport, a natural
harbor formed at the mouth of the Umpqua River. Reedsport fishermen, like sailors all over the world, are superstitious. ''To survive in his trade,'' says folklorist Horace
Beck, ''the sailor must be particularly aware of the unusual.'' Indeed, many of these superstitions depend on the
sailor's ability to detect minute changes in the weather or
subtle signs among seabirds. Other superstitions may
derive from obscure rationale, often based in metaphor and
analogy (as in painting the hull green, the color of money,
to assure good fishing).

Some of the practices found at Reedsport simply involve good sense. Painting a boat hull black, for instance, causes the wood to gather excess heat, encouraging cracked seams. Leaving an engine hatch open exposes the crew to obvious dangers, as happened to Michael O'Dell's informant (see Newport, p. 26), who caught her shoelaces in the engine flywheel and lacerated her leg. However, most nautical superstitions depend on association. Saying that cobwebs on board portend heavy fog is one such example, as is the notion that the words "pig" and "rabbit" metaphorically challenge the boat's seaworthiness. Nailing a silver coin to the mast is an ancient tradition, a variant of "buying the wind," as found in classical mythology. Most sailors, however, use small coins, wary of purchasing a squall or a gale.

PIGS, RABBITS, AND HATCH COVERS

☐ *Never say the words "pig" or "rabbit" on board. Pigs and rabbits are notably bad swimmers.*

☐ *Paint the boat hull green for good fishing. Blue hulls are an offense to the sea-gods, and black hulls portend death.*

☐ *Never leave a hatch cover turned upside-down on the deck.*

☐ *When returning to the dock to fetch something forgotten, you must mark a cross in the wood of the dock.*

☐ *A circle around the moon means that there will be a storm.*

☐ *To find cobwebs on board a ship means that you will encounter heavy fog.*

☐ *If a bird lands on your boat, expect rough weather.*

☐ *Never leave port on a Friday.*

☐ *If you lose a shirt overboard, expect evil luck.*

☐ *The worst thing you can have is a hand who comes on board with a black suitcase. Most captains won't even let 'em step on board with a black satchel.*

☐ *It is bad luck to mention the name of a boat unless you own it. Also, owners seldom change the name of a boat when they purchase it. Some boats have resold four or five times, and the current skipper has no idea how it was named.*

☐ *For good luck, nail a silver coin to the top of the mast.*

☐ *If you see shooting stars at night, the next day the wind will blow in the direction that the stars were heading.*

☐ *If a storm is brewing, the sea gulls will fly way up high and circle in the air. Never fails.*

☐ *If a ship comes sideways off the rails when it's launched, it will never have the luck. A lucky boat slides smoothly off the rails into the harbor, straight as an arrow.*

☐ *Nobody should wear anything black on a boat—especially shoes.*

☐ *Nighttime red and morning gray,*
   It's sure to be a fishing day;
   Nighttime gray and morning red,
   Brings the rain down on your head.

Scottsburg

Douglas County. Scottsburg was founded in 1850 by Iowa emigrant Levi Scott. In 1846, Scott had been part of the original party that traversed the Applegate Trail. Scott was prominent in the territorial legislature from 1852 to 1854, and Mt. Scott in the Crater Lake National Park is named for this pioneer settler.

Scottsburg lies in a steep valley of the Umpqua River in an area heavily wooded with fir and cedar trees. Until the Elk Creek Tunnel was blasted through the mountainside for the construction of Highway 38 (from Drain to Reedsport), Scottsburg was somewhat isolated from the Willamette Valley, but a major hub nonetheless, receiving freight from San Francisco and transport wagons from Southern Oregon towns. In 1953, a local storyteller recounted a startling moment in the early history of boomtown Scottsburg.

THE RELUCTANT CORPSE

Back about a hundred years or so, Scottsburg was quite a town. The riverboat would come up from the San Francisco ships, and the mule trains from Jacksonville and towns inland would meet. The trains would take the supplies over the mountains. The bricks for the first church in Jacksonville were hauled from here and, one time, a printing press. Back then, you could count 500 mules grazing on the mountainside around here.

There were twenty-one saloons in town, and they used to be roaring twenty-four-hours-a-day. There were about a dozen whorehouses in town, too. That old house where Henry Jackson and his family lived used to be one of the liveliest. The stagecoach driver used to have a hell of a time getting the passengers away from the bars and the girls. Fast as they'd load 'em in, they'd tumble out the other side. Took the driver hours to get started. Finally they started loading the passengers the day before. They'd load all the drunks aboard and take them out to the old Johnson place and let them sleep it off, then start out early the next morning.

The Johnsons had a boy—boy or man, you couldn't tell—who was a hunchback. He was a town favorite. Every Saturday he went into town, and the boys in the barbershop would give him a dime; over at the drugstore, someone would always buy him a soda. He pretty much had the run of Scottsburg. Well, one day the young man got sick. He wasn't real strong ever, I guess. He finally died, and they had to bury him; that was before there were undertakers here to preserve the body, so they had to get it done.

They got him a coffin from somewhere and put him in it, but because of the curve to his back, he wouldn't lay down the right way. They took all the cushions out and all the padding and tried it again, but he still wouldn't fit right, so they had to tie the lid on with rope.

Well, they were holding the wake for him that night, and pretty near everybody in town turned out. All those old boys were pretty drunk, sitting around there boozing all night and talking about how much they liked the youngster. About that time, rigor mortis had started to set in. I don't know if the rope was rotten or what, but all of a sudden it broke. The lid popped off, and that hunchback sat up all of a sudden.

Man, those guys were out through closed windows; they took doors off the hinges; they just about trampled each other getting out of that place. Some of them could never be talked into going back 'til the longest day they lived.

Seaside

Clatsop County. Population 5,300. On January 1, 1806, after Lewis and Clark had reached "the end of the Trail," they built a salt cairn at the Clatsop village of *Ne-co-tat*, using the cairn to turn seawater into precious salt for the return journey. According to Sally Blisset Taylor, who grew up in Seaside, the name of the town was inspired by Ben Holladay's Seaside House, a famous resort built just south of the Clatsop settlement.

In the 1870s, the Seaside House provided entertainment and sport for some of the Northwest's best-known citizens. But Seaside gradually became a weekend getaway for great numbers of people who enjoyed its brilliant beaches, boardwalk, and arcades as well. Seaside today is also a favorite retirement community, and among the stories told in leisure time is Victor Olson's account of deer hunting in the hills behind Cannon Beach, recorded at Bill's Tavern in Cannon Beach by Peter Lindsey.

A LONG SHOT

This here feller went out hunting, and he drove up into the country. And he seen this deer walkin' along, and he got out his big old powerful Magnum rifle. He watched this deer for a little while, and about the time he got his sights set on it, the deer jumped behind this big tree.

That made him madder than the dickens, so he whirled around with his rifle and shot the other way! Shot it behind him! And it was the last day of hunting season, so he just emptied his rifle out, got back in his car, and drove home.

So, next huntin' season opened up, why, he went back up to this same spot. Here come a deer walking up there, and he loaded his rifle right quick, and he pointed it, and he went to pull the trigger. Just about the time he went to pull the trigger, the darn deer jumped behind a tree! So he pulls his rifle back and all at once the deer jumps straight in the air and dropped over dead.

So he walked around behind the deer and looked at it. And that bullet that he'd fired the year before went around the world and come back and smacked that deer dead center.

Siletz

Lincoln County. Population 932. The town of Siletz is one of many coastal landmarks named after the Siletz Indians, a tribe that lost its reservation in 1925 under pressure from the United States government. The name Siletz originally described only the southernmost Salishan tribe on the Oregon Coast.

In 1976 Peter B. Hilton interviewed two young Caucasian women, Veronica and Rebecca, who had grown up in the town of Siletz. Both recalled the story of the Whistleman, and Veronica said she had often seen him, a nondescript Indian man in baggy pants continually walking the roads near Siletz. "What I imagined to happen," said Veronica carefully, "was that you would see him, and then, three or four miles down the road, you would see him again going in the *same direction*. And you were in the car, and he was walking. And this would happen, you know, over and over on the way to Siletz or going the other way.'' While occasionally punctuating their talk with nervous laughter, Rebecca and Veronica called this vague figure the ''Owl Man.'' Sometimes, they said, he walked through Siletz whispering in a raspy voice, ''Whistleman goin' to get ya.''

Among most Native American tribes, the owl has great power; it is wise to heed the owl's warnings. Here is a typical version of the story of Siletz Owl Man.

THE SILETZ WHISTLEMAN

Around the town of Siletz, people used to talk about the Whistleman. Every once in a while you could drive along the roads near the town and see a round little Indian man in baggy pants—an old man with no distinctive features. But after driving four or five miles, you might see him again, walking the same direction as before.

The Whistleman was well known to the Siletz Indians. They called him Toemannah, *meaning ''part owl, part man.''* Toemannah *was a shaman with magical powers who could turn himself into an owl whenever he wanted. The Siletz feared and respected him, and they knew that his call could be the signal of approaching death.*

The Indians often put out fish for Whistleman, down by the river. And they paid special attention to his call. One time a pair of Siletz loggers were down in a deep canyon surrounded by sheer walls. All of a sudden they heard Toemannah*'s cry, and one said to his partner, ''Let's get out of here.''*

Sure enough, a few minutes later after they had climbed out, the canyon walls began to cave in. Within a few seconds, the canyon was filled with dirt and twisted trees.

Some people say the Whistleman is gone. One day a man was walking into Siletz to buy some supplies. He saw an owl and shot it. The owl fell into his path and bled on the ground before him. Then that man finished his trip into Siletz, bought his supplies, and returned on the same path. When he approached the spot of the shooting, there was a much bigger pool of blood. And he also noticed blood spots moving away from the trail. So the man followed the blood stains through the brush to a shack. There he opened the door and went inside. Sitting in a chair was an old Siletz man, covered with blood. Dead.

Tillamook

Tillamook County. Population 3,986. After a succession of early attempts at naming this harborside community, locals finally settled on Tillamook, an approximation of the name for resident Salish Indians. Tillamook Bay, one of the largest ports on the Oregon Coast, is a rich source of clams and other shellfish.

Before the arrival of the settlers, the coastal Indian tribes took advantage of abundant marine life, preparing fish soups, chowders, and baked fish. Inland, camas lily was available, along with wild nuts and many types of berries. Tillamook women and girls harvested the bulbs with digging sticks, then placed the camas in earthen ovens with fire-heated rocks. Then they covered the camas with layers of leaves and allowed two or three days for the bulbs to bake. The Indians ate the camas immediately or dried it in the sun, packing the vegetable into large loaves for storage. Other vegetables included wild wheat, acorns, tarweed seed, and *wapato* roots, which grow in water. The women prepared acorns by pouring hot water over the ground nuts in a process that removed tannic acid, leaving a mush that could be pounded into a flat bread. Of course, all Native American tribes made use of game, especially deer and elk, and harvested wild berries of many kinds.

Pioneer settlers at the Oregon Coast also ate heartily, learning some foodways from their Native American predecessors. Gerry Highsmith, a longtime Tillamook resident, recounted two traditional recipes in a 1983 interview.

SLIP-GO-DOWN

You asked me about recipes. I do remember two. The first one is a dessert, and I'm sure every pioneer woman made it. In our family it was called slip-go-down, and it was just simply berry juice that was strained through many thicknesses of cheesecloth until it was very clear, and then it was thickened with cornstarch. Sometimes Mama made it thin, and we ate it just like you would shortcake. Sometimes it was quite like Jello. If it was thicker, then we ate it with a spoon, out of a dish. We lived on a farm, so we always had cream. We would eat it with cream on top. We picked all kinds of berries—blackberries, salmonberries, thimbleberries, salal, and all kinds of berries that grew. And we made slip-go-down, no matter what kind of berries.

SALMON STEW

The other recipe is from the Freeman side of my family. I don't know if Grandma Freeman got it from the Indians or not, but they had a special pot (Grandma had the pot, not the Indians)—a large pot, probably about a three-quart pot. Cast iron. They would fill it about one-third full of water and put an awful lot of salt in it. And then there was a strainer that sat inside. They would not peel the potatoes, just cut out the bad spots and put them down in the water. And it would be boiling when they put them in, and then in the sieve portion, they would put carrots, onions, celery (if they had celery). The water would just barely touch the bottom; these things were steamed.

They would cook that all together for about fifteen minutes, and then they would take salmon chunks and lay them on top of these vegetables. And then, you see, mushrooms grew wild at our place. The last few minutes, just the last few minutes before it was done, they would cover the whole top of the stew with wild mushrooms. Morels, I think they were. They were plentiful at the time, and they would put those on top, and they cooked just a few minutes. And that salmon was juicy! It tasted like all those good things underneath, and it was soooooo good. It took them just about a half hour from the time they started. Of course, we caught fish right off the banks—great big, fine salmon—and it was good eating.

Yaquina Bay

Lincoln County. The bay and Yaquina Head bear the name of a local Indian tribe, members of the Yakonan language family. Yaquina Bay is well known for commercial fishing and shellfish harvesting. Yaquina Bay oysters, first discovered in 1861, were for years the featured delicacy at New York's Waldorf-Astoria Hotel. Yaquina Bay was a boom-town in the 1880s, the economy fueled mainly by shipping

trade. In 1887, a total of 144 ships cleared the harbor at Yaquina Bay.

The Yaquina Head light station, erected in 1873, was built in this location by mistake. Materials for the light-house, destined for Otter Crest, were erroneously delivered to Yaquina Head. In the confusion, the lighthouse was built on its present site. The 162-foot building still uses its original lenses, manufactured in Paris in 1868, and the Yaquina Head light can be seen from nineteen miles at sea.

Virtually every lighthouse in America has its own ghost or spirit. The second-oldest lighthouse on the coast, isolated and open to the elements, can be an eerie place. In 1978 Cheryl Lynn Phillips, a folklore student, contributed to the Mills Archives her version of the haunted-lighthouse story, one she heard as a young girl living in Florence.

A STRANGE DISAPPEARANCE AT THE YAQUINA BAY LIGHTHOUSE

As the story goes, there was this girl whose father was the captain of a ship, and he was out to sea, and the rest of the family took care of the lighthouse. While her father was at sea, she invited a bunch of friends over for a picnic, and after the picnic was over, they were all going down. . . . (The lighthouse was on top of a hill.) And they were all going down to the bottom of the hill, and when . . . they got about half-way down, the girl who was the caretaker of the lighthouse remembered that she had forgotten her scarf in the lighthouse and ran back to get it, and she had only been inside for a minute when all her friends heard a scream. They ran back to the lighthouse to see what had happened, but they couldn't find her. All they found was a scarf lying in a pool of blood, and the pool of blood led to a wall that had never been there before. . . . They never did find the girl or figure out what happened to the room that had been there.

The Willamette Valley

The Willamette Valley, 125 miles long and 30 to 60 miles wide, is an area of flat, green prairie generously adorned with rolling hills and buttes. Evergreen trees cover the hills, including fir, hemlock, cedar, spruce, and oak. Beside the many streams, groves of alder and willow flourish. Until the railroads were completed in the 1870s, the Willamette River was the major carrier of commerce. Steamships traveled upstream as far as Springfield and along many Willamette tributaries, including the Tualatin and Yamhill rivers, and towns such as Harrisburg, Albany, and Gladstone grew wherever there were ferry landings and mill sites. Since the earliest days of white settlement, the Willamette Valley has been a significant center of Oregon history.

Few people who took the Oregon Trail were either wealthy or poor; it took money to finance the long overland journey, and a majority of the travelers were farmers who had already known moderate successes. Between the years 1840 and 1860, more than 53,000 emigrants settled in the Willamette Valley. They joined earlier groups, including the "Rocky Mountain Boys," aging trappers who,

along with their Indian wives and children, had settled on the Tualatin Plains. Just across the Columbia River were the aristocratic gentlemen of the Hudson's Bay Company, with their fine manners, fine wine, and fine furnishings. Also, living near French Prairie were clusters of French Canadian adventurers. Merchants arriving by ship from New England comprised yet another distinct company. Despite various backgrounds, most of the early settlers were young, determined, and headstrong; nearly 95 percent were under the age of forty-five.

The increase of settlers had an ill effect on the Hudson's Bay Company, undermining established trade patterns and increasing competition. Even so, Dr. John McLoughlin, chief factor of the company, aided the newcomers with lodging, food, credit, and counsel. He supplied them with seed for their first crops and with articles necessary to set up housekeeping, asking only that the loans be repaid at harvest time. McLoughlin, the husband of an Indian woman, ignored the rules forbidding retired trappers from settling in the area with their native wives. Moreover, he served as judge and jury for Oregon law and order, administering justice less with an Old Testament exactitude than with flexibility and compassion. A formidable man, more than six feet tall with long white hair and eyes of grey steel, he was nicknamed Great White Eagle by the Indians. Although not always popular among the diverse populace, McLoughlin gained universal respect. During the formative years of settlement, McLoughlin was reigning monarch of a domain that stretched from California to Alaska and from the Rocky Mountains to the Pacific Ocean.

Following McLoughlin's advice, Jason Lee led the first missionaries into the Willamette Valley in 1834, locating a mission on the Willamette near its confluence with the Columbia River. These Methodists brought great zeal and good intentions, but little understanding of the Native Americans, who showed total indifference to Christianity and rarely wore clothes. The Methodists could not convince the Indians that their ageless customs were sinful, especially when most of the trappers and other adventurers habitually laid waste to the Ten Commandments. Nonetheless, the industrious missionaries made contributions to Oregon pioneer life. A Methodist school in Salem

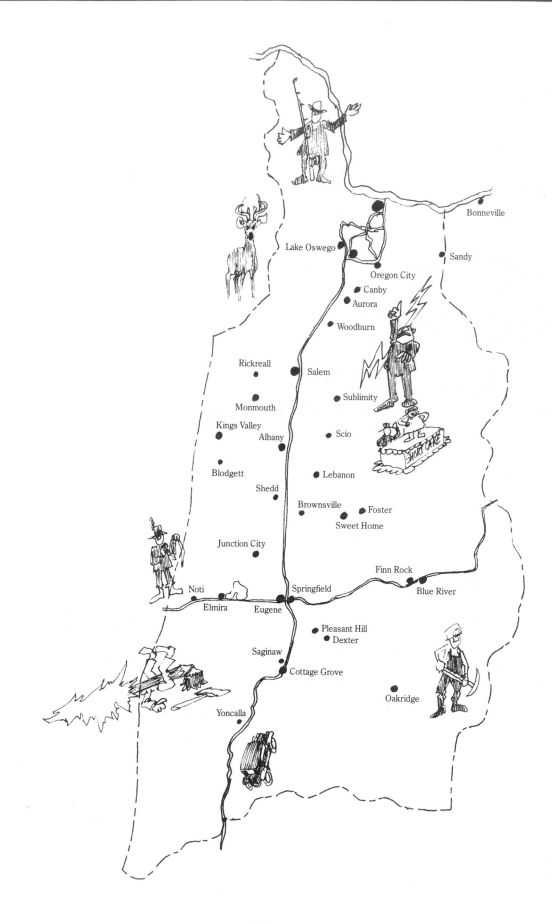

Bonneville

Lake Oswego

Sandy

Oregon City

Canby

Aurora

Woodburn

Rickreall

Salem

Monmouth

Sublimity

Kings Valley

Albany

Scio

Blodgett

Lebanon

Shedd

Brownsville

Foster

Sweet Home

Junction City

Finn Rock

Blue River

Noti

Springfield

Elmira

Eugene

Pleasant Hill

Dexter

Saginaw

Cottage Grove

Oakridge

Yoncalla

John McLoughlin

eventually became Willamette University, and despite minimal successes in proselytizing the Native American residents of Oregon, Jason and Daniel Lee demanded propriety from the new settlers, helping to establish Oregon as the most civilized of the new western provinces.

In a speech before Congress in 1838, Jason Lee made it clear that Oregon was no place for the "reckless adventurer" or the "renegade of civilization." The Oregon Territory, he said, should be the home of only "pious and educated young men." In particular, Reverend Lee railed against the growing influx of Californians, those "unprincipled sharpers of Spanish America," foreshadowing by 100 years the Oregon spirit of isolationism. Apparently Lee's words had some impact. On first arriving in the West, well-known Oregon pioneer Jesse Applegate wrote to his brother that "almost all the respectable portion of the California immigrants are going on the new road to Oregon, and nearly all the respectable immigrants that went last year to California came this year to Oregon." In *Empire of the Columbia*, Dorothy Johansen repeats a popular item of folklore; apparently there was a hand-lettered sign outside Fort Hall pointing to "Oregon." Those who could read followed the northern route to the Willamette Valley; those who could not, blundered into California.

As the Valley communities continued to grow, legal problems arose, primarily because no nation held title to the Oregon land. "Joint occupation" was the rule of the day, with both Great Britain and the United States laying claim to the country. The death of prominent pioneer set-

tler Ewing Young brought the problem of "joint occupation" into the public forum. In 1834, Ewing Young had arrived from California, driving large herds of cattle; at his death in 1841, he left no heirs, and the cattle roamed free in the Chehalem Valley. Soon wolves and panthers gathered to prey on the calves, and the settlers decided to call "wolf meetings" to organize a bounty hunt. It was agreed that each person present should contribute five dollars toward a bounty on wolves, bears, bobcats, and panthers. The "wolf meetings," however, soon gained another purpose. Meeting at the home of Joseph Gervais, the settlers appointed a committee of twelve to consider the need for a provisional government in Oregon.

The third "wolf meeting" at Champoeg was tumultuous. The British subjects were crying "sedition," and the Americans called for separation from the rule of the Hudson's Bay Company. The French Canadians withdrew to themselves. At length, irrepressible trapper Joe Meek shouted enthusiastically, "Who's for a divide? All in favor of the report and an organization, follow me!" After a few minutes, fifty men stood with Meek, and fifty men stood their ground. At that moment two French Canadians stepped forward and made history; Etienne Lucier and F. X. Matthieu walked casually to the American side, breaking the tie and deciding the issue for the United States.

Joe Meek

In 1845 a provisional government was formed at Champoeg, and George Abernathy became the temporary governor. Abernathy chose J. Quinn Thornton as his envoy, and Thornton embarked by sea for Washington. The provisional legislature, however, preferred Joe Meek as their envoy. He was appointed "Envoy Extraordinary and Minister Plenipotentiary for the Republic of Oregon to the Court of the United States." Given $500 for travel, Meek threw an enormous party for all his friends and rode off with a hangover to solicit his way across country. When he reached the Mississippi, Meek depended on charm to pay his steamboat passage, declaring himself "Envoy Extraordinary" and cousin to President James K. Polk.

On March 3, 1849, the day before leaving office, President Polk appointed General Joseph Lane governor of the Oregon Territory, after failing to interest Abraham Lincoln in the position. Asked if he would be willing to serve in the western territory, Lane responded, "I'll be ready in 15 minutes." Perhaps Lane later wished he had taken longer to decide about the governorship. In the 1850s, the increase of settlers fomented Indian hostilities in the Oregon Territory. With the ever-increasing encroachment upon their lands, the Native Americans found themselves losing traditional hunting grounds and camas fields, and large numbers of their people were falling prey to smallpox. In time, scattered Indian attacks increased. The Cayuse Indians attacked the Whitman mission; the Rogues battled settlers in Jackson County. All over Oregon, Indians were fighting to retain rights to their lands.

In the midst of the Indian uprisings, gold was discovered—first in California and then in Oregon. People from all walks of life joined the mad rush to the goldfields. In 1849, within a few months of the news from Sutter's Mill, two thirds of Oregon's adults had left for the California gold strikes, leaving fields fallow and business doors locked. However, many of these Oregon miners acquired easy fortunes, returning with $30,000 or $40,000 in gold dust, money to pay off debts, improve businesses, and buy property. Those who stayed home profited, too; miners needed lumber and supplies. Soon the price of wheat soared to $4 a bushel; flour sold at $15 a barrel; and timber brought $100 per thousand feet. In a matter of months, the crude cabins of Oregon settlers were often replaced with the kind of homes reminiscent of New England or the Deep South.

Another thing Oregon shared with the South was the divisive issue of slavery. On June 26, 1844, the provisional legislature enacted a paradoxical law: white Oregonians could not legally own slaves; nevertheless, blacks could not remain in Oregon as free citizens. Oregon law stated that "slavery and involuntary servitude shall be forever prohibited in Oregon." However, free blacks could not remain in the territory as adults. In fact, "if such a free negro or mulatto fail to quit the Oregon country, he or she may be arrested upon warrant issued by a justice of the peace and if found guilty upon trial, the justice shall issue an order to any competent officer, directing said officer (giving 10 days notice with at least four written advertise-

ments) to publicly hire out such negro to lowest bidder who will obligate himself to remove such negro from the country within six months (signing bond of at least $1000) after such term of service." Such were the foundations of Oregon's onerous *sundown laws*.

The legislature's edicts were not always obeyed. Colonel Nathaniel Ford came from Missouri with three black slaves and settled in Polk County. Two of the slaves, Robbin and Polly, married and had several children. Although they gained their freedom and established a home near Nesmith's Mill, the couple lost their children to Ford, who retained them as his property. In 1853 Robbin obtained a writ of habeas corpus and regained the custody of his children. Even more shocking is the widely circulated story that Governor Joe Lane, admittedly an opponent of the abolitionists, continued to keep a slave on his Roseburg farm until the late 1870s. Soon the slavery issue erupted into open forum. In small communities, both Union and secession meetings were held. One Oregon newspaper was suppressed for declaring the southern leaders "the glory of the land" and referring to Union soldiers as "the enemy." The official flag of the Confederacy flew openly in several communities; towns such as Monroe, Corvallis, and Albany supported lodges of the Knights of the Golden Circle, a predecessor of the Ku Klux Klan.

Slavery, like most legal matters in pioneer Oregon, was a relative proposition; throughout the legal system, justice was dispensed irregularly. According to *Oregon Oddities*, in 1875 a ten-year-old boy from Multnomah County was convicted of stealing candy; he served his full three-year sentence in the Oregon State Penitentiary. At the same time, "a man sentenced to life for murder was pardoned after four months." Except in the cases of dangerous candy thieves, early Oregon law was forgiving and incompetent. The first 100 Oregon convicts tried for crimes ranging from larceny to murder received sentences averaging only three years. "Several of this number," says the *Oddities* editor, "were pardoned, and 73 escaped, reducing the time actually served to an average of one year." In a fifteen-year period from 1861 to 1875, every single man serving a life term in prison either escaped or drew a pardon.

Always the population center of Oregon, the Valley is still home to 60 percent of the state's people. Eight of Oregon's ten largest cities lie somewhere between the Columbia River and Cottage Grove, the north-south boundaries of the Willamette Valley. For much of the length of the Valley, the Willamette River meanders lazily. The stream passes Springfield, one of Oregon's largest mill towns; Eugene, home of the University of Oregon; Corvallis, the "heart" of the Valley and location of Oregon State University; Salem, the state capital; Oregon City, the seat of provisional government in the 1840s; and Portland, Oregon's only true urban center.

The Valley has a remarkable diversity in place-names,

some historical, some fanciful, and some colorful. The Pudding River, located east of Salem, was named by two French trappers, Joseph Gervais and Etienne Lucier, who came upon a herd of elk and shot some of the animals. Immediately the Indian women in the party made blood pudding from the kill, and the Frenchmen later christened the stream "Riviere au Boudain," or Pudding River. In 1880 robbers reputedly buried their loot in a clearing west of Mt. Hood; the location where treasure hunters dug for the cache became known as Horse Thief Meadows. In Lane County, the German community of Coburg was named for a Prussian stallion from the old country. Near Salem, Murder Creek ran red with blood when two men fought over a pair of boots. In the Blue River area, a wagon-train cook baked up a batch of stone-hard sourdough biscuits; rather than complain to the source, the victims christened the spot Deathball Rock. Gales Creek in Washington County was named for Joseph Gale, master of the *Star of Oregon*, first ship built in the state.

Swisshome, Helvetia, and Bohemia all tell the stories of Swiss-German immigrants, as does the town of Berlin. Mt. Angel is the Americanized version of Engelberg, a town in Switzerland. Orient, near Gresham, was the homestead of Oregon's first Japanese settler, Miyo Iwakoshi, the 1880 bride of Andrew McKinnon. Multnomah County's Ban was named after a Japanese mill owner who entered Oregon in 1891. In the Eugene area, Danebo is home to great numbers of Danish settlers. Champoeg is clearly of French origin, perhaps a French Canadian reference to the abundance of "weeds" in the area.

Benton County's Buttermilk Creek derived its name when local "smelling committees" discovered that a creamery was discharging its excess buttermilk into this tributary of Mary's River. Near Monroe, the Long Tom River once supported prospectors with their portable sluice boxes, called "long toms," although one longtime Oregon resident says Long Tom derives from the Chinook Jargon *lumlum*, meaning "rum" or "whiskey"—not a bad guess considering the number of Whiskey Creeks in Oregon. In Columbia County, Bachelor Flat was home to a large number of unmarried men; for those who preferred female companionship, Washington County's Blooming provided a place for bachelors to pick flowers before going courting.

Gray Eagle Bar in the Willamette River gained its designation when a steamer stuck on its sands for several days, and Fashion Reef near Multnomah Falls was the final resting place of this Columbia River steamer. A tributary of Hills Creek, TNT Creek was named when a mule jettisoned a box of dynamite on its banks while workers were building a trail. Clackamas County's Splintercat Creek takes its name from a legendary animal that stalks the woods, splintering branches with its tail—a feline known around Northeastern Oregon's town of Unity as the "beaver cat." Tom Dick and Harry Mountain, of course, has

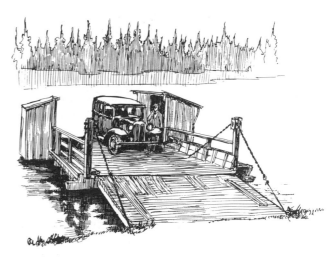

three distinctive peaks; Inch Creek near the Salmon River covers about one inch on most Oregon maps.

Enola in Clackamas County came from "alone" spelled backwards, a reference to a solitary settler, and Ten O'Clock Church gained fame when United Church of Christ members, unable to afford a timepiece for their church tower, painted a clock face with the hands permanently fixed. Nofog, of course, has no fog, and Gone Creek is, well . . . gone.

Albany

Linn County. Population 29,161. This community, settled before 1850, was named for Albany, New York. At one time it was known as New Albany. Among other things, Albany is famous for the pencil sharpener, invented by Dr. E. O. Smith.

Perhaps the biggest news to come from Albany since the pencil sharpener is the sighting of a seven-foot, 400-pound albino creature in the Conser Lake area, some five miles northwest of the Albany Wah Chang chemical plant, an unmistakable Oregon landmark. The creature, resembling a cross between a gorilla and a polar bear, first made its appearance late in 1959, running alongside a truck making a night delivery to the mint fields. According to Mike Helm, who summarizes these events in *Oregon's Ghosts and Monsters*, the truck driver gunned the vehicle to a speed of thirty-five miles per hour, but the monster continued to keep pace. Later, on August 5, 1960, journalist Betty Westby reported a monster sighting near Conser, the news appearing in a guest column of *Greater Oregon*, an Albany weekly.

> Last Sunday night seven teen-agers from Albany received the fright of their lives when the creature appeared in the lanes of Conser Lake (road) where they were out for a moonlight stroll. . . .
> Two of the boys had been lurking in the lane in order to jump out and startle their friends when they heard a crashing noise that they said was too large for a human source to cause. A seven-foot creature, white in the moonlight, its features indistinguishable, came squishing down the lane, making noise, said one boy, as though he had water in his overshoes. The youngsters could not distinguish any garments, however, and described the same furry appearance of which the mint truck driver had told in his first encounter.

After the story was reported on radio KGAL in Albany, the Conser Lake lowlands became swamped with monster-hunters, many of them toting guns. Within the week, one Albany resident claimed to have wounded the monster in the shoulder. In short order, reporter Westby hurried to the scene, where she discovered "heavy impressions of a great, spraddling foot, similar to a wedge or duck foot," the impressions falling "six and seven feet apart." After these reports were filed, Linn County police officers released two hounds around Conser Lake, but the dogs were "literally torn to ribbons," according to Westby. Even today, the Conser monster remains a mystery, perhaps still hiding in the fens around Conser Lake.

Aurora

Marion County. Population 564. Dr. William Keil founded this community in 1857 and named it after his daughter, Aurora. Keil was the leader of the Bethelites, a group of Christian communists. These hearty Germans established a religious commune first called Aurora Mills, with Keil as the first postmaster. But the name was changed to the present Aurora in 1894. This group of religious idealists first operated as a group in Pennsylvania before moving to Bethel, Missouri, and then on to Oregon Territory. After establishing their commune, the Bethelites attracted many newly arrived German immigrants.

Dr. Keil's German immigrants were industrious workers whose products gained a reputation for excellence during the early days of Willamette Valley settlement. In Aurora, no cash changed hands, however. According to Keil's communist methods, only barter and exchange were allowed. One of the Bethelites' most popular products was Golden Rule whiskey, a popular medium of exchange in old Oregon. Ironically, it was a prime factor in the Bethelites' safe journey across the Oregon Trail at a time when many wagons were besieged by Indians, as the following "history" demonstrates. Details of Willie Keil's journey come from two sources. The first is Stewart Holbrook's *The Far Corner*; the second, an oral history that Jean Campbell gathered from Frances Blair, a woman who had spent time with the German community in Aurora and had once visited Willie Keil's final resting place near Menlo, Washington.

WILLIE KEIL AND THE "GOLDEN RULE"

Dr. William Keil's German commune, based on common ownership, equality, and cultural achievement, was established in 1844 in Bethel, Missouri, not far from Independence, the organizing point for many of the Oregon Trail wagon trains. "Oregon Fever" soon spread to the Bethelites, and the group prepared to travel west, where they could expand their ministry and acquire cheap land for cultivation.

After two months of frenzied preparations, the 250 members of the commune began to pack their wagons for the trip to the New Canaan. Dr. Keil had several children, but only one son. Willie Keil, who was about sixteen years old, asked his father, "Could I please drive the lead wagon?" Dr. Keil agreed, and Willie could hardly wait for the day of departure.

Willie did not live to see the train on its way. Four days before embarking, Willie Keil became sick with a fever. In two days he was dead. His grief-stricken father knew he must somehow keep his word to the boy; and with the Bethelites' help, Willie Keil led the wagons west. The artisans built a lead coffin and filled it with Golden Rule whiskey. At the head of the column of thirty-four rigs was a special hearse with open sides, the wagon containing Willie Keil's coffin and several gallons of whiskey. Over the coffin was a crossbar outfitted with hundreds of bells, which rang as the wagon rumbled across the prairie.

In 1855 the train moved away from Bethel with the emigrants playing guitars, zithers, flutes, and drums. The Bethelites accompanied the train to the tune written by Keil for his son's funeral, "Das Grab ist Tief und Stille." The procession was led by a brass band and a *schellenbaum*, an umbrellalike structure with bells attached. When the wagons arrived in Fort Kearney, they found that the

Sioux and other plains Indians were attacking virtually every wagon to cross the Oregon Trail. Without fear, Keil said, ''The Lord will preserve and guide us.''

Shortly beyond Fort Kearney, a small party of Sioux halted the procession, but not to raid the wagons. The hearse was fascinating to the Indians. They came to investigate the music and the bells, stopping the train to demand access to the lead-lined box. Dr. Keil, without any objection whatsoever, opened the casket and showed the Indians Willie's body floating in alcohol. The Indians were petrified; they wondered what kind of God would allow such things.

After that first incident, the Bethelites were assured safe passage. As they traveled from town to town on the journey west, they heard repeated tales of atrocities and massacres; but the Indians who approached the wagon train came only to view the body. At one point a huge band of warriors lined up alongside the hearse, riding single-file past Willie's body while the Germans sang their dirge. Every once in a while, the Bethelites would round a small hill or pass a bluff and find a newly killed buffalo or elk—a gift to pacify these strange people, the Bethelites.

Blodgett

Benton County. Founded as Emrick in 1888, this community on Mary's River was finally named Blodgett after a Corvallis-area settler. In Blodgett's churches, one of the most popular hymns was ''Beulah Land,'' a standard tune in Protestant congregations throughout Colonial America. The words of the hymn describe a land of heavenly abundance.

BEULAH LAND

I've reached the land of corn and wine,
And all its riches now are mine.
Here shines undimmed one blissful day,
For all my night has passed away.

Chorus:
Oh, Beulah Land, sweet Beulah Land,
As on thy highest mount I stand,
I look away across the sea
Where mansions are prepared for me
And view the shining glory shore,
My heaven, my home for evermore.

As the pioneers started west, they sang this song and pictured a heaven on earth—their Beulah Land. However, the wanderers sometimes discovered that their destinations were not exactly ''the land of corn and wine.'' As a result, several parodies reconstructed the image of the Promised Land. For those who reached Oregon, there were also some disappointments. In Central Oregon the parched newcomers sang their own laments about cloud-

less skies and barren dirt (see Bend and Fort Rock, p. 101 and 105). On the ''wet side,'' the mud-caked Willamette Valley settlers sang ''Beulah Land'' parodies with emphasis on the incessant rains. In most variants, such as ''Oregon Girls,'' there is a grudging recognition that constant Oregon rain has some benefits—in this case, ''flowers that in springtime grow/and many shrubs that bud and grow.''

OREGON GIRLS

We've reached the land of rain and mud,
Where trees and flowers so early bud,
And where it rains the blessed day
For in Oregon it rains always.

Chorus:
Oh! Oregon, wet Oregon,
As through the rain and mud I run,
I stand and look out all around,
And watch the rain soak in the ground.
Look up and see the waters pour
And wish it wouldn't rain no more.

A sweet perfume is on the breeze;
It comes from fir and alder trees
And flowers that in springtime grow
And many shrubs that bud and blow.

Chorus:
Oh! Oregon girls, wet Oregon girls,
With laughing eyes and soggy curls,
They'll sing and dance both night and day
Till some Webfooter comes their way.
They meet him at the kitchen door
Saying, ''Wipe your feet or come no more.''

Another Oregon version of ''Beulah Land'' was composed by a wood-cutter who was spending the winter in the Blodgett area about 1920. In 1982, Ruth Wright, a transplanted Kansan, added the last verse. Twilo Scofield collected the words after a folk-song performance in Salem in 1983. In typical style, ''Webfoot Land'' reveals the singer's ambivalence about the Valley, a place that is hard to endure in a downpour, but lush and green when the sun finally peaks through.

WEBFOOT LAND

I've reached the land of mud and rain;
I've struggled long this land to gain.
And now that I have reached the spot,
I sometimes wish that I had not.

Chorus:
Oh, Webfoot land, wet Webfoot land,
As in my house I sadly stand
And gaze with-out through dripping pane
And wonder when 'twill cease to rain,
I often wish that I could fly
To land where it was sometimes dry.

It rains at morn, it rains at eve,
It rains at night, there's no reprieve.
Day after day, it's just the same—
I often wonder why I came.

The people ride around in hacks
With green moss growing on their backs.
They leave their apples on the trees
And dig potatoes when they please.

If ever I do get the cash,
For eastern lands I'll make a dash.
I'll live where I the sun can view
And have my clothes look dry and new.

Then when my garden gets too dry,
And when for gentle rain I cry,
Or shoveling snow makes blistered hand,
I'll run right back to Webfoot land.

Blue River

Lane County. Blue River is a village at the juncture of the Blue and McKenzie rivers, notable for the pure blue water flowing downstream at this point. Blue River is a productive fishing spot, and during the season it is a popular gathering place for anglers from the Valley and beyond.

Anglers usually have their special theories about when and where to fish. Some always look for a drizzly, overcast day; others wait for a precise water temperature. Richard Mitchell's companion had his own method of locating the big ones: "I used to go fishing with a guy who would get into the boat, sit down, and unzip his pants. He would look at his penis to see which way it was turned. If it was lying toward the left side, he would fish out that side of the boat; if on the right, he would fish that side. If it was lying straight, he figured fishing would be poor."

In 1985 Harry Tackett, an Oregonian transplanted from Texas, heard this extraordinary lie, a *Münchausen*, from an old fisherman one morning in a cafe at Leaburg, approximately twenty-five miles below Blue River on the McKenzie Highway. Tackett, himself a yarn-spinner and purveyor of "aggie" jokes, recognized immediately the germ of a familiar story. "I used to tell one something like this myself," he told Tom Nash in Ashland. A similar story

appears later in the section on Frenchglen, attributed to Tebo, the Wild West storyteller of Pete French's P Ranch.

SYLVIA

Blue River has always been my favorite fishing spot, but I don't know if I can ever go there again. It's a sad story, really, but one I can't seem to keep to myself. It all began in 1924, the year before the Blue River Inn burned down. But the fire was a lesser tragedy than the loss of poor Sylvia.

One day in the middle of a McKenzie River downpour, I hooked into a good-sized rainbow trout. When I pulled the fish up on shore, I saw there was something special about this one. She had deep brown eyes and a kind of pleading look; she was also bleeding from lashing against the rocks. So, in a moment of compassion, I took the fish back to my cabin and filled the tub with fresh water. I nursed that fish back to vitality, and she seemed to show her appreciation in those deep eyes.

In a while, I discovered that my fish could spend short periods of time out of water. Eventually the trout learned to prop herself up on a fin on top of my desk. Within weeks, she could spend hours at a time out of the tub, and after six months she had a room of her own and never thought more about her life in the river.

Then I noticed that my fish wanted to communicate. So, on a hunch, I took her to the veterinarian at Vida. Dr. Jonathan Pinehurst suggested a simple operation, and after administering a bit of novocaine, he commenced with the tongue clipping. In no time at all, my fish was trying to speak. With her first words, she said her name was "Sylvia."

Sylvia proved a wonderful companion. She became a brilliant conversationalist, and one day I came home to find her on the front porch giving fish-tips to anglers for 50 cents apiece. She also arranged a series of nature lectures at the Blue River Inn and attracted a small but dedicated local audience. One day, however, Sylvia decided she was lonely; so, at my suggestion, she joined the first grade class at Blue

River Grade School, where Mrs. Katz taught Sylvia to read, although one of the students had to turn the pages for her.

School, however, proved to be Sylvia's downfall. One June day, the class followed Mrs. Katz on a picnic outing to a park just outside of town. While the children were playing on a dock at the stream-side, one of the boys started rough-housing, and my poor Sylvia fell into a deep pool of the Mc-Kenzie River.

Despite the noble efforts of Mrs. Katz, who came as soon as she was called, there was nothing that could be done. Before anyone could save her, Sylvia drowned—in the very pool that she had once called home.

Bonneville

Multnomah County. Washington Irving popularized the name of this western explorer in his book *The Adventures of Captain Bonneville.* McArthur, in *Oregon Geographic Names,* suggests that this West Point graduate may have been the first white explorer into Wallowa County. In 1933 the Columbia River was changed forever with the opening of construction on Bonneville Dam.

In 1941 Woody Guthrie was hired as a ''public relations consultant'' by the Bonneville Power Administration in its battle to overtake small power companies operating on the Columbia River. At this time, the Bonneville authorities were trying to provide a cheap source of power for the Northwest. Largely because Guthrie's songs were so convincing, public power won the voters' approval. In twenty-six days Guthrie wrote twenty-six ballads—among them ''Roll on, Columbia''—and received $266.66 for his efforts. In 1942 the power administration created a movie, *The Columbia,* that featured several of Guthrie's songs; the film was destroyed in 1953 under orders of Douglas McKay, interior secretary under Eisenhower.

ROLL ON, COLUMBIA

1. *Green Douglas fir where the waters cut through,*
    Down her wild mountains and canyons she flew,
    Canadian Northwest to the ocean so blue,
    Roll on, Columbia, roll on.

Chorus:
  Roll on, Columbia, roll on
  Roll on, Columbia, roll on
  Your power is turning our darkness to dawn,
  So roll on, Columbia, roll on.

2. *Other great rivers add power to you,*
    Yakima, Snake and the Klickitat, too,
    Sandy Willamette and Hood River, too,
    Roll on Columbia, roll on.

Chorus

3. *Tom Jefferson's vision would not let him rest,*
    An empire he saw in the Pacific North-west,
    Sent Lewis and Clark and they did the rest, so
    Roll on, Columbia, roll on.

Chorus

4. *At Bonneville now there are ships in the locks,*
    The waters have risen and cleared all the rocks,
    Ship-loads of plenty will steam past the docks, so
    Roll on, Columbia, roll on.

Chorus

5. *And on up the river is Grand Coulee Dam,*
    The mightiest thing ever built by a man,
    To run the great factories and water the land, it's
    Roll on, Columbia, roll on.

Chorus:
  Roll on, Columbia, roll on
  Roll on, Columbia, roll on
  Your power is turning our darkness to dawn,
  So roll on, Columbia, roll on.

Brownsville

Linn County. Population 1,273. Brownsville, lying at the foot of the Cascades, was named for an early emigrant, John Brown, one of Oregon's first black landholders.

''Springfield Mountain,'' believed to be America's oldest folk song, has many variants. Three versions are included here. Originally written as an elegy in 1761, ''Springfield Mountain'' borrows its melody from the ''Old Hundred,'' commonly called The Doxology. The first version recalls the death of Timothy Myrick and ends with a warning to the faithful: Remember God, for death may come at any moment.

SPRINGFIELD MOUNTAIN

On Springfield Mountain there did dwell
A handsome youth was known full well;
Lieutenant Merrick's only son,
A likely youthful twenty-one.

On Friday morning he did go
Down to the meadows for to mow.
He mowed, he mowed all around the field
With a poisonous serpent at his heel.

When he received his deathly wound,
He laid his scythe upon the ground.
For to return was his intent,
Calling aloud long as he went.

His calls were heard both far and near,
But no friend to him did appear.
They thought he did some workman call;
Alas, poor man, alone did fall.

Day being past, night coming on,
The father went to seek his son,
And there he found his only son,
Cold as a stone, dead on the ground.

He took him up and carried him home
And on the way did lament and mourn,
Saying, "I heard, but did not come,
And now I'm left alone to mourn."

In the month of August, the twenty-first,
When this sad accident was done,
May this be a warning to you all
To be prepared when God shall call.

A later version, sometimes called "The Pesky Serpent," describes a stricken young man and his intended wife; the woman, who sucks the poison from his wound, infects her own rotten tooth, and the poison kills them both. Wayne Tabler, who as a young man spent his summers working on a hay bailer near Brownsville, says there were plenty of rattlesnakes in those hills; he gathered up a couple of rattlers every day in the machinery. "Brownsville Mountain" was recorded by Walter Bolton in Eugene in 1970.

BROWNSVILLE MOUNTAIN

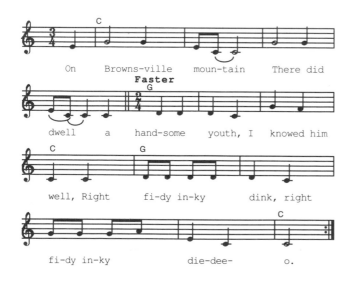

On Brownsville Mountain there did dwell
A handsome youth, I knowed him well
Right fidy-inky-dink
Right fidy inky di-dee-o.

This handsome youth one day did go
Down in the meader for to mow hay
Right fidy-inky-dink
Right fidy-inky-di-dee-o.

He had not mowed half round the field
When a rattlesnake come and bit him on the heel
Right fidy-inky-dink
Right fidy-inky-di-dee-o.

Oh, Johnny laid upon the ground
He closed his eyes and he looked all around
Right fidy-inky-dink
Right fidy-inky-di-dee-o.

"Oh, Johnny dear, why did you go
Down in the meader for to mow hay
Right fidy-inky-dink
Right fidy-inky-di-dee-o."

"Oh, Sally dear, I thought you knowed
'Twas Pappy's hay and it had to be mowed
Right fidy-inky-dink
Right fidy-inky-di-dee-o."

Oh, Johnny laid upon the bed
In half an hour he went dead.

"Rattlesnake Mountain" is the third variant of this popular tune, one that adds a laconic warning against the wiles of unmarried pioneer women. Wayne Tabler collected this version while working on a Brownsville farm in 1946.

RATTLESNAKE MOUNTAIN

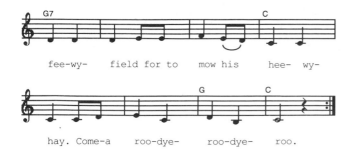

fee-wy- field for to mow his hee- wy-

hay. Come-a roo-dye- roo-dye- roo.

On Rattlesnake me-y Mountain I did dwee-wy dwell
When I heard a stee-y story I'm 'agonna tee-y tell
Come a roo-die-roo-die-roo.

A nice young mee-y man in the month of mee-y May
Went down in the fee-y field for to mow his hee-y hay
Come a roo-die-roo-die-roo.

He had not mow-y mowed half 'round the fee-y field
When a rattle copper snee-y snake come bit him on the hee-y heel
Come a roo-die-roo-die-roo.

He jumped up hee-y high and he looked all a-ree-y round
Then he closed his ee-y eyes and he fell to the gee-y ground
Come a roo-die-roo-die-roo.

He said, "Little b-y bird, go and tell my gee-y gal
I'm 'a rattlesnake bee-y bit and I need my See-y Sal."
Come a roo-die-roo-die-roo.

"Oh, Johnny dear-y dear, why did you go-y go
Into the fee-y field the hay for to mow-y mow?"
Come a roo-die-roo-die-roo.

"Oh, Sally dear-y dear, I thought you knee-y knowed
When the hay gets ree-y ripe, it's got to be mee-y mowed."
Come a roo-die-roo-die-roo.

"Oh, Johnny dear-y dear, I'll save your lee-y life
If I may be-y be your sweet little wee-y wife."
Come a roo-die-roo-die-roo.

She grabbed his lee-y leg and made him squee-y squeal
And sucked that pizen blood all out of his hee-y heel
Come a roo-die-roo-die-roo.

So come all young me-y men and a warning tee-y take
Don't ever get bee-y bit by a rattle copper snee-y snake
Come a roo-die-roo-die-roo.

When a rattlesnake bee-y bites, it hurts like a knee-y knife
When a woman bee-y bites, you're bit for the rest of your life
Come a roo-die-roo-die-roo.

Canby

Clackamas County. Population 8,936. Canby was named for Major General Edward Canby, a casualty of South Central Oregon's Modoc Wars. In 1873 in the Lava Beds below Klamath Falls, General Canby, Alfred B. Meacham, and the Reverend Eleazar Thomas entered a peace conference with Captain Jack and his representatives. The Modocs attacked the unarmed men, killing Canby and Thomas, and partially scalping Meacham, who survived.

Canby lies in a bountiful agricultural area. It is surrounded by lush farms, where harvesters gather crops of all kinds, including green beans and turf grass. The soil in Canby is dark and rich, gently irrigated by the profuse rains and protected by the "wet side's" temperate climate. A native of Canby reports that zucchini squash grow especially fast in the local soil: "One year, a few hours after I planted zucchini seeds, the dirt began to fly, and the zucchini vines came bursting out of the ground from all directions. I turned to run, but the vines overtook me less than 50 yards from the seed hill. Why, I had to cut myself free with my pocket knife, or I would have been crushed to death by a sizeable zucchini squash that was growing right on my chest."

Although the growing season is long and bountiful in Canby, Willamette Valley residents pay for this lushness when they endure the insistent rains. In 1971, Betty Ann Woolley contributed this story to the Mills Archives, a typical joke about the Valley weather.

TOO WET TO BURN

A man won a lottery, and the prize was a visit to Hell. When he arrived, he was met by the Devil, who gave him a guide and sent him on his way. The man observed all the circles of Hell, and he noticed one in particular where a demon was shoveling bodies into a fiery furnace. He was puzzled, and when he was ready to leave, the Devil asked him how he enjoyed his visit. The man said frankly that he hoped he would not have to come back.

The Devil then asked him if he had any questions. "Yes," said the visitor. "I came across a demon shoveling bodies into a furnace. Every once in a while he would put one aside, but I can't figure out why."

"Oh," laughed the Devil. "Those are Oregonians. They're too wet to burn."

Cottage Grove

Lane County. Population 7,354. Cottage Grove has always been an important junction in Oregon; the Coast Fork of the Willamette River flows through the city, and the railroad has connected here since the 1870s. At various times in pioneer history, the Cottage Grove area was called Lemati, a misspelling of the Chinook Jargon word for "mountain" (*lemiti*).

The Bohemia mines dot the Cottage Grove hillsides, especially along Sharps Creek, Champion Creek, and Horse Heaven Creek. Most of the Bohemia claims have colorful names, including Knickerbocker, Quick Step, Professor, Holy Smoke, Confidence, William Tell, Oversight, Oro Platta, Sedan, Holy Terror, and Lost Providence. Obviously the names of the gold strikes suggest a mixture of broad confidence and irony—necessary components for men burrowing underground in dangerous yet profitable labors.

Unlike most Oregon gold country, the Bohemia mines have no population of Cousin Jacks, Cornish immigrants who spread stories of "Tommyknockers." Nonetheless, according to James C. Baker, the Bohemians and Swiss who work in Cottage Grove's mining district trade plentiful tales of the "noisy spirits who act benignly and maliciously." Tommyknockers can cause cave-ins, steal lunches, or drop rocks on the shoulders of miners; they also might warn the workers of loose overhangs or lead the lucky "hard-rock" to the mother lode, depending on the whims of the underground gremlins. Says Baker, the technique of tapping walls with a prospecting hammer to look for water pockets or solid veins is called "tommyknocking."

Early Oregon miners, like the mules who worked for them, could be stubborn and willful. H. L. Barton says that one Bohemia miner was feuding with the local mailman, whose route required a daily ski trip back and forth through the hills between Elephant Mountain and Bohemia Mountain. The miner gathered up a half a ton of ore from his claim and mailed it in large packages to the Bohemia District Mining Office.

MINERS' HARDTACK

A staple in Bohemia mining country was hardtack, a dry and hard wafer that was easy to prepare and appropriate for the damp, hot conditions underground. Hardtack was a food fit for a miner's spartan life—tough and hard as the occupation itself, and sometimes called "jawbreaker" by the miners. For hardtack, first make a stiff mixture of the following ingredients:

> *1½ cups of graham flour*
> *3 cups of unbleached white flour*
> *½ cup of cornmeal*
> *½ cup of lard or shortening*
> *1½ cups of milk*
> *1 teaspoon of sugar*
> *1 tablespoon of salt*

Then lightly grease several cookie sheets and sprinkle them with flour. Dust a chunk of dough (about the size of an egg) with flour, place it in the middle of the cookie sheet and slightly flatten it with your hand. Now roll the dough out to cover the surface of the baking sheet, making it as thin as possible. Dust the dough with flour when necessary to prevent sticking. You may want to use a flour sock on your rolling pin. Trim off excess dough and return the mixture to the mixing bowl. Bake the unleavened bread in a 400-degree oven. When the edges are brown, turn it over. Continue baking until the flat bread is nearly as stiff as cardboard. Turn it once more and, when the hardtack actually is the

consistency of cardboard, remove it from the oven. The hardtack may be eaten when freshly baked and hot, but will last indefinitely if kept dry.

Dexter

Lane County. According to Randall V. Mills, this community was initially named Butte Disappointment by Elijah Bristow, because in 1848 Bristow and a band of pioneers, while chasing Indians near Fall Creek, got lost and found themselves in the disappointing predicament of having wandered up the wrong side of the swollen Willamette River. When they discovered they were lost and had to retrace many miles to cross the stream, they named their landmark Butte Disappointment.

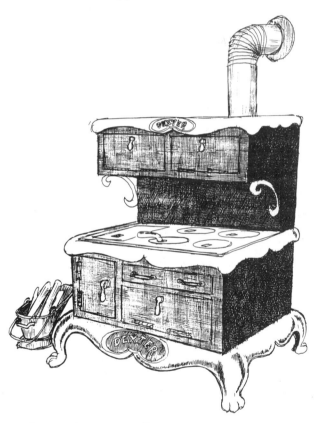

Later, when a post office was established in 1875, the postmaster, Samuel Handsaker, changed the name to Dexter. A surviving son wrote to the *Eugene Register-Guard* in the 1950s to explain the origins of the place-name. "It is my opinion and only my opinion," wrote John Handsaker, "that my father took the name [Dexter] from our cookstove. I have never heard the name used in any other connection." Handsaker said that the cookstove was important to the family because his mother taught the children their "letters" by having them trace their fingers over the cast-iron captions on the front of the Dexter Cook Stove in the kitchen.

A longtime storyteller in the Dexter-Lowell area was Vern "Pappy" Hucka, a man who settled on Fall Creek in 1917 and lived there until 1964 when the Army Corps of Engineers placed a dam on the river. Here are two stories involving "Pappy" Hucka, as recalled by his son Bill and recorded by Carol Knox.

A NEW BREED OF FISH

Every once in a while my dad used to go off fishing for a few days—just mainly to get away from mom and us kids for a while, I think. After all, the creek ran right in front of our house. Anyway, he'd been fishing one day and caught a good limit of trout, but he hadn't been too careful about how legal he was. So at the end of the day he builds a nice little fire, and he commences to cooking these little fish. Just as he got them sizzling in the pan, up walks the local game warden to inspect his fish.

"Say, Pappy," he says, "these fish don't look like six-inchers to me."

Well, my dad says, "It may be true they're a little short in the body. But, John, I'm telling you, those fish had the biggest damn heads you ever saw in your life. Must be some new breed."

AN UNBEARABLE TALE

My dad's friend Charlie was over at our house one evening. We were all sitting around, and Charlie started telling us about one time when he got clawed by a bear. He said, "This bear just jumped out of the blackberry bushes, and he was growling and snarling. He was a real giant, and vicious . . . just plain-ass mean. Slobber was pouring down out of his mouth, and his eyes were red. He reaches out his paw and rakes my arm, up one side and down the other—nearly took all the meat right off. I've got a terrible scar from it."

And he began rolling up his sleeve, and we were all watching, and he says, "By God, that's right. I remember now. That was my brother the bear clawed."

Elmira

Lane County. Perhaps the original name of this spot, Duckworth, is more descriptive, considering the wet weather and nearby Fern Ridge, a waterfowl habitat. However, in 1884 a local blacksmith convinced postal authorities to adopt the name of his favorite spot in California, and the title Elmira has endured. In 1971 Anne Hubbard gathered several folk beliefs and contributed them to the Mills Archives.

ELMIRA-AREA SUPERSTITIONS AND CURES

☐ *Do not butcher a pig, calf, rooster, duck, or goose—or dehorn a cow—unless the sign in the almanac is right. That is, the sign must not be in the heart.*

☐ *Don't bring digging implements into the house or there will be a death in the family.*

☐ *If you plant a cedar tree, when it grows large enough to shade a grave, someone in the family will die.*

☐ *For curly hair in a child, rub its head with goose oil after washing.*

☐ *If you see some kind of horrible sight during pregnancy, it will leave a corresponding mark on the baby.*

☐ *If a woman has hemorrhages, place the pages from a slick magazine, such as* Ladies Home Journal *or* Saturday Evening Post *under her. Then raise the lower end of the bed six inches.*

☐ *For warts, steal your mother's dishrag and bury it after rubbing it on your warts.*

☐ *If green toads jump back and forth across your path in the garden, you will soon receive money.*

☐ *At a wedding shower, the number of ribbons broken when unwrapping packages indicates the number of children that will be born.*

☐ *One way to get worms is to walk on the lawn at night barefoot.*

☐ *If you grind your teeth at night, it means you have worms.*

☐ *Operations above the heart—such as having a tooth pulled—must be done when the almanac sign is above the heart. Operations on the feet or legs must be done when the almanac sign is below the heart. Otherwise there will be excessive bleeding.*

☐ *It is especially good luck to wear one simple bracelet for each of your children.*

☐ *Never start sewing on Friday because you will never finish the garment.*

☐ *At a wedding shower, it is bad luck to break the ribbons on the packages.*

☐ *Leaves turned to their undersides means rain is on the way.*

☐ *If the winter sky is green, there will be cold weather.*

☐ *If the fire "says" snow with fine sparks popping out, it will snow shortly.*

☐ *If someone gives you a knife as a present, you must give at least a penny in return or the knife will eventually cut you.*

☐ *Evening red and morning grey sets the traveler on his way; evening grey and morning red keeps the traveler in his bed.*

☐ *When the horses are always tired and lathered in the morning, witches are riding them at night. To keep witches from the stable, put a broomstick crossways at the barn door.*

□ *A "witch's knot" in a horse's tail means that witches are "borrowing" the horses at night. The knot pulls their eyes permanently open, and the horses eventually die of exhaustion.*

□ *If you leave the house and forget something, you must return to the house and sit down before leaving again. Otherwise you will have bad luck.*

□ *If a bird flies up to the window or hits the window, either there will be a death in the family or a close friend will die.*

□ *A portent of death occurs when you hear a gate open and shut, even though no one is there.*

□ *If your coffee or tea has bubbles around the top, you will receive money in the near future.*

□ *A small spider on the ground before you means good luck.*

□ *If you find an open safety pin, you will get good luck from the direction of the open end. You must pick up the pin and close it to secure the luck, however.*

In 1970, Karen Larson interviewed Laura Wilder, an Elmira farm wife. Wilder had seen Elmira-area Indians use folk remedies to cure many ailments. On one occasion, Wilder says, the cure was especially unusual.

ANGLEWORM SALVE

The patient was a young boy with a lame leg. This Indian woman took some angleworms and put them in a glass jar. She put the jar in the center of a pan of cornbread batter. The cornbread was baked and when it was done so were the worms. They had turned to an oil. She rubbed this oil on the boy's lame leg, and soon he was walking around as well as anybody.

Eugene

Lane County. Population 112,264. Early travelers called this Willamette Valley town Skinnerville or Skinner's Mudhole, after its first resident, Eugene F. Skinner, who built his cabin in 1847. In 1853 the place became Eugene City; by 1889 the name had been shortened to Eugene. Skinner's wife, Mary Cook Skinner, was the first white woman to reside in Lane County and was directly responsible for the name Eugene; she argued that Skinnerville was hardly appropriate for a town that wished to earn the trust of visitors.

Eugene must have become a popular stopping place for single women in the 1860s because, only twenty years after Mary Skinner's arrival, the local bachelors were getting remarkably picky. Consider, for example, this forthright advertisement in the *Eugene Guard* for July 31, 1869:

> WANTS A WIFE: A bachelor without encumbrance is desirous of obtaining a wife. She must be accomplished, able to milk cows and play the piano forte; she must be fond of children, willing to mend their clothes, and a good hand to raise chickens. The advertiser scorns to marry for money, but it is of the utmost importance that the lady's relatives furnish a written character of her ability and worth, and as a trifling matter, said friends would also be required to deposit $500 with the advertiser as a proof of their judgment that the lady is what she says she is. No widow, grass or otherwise, need apply.
> —R.S. c/o Post Office, Eugene City

Even without answering such ads, women knew too much about labor and hardship in the early years of Willamette Valley settlement. Fred Lockley's *Conversations with Pioneer Women* chronicles, among other things, the endless drudgery of pioneer settlement. For most women, the end of the trail was the beginning of unrelieved scrubbing, cooking, and cleaning. In a 1933 interview with Lockley, Rebecca Heater Hess remembered her young life on a pioneer homestead: "During the 66 years I have lived on that farm I have managed to keep busy, taking care of my ten children, and milking six or seven cows night and mornings, besides making bread, doing my housework, and keeping the children's clothes mended." The typical sentiments of women such as Hess later found expression in a popular song called "The Housewife's Lament," a lyric found penned in the diary of Sara Price, who lost two sons at the outbreak of the Civil War.

THE HOUSEWIFE'S LAMENT

1. *One day I was walking, I heard a complaining*
And saw an old woman, the picture of gloom.
She gazed at the mud on her door-step ('twas raining)
And this was her song as she wielded her broom:

Chorus:
"Oh, life is a toil, and love is a trouble,
Beauty will fade, and riches will flee.
Pleasures, they dwindle, and prices, they double,
And nothing is as I would wish it to be.

2. *"There's too much of worriment goes into a bonnet,*
There's too much of ironing goes into a shirt.
There's nothing that pays for the time you waste on it,
There's nothing that lasts us but trouble and dirt.

Chorus

3. *"In March it is mud, it is slush in December;*
The midsummer breezes are loaded with dust;
In fall the leaves litter, in muddy September
The wallpaper rots, and the candlesticks rust.

Chorus

4. "It's sweeping at six, and it's dusting at seven;
   It's victuals at eight, and it's dishes at nine;
   It's potting and panning from ten to eleven;
   We scarce break our fast till we plan how to dine.

Chorus

5. "There are worms on the cherries and slugs on the roses
   And ants in the sugar and mice in the pies;
   The rubbish of spiders no mortal supposes
   And ravaging roaches and damaging flies.

Chorus

6. "Last night in my dreams I was stationed forever
   On a far distant isle in the midst of the sea;
   My one chance for life was a ceaseless endeavor
   To sweep back the waves as they swept over me."

Chorus

7. Alas 'twas no dream for ahead I behold it,
   I see I am helpless my fate to avert.
   So she lay down her broom, and her apron she folded,
   She lay down and died and was buried in dirt.

In 1974 Karin Smith interviewed several Eugene women who had emigrated from other countries, including Britain, Sweden, and Germany. Smith recorded a long list of domestic beliefs and superstitions from Ethel Gilmour, Joan Cadwell Shumate, Eva McKenney, Margot Sherman, and Ann-Mari Carroll. These beliefs show different ways of coping with age-old concerns, such as birth, death, and marriage—most of them stemming from local or regional traditions in the European countries where the women were born.

OLD-COUNTRY BELIEFS AND CUSTOMS

☐ *When you are expecting a baby, and you get scared, and you touch your stomach, the baby will have a red spot [Germany].*

☐ *My mother used to say, "If you carry it [the baby] in the front, it will be a boy; if you carry it all around, it will be a girl." I carried David [her son] in the front [Britain].*

☐ *You're not supposed to reach up [when expecting a baby]. It's supposed to strangle the baby—the cord [umbilical cord]. David was almost strangled [Britain].*

☐ *Red is anger. It stirs up the emotions to eat, to get mad, to lust. No, red is not the color to have in the house, I don't think. Not in big ways. Blue, green is a healing color. Blue is very good. You should always sleep in blue. I sleep in blue, and I have blue sheets and a blue bedspread [Britain].*

☐ *When we have an eye infection, at home, we rub it with a gold ring. A wedding ring. Rub it with a gold wedding ring, and it goes away. It's something in the gold, I suppose [Britain].*

☐ *To get rid of freckles or warts, put a slug [snail] on them [Germany].*

☐ *To get rid of warts . . . ha, ha . . . you are supposed to stick the finger with the wart . . . into . . . well, the pot under your bed—you know what for—and this will help, if you never wash it off, until the wart is gone [Germany].*

☐ *You know what I did when I was going to school, too? You picked a dandelion and you squeeze the milk out of it and put on the wart, and it disappears. I've done that [Britain].*

☐ *I've used a remedy for warts, and it works. We read in a folk book about taking a green pea, splitting it open, and rubbing it on a wart, and then wrapping it in a piece of paper and burying it in the ground. And when the pea withered in the ground, the wart would be gone. And I've done that twice, and it works [Britain].*

☐ *If you make a wish, and your partner is sneezing at the same time, this wish will come true [Germany].*

☐ *When the bride goes to church, she has to enter on someone's left side and leave on someone's right side. This is to assure that the marriage will be a happy one [Germany].*

☐ *In August when it is such a pretty moon, we have crawfish parties in the evening in August. And there we have big, big paper lamps that open (These are shaped like moons.) [Sweden].*

☐ *They say at home that if you get a haircut, you should get your hair cut when the moon is coming up. It grows faster [Britain].*

☐ *If someone says the same word at the same time as the other, then both are allowed to make a wish, and it will come true [Germany].*

☐ *If your feet itch, you're going to travel on strange ground [Britain].*

☐ *We used to have a saying at home, "Rain before seven, fine before eleven." So, if it rained early in the morning, you could be sure that the weather would clear up by noon, at least [Britain].*

☐ *When the backs of the leaves show on the trees, it's going to rain—when they look silver [Britain].*

☐ *If you sit opposite a table corner, you're going to get a "mean" mother-in-law [Germany].*

☐ *If you have something left in your cup (like coffee, for example), you may not fill it up again. You have to throw the rest away and then fill it up. If you don't do this, you will get a "mean" mother-in-law [Germany].*

☐ *At midsummer, which is a big holiday at home, at midsummer, you got out and pick seven different kinds of flowers, and then you put them under your pillow, and then you will dream about your future love [Sweden].*

☐ *We chime in New Year's. We open the back door and take a broom and sweep out the old year, and then we open the front door and let the New Year and the good luck in [Britain].*

☐ *Each January . . . grandmother used to have the priest come to her house to bless all four corners of it, so that "peace" would be in the house [Germany].*

☐ *A long time ago . . . we had small, what we called Tomteguber, which is the word for Santa Claus, but they [are] really small, small. And they live in the house, and they have good ones and they have bad ones [Sweden].*

☐ *When moving into a new home, the first thing that has to be carried inside is salt and bread; otherwise, you will be hungry in the future [Germany].*

☐ *Before . . . grandmother used to cut bread or a cake, she would make a cross with the knife on top of it. This was to make sure that no one in the family would be hungry in the future [Germany].*

☐ *A lot of farmers will sow grain while the moon is coming up, and then they don't sow after the moon is full [Britain].*

☐ *You may not step on a grave. It will make the dead spirits mad, and they will make you stumble later [Germany].*

☐ *We had a bird fly in the house on West 36th Street, and each time, somebody died. It was once my uncle and my grandmother. We had a bird loose. It just flew in the window [Britain].*

THE TICKING SPIDER

Told by Ethel Gilmour from Gorby, England

We have a spider in England they call a "ticking spider," and the only time a ticking spider makes noise is when somebody in the house is going to die. My mother believed that and that happened when her mother and her father and anybody that has been in our family has died. While my mother was alive, we heard the "ticking spider" and never heard it since.

The only thing we had with the spider is the "ticking spider," and you can't ever find that spider—you can't ever find it. It ticks like a clock—constantly. And as soon as that person's dead, it ticks no more. It doesn't make any more noise. And that has happened. . . . I've heard it myself, I've heard them.

It's just an omen. It used to worry my mother something terrible. It used to worry her terrible, when she heard this, she'd be all over the house looking for that thing. You cannot find them. The minute somebody in the family dies, it stops. And you don't hear it anymore. I've looked for it. I've never heard one since.

My aunt that died, she believed in them, too. She had the spiders, too. We've never ever found it. . . .

Finn Rock

Lane County. This landmark alongside the McKenzie River was named for Benjamin Franklin "Huckleberry" Finn, a celebrated storyteller and, by his own admission, "the biggest liar on the McKenzie." Finn claimed to have been the "real" Huckleberry Finn whom Mark Twain wrote about; allegedly the two men had met on the Mississippi while piloting riverboats. When asked why he had given up such an exotic life to travel all the way to Oregon, Finn replied, "I got into debt, and I told my creditors I'd pay 'em in fur. Well, I went to Missouri, but that weren't *fur* enough, so I come on out West." Finn took great pride in

his reputation as a yarn-spinner. It was widely reported, in fact, that of the three biggest liars in the McKenzie Valley, "Old man Pepiot was one, and B. F. Finn was the other two."

"Huckleberry" Finn stories are favorites in the Mc-Kenzie River area, and several people have collected variations of "Huck Finn" tales for the Mills Archives, including Charlene Walker and James C. Craig. Another useful source of Finn stories is Susan Mullin's article in *Northwest Folklore*, entitled "Oregon's Huckleberry Finn: A Münchausen Enters Tradition."

Folks from all over the Valley liked to listen to Finn spread his stories, and he had a constant supply of visitors, but he was not above pulling their legs, no matter how far the gawkers had traveled, as shown in this whopper collected by Dexter resident Charlene Walker.

A PREMATURE FUNERAL

"One time," says George McCornack, "Orel O'Brien was driving a stage up to McKenzie Bridge, and he saw old man Finn walking along the side of the road. He said, 'Hey, Mr. Finn! Stop and tell me a lie!' "

"Finn said, 'I haven't got time, I haven't got time. Old man Pepiot has just died, and I'm going down to start the mill up to saw out some lumber for his coffin.' "

" 'Course, they all knew old Pepiot, so they dashed on up there, and old man Pepiot was sitting out on the porch playing his fiddle. So, Finn didn't stop and tell 'em a lie; he told 'em a lie and went right on."

Perhaps the most widespread McKenzie narrative tells how Finn Rock came to rest in its present location. In 1974 a University of Oregon student interviewed a Eugene dentist and heard the Legend of Finn Rock. "When I was young," said the student folklorist, "[my father] used to tell us, 'There's Huckleberry Finn Rock.' I never knew why he called it that until I did this project. I think *his* father told him this story when he was young." Here is one of many available stories behind the naming of Finn Rock, a notable promontory alongside the McKenzie River Highway, east of Springfield.

HOW FINN ROCK GOT ITS NAME

Huckleberry Finn used to live on the Mississippi River, and when he retired, he moved to Oregon and lived up the McKenzie River at Finn Ranch. And, uh, every fall he'd go hunting, and the way you hunt on the McKenzie River was you stand beside the river and wait 'til the deer came by, and then you'd shoot one, and after it got out in the middle of the river, you'd go drag it out and put it on a mule and carry it back home.

And the highway used to go around Finn Rock, and it was hard to get around the rock and alongside the river. And [Finn] was coming around there with his mule with the deer on the back, and every time he'd go by, [the deer would] fall in the river. And so he got mad about it. So he hooked his mule up to this rock and just pulled the rock out of the way. And that's why the highway goes where it does now. It goes through the rock. That's why they call it Finn Rock.

Finn gained his reputation not only as a storyteller but also as a local character. In 1970 Charlene Walker coaxed George McCornack into telling about Huck Finn's masterful deflation of a loud tourist. This story is similar to "Black Powder Loads Is Slower," (see Gold Beach, p. 79 a tall tale told about Hathaway Jones, Southern Oregon's competitor in the "greatest Oregon liar" contest.

"THEM DAMNED 'KALARUP' GUNS IS NO GOOD"

When he got to be an old man, they used to have him around the hotel to lie to the tourists as they came through. One fella came up there with a new Winchester automatic rifle, which he was very proud of and did a lot of bragging about.

After he'd talked himself out, old Finn says, "You know, them damned kalarup guns is no good. My boy Willie, he had one. We went across the river the other day, and I sat on the river, and he said he'd go and chase one in to me. He went up the ridge about a half a mile, and he jumped one and shot at it. It come right down the ridge to me. You know, when that deer went by me, that bullet was still three feet behind him, and there was drops of sweat as big as your fist falling off that bullet, and it just couldn't catch him. I tell you, them damned kalarup guns is no good."

Foster

Linn County. The name Foster apparently came from the operator of a local mill. Foster is a logging town forty-five miles southeast of Albany in the Cascade foothills.

While growing up in the Foster area, Twilo Scofield heard her father, a logger, talk about the men of the woods. He called them "timber-beasts." Loggers are hard-working men, rough and tough both in speech and behavior. Faced daily with dangerous work, the "timber-beast" becomes larger than life, laughing at the occupational risks and fears. One bit of backwoods lore, capturing the swagger of the typical Foster logger, is "The Timber Beast," written by Scofield from memories of her father's tales and stories. "In what other occupation," joked her father, "could you expect two moonlight rides and a picnic lunch?"

THE TIMBER BEAST

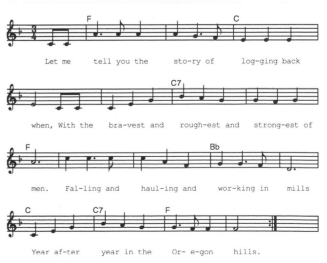

Let me tell you the sto-ry of log-ging back when, With the bra-vest and rough-est and strong-est of men. Fal-ling and haul-ing and wor-king in mills Year af-ter year in the Or-e-gon hills.

Let me tell you the story of logging back when,
With the bravest and roughest and strongest of men,
Falling and hauling and working in mills
Year after year in the Or-e-gon hills.

Logging's the finest work man ever found,
Wildlife and wilderness beauty abound.
Two moonlight rides and a big picnic lunch,
All day in the woods with a fun-lovin' bunch.

Yes, loggers are men of the toughest and best,
Each day for fun we are put to the test.
We take off our boots and our socks when we meet
And kick frozen knots off the logs with bare feet.

We'd build us a splash dam where the waters run low,
Then we'd pile all the logs in the dry bed below.
When it was filled up and not room for one more,
We'd open the gates, down the river they'd roar.

Out on the water the pond monkeys dance,
With peaveys in hand they retreat and advance.
Twirling and burling, their feet never stop.
Takes a mighty fine man just to stay up on top.

The rain came down hard and the river did flood.
We labored to save her with sweat, tears, and blood.
We tried hard to save her but we didn't know how,
Where once stood our sawmill, the river is now.

The flood took our mill and it took the crew, too,
But those boys around Foster, they knew what to do.
They rode that wild sawmill, stayed on 'til the end,
And they fired her up on the next river bend.

We scarce had rebuilt her when we had a big fire,
The flames caught the logs and rose higher and higher.
The boss, he said, ''Boys, you may think I'm a fool.
But we'll start to rebuild just as soon as she's cool.''

The Timber Beast works 'til he's tired and old
In the rain and the wind, the sleet and the snow.
Says he, ''When I die, it can't do me no harm.
To choose hell over heaven, at least I'll be warm.''

Junction City

Lane County. Population 3,666. In the 1870s, railroader Ben Holladay formed a plan to build a rail line in the far western part of the state. It was to join his eastern rail line just west of Eugene. Even though the west line was never built, the proposed junction of these rail lines came to be known as *Junction City*, a name that became more appropriate in the early half of this century, when two main branches of the Pacific Highway joined there.

When the first automobile to cross the continent pulled into the toll station of the Santiam Wagon Road on June 20, 1905, the tollkeeper had no idea how to describe the iron beast nor what rate to charge. Finally he determined the Oldsmobile of Dwight B. Huss to be a road hog and levied the usual fee for swine of three cents. In later years, when the automobile road hog came to the Willamette Valley, there were no traffic laws, no road signs, and not much driving expertise. Most of the farmers who

picked up these strange contraptions in Eugene and Salem had never driven anything but a horse before. Consequently, the first Junction City drivers were in for some adventures, as explained by Clarence A. Pitney, an early settler.

WHOA! WHOA!

Miller Nelson, a close neighbor, placed seven good-sized fence posts in his garage to stop his new Overland when he drove in. He began yelling ''Whoa! Whoa! Whoa!'' and went clear over the posts and pushed an extra strong wall out about three feet.

Another man's car didn't stop with the usual string of ''Whoa's,'' and he drove right on through his garage. And forgetting how to stop the thing, he drove around until he ran out of gas.

Still another driver stood up as he entered the garage and pulled so hard that, when it didn't stop with the ''Whoa's,'' he pulled the steering wheel right off the post. . . .

My brother Cecil was raking hay with a dump rake, near the road at our place, when one of these new contraptions that Hattie [the horse] hadn't seen before came along. Old Hattie ran and started kicking, which laid the skin on Cecil's shin wide open for about seven inches. Don Hicks, living in Junction City, had a Reo Runabout, a one-lunger that was cranked from the side. After getting our phone call, he came out at the incredible speed of fifteen miles per hour. No, we didn't laugh, but viewed the feat with awe.

King's Valley

Benton County. King's Valley was named for its first settler, Nahum King, who settled there in 1845. The flour mill at King's Valley has been in operation since 1853. King's Valley lies in the heart of the coastal logging country, and Oregon loggers, as everyone knows, are tough.

Tony Hill, an Alsea resident, was felling timber in the woods near Alsea when his partner, a man living on the family homestead, stopped to tell the story of "The Log Truck Driver and the Bikers." This narrative underscores the quiet self-confidence of Benton County woodsmen and, at the same time, calls into question the intelligence of outsiders who cannot mind their own business. According to Hill, the storyteller claimed that these events actually happened in Benton County near the year 1975.

THE LOG TRUCK DRIVER AND THE BIKERS

There was a log truck driver who stopped at a cafe for a cup of coffee—I think it was around King's Valley. While he was drinking his coffee and just relaxin', three Hell's Angels kinda guys came roarin' up to the cafe. They came in real loud, just like they owned the place, just actin' like they always act, and they saw there was just the logger and the waitress in the cafe. They started harrassin' the guy—makin' jokes about him, puttin' salt in his sugar, bein' rowdy, stuff like that. But the logger didn't do anything, just sat there and drank his coffee, calm and not payin' much attention to 'em. Pretty soon he just paid and left. The bikers hooted after him and sat down to order. The waitress came up to take the order, and one of 'em said, "I thought these guys out here were s'posed to be tough. He sure wasn't much of a man."

The waitress says, "I don't know how much of a man he is, but he sure ain't much of a driver. He just backed over three motorcycles in the parking lot."

Lake Oswego

Clackamas County. Population 30,305. Originally called Oswego, this townsite was named after Oswego, New York. Some early pioneers called the area—lake and town—Sucker Lake. Perhaps the early name is worth

recalling, considering the supreme act of folly that once took place on the shores of this Portland-area lake. Here is the story of the *Tomonos* rock, compiled from materials gathered by the Writers' Program of the WPA in the late 1930s.

THE TOMONOS *ROCK*

The third largest meteorite ever discovered in the world—and the largest found in this country—was once heisted.

In 1902, Elias G. Hughes, a farmer, found the meteorite while prospecting in the hills around Oswego with his friend William Dale. At first the two men thought they had found a reef of iron buried in a side hill, but they later realized they had found a huge rock from outer space. Hughes and Dale vowed to keep their find a secret, and Dale immediately left the country in order to gain financing for the purchase of the property where the meteorite rested.

When Dale did not return by the summer of the next year, Hughes himself attempted to buy the hillside property, but the owners, Oregon Iron and Steel Company of Oswego, would not sell. So, with great care, Hughes devised a capstan, anchoring it with a logging chain, and hoisted the rock onto a crude log wagon, attempting to drag the meteorite onto his own property. For three agonizing months Hughes and his fifteen-year-old son fought with this unusual load. Some days the meteorite progressed only a few feet; on other days Hughes and his son managed ten or twenty feet. One glorious day, the pair dragged the 31,107-pound rock a total of fifty feet toward home.

During the entire summer labors, Hughes was not observed by anyone, even his neighbors. When he finally dragged the rock onto his own land, Hughes built a shed to cover the meteorite and announced a viewing fee of twenty-five cents.

But Hughes made only a few dollars from his exhibition before Oregon Iron and Steel filed suit for recovery of their meteorite. To confuse matters more, a third party—the man whose property lay between the excavation site and Hughes' shed—claimed the rock. The neighbor even showed proof of his claim: a huge empty crater on his property, where the Willamette Meteorite (no doubt) landed. Unfortunately, the third litigant was soon discovered to have made the crater himself with a crackerjack dynamite charge. On July 17, 1905, the United States Supreme Court proclaimed Oregon Iron and Steel the rightful owners of America's largest meteorite.

During the lower court trial, several Native Americans were called to testify, all of them avowing the long history of the Willamette Meteorite, called Tomonos *by the Indians. The Klickitats said in court that the rock had come from the moon and was a sacred stone possessing magical powers. Before going to battle, said testifying Klickitats, their ancestors would wash themselves and their arrows in the rainwa-*

ter standing in the deep basins of the meteorite, the Indians believing that this indulgence would assure their success in war.

After the Supreme Court judgment, Elias Hughes had to relinquish his claim to the stone he had carted many thousands of yards through the hills. He was left with only a chronic sore back. Oregon Iron and Steel began advertising that it was handling iron ore from ''both heaven and earth.'' Subsequently the Willamette Meteorite was displayed in the Mines Building at the Exposition Center in Portland, but was later moved to New York, where it was displayed in the American Museum of Natural History. In 1938 the curator of the museum sent a 181.1-gram chunk of the Willamette Meteorite as a gift to the University of Oregon.

Lebanon

Linn County. Population 10,855. This location east of Salem was first settled in 1848 and called Kees Precinct after the first immigrants. McArthur says that in 1851 Jeremiah Ralston, a pioneer from Lebanon, Tennessee, established the town boundaries and named the site Lebanon.

In early June Lebanon hosts the Strawberry Festival, an annual event since 1909. Usually the celebration includes athletic events, strawberry judging, and coronation of the Strawberry Queen. Also the Lebanon growers bake a huge shortcake, measuring twelve by fifteen feet, large enough to serve 10,000 visitors. Here, from the pages of the WPA's *Oregon Oddities*, is the recipe.

WORLD'S LARGEST STRAWBERRY SHORTCAKE

288 pounds of sugar
108 pounds of shortening
800 eggs
118 quarts of milk
20 pounds of baking powder

375 pounds of flour
2 quarts of flavoring
5 pounds of salt
21 gallons of whipping cream
1600 pounds of strawberries
45 gallons of table cream

Many Lebanon settlers came across the Oregon Trail with the Ralston wagon train. But even after arriving in the Willamette Valley, the frustrations of emigration did not disappear. In 1974 Tanis Knight collected this tale reminiscent of ''searching for a needle in a haystack.''

THE LAST NEEDLE

Mrs. John C. Wood of Lebanon told me this story of early Lebanon that was told to her by Mrs. Hulda Miller, daughter of one of the pioneer families who made the trip west with the Ralston wagon train:

''The original wagon train was by nature very self-sufficient, and the settlers had to construct their homes before any manpower could be spared for the trip to Oregon City to replenish supplies. Among the items that were in painfully short supply were pins and needles. Eventually the ladies of the settlement were down to their last needle. This was rationed out among all families on a share-and-share-alike basis.

''When it came time for Mrs. Miller's parents to pass the prized needle on to the next family, it could not be found. Panic-stricken, the family began a frantic search. The straw that littered the floor was swept up and gone through with a fine-tooth comb. Dirt which had been swept into cracks in the flooring for added protection against the cold was swept back up and sifted. No needle was found.

''The careless people were practically ostracized by their neighbors when, after five weeks of fruitless search, the offending needle turned up sticking jauntily into a piece of sewing that had been overturned in the initial search. The needle was promptly turned over to its rightful users and the family was restored to the good graces of the community.''

Monmouth

Polk County. Population 6,278. Monmouth, named after Monmouth, Illinois, was the site of Monmouth University, founded in the mid-1850s by members of the Christian Church. Monmouth is the present location of Western Oregon State College.

In 1972 the U.S. Olympic Committee received an application from the town of Monmouth to sponsor the 1976 winter games in that city, with alpine and downhill events scheduled for Cupid's Knoll, an impressive 319-foot mountain in the center of town. In support of its application, the Monmouth City Council forwarded an Olympic budget of $2.25 to event organizers. To everyone's surprise, Innsbruck, Austria, became the host city in 1976. Monmouth officials continue to believe that international politics played a role in the hasty decision.

For students at Oregon College of Education (now Western Oregon State College), Cupid's Knoll featured sport of a different kind. On Friday and Saturday nights, sedans and coupes climbed to the top of Cupid's Knoll, where students watched the lights of Corvallis flickering in the distance. Of course, wherever young people gather to watch the "submarine races," people tell the story of "The Man with the Hook," patterning the details to fit local landmarks. In 1968 folklorist Linda Degh uncovered forty-four variants of "The Hook," signaling its popularity as an urban belief tale. One version was remembered in 1988 by Arlie Holt, who was an Oregon College of Education student in the early 1950s.

THE MAN WITH THE HOOK

One Saturday night after a dance at the college, this guy named Dale took his date up to Cupid's Knoll. It was in October, and the weather was still pretty good, but too cold to leave the windows down.

So Dale and his date were sittin' there watching the lights, y' know, and Dale decides to get some soft music on the radio. Romantic stuff. And pretty soon he puts his arm around her, and she doesn't move it, so he kisses her a few times. Just then, there was a soft scraping on the passenger door, so Dale reached over and pushed down the lock. Then they went back to what they were doing.

Pretty soon, the music stops, and there's this news bulletin: "A man has escaped from the state mental institution in Salem, and he's been seen in the Monmouth area." It turns out that the guy is a mass murderer, and when they finally arrested him, he tried to jump through a picture window, so he's lost a hand. "Be on the lookout for a man with a hook on his right arm," says the radio.

So Dale's date gets freaked out, and she wants him to leave right away. He tries to ignore it, but she's so shook up that she won't stop shakin'. So finally he slams the car into reverse and squeals outta there. All the way down the hill he won't talk to her, 'cause he's so mad. Finally they get to the dorm, and he goes around to her side to open the door. There was something shiny on the door, but Dale couldn't make it out at first. Finally he got close enough. There, hanging by the door handle, was a metal hook, covered with blood.

Noti

Lane County. Noti's naming is a matter of conjecture, but one story is the most colorful. According to old-timers in the small Valley town on the way to the Coast, an Indian and a white were traveling from the seaside town of Florence to Eugene. They had only one horse, and in order to

make rapid progress, they were "riding and tying." In this manner, one of the men would ride the horse twenty miles while his companion walked. At the end of the twenty-mile segment, the rider would dismount, tie the horse at a predetermined spot, and begin walking the next twenty-mile stretch. When his companion reached the tied horse, he would mount up and ride past his traveling mate to the next "tying place." Apparently the Anglo agreed to tie the horse near the present location of Noti. However, he did not keep his promise and rode on toward Eugene. When the Indian discovered he had been "double-crossed," he said, "Hmmm. Him no tie." In that phrase the community earned its name.

Noti was once a popular area for Indian gatherings. The Indians living near Cooper's Island (now covered by Fern Ridge Reservoir) met each year for a powwow. They came to hunt ducks, to gamble, to race horses, and to trade. In the Fern Ridge area, it is still easy to uncover arrowheads, and there is one huge mound where nothing whatsoever will grow, according to residents, who believe that the mound is filled with charmed artifacts. The Noti-area Indians left more than artifacts in the Noti region, however. Many of the folk cures and remedies, here collected in 1971 by Anne Hubbard, date back to the era of Skookum John and his wife, Sally, Native Americans who for many years made their home in the Noti area, arriving in 1852 or 1853, and working for Eugene pioneer Cal Young until their deaths.

FOLK CURES AND REMEDIES

☐ *Egg lining (the membrane between the egg and the shell) is a good poultice for infected eyes.*
☐ *Catnip tea is good for insomnia and colic.*
☐ *Sage tea cures worms.*
☐ *Bacon rind and cayenne pepper wrapped around the throat is good medicine against a sore throat.*
☐ *For kidney stones, boil beets with their tops on and drink the liquid.*
☐ *Puff balls from an oak tree will stop the bleeding from a bad cut.*
☐ *Proud flesh—that is, a sore or cut that does not heal—should be treated with burnt powdered alum.*
☐ *Asthma is eased by crumbling leaves from a myrtlewood tree into your pillow and breathing them while asleep.*
☐ *For an earache, soak cotton in goose oil and place it in the infected ear. Be sure the oil is warm.*
☐ *As a pneumonia jacket, take cloth, such as an old bed sheet, and cut holes for the arms. Mix together eucalyptus oil, a small amount of turpentine, hogs' lard, nutmeg, and flour. Apply this mixture to the cloth and wrap it around the victim.*
☐ *Beet juice is good for gall bladder trouble.*
☐ *Sassafras tea will insure pure white skin for a baby if the mother drinks it daily while pregnant.*

□ *For nosebleed, take a spent shot lead bullet, drill a hole in it, and hang it around your neck so that it swings over your heart. You will never have a nosebleed again.*

Oakridge

Lane County. Population 3,060. Once known as Hazeldell, the town of Oakridge is a logging center in the Willamette Pass area, east of Eugene.

Logging is rich in occupational lore, with an unusual emphasis on naming. Even personal names give way to conventions in the woods. In the pioneer lumber camps, any Swede with a name difficult to pronounce was entered in the payroll books as Johnson. From then on, the man would be known by that name, despite his protests. Sometimes a man could not shake a logging nickname, even among his own family. For example, Laura Wilder of Elmira told one student folklorist, ''Did you know my husband's name isn't really *John*? It's *Clinton*. He got that name in the loggin' camps. The first time Johnny went to work up there he wore his bib overalls. Well, loggers always wore their pants cut short just below the knee. When they saw him comin', one hollered, 'Here comes a John Farmer for sure!' After that, they always called him *John*.''

There is a story for virtually every term used in the woods. For instance, consider the *donkey engine*. According to a former personnel director of the Guistina Lumber Company, ''The first *donkey* that was taken to the woods was an upright spool, instead of the horizontal drums used today. About twenty-five or thirty loggers gathered around to see if it would pull anything. Since all the logging at this time was done by horses, everything was related to horsepower. So while they were waiting to see if it would pull the logs, they got to kidding. Somebody said, 'What is less than one horsepower?' The answer was one donkey power. That is how the name was started, and to this day it's still referred to as a *donkey engine*.''

Stories of logging camp initiations are rampant in the Oregon woods. The loggers' hazings serve a psychological purpose, reminding the greenhorn of the dangers of the job and the necessity of close cooperation. In testing the newcomer's temper and wit, the logging crew protects its interests and asserts its personality. Some of the most common initiation rites are described in the Mills Archives collections by Jeri Johnston, Trudy Cooper, Bill Agee, Greg Hamilton, and Valerie Grobe.

THE LOGGER'S INITIATION

One day a new green guy came into camp. Things had been a little slow, and the old-timers decided to liven things up at the expense of the new man. So the first day they sent him down to the equipment shack for a left-handed monkey wrench. The next day, they caught a bunch of yellow-jackets and put them in the green guy's lunch pail. When his wife opened the pail that night, they flew all over the kitchen, and the husband spent an hour chasing down the bees.

On the third day, Arky Andy was setting chokers—wrapping wire cable around a log. As sometimes happens, there was no clearance under the log to set the choker, meaning somebody had to dig a path for the cable. Instead, the old-timer said, ''Go up to the landing and get me a choker hole, kid.'' The green guy walked the quarter mile back to the landing and asked the boss for a choker hole. After the laughing subsided, the kid could feel the crew's eyes on him all the way back down the hill.

But the green guy finally got some revenge. A week or so later, the men were building a shed at the landing, and Arky Andy cut a two-by-four about four inches too short. With a wink at the crew, he said, ''Hey, kid. Take the crummy and go down to town and get me a board stretcher.'' So the green guy got in the truck and drove into Oakridge. But by now he was getting a little smarter. He looked through all the supply houses in town and finally found a corrugated fastener for stapling pieces of wood together. Its brand name was The Board Stretcher. He bought one for $26.50, charged it to the company, and brought it back to the job. Arky Andy got stuck with the bill.

Despite the larger-than-life image of the log truck driver in the King's Valley story of ''The Log Truck Driver and the Bikers,'' there is a natural antagonism between loggers and drivers, each feeling that the other ''has it made.'' This rivalry is best shown in the esoteric/exoteric lore of the professions; loggers trade stories among themselves that make fun of the drivers, and the drivers swap jokes that create cohesion in the group. In 1975 Jeri Johnston collected this joke about the deficiencies of ''truck drivers'' from a logger working out of Glide. Not surprisingly, the logger wished to remain anonymous.

THE CHOKER SETTER CONTEMPLATES BRAIN SURGERY

There was this old choker setter that went down to a doctor to get a new brain—tired of settin' chokers, wanted something different. And the doc says, ''Well, I got quite a few selections here. Take your pick.''

He says, ''Well, whaddaya got?''

And [the doc] says, ''Well, I gotta lawyer.''

Choker setter says, ''No, I don't wanta be no lawyer.''

Doc says, ''Well, it's a hundred and fifty.''

''No.''

''Well,'' he says, ''I got a doctor's brain here. You could be a regular brain surgeon.''

''How much are they?''

And he goes, ''A hundred and fifty.''

''No,'' he says. ''I don't want that.''

He goes, ''Well, I got a fireman . . . a fireman's brain. I got one I'll sell you. They're a hundred and seventy-five.''

Choker setter says, ''Nah.'' So the doctor says, ''Well, I got one here. This might be what you want: truck driver.''

Choker setter says, ''Truck driver, huh? Now that might not be too bad.'' He says, ''What's the price on them?''

Doc says, ''Five hundred dollars.''

And the choker setter took a double take and says, ''Well, now, I wonder why they're five hundred dollars?''

And the doc said, ''Well, it's the only brain you can get [that] ain't been used.''

Log truck drivers have their own folklore, of course. Jeri Johnston's sister heard this joke from a log truck driver, a version that shows log hauling in a different light—as a dangerous and freewheeling profession requiring steel nerves.

ST. PETER AND THE LOG TRUCK DRIVERS

Two priests . . . went up to St. Peter and they said, ''St. Peter, could we get into heaven?'' And St. Peter said, ''No way.'' And they couldn't figure out why he wouldn't let them into heaven.

Anyway, then these two loggers started coming up. They were just singing and cussing and drinking on the way up to heaven. They come up and they go, ''Hey, St. Peter, could we get into heaven?''

And, um, he said, ''Sure, just go on in.'' And the priests just looked at each other, and they looked at St. Peter, and they said, ''Well, how come you let the two . . . log truck drivers into heaven? They been sinning all their lives and cussing and drinking and going out, and we've led such a good life.''

And he said, and St. Peter said, ''Those log truck drivers scared more hell out of people than you'd ever think of doing.''

Oregon City

Clackamas County. Population 14,639. Dr. John McLoughlin, chief factor of the Hudson's Bay Company, established a residence alongside the Willamette River in 1829 and called the place Willamette. When the town was platted by McLoughlin in 1842, the name Oregon City prevailed, and the townsite became the seat of government until 1849. Overlooking the Willamette River Falls at Oregon City is a bust of McLoughlin, the ''Father of Oregon.''

Oregon City was a paradise for pioneer entrepreneurs. James B. Stephens, a cooper, settled there in 1844 and bought a sizeable portion of the present town for $150. After selling off many of the lots to land-hungry emigrants, Stephens was able to fill one of his handmade barrels with cash. In fact, he finally abandoned the barrel-making business and bought a bank. Even the governor made money—literally. At Oregon City, George Abernathy, provisional head of state from 1845 to 1849, minted his own coins from flint chips, inscribing the stone with his name and the coin's value. These chips were known as *Abernathy Rock*. Others put their faith not in Abernathy Rock nor Beaver Money, but in tradeable commodities, as shown by an *Oregon Statesman* advertisement for April 18, 1861:

WANTED
1000 DOZEN EGGS
100 DOZEN CHICKENS
500 CATS IN GOOD CONDITION

FOR WHICH THE HIGHEST MARKET PRICE WILL BE PAID IN GOODS, IF DELIVERED BY THE 10TH OF MAY. NOT LESS THAN 10 CATS TAKEN FROM ANY ONE PERSON.

—Dement Wilson, Oregon City

In 1974 folklore collector Ellen Kyle gathered several stories about horse training and care from an Oregon City horse trainer, who made a special point of warning that ''no inexperienced person should try these remedies or training methods.'' The collection features beliefs prevalent from pioneer times to the current era and serves as an interesting comparison with the horselore of Southeastern Oregon (see Fields, p. 151).

OREGON CITY HORSELORE

□ *A friend of mine, ol' Johnny Newp, is the talkin'est, drinkin'est man there ever was. Even now, he's 60–70 years old and can sit drinking beer and telling story after story 'til dawn, and the space around his seat looks like a brewery store-room. An' that's without any runs to the bushes. In all the years I've known him, I've never seen Johnny drunk or make any runs. He was the son of the man who owned the livery stable in Oregon City, back in the early days. When the cavalry came through buying horses, he and his brother used to hafta swim 'em across the Willamette 'n back. Any horses that swam high, the cavalry paid five dollars more for, 'cause they could pack perishables on 'em fording rivers.*

☐ *You can't work around horses if ya eat horse meat. Can't do nothin' with 'em cause they can smell it on ya—turns 'em all snorty and wild-eyed. Same as wearin' colognes and deodorants; it tends to make cattle and horses nervous— makes 'em fear you 'cause it's unnatural. Attracts bees to sting, too.*

☐ *Don't ever buy a roan or an Appy [Appaloosa] horse, 'cause you'll never make no money offen 'em. They got tempers as make 'em miserable to ride, and ya never can sell 'em cause no one wants to buy 'em.*

☐ *My daddy once cured himself of rheumatism. He had a young, broncky team of horses hooked to this old wagon, driving 'em around trying to gentle 'em down a little. Well, they was full of vinegar and broke the tongue out of the wagon and ran off. Dad held onto the reins 'cause he didn't want to lose them horses. He was runnin' along behind 'em takin' 20 feet at each step, 'til he finally lost 'em by tripping and burying his head in the sand, causing him to bite his pipe right in two! When he rolled up, the rheumatism was gone 'n didn't bother him again for another 20–25 years. It just flat jerked it out of him*

☐ *To cure a horse of rearing and throwing its head, fill a balloon or plastic bag with warm water and carry it with you while riding. When the horse starts to throw his head, hit him between the ears with it hard enough to bust the bag. The water draining over its head gives a horse the impression it's been hit hard enough to bust the skin. This makes an impression on an animal, and lots of times does work. For an extreme animal that continues rearing, a strong 2 x 4 often has a great and lasting effect.*

☐ *Once, when I was a boy, I had this pitch-black horse. One day I got back home from a purty long ride, an' put the horse in his stall. We was low on grain, but I wanted to make sure that horse got his share cause he worked so hard. Well, I scraped the bottom of the barrel for him—took me a while, too—but the damn critter kicked my hand while I was pouring it into the manger. Well, made me so mad, I grabbed a handy pole to whack him with, but on my second swing I knocked out the light. There I stood in a pitch-dark stall with a pitch-black horse out there somewheres, already tearin' mad at me for whacking him across the back! Well, I got outta there somehow with my head still on, but first I sure went from cussing to the sweetest talk ya ever seen.*

☐ *If you have a plain-colored horse you want to fancy up a little, all ya need is some potatoes. Say you have a horse with three uneven white stockings where you want four even stockings. All ya have to do is boil some potatoes with the skins on, take 'em out and mash 'em up and put them hot on the horse's legs. It cooks the roots and bleaches the hair, so it*

comes in white. Same as with a plain black horse; to getcha an Appalousy, just put a little of that potato here and there on its rump. Gotcha some spots

☐ *I've been castrating my own animals for several years now, an' I always operate according to the moon. I won't operate on an animal 'til, 'cording to the moon, the sign is the one farthest away from the heart, which is Pisces (feet), 'cause when the sign is at the lowest point, there'll be less swelling and bleeding in an operation, or any other type of wound, cut or incision—and faster healing, too. This belief was handed down from my Dad, who used it whenever he docked sheep's tails. Doing cutting [castrating] by the signs lessens your chances of losing an animal, partic'ly dogs or horses 'cause they're more ticklish to do that sort of job on.*

I'm talkin' percentages now, not proven fact, 'cause science will prove me to be a liar—but it works. Same with vets: 90 percent of 'em won't admit the amount of bleedin' or swellin' has nothing to do with the moon or signs. I know a lot of old folks who won't even have an operation, or let their kids have one, unless the right sign and the moon are together. The same's true for butchering—ya shouldn't butcher unless the sign is on the heart (Leo), for more freer bleeding in draining blood from the carcass.

Pleasant Hill

Lane County. According to legend, the early settler Elijah Bristow climbed this gentle slope in 1846 and exclaimed, apparently in the hearing of someone with a pencil, "What a *pleasant hill.*" In recent times Pleasant Hill has become best known as the location of Ken Kesey's farm and resting place for *Further,* the famous Merry Pranksters' psychedelic bus.

In 1974, Eugene resident Joann Low talked about the "good old days" with her father; when he was a boy walking the hills south of Eugene, he found that a good hunting dog was a wonderful companion, at least until the dog was crossed.

THE WORLD'S SMARTEST HUNTING DOG

When my dad was a boy, he had a hunting dog so smart that all my dad had to do was put a drying board outside, and the dog would bring back an animal whose pelt would fit the board. If we wanted a rabbit, he put out a board the right size to dry a rabbit pelt; if he wanted a muskrat, he put out a muskrat board and so on.

Well, this dog became the wonder of the countryside, and people would come from miles around, just to see and maybe pet him. This went on for quite some time, but one day, the dog did not come home at all. Well, dad had quite a time figuring out what happened, 'til he happened to see his mother's ironing board leaning against the house, and right where he usually put the pelt board.

Well, he didn't figure he'd ever see that dog again, knowing how proud he was, but one day, six or seven months later, here come the dog, dragging a coonskin coat, and a college kid right behind him, yelling that darn dog had stole his coat.

Well, my dad had to give the coat back, and his dog never did hunt again. I guess he figured it weren't no use, if dad was just gonna hand the skin back to the critters he caught.

Portland

Multnomah County. Population 433,666. Oregon's largest city was once called Stumptown, an allusion to the ravaging of the trees by Oregon Trail emigrants when they began to build houses. In 1845, however, the name had worn thin, and two newly arrived easterners agreed that Stumptown needed a classier name, but they argued for days about the choice. Finally Francis Pettygrove and A. L. Lovejoy tossed a coin to decide between the names Portland and Boston.

Portland's stumps were not usually a problem, but in the early 1860s a flood of the Willamette River made it necessary for people to row across town to work. During the flood, the submerged stumps caused navigational problems in downtown Portland. Shortly thereafter, the merchants of the city decided to clear the streets and lots of stumps, creating the green, appealing Portland of today.

One of Portland's less verdant areas is the wharf region of Burnside Street near the Steel Bridge, known in earlier times as the Big Eddy because the Willamette River cast up flotsam and jetsam near the foot of West Burnside. In those days, the flotsam and jetsam also included Third Avenue men and women who were "just passing through" or looking for work. George Estes,

interviewed in 1939 by WPA folklorists, told of a remarkable incident in a flophouse near the Big Eddy.

THE GOLD BRICK

One day I was approached by an acquaintance, a young fellow of no means, who asked to speak with me confidentially. He said that he had made the acquaintance of a miner who at that very moment was waiting for him in a room in a Burnside Street lodging house, and who had possession of a gold brick worth twelve thousand dollars, which could be bought for three thousand. He said the miner was badly in need of money and had come by the brick "never mind how." It looked like a splendid investment. Now, as it happened, my bank balance—because of frugal personal habits—stood at a sum just about ample enough to take care of such an investment. Three thousand dollars becomes twelve thousand dollars—just like that. No long, tedious slaving, scraping, and waiting for slowly amassed principal and small annual interest accruing to do the job.

I hastened to the bank and drew out the three thousand. My acquaintance and I hurried down to the miner's room, anxious to get there before someone else did, or before he changed his mind. He was there. I bought the brick. Certainly I was excited. My eyes bulged. The brick was golden yellow and heavy as lead. I left the miner's room and, with the winged heels of a Mercury, ran over to the shop of a jeweler and goldsmith who was a very good friend of mine. I wanted him to appraise, and perhaps buy, my twelve-thousand-dollar brick. My friend was out when I entered. It was some little time before he returned. I jumped up and hurriedly told him of my good fortune. He face turned ashen. He clamped his head with both hands in anguish and cried, "George, George! What have you done? You bought a gold brick down on Burnside Street? Oh, George! You damned fool! Give me the brick. Run down to Burnside Street and see if you can find the fellow that sold it to you! Get the marshall! Hurry! Run!"

Needless to say, I ran—but I arrived too late. My miner had checked out and disappeared in the brief interim that followed the transaction. And here is why I say "luck" played a major role in all of the incidents of my life: whether for good or ill. I wended my way slowly back to the shop of my friend, the goldsmith. I was callow. I had never heard of anyone being gold-bricked. At that time I hadn't heard that the Brooklyn Bridge was being "sold" by prosperous-looking New Yorkers to bucolic-looking strangers on an average of once a week. I walked into the shop of my friend—beaten, defeated, despondent. He jumped up excitedly at my entrance, shouting.

"George, you're the luckiest damn fool in the world. I've tested your gold brick, and it's solid gold to the core. An ingot worth pretty near what your miner said it was."

Now there's a gold-brick story with a different twist.

Many immigrants established businesses in the Burnside area around the turn of the century. Among the most widely recognized was Erickson's Bar. In the early 1880s August Erickson, an immigrant from Finland, established a drinking emporium unrivaled in the western world. At a time when having the longest bar was synonymous with having the best facilities, Erickson's bar measured 684 feet. The establishment itself covered an entire city block, ranging between Second and Third streets on Burnside. Erickson's Bar actually included five bars that ran continuously around one gigantic room.

In addition to being the largest, Erickson's Bar was also one of Portland's most elegant drinking establishments, furnished with ornate fixtures, huge mirrors, and classic statuary. The bar housed a $5,000 pipe organ and a full-sized concert stage. Ladies were permitted in a mezzanine with small booths, but never allowed on the main floor. Erickson's was a workingman's bar, a proper club for miners, sailors, and loggers from the Big Eddy. Erickson's eventually became so popular that one man looking for another could simply wait at the bar until the fellow would appear. In the 1880s mailmen made regular deliveries to Erickson's Bar, hand delivering their packages at the rails.

Stage shows at Erickson's were lavish, with beautiful show girls from all over the Northwest gracing the stage. Even the bartenders had class, wearing starched white shirts and vests adorned with heavy gold chains. Erickson advertised a free "dainty lunch," usually including huge haunches of beef and slices of sourdough bread slathered in mustard made on the premises. Stacks of Finnish flatbread lined the counters, flanked by platters of sausage and Scandinavian cheese. The sixteen-ounce schooners of beer sold for five cents, and the red whiskey featured a portrait of Erickson on the label.

An Erickson's customer had five chances to be civil. He could drink in one bar, get thrown out, go to the next bar, get thrown out, and continue around the block until gaining the dubious honor of having been ejected five times by the same bouncer. Erickson chose his bouncers carefully, wishing to find men who could get along with people first and, failing that, propel them well clear of the front door. The bouncers were good-humored men but able to throw a convincing punch when necessary. Perhaps the most famous was known as *Jumbo*. Weighing better than 300 pounds, Jumbo discovered that his best tactic was to fall upon the unwanted customer. It was convincing, agreed Jumbo's victims.

When Prohibition came along, Erickson adjusted to the times, serving *near-beer* and charging a small fee for the "dainty lunch." But the heyday of Erickson's Bar had passed. When the proprietor died in 1925, the bar soon fell into decline.

In Portland's rainy weather, walking along the muddy streets was a problem of propriety for a pioneer woman. According to custom cited in the *Morning Oregonian* for February 28, 1852, "to lift the robe in public is a dangerous experiment." In the view of the *Oregonian* editor, a woman of style and class somehow was obliged to avoid muddying her petticoats while, at the same time, "revealing nothing beyond the top of a well-laced boot." On the other hand, there were immigrants to Portland who profited from a well-timed display of hosiery, including the "working girls," whose badge was a pair of striped stockings. In "The Girl with the Striped Stockings," the narrator is a "john" who "got rolled" by one of these distinctively dressed prostitutes.

THE GIRL WITH THE STRIPED STOCKINGS

One rai-ny day I'll ne'er for-get The pret-ti-est girl I ev-er met. And when she raised her skirts to the wet, I saw she had stri-ped stock-ings on! She was al-ways out when the wind blew high, When the

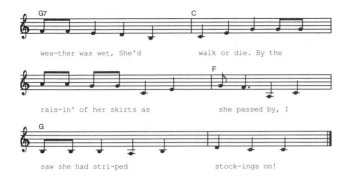

wea-ther was wet, She'd   walk or die. By the

rais-in' of her skirts as   she passed by, I

saw she had stri-ped   stock-ings on!

1. *One rainy day I'll ne'er forget*
   The prettiest girl I ever met.
   And when she raised her skirts to the wet,
   I saw she had striped stockings on.

Chorus:
   She was always out when the wind blew high;
   When the weather was wet, she'd walk or die.
   By the raisin' of her skirts as she passed by,
   I saw she had striped stockings on.

Chorus

2. *Oh, the color of her hose was red and yeller.*
   She says to me, "You're a mighty fine feller."
   I escorted her home under my umbrella—
   The girl with the striped stockings on.

Chorus

3. *And when we parted in the rain*
   She said, "We'll never meet again."
   And so she hooked my watch and chain,
   The girl with the striped stockings on.

Chorus

Despite discriminatory exclusion laws, some blacks settled in the Portland area toward the turn of the century. By 1900, nearly 70 percent of Oregon's African Americans were living in Portland. However, it was not until the 1940s that blacks came to Oregon in large numbers, as jobs opened in the shipyards and in defense plants. The first blacks in Portland fought the usual prejudices, and according to Elizabeth McLagan, author of *A Peculiar Paradise*, it was not unusual to find workingmen sleeping in alleys or on the billiard tables of bars during the war years. In the beginning, Oregon laws effectively discouraged integration. Portland labor unions prohibited black membership until 1949, and the Oregon Public Accommodations law did not pass the legislature until 1953.

In recent decades, African Americans have made homes in many Oregon communities, primarily on the "wet side," but not exclusively. Charmaine Coleman came to Eugene, like so many members of an ethnic minority, with some concerns about the attitudes of established Oregonians. "It is very important for African-Americans to be called by their proper names. Nicknames don't sit well with us," she explains. For years, blacks had to

endure being called "Sister," "Auntie," "Boy," or "Girl." Even today, says Coleman, African Americans remain sensitive about names.

Charmaine Coleman grew up in the South, where African American folklore had a powerful community impact. In the South, she says, "sometimes children are named before they are born because of a warning or prophecy. This practice is common. An old Creole conjure woman who was respected for her intuition and wisdom told my mother, 'That's a girl, and you better name her *Charmaine*, 'cause it means *little bird*.'" She also remembers a strict discipline and community respect for elders. As a girl, Coleman played counting-out rhymes and clapping games, especially during evenings when parents would gather on porches to visit and to supervise the children. "One of my favorite games," says Coleman, was "Little Sally Walker," a counting-out game.

LITTLE SALLY WALKER
(a counting-out game)

Little Sally Walker
Sittin' in a saucer,
Rise, Sally, rise.
Wipe your weary eyes.
Put your hands on your hip
And let your backbone slip.

Oh, shake it to the east.
Oh, shake it to the west.
Oh, shake it to the one
That you love best.

Then you close your eyes, go around the circle, and point to someone to become the one in the middle. You say it kind of sassy, you know.

MISS MARY MACK
(a clapping game)

Miss Mary Mack, Mack, Mack,
All dressed in black, black, black,
With 24 buttons, buttons, buttons,
Up and down her back, back, back.

She asked her mother, mother, mother
For 15 cents, cents, cents,
To see the elephant, elephant, elephant
Jump the fence, fence, fence.

He jumped so high, high, high
He touched the sky, sky, sky
And he never came back, back, back
'Til the Fourth of July, -ly, -ly.

Charmaine Coleman also remembers some favorite African American foodways—methods for preparing foods such as beans and hamhocks, cornbread, pound cake, lemon pie, sweet potato pudding casserole, and chicken feet gumbo.

SWEET POTATO PUDDING CASSEROLE

Sweet potatoes, cooked and mashed, are mixed with cream, eggs, cinnamon, and nutmeg—as you would mix filling for a pumpkin pie. The mixture is baked as a custard.

Poured into a crust, it becomes sweet potato pie. There is a saying among Afro-American people: "We don't eat pumpkin pie; we eat sweet potato pie."

CHICKEN FEET GUMBO

This dish used to be common fare. Now it is usually made for very special occasions:

Make a roux the consistency of gravy. In it you would put chicken feet with the nails removed. (Chicken feet add a delicious flavor to the gumbo and are filled with nutrients). Then you would add pieces of chicken, salami, sausage, or other meat, as well as okra and maybe some corn. You can put a tomato base to it and season it with file gumbo.

Rickreall

Polk County. In *Oregon Geographic Names*, Lewis McArthur summarizes a long-standing debate about the naming of this farm community west of Salem. The name may have come from the French *la creole* or from Chinook Jargon *hyak chuck*, "swift water." At any rate, the town was called Dixie during the Civil War period, when the population was increased by the addition of several southerners. Today Rickreall has a large Spanish-speaking population.

Hispanics are by far the largest minority in Oregon, and the Spanish-speaking populace has a rich and fascinating body of folklore. Belief in the *mal ojo*, or "evil eye," is widespread among migrating Hispanic women, for the *ojo* is often cast against a beautiful child, bringing lethargy, sickness, or even death. The cure for the *ojo* often comes from *curandera*, women with supernatural healing powers; their spells offset the evil done by *brujas*, witches, and evildoers. In some Mexican communities, spells and incantations, part of the occult world, may be mixed with Catholic rituals, such as the recitation of a "Hail Mary" or an "Our Father." Rites of magic, such as those described below, call for special instruments—an unbroken egg, special powders, eucalyptus leaves—to cure *empacho*, "depression and listlessness," or *espanto*, "the horror." Typical of incantation rituals, the rites must be performed at a crossroads, where spirits congregate.

In 1974 Karin Smith collected tales of *brujas* and *curanderas* from a Hispanic woman living in Eugene. These legends, like Hispanic *llorona* stories (see Phoenix, p. 88), circulate mainly among women of childbearing age.

WITCHES AND HEALERS

In Mexican communities there are always one or two women who were the curanderas. *They healed with prayer, herbs, and weeds. It seems to me that they were always old women—I mean real old, like over a hundred years old. They had magical powers. They knew prayers for everything, and they knew how to talk to the devil, too. They always* dressed in black from head to feet and always had a black rebozzo. They wore all kinds of things dangling from their necks.

In our town there was only one, since we lived in a farming community. Her name was Dona Luisa. We knew she was a witch. Sometimes we would drive by her house (an old shack), and always there was a ladder leaning on the wall leading up to the roof where she would climb for her takeoff. My mother always told us that Dona Luisa flew at night. According to my mother, Dona Luisa did many evil things. Every time we went by her place we would cross ourselves and pray an Ave Maria *and a* Padre Nuestro. *If a young man wanted a certain girl to fall in love with him, and she refused him, he would go to Dona Luisa, who would give him something to put in her drink or some powder to rub on his hands when he touched her. If this failed, Dona Luisa would fly off on her nightly visit and soon the wedding bells would ring.*

THE EXORCISM OF THE "EVIL EYE"

I was born in a country of brujas *and* curanderas. *When I was very little, people used to get sick a lot. Always someone had* empacho *or* espanto, *or children had* ojo.

Once when I was very young, a close friend of my mother's had a baby boy who was very beautiful. One day she came over to our house in a very hysterical condition. Someone had made ojo *at her baby, and the baby was very sick—so sick, in fact, that he most likely wouldn't live through the night. Dona Luisa was out on one of her flying trips, and there was no one to* curar *the baby. So she came and begged my mother to do it. My mother knew all the prayers and set out to save the boy's life.*

Ojo *is when someone looks at your baby and wishes it was theirs. If the person wishing the baby was theirs touches the baby, the baby will get sick and die within a few hours. So my mother had to do the ritual. No one was allowed at this ritual except the* curandera *and the mother of the child. I hid and witnessed it all.*

First, they took all the clothes off the child and laid him on a blanket on a table. Then my mother took an unbroken egg and rubbed it all over the baby, all the time praying Ave Marias *and* Padre Nuestros *and other prayers I couldn't recognize. After many, many prayers, she picked up the baby and took him outside and started walking down the road, followed by the mother, who carried a bucket of lime and an armful of eucalyptus leaves, all the time praying in a mournful tone.*

When she reached the crossroads, she stopped and ordered the mother to make a cross of lime on the center of the crossroads, after which she laid the eucalyptus leaves in the form of a cross. Then she laid the baby on the cross. Then the prayers began. My mother would pray out loud, and the mother would echo her prayer. They prayed and prayed for hours and hours, and when they knew it was past midnight, they picked up the baby and started walking back home, all the time praying and echoing. When they got home, they made a cross of lime and eucalyptus leaves again, this time on the bed, and they laid the baby on it. My mother then took the egg which she had rubbed him with and which she must have had on her person all this time, and she again rubbed the baby all over his body. Finally, she broke the egg into a cup and set it under the bed. And after another prayer, we all went to bed.

Next morning the egg in the cup was green, and the baby was well. My mother told me that the green in the egg was the evil that had been in the baby.

Saginaw

Lane County. Saginaw, named for the town in Michigan, is a timber community on the outskirts of Cottage Grove. In 1970 Tina Wegelin asked her uncle, Will Norwood, to write down some stories from earlier years. Norwood penned ''The Ox Breaker,'' a tall tale about the era when there were no log trucks on Lane County roads, only ox-driven wagons. Naturally, someone had to break the oxen to the harness, and a man named Jones had that task. According to Wegelin, her uncle wrote the story out by hand, adding it was ''a pity someone who knew how to write didn't take the story and write it up 'good' and make some money off it.'' (We've done our best, Mr. Norwood—T.N. and T.S.)

THE OX BREAKER

Mr. Jones was an ox breaker. Some oxen were hard to break, but Jones had a scheme he thought would work with the worst ones. He made a small corral with a long chute leading to a larger corral. Between the pens was a chute, about four feet wide and 200 feet long. Once the ox left the first corral, he would have to buck straight ahead and could not spin or swerve.

Well, to help him stay on for the full 200 yards, Jones got some pitch and put it over the seat of his pants. Then he grabbed the ox's tail and threw it over his shoulder, an old-timer's trick for hanging on, and he picked up a sturdy three-foot stick. They got started down the chute, with that ox bucking straight ahead. When Jones said ''Haw!'' he hit that ox on the right side of the head, and when he said ''Gee!'' he hit him on the left, hoping to train the animal to turn. Sure enough, the ox bucked like a devil all the way down the chute, and by the time he hit the large corral, the animal was exhausted.

Afterwards, Jones started to get off but couldn't. He was stuck fast in the pitch. So he called for help from a neighbor, but three men couldn't pull him off. So they put a pulley over a tree limb and tied the rope under his arms. They reefed and reefed for a long time. Finally they pulled Jones right out of his pants! He hung there in the air wearing only his shorts.

After Jones got down, they tied the rope to his belt and jerked until the pants came loose, tearing up a big chunk of ox fur at the same time. Mr. Jones's wife boiled those pants for an hour or so and couldn't get them clean, so she cut about twelve inches out of the seat. But she didn't have any denim for a patch, so she looked around and found an old sheep hide. She sewed it over the hole. After that, Jones could sit down anyplace and have a cushion under him. When he went to church and sat on those hard pews, he went right to sleep without even waiting for the preacher to start the sermon.

Pretty soon every man in the neighborhood had wool to sit on. Wool hides, usually worth six-bits, suddenly cost $3 or $4 each. Mr. Jones tried to get a patent on his invention but failed because a man in Arkansas had already thought of the idea. But Jones made money anyhow. In the spring when Cottage Grove's weather got warm, he would shear his neighbors' pants for twenty-five cents apiece—and sell the wool besides.

Salem

Marion County. Population 106,942. The first wagon trains to reach this location on the Willamette River gathered at *Chemeketa*, a ''resting place.'' Around 1844 the location was renamed Salem (Hebrew *shalom*, ''peace'') after the town in Massachusetts. The name Chemeketa is retained in the community college located in the city.

Salem became the capital of Oregon in 1851, replacing Oregon City. Some people say that legislators are a humorless lot; of course, those people have not read recent property tax legislation. In fact, there is considerable levity in the lawmakers' chambers. For instance, in 1981 the house speaker stood to announce Rick Bauman's birthday, but he got the date wrong. Bauman replied, ''It's not my birthday. That's three months from now!'' Representative Norm Smith then took the floor and said, ''I move that we change Representative Bauman's birthday to today.'' The motion carried, with only one dissenting vote. In 1921, a man named Stannard was elected to the House, but on the way from the Coast, he died. According to Cecil Edwards, Senate historian in 1981, the Credentials Committee seated Stannard anyway. Being dead was not one of the reasons listed in the bylaws for being denied a House seat.

Salem stands not only as the legal center of Oregon, but as its historical center as well. The State Library and State Archives are good places to discover traditional recipes and foodways, many contributed by homesteading women and nineteenth-century immigrants. Food preparation and foodways have always played a major part in women's lives, so it is not surprising that trading recipes has been a popular practice since the 1850s. Still today, researchers and browsers commonly find recipes tucked away in old books, family Bibles, journals, diaries, and letters. It seems only natural to list a broad sampling of Oregon recipes under Salem, the capital city. Some of the foodways were contributed by Fern M. Smith or Diane Llewellyn; others come from Twilo Scofield's personal collections; still others have taken the most common route, traveling anonymously from kitchen to kitchen before being recorded in this book.

CORNSTARCH

Berta K. Barker, Salem, 1969

This recipe was brought from Pennsylvania by Mrs. Barker's mother:

Gather white field corn when ripe enough that the milk is set but not hard. Husk and "whisker" the corn. Slit each row of kernels with a sharp knife. In a tub half filled with water, place the washboard (which has been thoroughly cleaned and scalded). Start rubbing the ears of corn on the washboard until all the corn is off the cob.

Skim the hulls off the water and strain the remaining milky mixture through cheese cloth. Let it sand until the starch settles to the bottom. Pour the extra water off the top. Spread the starch on a sheet to dry in the sun. Store the starch in fruit jars.

CORNSTARCH PUDDING

This was a popular recipe in early Oregon, since most households had the ingredients in stock:

> 6 tablespoons of cornstarch
> ⅔ cup of sugar
> ½ teaspoon of salt
> 4 cups of scalded milk
> 2 teaspoons of vanilla
> cinnamon to taste

Mix the cornstarch with sugar and salt. Add the cold milk and stir until smooth. Then pour the mixture slowly into the scalded milk, stirring constantly. Cook the potion for 15 minutes in a double boiler at a slow boil, stirring the pot constantly until the mixture thickens. Continue to stir the pudding occasionally during the remainder of cooking time. Cool it slightly and then add vanilla. Pour the pudding into bowls and sprinkle cinnamon on top. Chill.

MINCEMEAT

Mamie Tabler, Foster, 1960

> 4 pounds of lean beef
> 1 pound of butter
> 1 pound of brown sugar
> 8 pounds of apples (Jonathan or Spitzenberg are best.)
> 3 pounds of raisins
> 1 pound of citron, orange peel, candied fruit, or pineapple

> 2 quarts of sweet or boiled apple cider
> 1 pint of vinegar
> 1 tablespoon of salt
> 1 tablespoon of pepper
> 1 tablespoon of cloves
> 1 tablespoon of allspice
> 4 tablespoons of cinnamon
> 2 tablespoons of nutmeg

Cut the meat into small cubes and cook it with enough water to cover the ingredients until everything is tender. Then chop the apple to a fine texture and add it, with all the other ingredients, to the kettle. Then cook the whole mixture until the meat is tender and all the flavors are blended. Can the mincemeat while it is hot. If the mixture seems too thick, add the broth to the mincemeat.

COTTAGE CHEESE

Mamie Tabler, Foster, 1960

I remember my mother making cottage cheese with extra milk. That is, when we had more than enough for the family to drink. The cream was skimmed off the top for making butter, and the milk was set in a container on the back of the wood stove, where it got warm enough to separate. When the watery whey would separate from the solid part of the milk, my mother would drain it off and pour it in with the slop for the pigs. She would put the solid white part in a clean flour sack and hang the bag up over a pan, so the remaining whey could drip out. What was left in the bag was cottage cheese, to which she would add a bit of salt. There is nothing better than homemade cottage cheese with a bit of pepper and a tomato fresh from the garden.

APPLE TURNOVERS

Wash one pound of dried apples, removing bits of core and skin, and soak the apples overnight. On the next day stew in enough water to cover everything and, when the apples are soft, run the mash through a colander. Return the ingredients to the stove, add enough brown sugar to make the fruit rich and sweet, and cook until the mash is thick. Then cool it and add 1½ tablespoons of cinnamon. Line a dripping pan with pie crust, put in the fruit mixture, and cover it with an upper crust, gashing the top crust slightly to let the steam escape. Press the edges of the crust together and bake the turnovers, at first in a hot oven, then under reduced heat. When the turnovers are done, cut them into diamond-shaped portions and serve them hot with cream.

BREAD PUDDING

Frankie Hermann, La Grande, 1975

> 2 cups of stale bread, torn into pieces
> 3 cups of scalded milk

1 cup of sugar
1 cup of melted butter
2 eggs, slightly beaten
½ teaspoon of salt
1 teaspoon of vanilla or ¼ teaspoon of cinnamon

Soak the torn bread in milk and set it aside to cool. Add sugar, butter, eggs, salt, and vanilla or cinnamon. Stir the contents and pour everything into a buttered 9'' x 9'' baking dish. Bake the pudding for one hour at 325 degrees.

SWEET AND SOUR CABBAGE

Mrs. Lawrence Jenson, Corvallis, 1969

''This recipe was received from my grandmother at my marriage in September, 1953—just two months before her death at 102 years. She was born Emilie Hulda Wilhelmina (Hartwhich) Rave at Labes-Pommern, Germany, August 1, 1851.''

Shred cabbage and cook it until tender, but still firm. Drain and return the cabbage to the pan. Add one tablespoon of shortening and salt to taste. Simmer for about 10 minutes. Add one cup of diluted vinegar sweetened with white or brown sugar. Simmer on low flame about one-half hour. Onion or apple may be added.

KRAUTRONZA

Molly Lansing, Creswell, 1972

Take a rich hot-roll dough and roll it out. Cut it into big diamonds. Then make a filling of shredded cabbage, shredded carrots (about equal amounts), and chopped onions fried in grease until the vegetables are soft. Add lots of black pepper—large ground. Put the vegetable filling in the middle of the dough diamond and pinch the ends up so that it looks like a submarine. Bake it just as long as you would bake roll dough, at about 350 degrees.

DANDELION WINE

Vintie Holt, Bridgeport, 1973

''I like the wine better with white sugar than with brown.''

1 gallon of dandelion blossoms
1 gallon of boiling water
4 pounds of sugar
1 cake of yeast
4 lemons
4 oranges
bitter almond

Pour the boiling water over the blossoms and let it stand until the blooms rise, about 24 to 48 hours. Strain it into a stone jar, into which you dice four lemons and four oranges. Add four pounds of sugar and one cake of yeast. Stir it well and stand the jar in a cool place. Stir four or five times a day until fermentation starts. Keep the jar well covered. In two weeks strain the mixture and add a little bitter almond. Cork

it tightly and keep it in a dark, cool place. The wine may be improved by allowing it to stand in the jug for six weeks before the bottling, and I find the wine has a much better flavor.

Sandy

Clackamas County. Population 4,078. Sandy is a town on the Mt. Hood Highway, located near the Sandy River, which gave the town its name. Lewis and Clark's descriptions of the river contributed to its first name, the Quicksand River, later shortened simply to Sandy.

Oregon's independent settlers often came west to be free of others telling them what to do. Later generations of Oregonians often kept that spirit alive. One such woman was Nettie Connett, who made the town of Sandy her base of nearly legal enterprise.

NETTIE FINDS A WAY

Nettie Connett was a rugged mountain woman who lived in the area northeast of Sandy for most of her 84 years. She was a small woman, but tough and self-reliant, often operating just on the other side of the law.

Nettie, who drove a battered Model A pickup in the 1940s and 1950s, would pull into her ''office'' in Sandy, Irene's Tavern, spitting tobacco juice between her false teeth and cussing up a storm. She had numerous money-making adventures, such as selling Christmas trees cut from the yards of her neighbors. But most of her cash came from moonshining.

One day, while driving out of town, her truck filled with bottles of home-made liquor, Nettie was stopped by two policemen, who said, ''We're lookin' for Nettie Connett.'' When they explained that they suspected her of making moonshine, Nettie gave them a shocked look and offered to give the officers careful directions to the home of Nettie Connett. Before they drove away, she wished them luck and bristled a few times about ''such goings-on in our community.'' Then Nettie happily drove on to Oregon City, where she sold her entire truckload of ''shine.''

Nettie was also vague on the hunting laws of the state. Every year on the first day of the season, Nettie could be expected to drive through town, just after dawn, with a deer showing from the bed of her Model A pickup. Her friends at Irene's Tavern, however, noticed the odd fact that, while most of the deer taken on that morning were still steaming on the hoods of coupes and sedans, Nettie's deer always seemed curiously cold and stiff.

One year, Nettie made a little mistake on opening day, and she bagged a doe. Undaunted, Nettie got out her hunting knife and sewing kit, performing a hasty sex-change opera-

tion on the doe. When Nettie drove through Sandy that morning, trophy displayed, the doe was wearing an impressive rack of borrowed horns.

Scio

Linn County. Population 539. Most of the community was settled by emigrants who accepted Donation Land Grants from the Oregon Territorial government. Stories vary as to how Scio got its name. Some believe it was named for Scio, Ohio. Others say the name recalls a local Indian chief, Scioto. Among the most popular versions is the opinion that the town was named by Matilda McKinney, who said that the word meant ''peace.''

Perhaps there was peace in Scio, but it was probably not the work of its most famous resident, the Reverend Joab Powell, pioneer pastor of Scio's Providence Church. According to one longtime Scio resident, ''Joab Powell would preach on Sunday and then stay drunk the rest of the week.'' In 1973, a caretaker for the Providence Church argued that Powell never drank, but was ''big and scary-

looking'' and dressed in clothes that had never been cleaned. Powell was a fierce fire-and-brimstone preacher, who had his own way of describing sin and corruption. With his booming voice, fiery tongue, and burning evangelism, Powell managed to offend as often as inspire. ''Women,'' he said to one startled audience, ''are like oak trees—solid in the middle, but rotten at the branches.''

Despite his suspicion of women, Powell had to depend on his wife for the reading of Scriptures. Thoroughly illiterate, the preacher had Mrs. Powell read him the Bible passages and then committed them to memory. Powell would cram a chaw of tobacco into his mouth and then open church services with the phrase ''I am the *Alpha* and *omegy*.'' During his twenty-three years of preaching, Powell supposedly baptized more than 3,000 people in a cold stream flowing past the town.

Powell was famous enough to be asked to offer the prayer at the state legislature in Salem, the shortest one on record (see ''Unforgettable Moments in Oregon History,'' p. 4). Even so, he was not universally considered an upright citizen in the town of Scio. The preacher physically hurled disruptive members from the church and once thrashed a powerful blacksmith who was angry at Powell's proselytizing on French Prairie. One Sunday morning, according to Helen Myers Lowe, Joab Powell sent one of his thirteen children to a neighbor's house to buy some breakfast bacon. The neighbor's name was Paul. When the boy slipped into church service, his father was in midsermon, pointing to the New Testament and shouting, ''And what did Paul have to say about this?'' Surprised, the boy jumped up and replied, ''Paul says you can't have any more bacon until you pay for what you already got!''

The Oregon Trail provided a bitter journey for many people. By rough estimate, one person died for every ten feet of the trail. After considering the odds, some people prepared for the journey as though it would be their last. In one of many Scio stories collected by Tanis Knight in 1974, Mary Brown Knight describes the overland journey taken by a pessimistic pioneer ancestor.

THE WELL-TRAVELED CASKET

My great grandmother, Polly Crowley, whose family was one of the first to settle at Scio, came across the plains in 1846 from Tennessee. She was sure she would never make the trip alive, so she had a casket of walnut made before the trip started. This casket was hauled all the way from Tennessee to Oregon in the family's wagon. Inside, buried beneath the linens, was the family fortune of $10,000. That sum was a great amount of money in the mid-1800s.

Old Polly, who enjoyed poor health, as they said then, not only made the trip in good condition, she also managed to live for forty years after her arrival. She bore several children after arriving in Scio. When she finally did die, her son-in-law, who was a prosperous undertaker, could have easily made her another coffin. However, the family, known for thriftiness, used the same walnut coffin to bury the old lady.

Shedd

Linn County. According to Jack Norman, a mill was built in this location in 1852 on the banks of the Calapooya River. Because the mill sat at the base of Bunker Hill, the owner called his settlement Boston Mills. When the railroad came through, the lines passed through the farm of Frank Shedd, who was also hired to build the station. Naturally, Shedd became the new name of this timber center and logging community.

In a mill town logger lore is a staple in every barber shop, tavern, and cafe. The Northwest logger is a throwback to another era. Despite his relative "veneer of civilization," the timber-beast is unlike other Oregonians. "The wilderness is his workshop," says Wilbur A. Davis, "and he pits his strength and ingenuity daily against his rugged environment." Woods work is dangerous work, and it is nearly impossible to find a logger who has not been seriously injured at least once. Nonetheless, the Oregon logger is a prideful man whose tales and customs suggest a fatalistic lack of concern for his own safety, as evidenced by this lumberman's tale involving the *choker*, a cable attached to logs for skidding. After several skids, the normal choker looks like a pig's tail and has a tendency to get hung up on every bush and branch in the forest. "The Kinky Choker" circulates through most logging communities and may be found in several variants, including one about a Russian tourist, a Texas cowboy, and a very old woman.

THE KINKY CHOKER

A choker setter from Shedd went into Salem to catch an airplane, and he found himself on a small, beat-up little puddle-jumper with three other passengers: a Russian tourist, a Texas cowboy, and a very old woman. During the flight the plane developed engine trouble and started to go down. The pilot opened the door and said, "Grab those parachutes and jump for it!" And with those words, he abandoned the plane.

Well, the passengers looked under their seats and found only one parachute. The Russian went to the doorway and said, "Give it to the lady." Then he yelled "For the Revolution!" before he jumped. The Texan said, "I'm not gonna be outdone by no Russkie!" So the Texan pulled hard on his 10-gallon hat and said, "That parachute's for you, ma'am." Then he stood in the doorway and yelled "Fer the Alamo!" and jumped.

The old woman looked at the choker setter and said, "You're a young man with something to live for. I've got very few years left. Take the parachute." But the logger just handed it back.

"No, m'am," he said, "I got this kinky choker. The minute I jump out, sure as hell it's gonna' hang up on somethin'."

Springfield

Lane County. Population 44,597. Early travelers passing through the southern end of the Willamette Valley called this community Scantigrease, suggesting the scarcity of tallow and oils, necessities for wagon travel. Springfield is the most common town name in America, and emigrants from a similarly named town in Kentucky, Illinois, or Missouri may have settled here early on. Located near the confluence of the McKenzie and Willamette rivers, Springfield is a traditional mill town, the home for many loggers and others who work in the wood-products industry.

Springfield is a likely place to hear a popular Oregon song about the larger-than-life woodsmen. "The Frozen Logger" was written by Stewart Holbrook, H. L. Davis, and James Stevens of *Paul Bunyan* fame. One day after meeting at a writers' conference in Corvallis, the three men decided there were no Northwest loggers' songs that could be sung in mixed company. Hours later, "The Frozen Logger" was born. Over the years "The Frozen Logger" has circulated widely, a tune sung by people from all corners of the state who enjoy its humorous look at the lumber industry and its legendary characters. It has even been the subject of some hilarious parodies, including a Eugene version called "The Frozen Jogger."

THE FROZEN LOGGER

As I sat down one evening
In a timber town cafe,
A forty-year-old waitress
To me these words did say:

"I see you are a logger
and not just a common bum,
For nobody but a logger
Stirs his coffee with his thumb.

"My lover was a logger,
There's none like him today.
If you'd pour whiskey on it,
He would eat a bale of hay.

"Well, he never shaved the whiskers
From off of his horny hide.
He'd just pound them in with a hammer
Then bite them off inside.

"My logger came to see me
Upon one freezing day,
He held me in a gentle hug
That broke three vertebrae.

"He kissed me when we parted,
So hard he broke my jaw,
I could not speak to tell him
He'd forgot his mackinaw.

"I watched my lovin' logger
Sauntering through the snow,
Going gravely homeward
At forty-eight below.

"The weather, it tried to freeze him.
It tried its level best.
At one hundred degrees below zero
He buttoned up his vest.

"Well, it froze clean through to China,
It froze the stars above,
At one thousand degrees below zero
It froze my logger-love.

"They tried in vain to thaw him,
And if you'll believe me, sir,
They made him into axe-blades
To chop the Douglas fir.

"And so I lost my logger,
And to this cafe I come.
And here I wait till someone
Stirs his coffee with his thumb."

Some years ago another song began to circulate throughout the Northwest in many versions. As "The Logger's Sweetheart" was sung by more and more people, it finally evolved to a folklore response to "The Frozen Logger." Here, in a version sung by Bob Beers, is the log-camp sequel to James Stephens's popular lament. The narrator is a woodsman who describes his lost love.

THE LOGGER'S SWEETHEART

"Oh yes, my dear, I'm a logger
And I am lonesome too
For I recently lost my true love,
She much resembled you.

"We were working out of Oakridge,
Logging the country 'round,
My true love worked in a small cafe
A few miles out of town.

"She was a delicate hasher,
A hasher beyond compare,
With a tiny flick of her dainty wrist,
She'd flatten a grizzly bear.

"She had many good points about her,
And I can remember yet
How she let me use her flaming lips
To light my cigarette.

"One night we went on a party,
We went with a sawmill crew,
We all had a drink of whiskey,
My love had a quart or two.

"Well, you know how it is when you're playful,
The whiskey within you burns,
My true love challenged a buzz saw
And spotted it seven turns.

"Oh, she was easily winning
When by some cruel stroke of fate
She slipped and lost her footing
And was sawed into four-by-eights.

"So that's how I lost my true love
And that mill owner as a joke
Took all that was left of her carcass
And sold it for seasoned oak.

"Yes, that's how I lost my true love,
And I come to this small cafe,
And now that we've met each other,
We can plan our wedding day.

"We'll stand at the top of a mountain
And we'll sing to the stars above,
And at forty degrees below zero
We will consummate our love.

"Well, that's almost the end of the story,
There's only one thing more,
We wanted a great big family,
We've had babies by the score.

"The first year we had nine children
And the next year 79,
You see, when we found we could do it,
We'd have them ten at a time.

"My wife was a very good mother,
She nursed them one by one,
On one side she had straight whiskey,
On the other she had rum.

"Well, now when we're all at the table,
We count them, one by one.
Yes, we sit and count our blessings
And stir our coffee with our thumbs."

Sublimity

Marion County. Population 1,490. Established in 1852, the town was named Sublimity by settlers who found the location "sublime" in every respect. In 1857 the United Brethren Church established a school in Sublimity that later became Sublimity College. According to the WPA's *Oregon Oddities*, the first president was Milton Wright, a respected educator. Wright, however, was skeptical when students began to speculate about flying machines. "If God had intended you to fly," he said, "He'd have put wings on you." Two years later, Milton Wright returned to the East and began to raise a family, including two sons, Wilbur and Orville, who apparently did not listen to their father on the subject of flight.

Perhaps the early wagon-train emigrants called their town Sublimity because they found their destination peaceful and serene compared to life on the Oregon Trail. More likely, however, they were just relieved to have a few acres of land between themselves and Murilla Greenstreet Hobson. Folklore collector Jean Campbell recorded this legend about one of Sublimity's most hot-tempered citizens.

THE SHREW OF THE OREGON TRAIL

This occurred on a train—I don't know which train it was. I never did find out. But anyway, this Murilla Greenstreet Hobson is buried in Sublimity Cemetery. They were on their way to Oregon, and the Indians attacked, and they captured her. Now she was 17 or 18 years old—she was no kid—and she had a violent temper, just a violent temper. And it made her so mad that these Indians laid a hand on her.

And, the story goes, she kicked, scratched, and yanked their hair. She just fought back and really mistreated them— poor things. And Indians do have a certain respect for anybody who shows no fear; they're strong for that. And she certainly showed no fear; she just tore them apart.

Well, they brought her back to the wagon train, but they demanded white bread in return. Indians were very fond of white man's bread. They didn't have anything like that. They demanded white bread before they would leave, so Murilla said, "I'll make the bread. You sit down here."

Well, they wanted a cow, too. So they killed a cow and ate it raw—right then and there while they were waitin' for the bread. And she knew what she was doing. They had flour in one of the wagons that had kerosene spilled on it. And it was ruined, of course. So she made the bread out of that kerosene-flour, and the Indians ate it and it made them horribly, horribly sick. And she stood there yelling at them, "I hope it kills ya. Eat some more. I hope it kills ya!"

And when they finally got so they could stand up and walk without heavin', they went away. They were afraid of her by that time.

Sweet Home

Linn County. Population 6,797. In its pioneer glory, the current town of Sweet Home was called Buckhead, after a local tavern with antlers prominently displayed over the front door. In the rough-and-tumble era of settlement, the streets of Buckhead saw a disproportionate number of shootings, fistfights, and drunken riots.

Although changing the town name to Sweet Home softened the town's image, this East Valley logging town remained on vague terms with the law for many decades. During the Depression, Laura Wilder worked as a cook's helper in Sweet Home. "We'd go out and shoot a deer and hang it out back in the woods until it was gone," says Wilder. "The forest ranger was always dropping by to eat. He was the game warden, too, but when we served him venison we'd just call it something else, and so would he."

In 1971 Bonnie and Roy Phillips visited Sweet Home and a number of Willamette Valley locations, compiling a list of superstitions to be included in the Randall V. Mills Archives. In the Phillips collection, one speaker cites a superstition against carrying exactly thirteen cents but seems to overlook the fact that driving home from a tavern is dangerous for most people, regardless of pocket change.

WILLAMETTE VALLEY SUPERSTITIONS

☐ *"When I go fishing, I determine which way to go on the river by spitting in my left hand and slapping the right hand down on it. The way the biggest splatter goes is the direction I fish."*
☐ *"My mother always warned me to be careful in cleaning a chicken when I was pregnant. If you do not get the lungs out, the chicken will poison you."*
☐ *"When I am driving someplace and have to dodge an animal in the road, I always know I will have to dodge two others before finishing the trip."*
☐ *"I will never put 13 cents into my pocket (in addition to all the other no-no's about 13). Once my father had this amount—a dime and three pennies—in his pocket and was almost killed in a car wreck on the way home from a tavern."*
☐ *"My mom always told me it was bad luck to start a trip on Friday of any week."*
☐ *Three woods accidents will happen in a row involving men from the same line of work. The same is true for all occupations.*
☐ *If two people die within the same family, a third will die before the year has ended.*
☐ *After walking nine railroad ties, the first man a woman meets will be her sweetheart.*
☐ *"You can determine the sex of a child before birth if you hold a dime attached to a string before the stomach of a pregnant woman. If the head of the coin turns toward the stomach, the child will be a boy. If tails, it will be a girl."*

☐ *"Don't eat sauerkraut or pickles during menstrual periods, or the food will spoil."*

☐ *"When a person walks in your front door and out the back door, that is a sure sign you will have more company soon."*

☐ *"A snake will never die before sundown."*

☐ *"When a snake dies belly-up, it will rain soon."*

☐ *"If you steal a dishrag or piece of meat and rub it on warts, then bury the dishrag in the ground, the warts will go away."*

☐ *"To cure lovesickness: Take a dead chicken, a black candle, and a cigar, and put them in a box on his doorstep."*

Woodburn

Marion County. Population 13,504. No one is quite sure how the city acquired its name. Woodburn is the religious and social center for the Russian Old Believers, a group of people who migrated from Russia during the sixteenth century. Brutally persecuted in their home country, the Old Believers located colonies in Turkey, China, Brazil, Argentina, Alaska, and—eventually—Woodburn. In 1980 Kevin Dean researched the Old Believers community for the Mills Archives, interviewing a young member of the Woodburn society who was attending the University of Oregon.

Old Believers have maintained their customs and rituals for generations, despite centuries of isolation from their religious and ethnic roots. The Woodburn Russians retain their traditional costumes, foodways, and rituals, including the celebration of sixty-two special holidays. With few exceptions, they strive to remain isolated from the larger homogenous communities that surround them. Mostly farmers, some of the Old Believers have nonetheless worked as loggers or furniture builders; many have special skills in woodworking. The women sew, making traditional clothing and upholstery for hand-built furniture.

Girls in the Old Believer society usually marry by age fifteen, accepting marriages arranged by parents and then moving into the parents' home until the time of the next family marriage. The Russian women do not ever cut their hair. While growing up, a young girl wears her hair in a single braid; after marriage, she wears two braids, styling the hair over her head in the shape of a halo, covered with a cap called a *schmuda* and a colorful scarf. The Woodburn women also wear a sacred dress called a *senekai*, an apron, a belt, and a cross. Women's clothing is distinctive, intricately embroidered and decorated with bright colors.

Men in the Old Believer society wear their hair short, but they cannot shave after marriage, following half the obligation of Leviticus 19:27: "Ye shall not round the corners of thy head, nor mar the corners of thy beard." Like the women, the men wear a belt and a cross, but otherwise dress less formally, in jeans and a handmade shirt called a *rubashka*.

Food includes a variety of traditional Russian dishes, using beets, cabbage, meats, pancakes, and noodles. Food not only serves as a nutritional necessity, but also has religious and cultural symbolism. Bread and salt are symbols of hospitality and acceptance, as well as having religious connotations, including knowledge and wisdom. Occasionally outsiders visit an Old Believer home. After a meal, the guests' plates are thrown away or kept separate from the others. In the Old Believer society, only "insiders" may attend community gatherings, and members—especially women—are not supposed to talk to others in the Woodburn community.

During his interview with a woman from the Russian Old Believer community, Kevin Dean discovered that "it is not considered lady-like to use hand gestures while speaking." Anna was born in Hong Kong, later moved to Brazil, and finally to the United States. At the age of fifteen, her father arranged her marriage to a boy in Woodburn, but Anna rebelled and left the Old Believer society. Despite speaking Russian as a first language, Anna spoke clear and articulate English, betraying only a hint of an accent.

OLD BELIEVER WEDDING TRADITIONS

When you get married, you have a large feast and a celebration. The celebration used to last for a month. But in the United States, it only goes for . . . like, if you get married on Sunday, it goes on 'til Friday. All the relatives on both sides of the family drink, drink, drink. You drink, and then you go to sleep. Then you get up, eat breakfast, and start drinking. Meanwhile, the bride and groom and the best man and so on and so forth—all the people who came to the wedding—bring their gifts; they get a lot of money. They give gifts and money.

For every gift you give, the bride and groom have to thank you. They're all standing in front of you. Like, you'd be sitting here [Anna points Dean to a place], and I'd be the bride and groom, and you'd give us a dollar, and we'd give you a glass of wine, and you'd drink it up. You have to drink the whole thing up. We'd thank you. You'd thank us. And we'd give you another glass, and you'd give us some more money, and we'd thank you and bow to you, and we'd give you another glass of wine. Pretty soon, you'd give us a hundred dollars! That's the money the kids start off with.

You live with your husband's family. If you are the youngest in your family, your mother and sisters all move with you, too. Both your mother and father live with you. It's part of the custom. You live with your parents and take care of them. If you're the oldest boy, you live with your parents until the next kid gets married. Then you have to move out and make room.

Yoncalla

Douglas County. Population 930. This town was probably named by pioneer Jesse Applegate, perhaps a blending of *yonc* (eagle) and *calla* (bird). Jesse Applegate, one of the most famous of Oregon pioneers, was the first postmaster of Yoncalla.

In lumber towns such as Yoncalla, loggers often talk about the ever-present dangers of their jobs. Most loggers believe you should "quit the day before you're goin' to quit because that's when you always get hurt." Most loggers don't actually give notice; they simply *bunch 'er* or *go down the road*. In pioneer logging days, when jobs were plentiful and men followed the best work, it was often said, "There is one crew leaving, one crew workin', and one crew on its way." Because danger was a constant in the woods, men often sought out a *gyppo* unit, a small, independent outfit, one with experienced men and efficient equipment. If a man got stuck with a second-rate *highballin'* outfit, he might get *winnipuckered*—hit by a snapping cable—or decked by a *widow-maker*, a loose limb hanging in a tree.

Sometimes the logger's jargon gets confusing to an outsider or a greenhorn *Hoosier* and needs interpretation, as is shown in a story told by an old *snoose burner* about an accident in the woods. The story and various logging terms come from a 1973 Mills Archives collection by Trudy Cooper and from Wilbur A. Davis's 1950 article "Logger and Splinter-Picker Talk," included in the pages of *Western Folklore*. Many of these logging terms are still in use; others have been replaced.

THE HOOKER AND THE WHISTLE PUNK

There was this old hooker. *He wound up in the hospital and, boy, he was busted from one end to the other. The next day he woke up, and a nurse came in with her clip-board. "Well, sir," she said, "can you describe your accident? I have to make a report to the state."*

"Well, yes, ma'am," he said. "Everything is a little bit hazy, but to the best of my knowledge, we'd hooked onto this big ton. *I'd skinned a* mainline *ahead and the damn* donkey puncher *forgot to pick 'er up just a little bit, makin' the line awful tight. I hollered 'Whoa,' but the* whistle punk *musta' been sound asleep. He never slacked it off, never whistled or nothin'.*

"I bellered and bellered," said the logger, "and he finally shut 'er down. So I hollered 'Ho! Ho!' to the beaver, *and the whistle punk skinned it back. By that time the donkey puncher had pulled 'er in there so squeehawed into the crotch of this school marm that I couldn't unskin it."*

The nurse looked confused. "I'm sorry," she said. "I don't understand."

"Neither did that goddam whistle punk!" said the logger. "That's why I'm here!"

LOGGERS' JARGON

beaver: an inept man
brass nuts: the logging superintendent
bucker: the man who saws the logs into lengths
camp robber: a bird that scavenges at the logging sites and is said to be the ghost of a dead logger
chaser: the worker who unhitches the chokers
choker setter: fits the cable to logs for skidding
clam gun: shovel
cork boots: boots with steel caulks in the soles for traction
crummy: the crew car, aptly named—often festooned with beer bottles, chainsaw tools, and snoose cans
donkey puncher: the operator of the donkey engine for skidding logs
Dutch whistle: a piece of bark lying with the slippery side down
faller: the man who cuts the trees
fish eggs: tapioca
fool killer: an unsafe piece of equipment
gut-robber: the camp cook
gyppo: a small logging operator
hayburner: a horse
hell-howling: moving logs quickly from the brush to the road
highclimber: a timber topper
hooker: the man in charge of the *side*
Hoosier: a green man in the woods
jewelry: the blocks, tackle, and other hardware used in logging
mainline: heavy wire cable used to skid logs
"Make her out.": "I quit."
misery whip: crosscut saw
monkey-blankets: pancakes
pelican: one who chews enough snoose to distend the lower lip
pilgrim: a migratory worker
powder monkey: a man who handles blasting powder
salve: butter
sand: sugar
school marm: a Y-shaped crotch in a tree
side: the entire logging operation
skin: (v.) to drag
skyhook: where legendary woodsman Paul Bunyan hung his clothes at night; greenhorns to the woods are often sent after skyhooks.
snipe: a railroad worker
snoose-burner: a Scandinavian logger
squeehawed: crooked or misaligned
stumpjumpers: farmers who work in the woods now and then
Swedish condition powder: snuff
the brains: the company president or owner
timber-beast: a logger
tin clothes: waterproof clothing
ton: enormous log, perhaps weighing as much as a ton
whistle punk: gives signals by jerking the whistle cord of the donkey engine when the hook tender shouts commands

Canton Creek

Steamboat

Roseburg

Myrtle Creek

Riddle

Canyonville

Port Orford

Azalea

Glendale

Wolf Creek

Agness

Rogue
River

Gold Hill

Grants Pass

Gold Beach

Jacksonville

Medford

Logtown

Pistol River

Phoenix

Kerby

Cave Junction

Ashland

O'Brien

Lincoln

Takilma

Southern Oregon

In Southern Oregon, both at the Coast and inland, the discovery of gold led to the building of towns. Jacksonville, Gold Beach, and Port Orford grew up overnight during the early 1850s, as settlers from the Willamette Valley joined those men who had missed the "ophir holes" of the California rush and scrambled to stake out the new gold claims. These boomtowns needed materials and supplies, and the miners were willing to pay outrageous prices. Ashland Mills provided the flour to feed the miners and the timber for sluice boxes and "long toms." Roseburg flourished in 1852 as a supply station on the Oregon-California gold-rush route.

Settlement of the Southern region was marked by bloodshed. The Rogue River Indians and their associated tribes fought to protect their communities both from the desperate miners and from the secondary waves of immigrants who followed the Applegate Trail. Of the 242 immigrants killed in Oregon's pioneer era, 108 died in the Southern region. In 1852 during a square dance at Gold Beach, the Rogues attacked, killing twenty-three, including Indian agent Ben Wright, whose heart was barbecued and eaten at the site. But in that same year, gold was discovered at Sailor's Diggings, and the threat of death was not nearly enough to obstruct the sudden flood of miners and mountebanks.

The harshness of settlement is reflected in the graphic names for the cities, streams, and mountains of the South. Grave Creek, for example, was named for Martha Leland Crowley, the sixteen-year-old girl who died on the harsh trail and was buried beside a tall oak next to a pleasant stream. Her burial site, immediately despoiled by grave-robbers, later became the mass burial ground for six Indians killed in the 1856 Rogue River Indian Wars. Other testaments to violent clashes with Indians include Bloody Run (near Grants Pass), Dead Indian Road (east of Ashland), and Battle Rock (at Port Orford). The Rogue River, central landmark of the region, was named by French settlers as *Riviere aux Coquins*, or "River of the Rogues," a telling reference to the ferocity of the Native Americans settled in these valleys.

While life on the Southern Oregon frontier was difficult and risky, it was also colorful, as seen in other place-names

of the region. Politics offered some of the most interesting titles. Josephine County, for instance, was named for the daughter of a prominent miner; later the county seat, originally called Kerby, was temporarily named Napoleon in an attempt to capitalize on French history. Political sentiment was strong in the area during the settlement period. Waldo, the first boomtown in Southern Oregon, took the name of the Whig candidate in the 1854 California governor's election. Meanwhile, the politically charged atmosphere of the Civil War era divided the population into rival factions. In 1861 "Auntie" Ganung chopped down a large Confederate flag in the courtyard at Jacksonville. Three years later, the Republican cause was so unpopular that, in order to cast his ballot for Abraham Lincoln, Alex Watts had to shove his rifle barrel through the window of the polling clerk's office. In the midst of these controversies, the citizens of one Josephine County settlement chose to name their town Democrat Gulch. Despite the large number of Confederate sympathizers in Southern Oregon in the 1860s, Union Creek was home to several followers of the northern cause.

Politics was not the only source of fanciful names. Sailor's Diggings was so named because a group of ship-wrecked sailors discovered gold there in 1852. Kanaka Flat, west of Jacksonville, was settled by Hawaiian gold panners who were called "Kanakas" by the locals. J. T. Robinson established a dry goods store at Wonder, a town so far from the beaten paths that his few neighbors began to "wonder" where the customers would come from. In the early 1900s the Arnold brothers staked a meager claim at Bean Gulch, so named because the miners could eke out just enough gold to buy beans. Merlin was not named for King Arthur's wizard, as might be imagined, but after an obscure bird. David Loring, a Southern Pacific site engineer, noted the unusually large numbers of "merlins" at this rail stop. Puzzled ornithologists have suggested that Loring may have had the pigeon hawk in mind. Racial prejudice probably inspired the name Louse Creek, near Grants Pass. Originally called Grouse Creek, the stream banks were home to hundreds of hard-working and successful Chinese miners. According to the popular account, Grouse Creek became Louse Creek in the speech of the

Caucasian miners, who mimicked the Chinese pronunciation of the *r* sound in English.

Eight Dollar Mountain acquired its moniker when a miner, after paying that tidy sum for a new pair of boots, wore out the leathers in a single day of digging on the hillside. Jumpoff Joe Creek, the subject of numerous off-color variations, may have been named when a miner, being chased by Rogue Indians, was urged by his pals to take the only means of escape. "Jump off, Joe!" they yelled as he stood on a bluff overlooking a shallow pool of the creek. Gluttony perhaps contributed the name for Galice, a town west of Grants Pass. Each night a Rogue Indian would come into the camp of some French settlers, the brave asking "*wake tika gleece*," a request for bacon. The settlers, growing tired of the ritual, cooked up a stupendous batch of fatback and forced the Indian to eat every bite. He never returned, but the name Galice survived. Scaredman Creek, on the Umpqua watershed near Roseburg, acquired its name from hunters in the days when wolves were still quite plentiful in the Umpqua Valley. In 1851, Captain William Tichenor, while being harried by Indians, sent a scouting party from Port Orford in the wrong direction. This folly led the settlers to call the intended location Tichenor's Humbug, later changed to Humbug Mountain.

Southern Oregon extends from the Calapooia Mountains in the north to the California border in the south; it stretches from the Pacific Ocean to the Cascade Range. Southern Oregon hills are heavily timbered, and the mountains look down on broad, fertile valleys and plateaus. Because the land is rugged, the Umpqua and Rogue rivers have always been major transportation routes, especially during the pioneer era, when travelers could reach the Oregon beaches only by following the river canyons. Today parts of both rivers remain navigable, and visitors can join the mail boats for the thirty-two-mile run up the lower Rogue from Gold Beach, a tourist's delight, especially when the guides stop at Marial and Agness to tell Hathaway Jones stories.

Southern Oregon's geographic variety is best shown in Douglas County, where the elevation ranges from sea level to 9,182-foot Mt. Thielsen. Nearly 2.8 million acres of commercial timberland lies within the county's borders, including the largest stand of old-growth timber in the world. Here, nesting in the tops of these ancient trees, are Oregon's spotted owls, an endangered species whose protection, at least in the eyes of the logging community, threatens the continued existence of Southern Oregon loggers.

For many reasons—geographic, political, and economic—the South Coast is considered part of Southern Oregon. Towns such as Port Orford, Bandon, and Brookings have always been far enough from Salem and from Oregon's population centers to become invisible during the legislature's appropriation hearings. The lack of state funding for roads, bridges, and civic improvements has a long history throughout Southern Oregon, causing isolated citizens from Gold Beach to Prospect and from Roseburg to Ashland to see themselves as citizens of a separate place, sometimes called the State of Jefferson.

"Jefferson" is a name commonly found on storefronts and in advertising pamphlets throughout Southern Oregon. Ashland's KSOR radio has a "Jefferson Daily" segment; Grants Pass has a Jefferson Title Company; until recently, Medford had a Jefferson State Bank. Although Jefferson is a mythical community, people in Southern Oregon sometimes see themselves as Jeffersonians, members of an imaginary commonwealth named after the American president who consistently championed political and social self-reliance, who backed the Lewis and Clark expedition, and who was a staunch defender of states' rights. The State of Jefferson ties both disgruntled Northern Californians and isolated Southern Oregonians, both groups having been ignored and underfunded by their state legislatures since the middle of the nineteenth century.

Oregon's "North Jefferson" region was settled during the 1850s, after the discovery of gold in California. By the mid-1850s, even practical midwestern farmers and skeptical eastern merchants were being drawn by the gold-bug toward the increasingly popular Applegate Cutoff, the travelers turning south at Pocatello, Idaho, and wending into the heart of the Rogue River Valley. The most adventurous Applegate travelers stopped in the boomtowns of Waldo, Grass Flat, Jacksonville, Kirbyville, and Althouse to try their fortunes at placer mining, gold panning, or claim jumping. During the first years of the Southern Oregon gold strike, more than $100,000 in ore was passing weekly from the Jefferson region into San Francisco banks. Many fortunes were made in the digging fields of the Rogue River Valley in the 1850s, but not every miner took his fortune back to the homestead. Gold was worth $16 an ounce in those days, but so was salt. A room in a miner's hotel in Jacksonville or Sailor's Diggings cost $16 a day, with food consisting of venison, which the boarders themselves were obliged to shoot and dress. It was generally agreed that the hotel occupants paid their outrageous boarding fees primarily for the privilege of having salt with their deer meat.

The gold-rush settlers of the 1850s were quick to develop an identity crisis. When the California tax collector came through the fields, the miners declared themselves citizens of the Oregon Territory. When the territorial tax man rode into town, they were loyal citizens of California. In fact, the people of this isolated region wanted no part of Oregon statehood or California law. In January 1854, citizens of Southern Oregon, gathering in Jacksonville, met for the purpose of forming a separate territory, one to be joined with the northern counties of California. Furthermore, the group successfully lobbied against the statehood efforts that would have incorporated Southern Oregon; consequently, in the summer of 1854, a referendum on

statehood was rejected, with the southernmost counties voting against statehood by a margin of 723 to 20.

Early separatists proposed that the region be known as Jackson Territory, after the intended capital city of Jacksonville. Plans called for the region ultimately to enter the Union as a proslavery state. Although the Jackson movement was unsuccessful, recalcitrant Southern Oregonians helped to defeat statehood referenda in both 1855 and

1856, the Jacksonians not voting with the Republican consensus until 1857, when the statehood measure finally passed.

Nearly 100 years later, in the early 1940s, another serious effort at secession was centered in Port Orford. Contending that Salem had completely ignored Southern Oregon's needs for roads, bridges, and other civic improvements, Port Orford citizens rallied around the cause of the "Great State of Jefferson." The boundaries of the State of Jefferson were unusually large. As proposed by various secessionist speakers of the era, Jefferson would range from Roseburg in the north to Redding in the south—and from the Pacific Ocean in the west to the Cascade slopes in the east. As planned, Jefferson would enfranchise Southern Oregonians who had more in common with Northern Californians than with Webfooters and Bunchgrassers of the Oregon Territory.

In November 1941, a large group of Southern Oregonians met with miners and business executives in Yreka, forming an alliance for "promoting the development of the mineral resources of Northern California and Southern Oregon." Port Orford's mayor, Gilbert Gable, was elected "governor" of the new state, and the *Siskiyou Daily News* ran a name-the-state contest the day after. The name of Jefferson, already in popular use in Northern California, soon began appearing on billboards, letterheads, and flyers in Southern Oregon as well, particularly in Port Orford, where Gable spurred the movement with fiery speeches and news releases. Governor Gable enlisted popular support by proclaiming his opposition to sales tax, income tax, and liquor tax.

Unfortunately, Gable's fondness for untaxed liquor cost him the chance to govern his new state. While being interviewed by Stanton Delaplane of the *San Francisco Chronicle* late one night, the governor and the reporter drank a bottle of 100-proof rum. Delaplane staggered to a hotel room, where he began a series of articles that later won a Pulitzer Prize. Governor Gable staggered to his bedroom, where he suffered a fatal heart attack.

After Gable's death, the Jefferson movement shifted from Port Orford but lost none of its enthusiasm. Judge John L. Childs of Crescent City, California, was elected governor of Jefferson on December 4. Crews from *Time* and *Life* magazines were there, as well as a Hollywood newsreel company. Childs gave a "ringing speech of acceptance" on the courthouse lawn in Yreka on December 4, and Jeffersonians blocked Highway 99, the main interstate route, for several hours. The secessionists collected a road toll and handed out printed copies of the Declaration of Independence, which read in part: "You are now entering Jefferson, the 49th State of the Union. This state has seceded from Oregon and California this Thursday, November 27th, 1941."

Three days later, on December 7, the sobering news of Pearl Harbor pushed the State of Jefferson movement into history. In his last official act before disbanding the State of Jefferson, a subdued Governor Childs stood on the steps of the courthouse to declare war on California, Oregon, and Japan.

Ashland

Jackson County. Population 16,194. First called Ashland Mills, this community near the California border originally boasted a flour mill and a sawmill, both enterprises proving lucrative during gold rush days. In 1852 the town was named by its founder, Abel Hellman, in honor of his birthplace, Ashland, Ohio.

Some fifty years ago Angus Bowmer initiated the first cycle of Shakespeare plays in the small college town of Ashland. Today the Oregon Shakespeare Festival is the oldest outdoor theatre in America, boasting an annual attendance of more than 300,000 playgoers. From humble beginnings, the festival has come to be respected around the nation; in 1983, Shakespeare in Ashland won a Tony Award for dramatic excellence.

The players and producers can point proudly to distinguished alumni, including William Hurt, who once played Jamie in *Long Day's Journey into Night*; Stacy Keach, who was *Henry V*; Dick Cavett, a "very minor bit actor" in the sixties; and Charles Laughton, who signed to play *King Lear* in 1962, but succumbed to a heart attack before traveling west, probably when his agent told him how much the festival could pay.

Presenting live drama is a difficult and demanding job, and the artists and technicians tend to be a superstitious lot. Consider, for example, some of the customary beliefs about the theatre, gathered from festival members by Tom Nash in 1985.

OREGON SHAKESPEARE FESTIVAL SUPERSTITIONS

□ *Peacock feathers are very bad luck anywhere on stage. (Peacocks are strutting, vain creatures.)*
□ *It is good luck if a cat adopts the theatre as its home, but bad luck to bring a cat into the theatre under any other circumstances.*
□ *Never bring fresh flowers on stage, especially lilies or dahlias.*
□ *On opening night, give an apple as a gift to a first-time performer.*
□ *Shoes worn on opening night of a "hit" should be kept forever.*
□ *Green in costumes is bad luck (and also plays havoc with the lighting).*
□ *While on the set, never place a hat on a bed.*
□ *Actors late for rehearsals must apologize to* everyone involved *if the show is not to suffer from ill fortune.*

□ *Macbeth is referred to as "the Scottish play." The true title should never be mentioned in the theatre.*
□ *Never open a congratulatory telegram until the first night's performance is over.*

At Oregon Shakespeare, the most common folk belief is an injunction against whistling backstage. Mary Turner, one of Ashland's most venerable performers, says, "It is the strongest belief in the theatre." Joe Vincent, a twenty-year veteran of Ashland theatre, explains this superstition by referring to Elizabethan history. The first scenery men in Elizabethan theatres were conscripted from sailing ships, according to Vincent, and they brought their nautical customs with them. "All those workers were ex-seamen," he says, "who used whistle-cues to communicate in the earliest theatres. During a scene change they would be up in the riggings. The prohibition against whistling simply made sense. You might get someone seriously injured by whistling backstage at the wrong moment."

Le Hook, the scenery engineer at the Oregon Shakespeare Festival, lends credence to Vincent's theory. Although whistle-cues are no longer used behind stage, Hook admits that the lighting beam in the theatre is called the *scene dock* and the stays for securing ropes are called *belaying pins*. The curtains are the *shrouds* or *sails*, and the main lighting beam in the playhouse is the *first bridge*. Hook even has on his desk a copy of *Ashley's Book of Knots*, a kind of primer for nautical types.

Much of the folklore of the theatre invokes the fear of "freezing up" or "going north." Dropped lines, missed cues, and bungled entrances are serious matters in professional theatre, and the festival members often ritualize one error as a charm against others. For instance, a few years ago in *Winter's Tale*, a character played by Larry Ballard came on stage. Henry Woronitz was to turn and say, "And here's a very merry ballad." Instead, the line came out, "And here's a very Larry Ballard." This malapropism was not glossed over, but incorporated into future performances. For the rest of the season, "And here's a very Larry Ballard" became the standard line.

In similar fashion, Priscilla Hake Lauris as Mrs. Telford in *Trelawney of the Wells* once made a strange ad lib about "the queen" to cover a momentary "freeze." Thereafter, the mistake became a regular part of the script, so that some ad lib about a queen had to be slipped into each performance. To this end—and because the lines became more difficult to integrate cleanly into the drama—someone put a list of ninety queens on the wall in the Green Room, so that the players could choose to mention Victoria, Elizabeth, Eleanor of Aquitane, or even Ellery Queen. A standard greeting at the stage door that season was the weathered line "Who's the queen tonight?"

Sometimes a gaffe is so obvious that it cannot be glossed over, and the players must gather themselves and just go on. For such occasions the festival members pass around the Dummy Box. Begun more than twenty years go, this tradition calls for the quiet passing of a decorated box inscribed to the player who "goes north" at a critical moment in a play. In its twenty years, the award has been passed regularly, and now more than a dozen Dummy Boxes lie wrapped within the current one, each box a record of serious mistakes and threats to the success of a performance. Interestingly enough, when interviewed about traditions of the theatre, the most experienced member of the company, Shirley Patton, did not know about the Dummy Box. Having made no egregious errors in more than three decades of performances, she had not learned the secret of its existence.

Other traditions of the Oregon Shakespeare Festival are equally as interesting. Some say, for example, that the urn carrying the ashes of Angus Bowmer lies buried somewhere on the grounds of the new Bowmer Theatre. Angus's ashes, it might be said, consecrate the place as does the shadow of Thomas Becket on a pillar in Canterbury Cathedral or the ink-stained wall of Martin Luther's cell in Germany. Many festival members believe that the Shakespeare Theatre has stones from ancient Greece built into its outer wall. Others talk of the ghost of a festival technician, killed in the fifties in a fall; he regularly appears on opening nights. But perhaps the most haunting story of all is the one told about a famous Hollywood actor whose spirit periodically visits Ashland. This version, one of many, was told by Skip, a fledgling actor with the company, in the Green Room before a performance.

THE GHOST OF CHARLES LAUGHTON

In 1962, after a distinguished career in Hollywood films, actor Charles Laughton decided to fulfill a lifelong dream. Ever since his Academy Award performance in The Private Life of Henry VIII, *Laughton had wanted to play the title role in* King Lear. *For this performance, he chose the Ashland Shakespeare Festival and its theatre that authentically recreates the feeling of Shakespeare's own playhouse.*

The contracts were signed, and Laughton was finishing business in the Midwest on the eve of rehearsals for King Lear. *According to his agent, Laughton had become obsessed with the charm of playing Lear on the live stage and was working hard to learn the lines when he suffered a fatal heart attack in Kansas City.*

On the night of Lear's *opening in Ashland, the night was clear and warm. The audience settled into their seats, awaiting the trumpet call to announce the beginning of the play. As the lights dimmed, everything grew silent. Then, from the back of the theatre came a cold gust of air, blowing up onto the stage, pushing off the hats of the players and scattering them about the stage. At the same time, several people heard a low, eerie sound, like someone far away reciting the King's opening lines. Some say that Charles Laughton's ghost attended the first night's performance of* King Lear *in the summer of 1962 and that he still haunts every performance of the play in the Shakespeare Theatre at Ashland.*

Azalea

Douglas County. This small timber town was named after the abundant western azaleas and white azaleas that grow wild in the surrounding hills. Azalea is home to many families who make their living in Oregon forests.

Men in the woods value each other. Behind all the practical jokes and the outrageous stories is a camaraderie that is found only in the most hazardous professions. Even though affection is often expressed in practical jokes and stunts, there is usually a real dedication and commitment among the experienced workers in an outfit. Harry Stumbo, a Wolf Creek logger who often worked near Azalea, explains that spirit in a story about a fellow lumberjack: "I knew an old logger named Walt Boggs, who worked for a company out of Gardiner. He worked there twenty-five years, and he decided to quit and retire. And the old superintendent, who'd known him all that length of time, when Walt went up to get his pay, the old boy told him, 'Goddam you, Boggs. I knew you wouldn't last when you hired out.' "

But not all feelings are turned to humor in the woods. The men at Azalea and throughout Douglas County are serious about the dangers that face them every day. These fears often show in superstitions shared by the loggers. In times past, loggers would occasionally lean a stick up against a tree the day before cutting it. If the stick fell down during the night, the tree remained uncut. As Stumbo explains, there are inexplicable and dangerous forces at work in the woods.

"I'VE CUT TIMBER THAT I'VE FELT REAL BAD ABOUT"

I've cut timber that I've felt real bad about. I'd just go and sink a saw into 'em, and I'd say, "I just don't feel right about this." I'm not trying to say that trees are alive and have a personality or a consciousness, or anything like this, because I don't believe it. But I just think they have some control over their own selves. For no reason, they'll turn backward on the stump and fall right over the top of you if they can do it.

There was five of the best timber fallers in the state that gave up on this one tree. That's right. And you talk about superstition. This is the truth. It's still standing today. It's right there. And finally Allan, this old brother of mine, he was going to cut it. And he said, "You guys are all crazy. I don't know what's the matter with you." And he went down, and about an hour later he came back with his saw on his back and said, "To hell with it. I understand."

The motifs and patterns in ''The Curse of the Spanish Boots'' mark the story clearly as folklore and provide a good example of the tale. First, there are three sons and three scenes, a standard number in oral transmission. Second, the third son (and youngest), if not wise, is at least lucky; in Carolina ''Jack'' tales, the bumbling hero is always the third son. Finally, the tale has a moral ending: ''He went home and took care of his mother 'til she died.'' These storytelling elements reveal that ''The Curse of the Spanish Boots'' has circulated widely in the oral tradition, perhaps migrating from the Southwest, where Spanish boots are more common.

THE CURSE OF THE SPANISH BOOTS

Now this guy lived up above Canton Creek and had himself a little homestead up there and a real fine wife. Well, sir, that woman bore him three of the meanest sons-of-bitches you ever laid eyes on. They were lazy and shiftless—drunk most of the time, you know. Wouldn't do a damned thing to help out their Mom or Pop.

Well, sir, one day the old man went into Roseburg and bought himself a pair of the finest walkin' boots money can buy. He hardly got them broke in to where they was just fine, when one day while he was coming home, a six-foot rattler struck him in his left leg right above the ankle. That snake was so powerful, its fangs went right through the boot and into his leg. You know, that snake was an old one, and the older they get, the stronger the poison gets. Killed him almost instantly, I suspect. Least-wise he was dead when his son found him.

They didn't even care that he was dead. They took to fightin' over who was going to take what. They stripped the old man and just threw his body in the river for the fish, being too lazy to even bury him right. Well, sir, a fight started right then and there over those Spanish boots. Finally they drew lots and the middle son won. He didn't waste a minute's time pullin' them on either. So off they goes to spend the money they had stole off their dead father.

When they hadn't gone half a mile, the one who had won the boots started to lag behind—and it weren't a mile 'til they looked back and he was dead. The other two looked him over real close trying to figure out what had killed him. There weren't a mark on the boy, but he was dead as can be. Didn't make a lot of difference to them, though. They stripped him just like the father and dumped him in the river and took to fighting over them boots again.

This time they flipped a coin, and the oldest boy won. He pulled the boots on like before and off they went. Well, but this time it was getting to be late and night was coming on, so they decided to make camp. They had just started to get set up when the boy that had the boots says he ain't feeling so good and lays down. Weren't a minute later his brother turns around, and he is just as dead as can be.

That boy dropped down on his face, and he started to pray like he had never prayed before, 'cause he was convinced

Well, my God, it's the truth. It's just that some trees are going to kill you, and you feel it, and you know it. There's just no way you're going to fall that tree without getting killed.

Canton Creek

Douglas County. Canton Creek flows from the Cottage Grove area and enters the North Umpqua River about forty miles east of Roseburg. At Canton Creek in 1976, folklore collector George Braddock heard an unusual tale from prospector Al Renfro, a master storyteller.

that the Lord was punishing them for the way they had treated their kin. And he said how sorry he was and that, if the Lord would spare him his life, he would walk the straight and narrow always. Well, he stayed right there on his face for a long time waiting to see if he was going to die or not, an' all the time going on about being good from now on.

After a while he set up and it was all dark and getting cold, so he started up a fire and laid his brother out on the ground beside it, so he could get him ready for burying. When he got around to pullin' off the boots, that's when he saw it. Stuck in the side of that Spanish boot, just above the ankle, was a fang from that rattlesnake that had got broke off when he struck the old man.

And, you know, that boy stayed good to his word, too. He even went on home and took care of his mother 'til she died. Married and raised himself a right fine family. Hell, I damn near married his daughter. That's how I heard the story about the fang.

Canyonville

Douglas County. Population 1,224. In 1852 this important stage and rail location was called North Canyonville, but by 1892 the name was changed simply to Canyonville. The name is descriptive. Canyonville is a logging community, and at the Feed Lot Restaurant or Fat Harvey's Truckstop, stories about Oregon's spotted owl usually come with the blue plate special.

Old-growth timber in Southern Oregon provides a home to the spotted owl, an endangered species. In Douglas County, where logging provides most jobs, federal protection of the spotted owl remains a controversial issue. Open hostilities have erupted between Oregon environmentalists and timber industry employees throughout the county. In Glendale and Azalea, bumper stickers proclaim, "If it's hootin', I'm shootin'!" Lawn signs in Roseburg and Myrtle Creek say, "*Earth-Firsters* are loggers' speed bumps," a reference to human barricades that sometimes block logging roads. In storefronts at Drain, banners urge passersby to "Save a logger—eat an owl."

In 1990, Azalea Postmaster Jack Cornett heard a spotted owl joke in Canyonville and told it to Tom Nash. Cornett said that the spotted-owl issue is complex, even in Douglas County logging communities, with opinions dividing neighborhoods and even families. However, the loggers often let their jokes and stories speak for their point of view, as in this narrative from a Canyonville choker setter.

BIRDS OF A FEATHER

A forest ranger was walking through the woods and smelled smoke. Because it was summer and the woods were dry, he was alarmed. So he looked all over for the fire. After a long time he came to a small clearing and found a rumpled

man in tattered clothes cooking something over the fire. The man needed a shave, and his toes were sticking out of his shoes. There were feathers all over the clearing, and the ranger knew right away the man was roasting a spotted owl.

"You're in big trouble, buddy," said the ranger. "I'm gonna' have to haul you in."

The man looked up. His eyes were sunken, and his face was thin. "Can't you give me a break?" he said. "I lost my job in the mill. The bank repossessed my house, and my wife and kids left me. I had to sell my car, and I'm livin' out here in the woods like a bum. All because of the damn spotted owl."

The ranger felt pretty bad. After all, he thought, the owl problem was putting lots of people out of work. Maybe he couldn't help himself. "Okay," he said, "I'll overlook it this once. But don't let me catch you roastin' no more owls."

"Yessir," said the man. "Don't you worry."

So the ranger began to move away. But after walking almost out of the clearing, he began to get curious. He turned and said, "Say, tell me, what does a spotted owl taste like?"

"Well," said the man, "it's a little hard to describe, but it tastes a lot like a bald eagle."

Cave Junction

Josephine County. Population 1,130. The town bears the imprint of the nearby Oregon Caves, discovered in 1874 by Elijah Davidson and declared a national monument in 1909. The Oregon Caves, actually one cavern in a series of sub-terranean chambers, houses fantastic limestone formations; over the years, a combination of heat, water, and pressure has transformed the limestone into marble. Park rangers have christened the chambers with names such as Bridal Chamber and Satan's Backbone. Here is the story of the discovery of the Oregon Caves, as found in many sources, including the 1960 centennial edition of the *Grants Pass Daily Courier*.

ELIJAH AND THE BEAR

While hunting in October of 1874, Elijah Davidson followed a deer into a heavy thicket that revealed the opening of a large cave. Davidson gathered material, made a torch, and entered the cave, only to encounter a snarling bear, who also had designs on the unlucky buck. Davidson withdrew, but returned the next day to find the deer carcass and, next to it, the sleeping bear. After shooting the bear with his 50-caliber musket loader, Davidson investigated further into the opening, finally realizing that he had entered an incredible labyrinth of caves and tunnels.

In 1909 the 480-acre site was declared a national monument, and local miner Dick Rowley was named the first guide to the Oregon Caves, where he remained as the primary caretaker of the underground park for forty-five years. The poet Joaquin Miller was one of the most frequent visitors to the caves, and guide Rowley, a lover of the arts and letters, dedicated a lectern-like outcropping to the Oregon poet, calling it the Joaquin Miller Chapel.

To avoid getting lost in the years before electric lights spanned the cave walls, Rowley employed a trick from his mining days. Outside the cave entrance, Rowley would gather a pocketful of huckleberry leaves. As he wandered through the underground passageways, Rowley would leave a huckleberry leaf at every turn and crossroad, anchoring the leaf so that the stem pointed the direction back to the opening. In the event that his candle would blow out or the gas lamp fail, Rowley could find his way back to the sunlight by "feeling" the signs he had left behind.

Locals say that the Cave Junction area is a bit strange—a region where eerie lights fill the sky at night and where supernatural events seem almost commonplace. Perhaps, say the storytellers, it is because Cave Junction lies right on an earthquake fault line, or perhaps the rich deposits of gold, silver, platinum, copper, and other metals have created an imbalance in the earth's magnetic field. Maybe it is the ghosts of the Chinese miners whose graves were disturbed by Caucasians, who believed they were buried with their fortunes. At any rate, everyone agrees something terrible happened to a miner in the Cave Junction region. "The Ghost of Grisly Gulch" was collected in 1969 from a twenty-one-year-old Cave Junction man attending the University of Oregon.

THE GHOST OF GRISLY GULCH

Gene Kester graduated from the University of Chicago Medical School in 1896. But instead of practicing medicine, which was not the "gold mine" it is today, Kester decided to try the pick-and-shovel minings in the mountains and valleys surrounding the Oregon Caves. Kester had a friend named Joe, another miner, who lived in a cabin about a mile away at Grisly Gulch, a place known for its eerie sounds.

The two men often ate supper together, but Kester was reluctant to walk the worn trail from his cabin into the dark-

ness of Grisly Gulch. At night there was an unnatural whistling in the woods, and he repeatedly heard packs of coyotes howling, but there were no signs of animals on the trails. In fact, as far as both men were concerned, Grisly Gulch was avoided by animals altogether.

One night, as Kester was walking toward the cabin in Grisly Gulch, he heard a rumbling, half-hollow sound on the trail ahead. Kester jumped out of the way just in time to see a huge 150-pound oil drum roll by, crashing into the brush and trees where he had stood a moment before. Another evening, when Kester approached the cabin, he found his friend out in the mud investigating huge tracks—seemingly human, but three times as large as a man's footprints. There were deep nail prints at the toes. When Kester went home that night, he found Joe's missing straw hat. An immense bite had been taken from the brim.

Somewhat later, in early fall, Kester shot a deer near the mouth of the Caves. He invited his friend to dinner, but Kester kept the fire burning well into the night, and Joe did not show. At the first light of morning, Kester walked the trail to Grisly Gulch. As he approached, he saw a faint mist of smoke from the cabin's fireplace. The front door was wide open, and tracks in the snow led into the woods. At the top of a clearing, the tracks led into a small meadow and suddenly disappeared. Kester never saw Joe again.

Glendale

Douglas County. Population 692. When the railroad was extended south from Roseburg in 1881, the planning engineer, Solomon Abraham, named this spot Julia, after his wife. However, Abraham got into a squabble with his boss, who marked Glendale onto the maps. Some people have suggested that Abraham's petulant boss, A. F. Morris, named this location after his birthplace, Glendale, Massachusetts.

Despite the long hours, hard work, and difficult conditions of the lumber camp, loggers seldom make much money. And those who do make a few dollars have a hard time keeping it. That point is made clear in a story collected by Jeri Johnston about the logger who gets his big chance at a fortune.

THE LOGGER AND THE PHILANTHROPIST

A guy had a million dollars he was gonna give away, and he was looking for somebody to give it to, and so he found a guy that owned a service station, and he walked up to him and says, "Hey, what would you do if I gave you a million dollars?"

And the guy said, "Oh, I'd get a string of service stations from coast to coast and multiply that million by ten."

And the guy thought about it and said, "Well, you're kinda greedy. I'll look around some more. [Then he] found a guy that owned a restaurant and said, "Well, what would you do if I gave you a million dollars?"

And he said, "Well," he said, "I'd build a string of restaurants from coast to coast and multiply that million dollars by ten."

He says, "Well, you're a little greedy, too. I'll just look around a little more. I'll let you know." He was drivin' down the road, and he saw a guy walkin' along with his nose bag over his shoulder and riggin' clothes and everything, and stopped and says, "Hey," he says, "You look like an honest hard-working man," he says. "What would you do if I gave you a million dollars?"

The logger looked at him and said, "Well, I'd probably just keep on loggin' 'til it was all gone."

Gold Beach

Curry County. Population 1,531. Gold Beach was originally called Ellensburg, after Sarah Ellen Tichenor, the daughter of Captain William Tichenor, the famous explorer who figured prominently in the 1851 incident at Battle Rock (see Port Orford, p. 90). However, that name caused confusion with the Ellensburg in Washington Territory and was changed to Gold Beach by the postmaster, who based his choice on the number of placer mines erected there in the 1850s.

In the late 1800s and early 1900s, Gold Beach was one of the primary mail stops for the Rogue River mail carrier Hathaway Jones. The indefatigable Jones made his reputation as a storyteller in Gold Beach, Agness, Marial, and other towns on the Rogue route, which he traveled with his mule, Buckshot. Hathaway Jones, even though hampered by a severe cleft palate, was known to tell a few "windies" in his day, often signaled by his opening line: "You wouldn't believe this, but. . . ." Despite his twisting of credibility, says Curry County resident Joel L. Barker, "One could not call Hathaway Jones a liar in the actual sense of the word. They would have to say that he stretched the truth to its *unbustable* extent."

Sadie Pettinger recalled Hathaway Jones as a pleasant man with some education who was a natural storyteller: "Sometimes in the evening, especially in the late fall or wintertime, when it'd be cold and he'd be cold, he'd come in the kitchen, and he'd sit down and talk to me. I'd be goin' on in the kitchen. And we had a round table behind the stove where the family usually ate, and he'd sit there, and he'd cross his knee, and [chuckling] the stories would just roll out." According to folklore collector Dwight L. Clarke, Mrs. Pettinger felt that Jones had been slandered by writers for the *Oregonian* and by other storytellers who mocked his cleft palate. "I knew him well," said Pettinger. "And I'll say one thing for Hathaway: I never heard him tell anything against anybody."

Hathaway Jones was the subject of an extensive tall-tale collection. In 1974 Steven Dow Beckham published *Tall Tales from the Rogue River: The Yarns of Hathaway Jones* and was preparing a second volume of the old mail-carrier's yarns in 1990. However, Beckham is not the only collector of Hathaway Jones tales. In 1969, Joel L. Barker convened a meeting of appreciative Hathaway Jones fans in Grants Pass, telling a handful of "windies" he had heard from the postman's relatives and friends. Among them was a story about the best fireplace in Curry County, told with the characteristic nasal twang that often identifies a Hathaway tale.

HATHAWAY'S FIREPLACE: "A GOOD DRAW"

In the old days, fireplaces were built with one thing in mind—that was to draw good. Now a fireplace that "drew good," as they used the expression, meant that it did not smoke. The reason . . . of course that it didn't smoke was that it drew in enough air from the surrounding room that the heat, usually, and the smoke all went up the fireplace chimney.

One day—let us let Hathaway Jones tell it—his father had just completed a fireplace. Picture, if you will, an old ramshackle log cabin with a clapboard door, small porch outside, to which was tied a hound dog, and you have the setting. Hathaway Jones tells it this way:

"Pa, he built this fireplace, and boy did that fireplace draw. You never seen a fireplace draw like that. He shut the door and built a fire in this fireplace, and the first thing it did, it drew the door right off the hinges, sent it up the chimney. The old hound dog bitch [who] was about to have puppies was tied to the post of the porch, and then she came right behind that door; it pulled four pups right out of her, and before we could put out the fire, we have two more. That's drawing."

Others who gathered Hathaway Jones tales for the Randall V. Mills Archives include Dwight L. Clarke, Linda Barker, and Penny Colvin. Colvin's version of "Hathaway's Near Miss" was actually told by a tour boat captain as a "John F. Adams" story (the name of his boat); but the captain admitted that he had heard it originally as a Hatha-

way Jones tale. Here are some additional stories about Rogue River's cantankerous mail-hauler, taken primarily from the Mills Archives files.

BUCKSHOT TAKES THE HIGH ROAD

For his mail-hauling duties, Hathaway had a number of mules. But his favorite animal was Buckshot, a crafty and cantankerous old plug. One day Hathaway decided to cross the river to go bear hunting, and of course he took Buckshot along in case he got one. Pretty soon Hathaway spotted a good-sized bear, about 500 pounds, and he brought it down with his muzzle-loader.

Well, Buckshot protested, but Hathaway loaded that bear on the back of his mule and headed home. Buckshot was snorting and kicking and biting at the old man, but Hathaway kept plugging away toward the river until he could see his cabin in sight across the stream. So Hathaway led Buckshot down to the edge of the river, but the mule wouldn't go one step further. Finally the old man kicked her a few times in the stomach, but Buckshot wouldn't take another step.

So Hathaway had to unload the bear, pack it on his own back, and step in the cool waters of the Rogue River. Luckily, Hathaway was a good swimmer. He didn't have any problems until he got about halfway across, but then he found himself slipping deeper and deeper into the water.

Spitting and snorting, Hathaway barely made it to the other side. Gasping for air, he crawled up onto the bank. Right then, Hathaway got a glimpse of shadow, and he noticed that the bear on his back had long pointed ears.

"Sure enough," said Hathaway, "I looked over my shoulder and I seen that damned mule, Buckshot, ridin' right up top of that bear."

"BLACK POWDER LOADS IS SLOWER"

One day Hathaway was having an argument with a hunter at Agness about black powder and smokeless gun powder. "Black powder is ten times as slow as smokeless," said Hathaway. The other man disagreed, and the debate began to heat up.

Finally Hathaway said, "Let me tell you how slow them black powder loads is. Why, once I went out hunting with a man who had both kinds of loads—black and smokeless. So a big buck ran out in the clearing, and this fool made a mistake and put a black powder load in his rifle. Well, he shot dead aim, and that buck just stood there. 'My god,' he said, 'I used the wrong shell.' So he put in a smokeless shell and fired away. That buck dropped down right now.

"I decided to help out, so I ran out there with my knife to cut that buck's throat. And just as I bent over that deer, wham! Something hit me right in the rear where I kept my billfold. You might not believe this, but it was that black powder bullet. It'd just got there."

JENNY CLEARS THE TRAIL

I've heard this one for years. When Hathaway was carryin' the mail, why way up by Illahe, there was a big boulder in the middle of the trail and it'd make his mule Jenny mad, an' everytime she'd go around that trail, she'd kick at it.

So, anyway, he an' his mule were climbin' over this mountain, she gave a kick at that old boulder an' kicked it loose. It rolled down the canyon and up one side an' back an' forth, an' they watched it until they got tired of it.

Went on an' came back about a month later and looked over that canyon, and there was a streak of dust going up one side of the canyon and down the other.

HATHAWAY'S NEAR MISS

Hathaway was a heck of a shot. One fall there's a big flock of geese comin' up the river and landed on the gravel bar that shows itself in the late fall of the year. Hathaway picked up his old single-shot out of the house and went back down to the edge of the river.

Looked like a rough winter comin' on, an' Hathaway, being very fond of geese, wanted to get as many of 'em as he could. So he was goin' to be very serious about it. He took his time and stalked down to the river close to the geese 'n waited 'n waited for those geese. Finally they did it. They all got lined up and were takin' a drink of water at one time.

Old Hathaway raised the gun up to this shoulder, took a bead, and squeezed the trigger off. But the geese flew away, every one of 'em. Hathaway couldn't believe it. He'd never missed before.

Hathaway went down to that sandbar and waded into the water to investigate and see what he could find. Well, he found somethin' there that mornin' that he saved in a glass jar for years 'n years.

Hathaway had actually come as close to gettin' every one of those geese as a man possibly could. Hathaway picked up 27 goose beaks that mornin'.

Gold Hill

Jackson County. Population 935. Gold Hill was the scene of one of the earliest gold strikes in Southern Oregon. The real "gold hill," however, is not the slope where the town now stands, but the one across the Rogue River to the south, its massive scars signs of the tunneling and surface blasting of earlier years.

Gold Hill has an eerie atmosphere, and many Southern Oregonians consider the town and its surroundings "strange." Some people say that Gold Hill is magnetic, and they joke that it stands at the center of the earth. Others believe it is the ancient burial site of the Tekilma Indians, a location imbued with supernatural forces and powers and called the Forbidden Ground by the Tekilmas. As a child, Trudy Cooper was told that a meteor once fell on this land, altering permanently the gravitational fields. Since that time "horses shy away from the area, birds won't fly over it, and the Indians wouldn't go near it." Jack Schwartz, a world-famous lecturer on psychic events, reputedly owns land at Gold Hill, and rumors of a thirteen-story School of Psychic Phenomena have circulated through the Rogue River Valley for years.

Part of the local enthusiasm for stories about alien visitors centers on the majestic geologic landmark known as Table Rock, a tall, smooth butte standing starkly on the valley floor just south of Gold Hill. Table Rock is every bit as imposing as Wyoming's Devil's Tower, the destination for space visitors in Steven Spielberg's *Close Encounters of the Third Kind*; yet Table Rock is perhaps more inviting for inexperienced space travelers, its long, flat surface, strewn with wild flowers, forming an ideal runway.

Rogue River fishing guides tell their clients during a float past the impressive rock cliffs that "Table Rock contains old tablets from the sunken continent of Lemuria." According to the legend, Lemuria was an advanced civilization in the Pacific. The Lemurian scientists had long ago perfected space travel and were capable of affecting the laws of nature, such as gravity and magnetism. The Lemurians, who may sometimes be seen on Table Rock wearing long white robes, travel the universe, but return often to the butte, where they dwell under the surface in caverns hollowed out by powerful vibrations from a bell-like instrument. At night locals can sometimes see a red glow emanating from the top of Table Rock. This aura is a sign that the Lemurians are landing or departing.

The real matrix of strangeness in Gold Hill is the Oregon Vortex, so named because of its curious disregard for the laws of physics. At the center of the Vortex stands the House of Mystery. In this landmark, visitors usually find it impossible to stand erect; a thrown tennis ball will behave erratically. In the House of Mystery, a visitor standing on one side of the house appears taller than someone of the same height standing across the room. According to Ernie Cooper, who owned the House of Mystery in 1971, the Vortex deserves its eerie reputation.

THE OREGON VORTEX

You know, animals won't get near this place. They know something is funny about it. When the Indians lived around here, it was known as The Forbidden Ground because their horses spooked every time they came near it. They sensed it, you see. All the animals were afraid of it. If a dog was brought here, he would howl or lay down and whimper. And when the Indians or settlers tried to take cattle through, they just wouldn't go. They'd run clear around it. It's funny how the animals sensed it. Even today, if a family brings a dog to the House of Mystery, he howls and howls or collapses right here on the ground and won't move. It's real strange.

Animals, however, are not the only ones who find the Oregon Vortex unsettling. Persistent rumors suggest that the Vortex is the magnetic refueling station for ships from outer space. In fact, one Gold Hill resident reported for the Mills Archives a close encounter with alien beings.

GOOFER DUST

One night we heard a whining sound. High-pitched whine, a little like the hum the high-tension wires make. Woke me up. Woke Dad up, too. Patch [the dog] was still alive then, and he was out there, and he was scared. Just leaned up against my leg and whimpered. So I let him in the house.

This was before Ardeth died, too, and she heard it. Woke her up, and she stood out there and looked around, too. And that same night the Whitneys were driving up the road late and just past Jeroleman's Bridge, they saw a reddish glow towards Lokkens', but when they got up around the bend and could see where it woulda' been, it was gone. But red, and in the same place as before.

And y'know, Ardeth believed til the end that her cancer was caused by that glow. And she was worried about me. Even wrote to me clear from Portland when she was having her treatments, that I'd better watch out, that I'd probably gotten too much "goofer dust"—was what she called it. . . .

When I went to the hospital to get those tests on my head, Ardeth kept saying, like she was joking, that we'd stood out in the "goofer dust" too long, unprotected like that. She thought it was something supernatural from outer space.

Superstitions are a part of most people's lives. In fact, Wayland Hand of UCLA once suggested that most families share about fifteen folk beliefs. Among Gold Hill women, Trudy Cooper discovered an unusual number of superstitions about birth, an especially dangerous time in a woman's life. In 1973, one resident, remembering an earlier generation, talked about the relationship between birthmarks and prenatal accidents.

In Ma's day it was really believed that you could mark a child by what you saw or what you read. So women didn't even go out when they were pregnant. Aunt May once dropped an egg out in the chicken house, and it startled her, so she put her hand up to her head and, when her child was born, he had an opening in his head and a big growth like an egg out of it.

And Ma's mother, when she was about to have Aunt Lena, one day looked in the mirror and thought she was a bit pale, so she rubbed some rouge on one cheek. Lena, when she was born, had a red birthmark across the same cheek.

They thought they shouldn't read anything but poetry, y' know. They wouldn't be reading detective stories or anything like that. Just poetry and the Bible and aesthetic things.

There was a woman Ma knew who was thought to have marked her baby by trying to get rid of him when she was pregnant. He was always a bit strange, and then when he was about seventeen, he killed his mother and father and burned the house down.

The Gold Hill Cemetery, which has many gravesites dated in the mid-1800s, shares the curious reputation of the Oregon Vortex. In 1985 a version of the Gold Hill Cemetery legend surfaced in a folklore class at Southern Oregon State College.

A LONG NIGHT IN THE GOLD HILL CEMETERY

There's a pioneer cemetery in Gold Hill with lots of graves going all the way back to the 1850s. Lots of miners are

buried there, and the cemetery lies on land that was a grave-yard for the Tekilmas. Anyway, there's some sort of natural force field there, probably because the place is so close to the Vortex, where all the laws of nature get screwed up. There's some sort of disruption there, like at the Bermuda Triangle.

My friend's boy goes to Crater High, and he said this happened to a kid from Crater. These guys were out in the Gold Hill cemetery drinking a few beers. And it was pretty creepy out there, y'know. Lots of sounds in the woods and strange lights. Well, a couple of the younger guys were getting pretty scared, and this big football player named Jack starts in on their case. When they're good and freaked, he tells 'em about the hot and cold gravestones: "In the Gold Hill cemetery you can find two gravestones side by side. One hot and the other cold. If you lay down between the stones after midnight, you can't get up. They can't even pull you outa' there until dawn. First light of dawn, but not before."

Well, one of the younger guys just freaks out. He's sittin' right on top of a stone that's getting warmer and warmer. But the stone next to him has even a little frost on top. So the kid starts yellin' and screamin'. So Jack sees a problem here. He's afraid the cops are gonna' come and find out who bought the beer. So Jack says, "Calm down, man. I was just kidding. Look, I'll show you." And Jack laid down between the hot and cold stones. He folded his arms over his chest and closed his eyes and laid real still. Well, the crazy kid, he stops yellin', and pretty soon everybody started to laugh. A nervous laugh, y'know, like nobody'd really bought this story except the crazy kid.

But then Jack tries to get up. You can see his muscles twitchin' and the wild look on his face. He couldn't do it. A couple of guys go over and grab his arms, but they're folded tight across his chest, and they can't budge him. But his eyes are big as balloons, man, and his mouth is wide open, but nothing is comin' out.

Well, then things really got crazy. They drove into Central Point and got about half the football team. And they reefed on him until his arms were about to come off. But it was no use. He wouldn't budge until dawn. And Jack's been looney-tunes ever since. That was about the last time anybody tried that trick, I'll bet.

Jacksonville

Jackson County. Population 1,774. Jacksonville, established in the placer-mining era of 1852–53, was named for Jackson Creek, a small stream commemorating the man who first found gold on its banks. Gold mining continued as an important occupation in the Jacksonville area for more than eighty years, as shown in the Rainlight Films documentary *Undermining the Great Depression*. In fact, on January 26, 1935, after a period of heavy rains, the city of Jacksonville began to sink into a series of mine shafts beneath the town.

Townsfolk, weathering out the Depression by digging for gold tracings in their backyards and under their sheds, had added to the already-intricate maze of unsafe tunnels. When the heavy rains hit, the timbers of the makeshift mine shafts began to buckle; both horse-drawn carriages and cars began to disappear in the main streets of Jacksonville.

Jacksonville, once an important stop on the Southern Pacific rail line, was the county seat of Jackson County before the company rerouted its tracks through Medford. Jacksonville, however, has a rich political history, beginning with the 1880 visit of Rutherford B. Hayes, the first U.S. president to visit Oregon. Hayes, traveling with several dignitaries, including General William Tecumseh Sherman, stopped in Jacksonville at the French Hotel, owned and operated by Madame Derebaum. At that time, the French Hotel was famous on the West Coast as one of its finest establishments, an opinion not lost on Madame Derebaum as she figured the president's bill. In the morning, as President Hayes prepared to leave Jacksonville, the estimable innkeeper presented him with a bill for $100.00. The president, handing her $25.00, replied for all to hear, "Madame, we only wanted to rent rooms. We don't wish to *buy* your hotel."

In 1853, Jacksonville was little more than a wild mining town. Two years before, gold had been discovered on Jackson Creek, and at that time Jacksonville was perhaps the most rambunctious and wooly mining camp on the West Coast. Between 1853 and 1880, the little bank in Jacksonville run by C. C. Beekman processed more than $31,000,000 in gold dust. The streets were literally paved with gold, and it was not unusual to see a prospector sinking his pick into the ground at a street corner or even in someone's front yard. On one occasion, two men in the Jacksonville jail refused to leave when their term had expired; in attempting to tunnel to freedom, they had struck gold in the floor of their cell.

Into this bonanza in the year of 1853, rode the Reverend John Oberg, a Methodist minister. Immediately he saw the need for a church in this Godforsaken community. And, although there was plenty of money in Jacksonville, at any given time most of it lay on the gambling tables of saloons and hotels. Oberg found many citizens of Jacksonville who wanted a church, but few who were willing to donate.

So the good reverend decided to take his ministry to the places where it would do the most good. Night after night, Oberg set up his pulpit behind the rail of the Jacksonville Saloon or at the poker table in the United States Hotel, preaching and singing to the men of the goldfields and to the gamblers and painted women who "mined" Jacksonville in other ways. Every night Oberg showed up at the saloon strip with his Bible and songbook, ready to bring religion to the unwashed citizenry.

The saloonkeepers did not want to throw Oberg into the street, nor could the gamblers continue to deal cards while the minister was belting out "Bringing in the Sheaves." So the whiskey and the cards stopped until Oberg took up his collection. At that point the Jacksonville miners gave generously, hoping to bring the service to a speedy end and to discourage another visit the next night.

It was not long before Reverend Oberg had collected enough tithes from the rabble of Jacksonville's bars to construct a stately church in the middle of the city. That church, still standing today, later became a historic landmark and, even more, a tribute to the clever fund-raising methods of John Oberg.

AUNTIE GANUNG CASTS HER BALLOT

During the Civil War, Oregon was officially a free state. However, there were plenty of Confederate sympathizers in the state, including a band in Jacksonville. One evening the Rebels hoisted the Confederate flag on the pole in the center of town.

Although the Dixie flag caused quite a number of arguments and heated words in town, the northerners took no action, and the flag waved above the city for a whole day while the befuddled town council members met in a smoke-filled room to consider ways of handling the issue. As the men smoked their cigars and argued, "Auntie" Ganung took action. She decided that the travesty had gone far enough.

Armed with a loaded Colt pistol and a sharp axe, Auntie marched through the main street of Jacksonville and stood before the flagpole. Whack! The sound of the axe biting wood reverberated even to the council chambers. After a few quick blows, Auntie Ganung's axe felled the flagpole. The Confederates looked on in amazement, but no one tried to confront the robust woman as she marched back up the street displaying a satisfied smile.

The Confederate flag did not fly again above Jacksonville, nor did the town council replace the pole. For many years the wooden stump in Jacksonville's town square remained, a vivid reminder of Auntie Ganung's solution to divided loyalties.

Kerby

Josephine County. Kerby, thirty miles southwest of Grants Pass, was named after an early settler, James Kerby. When Kerbyville was declared the Josephine County seat in 1857, the name was changed to Napoleon. However, the name did not stick, and by 1860 residents were calling the place Kerby, a clipped version of its original title.

Kerby was founded by a man from Crescent City in the earliest mining days. The man was transporting a billiard table from California on the back of a pack mule, intending to deliver the table to a settlement farther north. Soon after arriving at the present site of Kerby, the mule staggered under the weight of the pool table and died from exhaustion.

"This place is as good as any for a billiard parlor," said the entrepreneur. Without even unstrapping the table from the dead animal's back, the Crescent City native began digging the foundations of the town of Kerby. Today Kerby is a quiet hamlet on the route from Grants Pass to the Oregon Coast, an outpost with a few filling stations, a store or two, and the inevitable truckers' cafe. Trudy Cooper collected this truck-stop story from her friend Freda in May 1971.

AT A LOCAL TRUCKSTOP

A truck driver stopped his truck in front of this restaurant and went on in. And the waitress came up to him and asked what he wanted. "The first thing I want is a lot of black coffee," he said.

So she went and got 'im some black coffee and come back and set it down in front of 'im and says, "Now, would you like to order?"

"Yes, I'd like two headlights, a couple of fenders, and a scorched top."

My gosh, she was mad. She went back to the cook and said, "What kind of an order is this? Two headlights, a couple of fenders, and a scorched top?"

"Why," he said, "that's simple." He says, "That's two eggs, a couple of pieces of bacon, and some toast."

So, it was late enough in the day that they had the lunch cooked, and amongst them was a great big pot of beans. So she got a plate and dipped 'im up a great big bowl of beans and took 'em out and set 'em in front of 'im.

He looked up at 'er and said, "I didn't order those."

"No," she said, "but I thought you'd like to gas up while you're waitin' for yer parts!"

Lincoln

Jackson County. Lincoln is a small community in the Siskiyou Mountains east of Ashland on the Greensprings Highway. The town was named for Lincoln, New Hampshire, by the Henry family, who moved their sawmill operation from New England to Oregon.

Tracy Lord, an Ashland native working in folklore at the University of Oregon, collected four versions of the ''Realfoot'' legend in 1975, and the following account is a composite of those variants. Lord noticed that her informants told ''Realfoot'' in typical legend style, exhibiting an aura of realism, despite the fact that Lord's storytellers had not observed the events firsthand. Nevertheless, details such as the precise weight of the bear and its eventual display in Sam's Sporting Goods Store make each

story seem verifiable. As with most legends, however, the search for verification is frustrating. A trip to the Yreka Museum or the shops around the Craterian Theater would probably not produce any tangible evidence of Realfoot's existence.

REALFOOT

In the year 1890, the Siskiyou Mountain area around Ashland was grizzly country. And the most notable of bears in these hills was Realfoot. His domain was from Mt. Pitt clear on down to Pilot Rock. When he was just three or four years old, Realfoot got caught in a trap set by a man named Greeves. And the bear, he lost three toes. This Greeves showed the toes around; they was almost five inches long.

Well, after losin' those toes, Realfoot got real mean. He would kill cattle, dogs, sheep, and anything else he came across—bite 'em right in the back. Sometimes he just left the carcass. He wasn't hungry—just mean.

So one day a bunch of trackers from the Wright family took out after Realfoot. He was easy to find because the track showed the deformed right foot. They caught up to him in the Greensprings up above Ashland. So the Wrights followed him over a little ridge and came upon him all snuggled into a wood rat's nest. That bear had torn that nest all to pieces, sticks and branches throwed everywhere. He was lyin' on his back asleep surrounded by leaves and sticks and piled brush.

These boys got up as close as they could and started firing. Old Man Wright had a 44–40 rifle, and Billy Wright had a smaller gun. So Billy said, "You shoot the head, and I'll get him in the heart." So they started shootin'. And Billy pumped ten shots into that bear, and his dad shot ten times. They never missed once, but the bear kept comin'. They had seven hounds and turned them loose too, but Realfoot just swatted 'em away like flies. Finally Old Man Wright put a bullet right between the bear's eyes, and he dropped like a felled pine tree.

Old Realfoot was so heavy they had to bring in a team of horses and a sled to haul him out. He weighed 1,892 pounds. They took him to the Wrights' ranch, and some guy from Hornbrook came up to stuff him. After that, he was sold to a man in California, and some people think he burnt up in the San Francisco Fire. But actually Old Realfoot was hauled around the country in a boxcar, and folks paid good money to see the biggest bear ever shot in this country.

About forty years ago, you could see Realfoot in Sam's Sporting Goods store across from the Craterian Theatre in Medford. And the toes are still on display in the museum in Yreka. They're mounted on a little bronze plaque in a display that explains the complete history of that bear.

Logtown

Jackson County. Population 0. At one time, Logtown lay six miles southwest of Jacksonville, at the confluence of Poorman's and Forest creeks. This once-prosperous site was named for F. Logg, a farmer on Forest Creek. In the previous century, Logtown was the supply point for several mines along Jackass Creek. The name Jackass Creek, hardly dignified, was changed after miners drew more than $10 million from the creek beds. Thereafter, Jackass Creek was known as Forest Creek.

The first full-time resident of Logtown was a woman who opened a store. One night she was robbed and killed. According to Ranger Lee Port, ''The story goes that the people believed in the superstition that the last object which the person sees is recorded in the eye before death. They brought [Peter] Britt out with his camera and attempted to photograph her eyes in order to determine the murderer.'' The negatives did not reveal the killer.

In the 1930s, when the WPA Federal Writers' Project workers toured Southern Oregon, they stopped at Logtown, once a thriving community with a schoolhouse, a miner's store, a Chinese store, the usual saloon, a blacksmith shop, and several dwellings. In the Depression, however, the WPA writers found only ''a few leveled spots on the hillside where buildings once stood, an old well, the corner of a fence, and a yellow-rose bush.'' The rose bush they mention is one of the most eminent reminders of the people who came to settle in the Applegate region during the pioneer era.

In the mid-1850s, John McKee and his family left Missouri for a new life in the West. But it was a sad parting. They left behind the grave of their young child, a child who had been the mother's favorite. Maryum McKee cried for days at the thought of leaving her child behind in the lonely grave on their farm. So, as John McKee loaded the wagon, Maryum walked to the small grave and cut a slip of the yellow rose that the McKees had planted in the young one's memory.

Across the plains and through the mountains, Maryum McKee cherished the rose cutting, keeping it in a tin can filled with moist papers. When after several months' travel the McKees arrived in the Applegate region, Maryum planted the yellow rose, a traditional symbol of remembrance, on the family homestead, where it served two purposes. The rose not only reminded the family of their lost child, but symbolized the presence of a woman on the homestead. Many such plantings remain evident today in the West as reminders of this pioneer tradition. Indeed, within a few years, the Logtown rose had taken firm root and soon covered the property in lush and beautiful blossoms.

The McKee family arrived in the Rogue River Valley and first settled near what is now Roxy Ann Butte, named for Maryum McKee's mother-in-law. When the McKees built their house, John, who loved to dance, made the living room big enough to accommodate two squares. Maryum and John McKee contributed much to the Applegate Valley over the years. John was a teacher and blacksmith, widely respected throughout the valley. As a mid-

wife, Maryum helped to bring countless children into the world and still had time to raise to adulthood her own brood of twelve children. Somehow, Maryum had time to cook, put up preserves, sew quilts, and offer kindness to all around her.

Although Logtown withered and died in the last century, the rose itself has remained hearty. In the 1960s, descendants of the McKees placed slips in McKee Park and at the site of the Pioneer Cemetery. Even today the yellow Logtown Rose, a remembrance of a lost McKee child, adorns the gates and posts of these historic spots near Jacksonville, not far from the green and lush Roxy Ann Peak.

''The Logtown Rose'' was written in 1989 from interview materials provided by Medford's Gladys Williams, a descendant of the McKees.

THE LOGTOWN ROSE

They packed up and left for a home in the West, Said

fare-well to friends dear and kind. A whole new life a-

wai-ted them there, But so much must be left be- hind.

It was such a short time since she plan-ted the rose On the

grave of her lost lit-tle one. And now she must leave and

ne-ver re-   turn At the   dawn of to-   mor-row's   sun.
Final ending
Whose   spi-rit is   li - ving   still.

They packed up and left for a home in the West,
Said farewell to friends dear and kind.
A whole new life awaited them there,
But so much must be left behind.

It was such a short time since she planted the rose
On the grave of her lost little one.
And now she must leave and never return
At the dawn of tomorrow's sun.

So Maryum took a slip from the rose,
Which she tended 'cross mountains and plains.
This symbol of love held close to her heart
Would grow in the Rogue Valley rains.

At their homestead in Logtown near Roxy Ann Butte
She placed that dear plant in the ground.
The yellow rose grew and flourished and bloomed,
Now all over the valley it's found.

What stories of life this rose could tell
As it's watched through the many long years.
Of the people who've come and the people who've gone,
Of their work, of their joys, and their tears.

So here's to the rose and long may it grow
On fence row and valley and hill.
A memory of Maryum's generous heart,
Whose spirit is living still.

Myrtle Creek

Douglas County. Population 3,060. The townsite, sold by
its founder for a yoke of oxen in 1851, was named for the
groves of myrtle wood, or *umbellularia californica*, standing nearby.

Myrtle Creek lies adjacent to the route taken by
Applegate Trail travelers who wished to push on to the
Willamette Valley after clearing the Cascade Mountains.
This theme is so persistent in Oregon tradition that histo-
rian Francis Haines has coined the story ''Goldilocks on
the Oregon Trail.'' In most versions of the legend, a Plains
Indian chief becomes enamored of the golden-haired
daughter of pioneers traveling the trail. In 1982 Lori
Lonergan heard from Olive Brown an oral history that has
been remembered in a family ritual.

GOLDILOCKS ON THE OREGON TRAIL

Somewhere out on the Oregon Trail, the wagon train
came across an Indian riding alone—a chief. He stopped
and talked to the settlers but then fixed his gaze on a young
girl with long, rather curly hair—very blonde and very pretty.

''He wanted to buy her for a wife for his son—or as a
daughter for himself—and they wouldn't sell her,'' says Olive
Brown. ''He couldn't understand why they wouldn't sell
her.'' After much talk, the settlers convinced the chief that
they loved their daughter too much to part with her. Finally,
the chief rode off, but returned shortly with a gift, a long
beautiful string of blue and white beads.

The chief handed the beads to the young girl in a gesture
of friendship. With a wistful look he rode off, leaving the
immigrants to puzzle over the strange encounter.

''They are tangled now, and the threads are very weak,
so they can't be used for anything except to just look at,'' says
Mrs. Brown. ''And those beads have been handed down in
the family to the first blonde child born into a generation.
Nancy was the one in her generation who inherited them,
and Karen is the one in her generation who is supposed to
inherit them. I am keeping them for her in an old Indian
basket.''

O'Brien

Josephine County. O'Brien was named for John O'Brien,
an early settler. The city was once the western gateway of
Sailor's Diggings, the first county seat of Josephine
County. In the 1850s and 1860s, Sailor's Diggings comprised a series of boomtowns, including Allen Gulch,
Browntown, Takilma, Althouse, French Flat, Waldo, and
O'Brien. Sailor's Diggings was approximately three miles
from the California border, just east of the Redwood Highway.

Sailor's Diggings was populated by sailors from an
unnamed ship harbored at Crescent City, the men leaving
their disabled craft to sail on the winds of gold fever. Thinking they were in California, the sailors were actually mean-
dering near the present site of Jacksonville when they
found several large gold nuggets in the Illinois River. When
the men returned to Crescent City for shovels, spades,
and timbers, they set off an alarm that cleared out both
Crescent City and the ships docked in its harbor. In a short
time, the news of the digs spread across the West. One
young Irishman, Mattie Collins, found a seventeen-pound
nugget in a stream bed in 1852. Soon after, Sailor's Diggings became a gold-mining metropolis.

Although Sailor's Diggings is now a group of ghost
towns, the region was once lively and thriving. In the mid-
1850s, Waldo boasted a bowling alley, cobbler shop,
butcher shop, blacksmith's shop, several stores, a Chinese boarding house, a courthouse, a billiard parlor, and—
some years later—a ballroom and a skating rink. In the
Waldo brewery of Jacob Marhoffer and Randall Sanns, local
miners could buy Sailor's Diggings Beer, a passable brew
made from Marhoffer's German recipe.

HOP BEER

Take five quarts of water, six ounces of hops, boil it three hours; then strain the liquor, add to it five more quarts of water, four ounces of bruised ginger root, and boil this concoction for twenty minutes. Then strain the mixture and add four pounds of sugar. When it has become luke-warm, put the liquid in a pint of yeast. Let the brew ferment. In twenty-four hours, it will be ready for bottling.

But the miners, who paid $16.00 an ounce for salt—the same price as an ounce of gold—found hop beer one of the few reasonable commodities in Sailor's Diggings. Apples, when they could be bought, cost a dollar each. When hard times hit and the claims began to sag, the miners sometimes found themselves hungry enough to eat miner's lettuce, a staple of both the Indians and the Waldo-area settlers. Growing along the stream banks of the Illinois River, miner's lettuce provided young leaves for salads and chewy shoots for boiled pottage. Very popular among the miners, this wild plant saved many a greenhorn from starvation in the early settlement days.

The mining was hard in the Illinois Valley. Miners worked with gold pans, shovels, and sluice boxes to sift the gold from the rocky soil, but they found the conditions trying. Eventually the mining companies began building huge ditches and culverts to employ hydraulic methods of mining required by the rough soil conditions around the digs. One day, John Valen and his friend Joe set out to bury a fellow miner in the Waldo cemetery. For hours they dug and sweated over the gravesite, finally hollowing out a suitable hole in the earth. Wiping the sweat from his brow, Valen turned to his friend and said, "When we get Mike in here, he'll never get to Hell. He couldn't get through this hardpan."

The Chinese miners, who often took up abandoned claims or bought ones considered "played out," kept the population figures of Sailor's Diggings high even after many of the Scots-Irish miners had left for the Canadian gold rush in the Frazer River Valley. At one point in the 1860s, more than 3,500 Chinese were registered (by poll tax) in Josephine County. Of course, there was a Chinatown in Sailor's Diggings. The Chinese miners as well buried their deceased in the hardpan of the Illinois Valley, but only temporarily. After a suitable time, the bones of the dead were exhumed from the land and returned to China for final placement in native soil. Today in the Waldo and Glen-Althouse area, it is not uncommon to find the open graves of the Chinese miners whose bones were removed from "foreign" soil a hundred years ago.

In mining, as in almost any dangerous occupation, greenhorns can expect little respect and possibly a good hazing. One such greenhorn got his revenge, however, as reported in the centennial edition (April 2, 1960) of the *Grants Pass Daily Courier*.

GREENHORN LUCK

A young man named Vaun arrived in Browntown broke. With true greenhorn innocence, he asked where there was a good place for him to do a little gold digging. Several old sourdoughs thought they would have a little fun and with mock dignity directed him to a big rock pile by the side of the creek running down the side of a nearby hill. The greenhorn took off. Within a few moments the old hands heard his delighted whoops. They followed him to the exact spot to which they had sent him and found him excitely regarding a huge nugget, later valued at $1000.

Declaring that so much money was more than the law allowed him, the erstwhile novice mined no more that day or again in those parts, departing on a horse purchased with the earnings from the nugget.

Phoenix

Jackson County. Population 3,163. Phoenix was originally called Gasberg, after the nonstop banter of a local woman who served meals at the stagehouse. Fort Grant, an outpost in the Rogue River Indian Wars, was located in what is now Phoenix. During the time of the fort's existence, prospectors, cattlemen, and ranchers deposited their gold dust with the Fort Grant paymaster, who converted the dust to ten- and twenty-dollar gold pieces at regular intervals when shipments came overland from San Francisco. In the meantime, the paymaster buried gold and coins in an iron kettle, carefully hoarding the secret of the stash's whereabouts. Unfortunately, one day he suffered a stroke. Unable to talk, he tried to draw a map to the "bank," but died before completing the diagram. Afterwards, the soldiers and locals prodded the entire Fort Grant area with an endgate rod, but the kettle was never found. To this day, the lost treasure of Fort Grant remains buried somewhere under the current town of Phoenix.

Phoenix is the center of the lush Rogue River Valley orchards. The Harry and David Company, famous for its pears and apples, stands at the northern gate of the city limits. Phoenix also has a large migrant labor population, many of them unregistered workers from Mexico. At Phoenix's *Clinica Azteca*, where Mexican women gather for health and prenatal care, folklorist Pamela Jones heard dozens of stories about *la llorona*, the "weeping woman." The *llorona*, who died after losing her children through neglect or infanticide, haunts the night hours, chilling the night air with her warning cry, *Ayyyy mis hijos*.

According to Jones, *llorona* narratives and songs are rampant among young women whose families survive on monthly incomes averaging $320—women whose love of family and children is mitigated by the fear of bringing new life into such an uncertain and foreign world. Jones, herself fluent in Spanish, slowly gained the confidence of the young women while offering health care at the Phoenix clinic. Initially Jones recorded the texts in Spanish, later translating the manuscripts to English for inclusion in the State of Jefferson Folklore Archives. In 1988 Jones published the *llorona* legends in *Western Folklore*. Because many of the informants were concerned about alerting the Immigration and Naturalization Service, Jones agreed to use only first names in her collection and to forego the use of a tape recorder. The first story, told by Ofelia, begins with a phrase that signals the *llorona* legend, ''There was a woman. . . .''

THERE WAS A WOMAN. . . .

[T]here was a woman who had children, two or three children. I can't remember which, and she lived in a town by a river. One day she went down by the river with her children to bathe and wash clothes. All the people of this town would go down to the river to wash. There was a big rock by the side of the river where everyone washed their clothes. This day the children were playing in the water and the river was very high. All of a sudden the river, which was moving so swiftly, carried the children away. The woman was frantic and she tried to save her children but she couldn't reach them in time. She was so sad that she went crazy with grief [she twirls her finger by her ear], and she would do nothing but walk up and down the side of the river and in the street crying out for her children. Her cry was long and mournful and so sad, but it was also a cry that would put goose-flesh on your skin and frighten you if you heard it. It would start out low and get louder and then slowly fade away as if she were crying softly.

They say that now after she died you could still hear her—just the sound of her voice in the air down by the river. In the place where she lived people often hear her crying and it is a frightening sound. . . . Yes, I did hear it once, or at least I thought I did. I heard it in the night. It was a long low moaning: aaaayyyah. Like that. I was ten years old, the age of my daughter now, and I can remember very clearly hearing the voice of la llorona.

A swift current was the cause of one *llorona*'s travail, and the theme of water recurs in another weeping woman story, this time told by Arlene.

My grandmother used to tell us that story. I can remember all of us kids would gather around her chair on the floor and she would tell us stories. From what I can remember of the story there was a woman who kept having children, she just kept having babies. I don't remember if she was poor or why she did this, but after she had her babies she would take them to the nearby reservoir or any nearby body of water and drown them. They say that as her punishment God would not allow her soul to rest. She had to wander the earth forever. The people of the village where she lived could hear her wailing night and day. That was grandmother's village. My grandmother, who is now ninety-seven years old, remembers

hearing the llorona *crying all the time when she was a young girl. She remembers the men of the village getting together in groups and getting their rifles to go after the* llorona *out in the country. I guess they were afraid or something and thought if they could shoot at whatever was making the noise that it would go away. They could see only a shadow, they couldn't really see her, only a shadow and hear the crying sound. The crying would move farther away as they got close. My grandmother used to tell us lots of stories but this one was one to remember. It really scared us kids. Especially because at night sometimes she would say: ''Now you kids be good or the* llorona *will come here.'' It was like saying the boogie man would come to get you, because her story was so eerie and because of what she had done to her children.*

When my grandmother was a girl she used to hear the llorona *all the time. That was ninety years ago. That was Old Mexico. Who knows what it was like then or how they lived. Everyone was poor. A woman could easily have had her babies out away from people and drowned them in the river. I wonder if they still hear her in Mexico today?*

Pistol River

Curry County. In 1853, a South Coast settler lost a gun in this river, suggesting the current name. Early immigrants to the area brought with them a favorite folk song, ''Old Mr. Fox.'' This version was gathered in 1969 from George Wasson, who learned it from his mother, Bess Finley Wasson Hockema. The family used to sing this song at family gatherings to the accompaniment of a ''squeeze box'' accordion.

OLD MR. FOX

Old Mis-ter Fox on a   moon-shin-y night

Stood on his hind legs   just a-bout right.   "I'll

have some meat for my   sup-per to-night, Be-

fore I leave this   town-e-o,   Be-

fore I leave this   town-e-o!"

Because the squeeze box player had to pause regularly to refill the bellows, "Old Mr. Fox" has exaggerated rests in each stanza.

Old Mr. Fox on a moonshiny night
Stood on his hind legs just about right:
"I'll have some meat for my supper tonight
Before I leave this town-e-o,
Before I leave this town-e-o."

He marched up to the farmer's gate,
There he spied an old black drake
"Mr. Drake, Mr. Drake come and go with me.
You're the finest old drake in this town-e-o,
The finest old drake in this town-e-o."

Mr. Drake looked up and he replied,
"No, Mr. Fox, I will not go.
If you never eat meat 'til you eat me-o,
You'll never eat meat in this town-e-o,
You'll never eat meat in this town-e-o."

Old Mr. Fox, he took his track back
Grabbed the grey goose by her neck.
Her wings went flip flop over his back
And her legs hung dingle dingle down-e-o,
Her legs hung dingle dingle down-e-o.

Old Miz Flip Flop lyin' in the bed
Raised up the window and poked out her head.
"Old man, Old man, the grey goose is gone,
For don't you hear her going 'crank crank-e-o,'
Don't you hear her going 'crank crank-e-o'?"

The Old man raised up in a mighty mighty rage,
Wiped out his mouth and it full of sage.
"Old Woman, Old Woman just let them go.
I'll make mighty music come-a-hime-e-o,
Make mighty music come-a-hime-e-o."

Mr. Fox, he ran 'til he came to his den,
There were the little ones, nine or ten,
The old ones eating up all the meat
And the little ones gnawing on the bone-e-os,
The little ones gnawing on the bone-e-os.

"Daddy, Oh Daddy, when you goin' back again?"
"I hope to the dingle dangle never to go again."
"Why?" (shouted by someone other than the singer)
"Oh, don't you hear the music come-a-hime-e-o,
Don't you hear the music come-a-hime-e-o,
Don't you hear the music come-a-hime-e-o?"

Port Orford

Curry County. Population 1,025. Port Orford was named after George, Earl of Orford, grandson of England's prime minister and nephew of England's well-known man of letters, Horace Walpole. On April 24, 1792, Captain George Vancouver spotted the landmark and named the area for his friend. Port Orford is the westernmost incorporated city in the lower forty-eight states.

Every July 4th, citizens celebrate the "Battle of Battle Rock." In 1851 the steamer *Sea Gull* stopped on the coast-line near Port Orford to discharge nine scouts. The men were immediately attacked by Coquille Indians. The colonists retreated to a large rock, accessible on foot at low tide but otherwise ringed with a pounding, swirling surf. For two weeks the inhabitants of Battle Rock, as it came to be called, held off the Coquilles, mainly with the aid of a small cannon. After one such skirmish, the nine men stole away at night, meeting successfully with settlers to the north.

Port Orford is perhaps best known for something that was lost: a meteorite. People have been scouring the coastline and Curry County countryside since the 1860s searching for the Port Orford comet. In 1859, Dr. John Evans, a Northwest geologist, found some interesting rocks in the area and sent them to New York for analysis. Among the samples was a chunk from a stone partially buried in the earth at a place called Bald Mountain. The geologic analysis of the fragment confirmed that the silvery-looking metal fragment was from another world.

Dr. Evans immediately forwarded the location of his meteorite to New York researchers, explaining that the rock weighing about 2,000 pounds lay on the "western face of Bald Mountain . . . in the Rogue River Mountains not very far from Port Orford, about latitude 42 degrees 35 minutes North and longitude 123 degrees to 124 degrees West." Unfortunately, Dr. Evans died before he could return to claim the meteorite, and his directions, while apparently clear, describe a huge gridpatch of land. Furthermore, there are three or four Bald Mountains in the region, none of them so sparse of timber as in the 1860s. Many seekers have claimed to find the meteorite, but so far the geologic hunters have failed to display anything more than an interesting pile of large rocks, all indigenous to Oregon.

In November of 1856, Judge D. J. Lowe sponsored a large fishing expedition to the Sixes River, north of Port Orford. Although the judge and his party had expected to dine beautifully on fresh steelhead trout, the fishing had been bad and the weather awful. Hungry and tired, they pulled in to Port Orford and settled at a poor excuse for a hotel run by a man named Billy Craze. The host himself was nearly starving, however, and he had little more than potatoes to offer his guests.

As the judge and his friends contemplated several hungry nights at Craze's hotel while waiting for transportation, prospects became more and more gloomy. "Let's go back down to the Sixes," suggested one fisherman. "Maybe we'll have better luck. I can't eat potatoes three meals a day and survive."

That night, while considering whether to brave the bad weather and return to the fishing grounds, Judge Lowe and his friends saw good luck blown into Port Orford on the winds of a storm. An immense wind—up to seventy-five miles per hour—tore at the reefs and drove the kelp inland from Cape Blanco, the seaweed sweeping ashore and forming an enormous seine. When the Port Orford travelers went to the beach, they found the kelp seine entangled with tons of fish, clams, crabs, and other sea fare. Mixed with the abundant potatoes, the sea bounty made an excellent chowder, one favored by the judge's party for many nights. As the judge later remarked, remembering the table at Port Orford's modest hotel, "We lived just fine."

Judge Lowe and his friends ate well, but their fare was not appreciably different from that of the Indians living near Port Orford. Here, for example, is a simple but delicious recipe from the first inhabitants of the Oregon South Coast.

INDIAN CHOWDER

The Indians soaked the clams overnight in a fresh-water stream and then threw them into a hollowed log containing water that had been heated to the boiling point by hot stones. After opening, the clams were scraped from their shells and placed once again into the log bowl, together with chunks of jerked meat or smoked venison, dried wild onions, and wapato roots. Early settlers in the Port Orford area fixed an appetizing counterpart of this chowder in a large iron pot over a driftwood fire, substituting bacon, potatoes, and ordinary onions for the original ingredients.

Riddle

Douglas County. Population 1,088. Riddle was settled in 1851 by Illinois emigrant William H. Riddle, whose descendants wrote their names in the pages of Oregon history.

Riddle retains some of the Old West flavor yet today, with its cardrooms, blackjack tables, and limited gambling ordinance. According to Jim Nichols, the dining room of the Riddle Hotel was also a popular poker room in earlier times, but it was hard for an outlander to ride out of town with much money. Invariably, the locals would sit the newcomer with his back to the big mirror on the wall, so that everybody could read his hand.

In the early years of this century, Riddle stood as an important rail stop on the Siskiyou line of the Southern Pacific. For a few years, in celebration of the fall plenty, Riddle residents gathered to throw a venison barbecue for their neighbors up and down the rail lines. All went well until somebody decided that the traditional cooking methods were just too old-fashioned.

According to documents collected in 1982 by Lori Lonergan, Riddle held its first venison barbecue in the fall of 1913. The hunting season was longer then, and the bag limits were bigger, so people from all over the Cow Creek region were glad to contribute bucks to the Barbecue Committee. The animals were stored in Roseburg until a few dozen had been accumulated.

The venison was quartered and suspended on iron rods over hardwood coals and drip-pans and periodically seasoned by men who dipped butter and spices from an oaken vat. People from Azalea, Canyon Creek, and Glendale all camped for the barbecue, bringing coffee and salads or pickles and relishes for venison sandwiches. It was all free, and everyone ate their fill. "In all my life long," said Claude A. Riddle in 1954, "I cannot recall any similar get-together where everyone seemingly enjoyed themselves so much as the people who attended the annual venison barbecue."

But events took a strange turn in 1916. After some members of the Barbecue Committee had complained about the hard work of roasting the venison, somebody mentioned a "barbecue expert" from Eugene who had secured a reputation for baking beef in a covered pit. "You've never tasted meat like this," said one man. So the agreement was made, and the Eugene cook arrived in town ready to show his style.

A pit was dug in the meadow—forty feet long and five feet deep. The cook built an oak fire and kept it going for two days. Finally the pit was ready, and the men loaded the neatly wrapped bucks into the hole, then covered it with dirt.

On the day in question, visitors rolled into town from all over Southern Oregon, many of them driving over dusty roads from as far as Cottage Grove and Grants Pass. There was a band and games and lots of entertainment. Everyone was having a great time right up until the moment when the boys began to open the pit. According to Claude A. Riddle, who described the 1916 barbecue in his book *In the Happy Hills*, the day's joy was soon ruined.

HERE LIES A BUM STEER

When the boys started to uncover the barbecued venison, an awful stench arose, and it was discovered that the meat had not cooked at all, but had only been heated enough to start it on the way to decomposition. The whole of the 21 bucks which were intended to appease our appetites and to give them something so delicious to eat that they would remember it all the rest of their lives—was a sorry unapproachable mess.

Well, there we were—a club with a broken heart. A great crowd of disappointed guests. But there was nothing anyone could do about it. The club members who had been instrumental in securing the services of the barbecue man scrawled on a sign "Here Lies a Bum Steer!" and placed it over the grave. The man who sold us the idea dashed to the hotel and shed bitter tears of remorse, while the rest of us somehow lived through the day. But we never had another barbecue, and in another year, we had no gun club.

The cause of the failure of the barbecue was laid to the fact that the ground was too sandy to hold the heat.

Rogue River

Jackson County. Population 1,757. Rogue River was originally called Tailholt because in the settlement era there was no bridge or ferry. To cross, a rider had to "grab 'holt of his horse's tail" and swim across.

Although history records no public hangings in Josephine County during its tempestuous mining days, there were more than a few whisperings of lynchings along the Rogue River in the settlement period. In 1984 Leslie Clason of Medford tape recorded the story of "The Creaking Mantel," told by a friend in Jacksonville who "used her voice to make sound effects, the creaking and groaning which set the mood of the piece." The informant also used her hands to gesture during moments of intensity. "At the end of the story," says Clason, "her voice got very soft and low, adding to the eerie tone she wished to convey."

THE CREAKING MANTEL

The story of the creaking mantel, one of my grandmother's famous ones, this occurred on an old dairy along the Rogue, and if I remember right, my grandparents were invited to a housewarming party that was held by some friends of theirs that had just built one of those modern-style, large ranch houses. And they had just moved out to this old country farm. And since this was a pretty big occurrence—this building of the new house—they had invited most of the people of the valley to come an' see their house an' since it was pretty chilly outside, all the guests gathered around the large fireplace in the middle of the room.

And everyone was talking an' havin' a good time, but as it neared midnight and the clock began to chime, the room

fell silent (pause). Because they were hearing strange creeeaking (narrator's voice creaks) and groooaning (voice groans). . . . It seemed to be coming from the wooden mantel on the fireplace that they were around. And between all this creeaking (voice creaks) and grooaning (voice groans), they heard stomping and whinneying of horses—all this commotion—and everyone was just amazed, you know. They couldn't believe what was happening right there before their eyes.

And so my grandmother, a few weeks later, she called them and wanted to know if they had found out anything about this, you know, what had happened. Was it some kind of practical joke or had she found out anything? And the hostess told her that she had went back and did some investigating of the property and had found out that the mantelpiece . . . had once been a part of a central beam of an old barn that had stood on the property, one that had been torn down before they built the house, anyway.

Apparently many years ago on that same date of the house-warming party, a man had been hanged (pause), and this occurred at midnight (pause) from the barn's central beam. This was done by a gang of outlaws who then fled, and the ghost of the man could still be, could still be heard on the anniversary of his death, just creaking and groaning as he swung from the beams, the rafters.

Roseburg

Douglas County. Population 16,703. The freight stop at the junction of Deer Creek and the South Umpqua River was first known as Deer Creek. In 1854 Aaron Rose donated three acres of land and $1,000 for a courthouse near the site of his tavern. Three years later the name of the post office was changed to Roseburgh and in 1894 altered to the current spelling.

Roseburg is a beautiful city surrounded by creeks of the Umpqua River watershed. Umpqua Valley storyteller George Braddock was one of many to collect stories told about the pioneer settlers on these riverbanks and streams.

THE COZY HEARTH AT THE McALDER HOMESTEAD

"My dad knew him and the Indian woman real well," said Al Renfro, a prospector. "You could always count on a good warm meal and a place to stay if you were ever out by their place." Old Man McAlder was widely respected in the City Creek area near Roseburg. When he married an Indian woman in his later years, he became very happy. She knew a little magic and always surprised him with some special cures and potions that were delightful. And the woman was always especially kind to travelers, who always met with the warmest welcome, a good fire, and wonderful food.

She was happy throughout her life, even though they never had any children. They built a nice homestead up in the hills, and Old Man McAlder saw to it that she had everything she wanted. But one day she took sick, and she knew she was going to die. She said that the Old Man had been good to her, and she appreciated her life in these hills.

The woman also said, "My spirit is always going to be in this house. I will never leave here."

With that, she died. Old Man McAlder didn't last much longer after that. One day in the next fall he took sick and died. The neighbors buried him right outside the cabin door.

Nothing ever came of the house afterwards. It just sat vacant. But one day a surveyor from Roseburg lost the surveying party in a storm. Darkness fell, and he was wet and without any food or matches for a fire. Then all of a sudden he saw a light on the hill.

When he got to the cabin, the surveyor knocked at the door, but no one answered. So after several tries, he carefully opened the door and went inside. There was a big fire going in the McAlder fireplace, a nice cozy bed with the covers turned down, and a big loaf of steaming hot bread on the table.

Takilma

Jackson County. This former gold-mining station on the Illinois River was named for the Takelma Indians of the Rogue River Valley. Takilma lies in the general area where gold was first discovered in Southern Oregon, part of the region known as Sailors' Diggings.

At Takilma, as in any goldfield or mining claim, the men in the digs were looking for a richer strike, a pure vein of gold like the Briggs strike—a yellow streak found by a teenaged boy where the gold, lying just at the surface, was enough to yield $32,000 worth of ore with little effort on Briggs's part. So, when news of the Frazer River strike swept through Sailor's Diggings, a great many men packed up their belongings and headed into the Far North country, in many cases abandoning claims that, with some honest sweat, would continue to pay handsomely for years. One such story concerning the rumor of an "easy strike" was told in the Takilma region by Southern Oregon prospector Al Renfro and collected for the Mills Archives by George Braddock in 1976.

ST. PETER AND THE OLD PROSPECTOR

It seems that a prospector died one day and went to heaven. He met St. Peter at the Pearly Gates greeting new arrivals. The prospector walks up and Peter says, "Oh, no, not another prospector. We already got too many. Why, they have the streets dug up, claims on every cloud; they even have a sluice set up on the heavenly river. I am sorry, but heaven won't stand for another prospector."

So the prospector sat down and thought for a while. He got an idea. He says to St. Peter, "Suppose I promise to get rid of some of those prospectors. Then can I stay?"

"Okay," Peter says, "I will give you a chance."

Well, the prospector, he starts right off gathering supplies for a big trip. He checks up on the gold market, actin' like he got in on some big strike. Then he lets fly a rumor that the streets of hell are paved in gold. Well, sir, it weren't a week 'til there was a steady flow of prospectors headin' out for hell.

About a month later, here comes the prospector past Peter at the gate, all loaded down with stash. Peter says, "Where you going? Aren't you happy here? You kept your promise. You can stay."

"Well, sir, I heard yesterday that the streets of hell are paved in gold, and I am going to go check out that rumor."

Wolf Creek

Josephine County. Wolf Creek was named for the abundance of these shy animals in the early mining days. Wolf Creek is not only famous for the Wolf Creek Tavern, where Jack London is purported to have penned sections of his famous novels, but also for the Six-Bit House. At a hairpin turn in the Southern Pacific rail line, this hostelry was available to travelers for seventy-five cents a night, a bargain compared to the dollar charged by other innkeepers on the Southern Pacific route. A more popular, but less likely, explanation involves a Wolf Creek hanging. The victim, a local Indian, had the indignity of being interrupted in his final moments by the innkeeper, who demanded the repayment of a six-bit debt even as the doomed man sat on horseback with a noose around his neck.

Today logging is the primary vocation of Wolf Creek residents. Cutting timber is one of the most dangerous jobs in the world. Consequently, the lumberjack, faced with the possibility of death or injury every day, tends to find amusement in the day-to-day details of his work. In order to have an outlet for the fears and anxieties of a job where one man's mistake might bring disaster to any number of coworkers, the logger enjoys practical jokes, outrageous tales, and shared superstitions, some of them not much changed since the earliest days of Northwest logging.

Bill Agee collected the story of "The Axe Man's Test" for the Randall V. Mills Archives in 1976. His informant, a twenty-five-year-old logger working on his third crew, "had himself been subjected to these initiations" and told the details with a certain good-natured resignation.

THE AXE MAN'S TEST

When you go out logging, usually new men have to get some initiation from the older fellas. There's a whole variety of things they do. One of the common ones is the axe man's test. They'll catch you around the landing, which is where they load the trucks and haul the logs . . . and get a chopping block.

When you're on your break or something, one of the old timers will get the axe and start chopping on the block. And he'll say, ''Have you ever taken the axe man's test?'' And most people don't know what the axe man's test is unless they've worked in the woods for a while. What you got to do is hit the same spot on the chopping block four times in a row.

They'll show you how it's done, which all seems quite simple. . . .

So you close your eyes and take one swing and then take another, and you feel like you're coming pretty close to the same spot. And maybe on the third swing they'll grab your gloves or your hard hat or lunch bucket or whatever's handy and put it on top of the chopping block. You come down and smash the hell out of it [he laughs], and everybody goes into hysterics.

Central Oregon

If a man escaped being scalped by the Indians, lost in the vast forests or deserts, poisoned by a rattler, eaten alive by a hungry wolf, coyote, bear or mountain lion, frozen by winter or dehydrated by summer, there were still no shortages of discouraging things to be taken into consideration. In modern Grant County, for example, cloudbursts have been known to move boulders and change the course of creeks. Temperatures in Central Oregon vary from as low as 25 degrees below zero to 110 degrees above and sometimes more. In the vastness of America there were at least a few lands with a more accommodating environment.

—David Braly, Juniper Empire

Parts of Central Oregon were once covered by a teeming inland ocean, as shown by the discoveries of Oregon's first geologist, Thomas Condon. In the John Day Fossil Beds, Condon unearthed the remnants of fish and mammals from the ancient sea. Elsewhere, Condon and his successors found the remnants of fish and sea mammals, as well as the bones of animals who lived by the seashore: three-toed ponies, camels, rhinos, and saber-toothed cats. Later, geological eruptions thrust these seabeds upward, forming domes and fault-block mountains. Soon the cutting action of the Cascade glaciers began to sculpt a geologist's paradise, a land of lava caves, high lava plains, rimrocks, buttes, cindercones, and glaciers. In recent history—only 6,000 years ago—towering Mt. Mazama erupted, leaving Crater Lake in its caldera and painting in greys the topography of Central Oregon. Today Central Oregon is a region of startling contrasts, where one moment the traveler drives through ponderosa and lodgepole pine, then abruptly enters desert land, covered with juniper trees and endless miles of sagebrush. In Central Oregon's Gilliam and Sherman counties, vast fields of wheat provide an abundant harvest. However, Deschutes and Crook counties are mostly desert lands.

Many say that Oregon's Old West is really east—east of the Cascade Mountains. Explorers and early wagon-train immigrants traveled across this part of the state to reach the coast and valley destinations, but some returned to Central Oregon, perhaps because the "wet side" was already becoming too crowded in the 1860s. Andrew Clarno was just such a man. When Clarno settled on the John Day River, says Lewis A. McArthur, author of *Oregon Geographic Names*, no one lived within a day's ride. However, soon Clarno heard that a friend had staked out a homestead about twenty miles to the east. So Clarno rode toward the present town of Fossil until he found his old companion. Climbing off his horse, Clarno said, "Bill, don't you think you're crowding me a little?"

In fact, by 1860 the ones who felt most crowded in Central Oregon were the Native Americans, notably the Wascos, Walla Wallas, Snakes, Tyghs, Klamaths, Modocs, and Warm Spring Indians, tribes who had for centuries carved trails through Central Oregon, following the deer and elk herds that were part of their natural food supply. Among the larger tribes were smaller Indian bands, their names as interesting as their ways: the Taih, or Upper Deschutes; the Wyam, or Lower Deschutes; the Tenino; the Dock-Spus; the Dalles; the Ki-gal-twal-la; and the Dog River Indians. While Andrew Clarno and his companions were moving into Central Oregon along these well-established hunting trails, Walapi Chief Paulina was organizing raiding parties to discourage settlement. In fact, pioneer settler James Clark was so completely discouraged by Indian attacks that by the year 1866 his settlement had become known as Burnt Ranch.

The influx of settlers actually began more than forty years earlier, however. By the mid-1820s they were discovering the wealth of the inland empire. Fur traders and explorers criss-crossed the countryside, seeking out pelts for the Hudson's Bay Company and marking rivers and mountains on rude maps. Peter Skene Ogden, one of the most colorful of the mountain men, first surveyed the land east of the Three Sisters and Mt. Jefferson, probably without realizing he was the first non-Indian to walk these trails. Ogden's excesses were also typical of explorers of his day. In his diary for 1827, Ogden notes that during a three-week traverse south to the Klamath River region, he and a companion collected 827 beaver and otter skins. As McArthur says in a line often quoted by Oregon conserva-

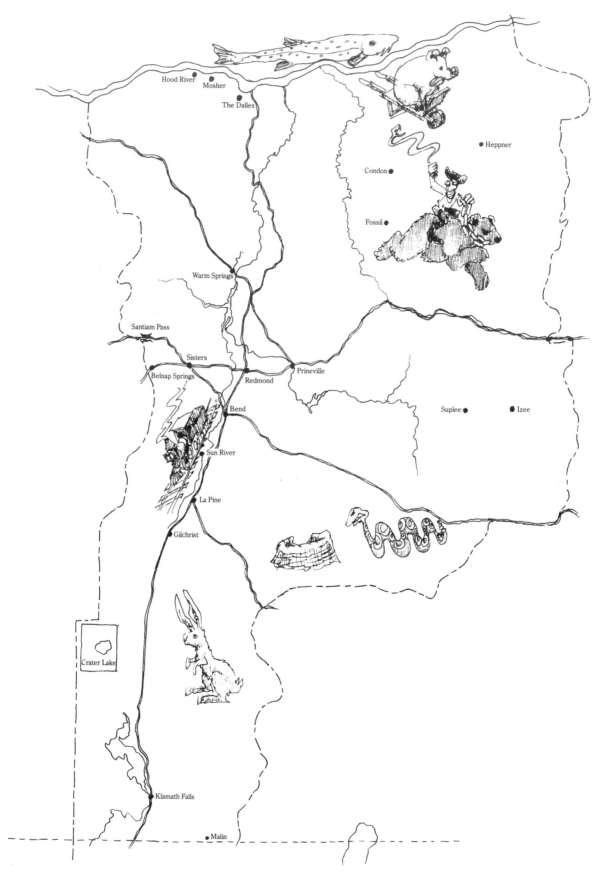

Hood River
Mosher
The Dalles
Heppner
Condon
Fossil
Warm Springs
Santiam Pass
Sisters
Belnap Springs
Redmond
Prineville
Suplee
Izee
Bend
Sun River
La Pine
Gilchrist
Crater Lake
Klamath Falls
Malin

tionists, it was small wonder there are "so many *Beaver Creeks* in Oregon and so few beaver."

In 1843, John C. Frémont, a U.S. Army lieutenant, traveled through Deschutes country and into the Klamath Basin. His guides were Kit Carson of frontier fame and Billy Chinook, a Warm Springs Indian. Frémont's party was searching for the mythical Multnomah River, believed to flow through the Cascades into the Willamette Valley. To aid in his "peaceful" expedition, Frémont hauled along a howitzer. After arriving in Klamath, the young engineer fired his cannon as a greeting, and the local Indians arrived shortly after bearing gifts. For good reason, the Central Oregon tribes received the news of settlers with suspicion and apprehension.

The year 1843 also marked a significant migration of settlers through the northern parts of Central Oregon, as more than 10,000 pioneers from Missouri braved the hardships of the Oregon Trail. Eventually more than 350,000 people traveled from Emigrant Park, Missouri, to Oregon, a trek of 2,200 miles, with 1,418 of those miles in Oregon Territory. The trip, averaging six months, was dangerous. Grave markers on trees, stumps, and rocks of the old Barlow Road commemorate the deaths of 672 emigrants, but it is certain that more than 30,000 people died during the mass exoduses to Oregon, causing the earlier settlers to call the route the "Bone Express." For the most part, the travelers were in great haste to get past the Cascades to the promised Oregon land; most followed the trail to The Dalles and then floated the remainder of the journey on the Columbia. But some feared the deadly rapids of the Columbia and instead chose to wind around Mt. Hood on the overland route blazed in 1845–46 by Samuel Barlow.

After months of travel, some newcomers to Oregon grew impatient. When Steven Meek proposed a high desert "shortcut" in 1845, members of the Blue Bucket Wagon Train paid Meek five dollars a wagon to take them south of the Oregon Trail and directly into the heart of the Willamette Valley. Somewhere east of John Day, Meek lost his way, and the Lost Wagon Train of 1845 circled for weeks in the late summer heat. The travelers drank tainted water and suffered from fevers and starvation; the animals literally left a trail of blood as they staggered across the rough and rocky terrain. Meek, warned by friends, stayed away from the wagon train because so many people who had buried relatives had threatened to shoot the scout on sight. However, the stories of death and hardship were secondary to the tales of yellow rock scraped from an unknown stream bed in a bright blue bucket. The children flattened out these stones for fishing sinkers and later threw them into a toolbox. Only after reaching the current site of Prineville did the travelers realize that somewhere in their wanderings they had crossed a stream littered with gold nuggets. During the last century and a half, many people have sought to retrace the steps of the Lost Wagon Train, hoping to discover the secret of Blue Bucket gold.

Until 1858 the U.S. Army, fearful of Indian uprisings, forbade settlement of Eastern Oregon. However, the discovery of gold quickly changed that policy. By the early 1860s, men who had vowed never again to set foot in the harsh country of Central Oregon were returning along the Oregon Trail with pickaxes and gold pans. Soon the Native American tribes revolted and were kept in check by the Army, excepting Teanamad, known by settlers as Chief Paulina, who left the Klamath Reservation in 1865, where he had been sent in exile; soon Teanamad organized the Walapi tribes for vengeance against the emigrants. In his first sweep through Central Oregon, Paulina killed scores of miners and settlers, creating the infamous Skull Hollow with the severed heads of his victims, and scattering the survivors back across the Cascades to safer lands. The Deschutes and Crooked river valleys were essentially abandoned, and the boomtown economy of Canyon City fell into severe depression. Only after Paulina was killed by rancher Howard Maupin in 1867 did serious settlement begin in Central Oregon, starting with the founding of Prineville in 1868.

Central Oregon cities grew up in a predictable pattern. Since this was range country, one of the first businesses was a blacksmith shop, followed, of course, by a livery stable. Homesteaders needed horses shod, farm implements repaired, and tools made. A mercantile store, a hotel, a church, a school, a post office, and several saloons completed the needs of a small town. From there, each town had its special priorities. Barney Prine built a racetrack from the Crooked River to the center of Prineville. Antelope residents created a community center and city hall, calling it Tammany Hall, anticipating by more than a century the political style of Baghwan Shree Rajneesh. Erroneously anticipating a long and prosperous gold rush, the government built a $105,000 mint at The Dalles, a building that never opened because the gold boom went bust.

Of course, after a few years of contending with gun-fighters, gamblers, and dance-hall girls, most communities tossed some money in the hat to build a jail. Unfortunately, according to historian David Braly, ''East Oregon jails were so bad that if a county wanted to get rid of a man, it had only to arrest him. That way he would be sure to break jail and flee the country.'' In 1882, for example, sheep thief Alva Tupper escaped from the Prineville jail simply by lifting a floorboard. In Redmond, says Joe McClay, whose father was city marshal in the first year of the city's existence, sometimes the prisoners needed a little help in escaping.

My dad was marshal then, when they built that and he'd take a prisoner down there, somebody'd get rough and they'd holler for him, my dad, to come get him. And he'd take them down there and throw them in that jail and tell them they'd better be quiet, or he'd see that they got a big fine next day. . . . Next morning he'd go down, open the door, and talk to them a little bit. He'd shut it and he'd say, ''What do you want for breakfast now?'' They'd tell him what they'd take for breakfast, and he'd say, ''OK, and I might be a little while before I get back. . . . I'm going to have a drink first.'' He'd go in the saloon and get his eye opener, as everyone did in those days, . . . and he'd leave the [jail] door unlocked, you see. Time he'd get back, why they'd be gone. And he never had no trouble. Never fined anybody. Never have any trouble with them coming back.

The law in Central Oregon was myopic, and some offenses counted more than others. As Braly notes, ''A man could shoot and kill ten men in gunfights without a word being said against him and then be hanged for stealing a horse.'' But it was cattle and sheep—not horses—that created open wars in the Central Oregon plains. After cattlemen had established a strong hold on the land, the

sheep ranchers came. Sheep became a problem to the cattlemen because the land was soon overgrazed, eaten down to where the grass could not recover. Soon sagebrush and juniper sprouted where once bunchgrass had flourished. Somewhere around 1896 cattlemen in the

Paulina area formed the Izee Sheep Shooters Association. Soon after, cattle ranchers were using knives, guns, and clubs to diminish the sheep population of Central Oregon. By the summer of 1905, the Crook County Sheep Shooters Association publicly claimed responsibility for the slaughter of nearly 10,000 sheep. The range wars also spilled over into Lake County, and 1904 marked the murder of Silver Lake merchant J. C. Conn, who had informed investigators about the business of the Crook County Sheep Shooters Association. However, because only one of the three bullets in Conn's body was found in his back, the coroner's jury ruled the death ''a clear case of suicide.''

In Oregon's High Desert, at an elevation near 3,000 feet, windstorms lasting several hours are common, raising huge dust balls that completely obliterate the horizon. When such a storm strikes, Central Oregon homesteaders simply say, ''Looks like the real estate is changing hands again.'' Periodically, land sharks have offered High Desert acreage at bargain rates, tempting the faithful with stories of waist-high grass and ample irrigation. Disappointed buyers arrived to find a different picture, especially in the 1930s and 1940s. Some gave up and left; others stayed and tried ''dry-farming'' because the High Desert had captured their hearts. Those who managed to endure occasionally woke to find half their homesteads and all their seed scattered over a neighbor's fields. As one homesteader said, ''It's just hell to get it all back again.''

The early settlers in Central Oregon were a rugged bunch, in many ways a reflection of the harsh and unyielding nature of a region where, according to Reub Long, homesteaders needed two essentials to survive—credit and water, both in short supply. Naturally, the place-names of the region are colorful and evocative, echoing the unforgiving climate, the struggle for survival, and the danger

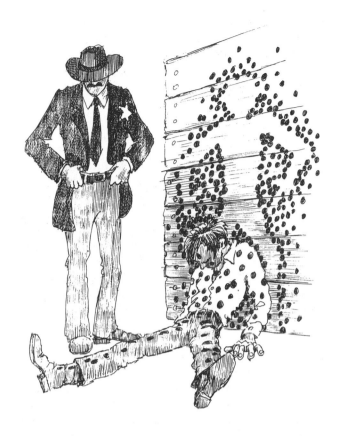

Heppner, has a huge boulder in the middle of town; this rock provided cover for a pioneer who was being chased by a band of Indians during the Bannock Wars.

Murderer's Creek saw the massacre of eight Grant County prospectors during the gold rush era. Battle Creek, flowing into the John Day River, marks the location where two Native American tribes fought each other in a major skirmish, ignoring for a moment the incursions of settlers. In the early 1900s, when the cattlemen in the Prineville area wanted to demonstrate their displeasure with sheepmen, the Crooked River Hanging Bridge gained its infamous name. Paulina in Crook County is named for Teanamad, the leader of the Walapi Paiutes who controlled huge sections of Eastern Oregon in the 1860s; Maupin, a small community near Antelope, is named for Howard Maupin, the rancher who shot Paulina.

Food and drink were natural concerns of the emigrants and travelers in Central Oregon, as expressed in the names left on landmarks. Wasco County residents were perhaps hungry when they named the Mutton Mountains for the flocks of mountain sheep grazing there. Hood River was originally called Dog River, a reference to the diet of pioneer travelers who chose dog meat over starvation. In the same way, Starveout gained its name in the rugged winter of 1884 when two loaded trains became stranded in deep Hood River snows. Unfortunately, the trapped travelers were far north of Bakeoven, the site of a Deschutes-area bakery. After crossing the Deschutes River on his way to the Canyon City gold strike, a German baker was attacked by Indians, who stole his horses. In true pioneer spirit, the unflappable German built a crude clay oven and began turning out a wide variety of breads, pastries, and muffins for the locals.

Needless to say, some of Central Oregon's place-names derive from the unhealthy life-styles of the early citizens. Sherman County's Bourbon was probably so named because rail hands, having tippled a bit too heavily, built this particular rail station crooked in relation to the path of the rail lines. Likewise, Lumtum Butte in Deschutes County bears a broad allusion to immoderate drinking. The word *lumtum* means "whiskey" or "rum" in Chinook Jargon. Even Mt. Vernon, which everyone assumes is an allusion to Colonial history and George Washington, recalls a popular and profitable Grant County racehorse. A small town on the Klamath River, just north of the California border, was named after Captain D. J. Ferree's bird dog, Keno, whose name celebrated a popular gambling game of the era.

Some of the place-names in the Big Bend land and the eastern valleys are simply colorful reflections of the settlers and their quirks. Klondike, once a station near Shaniko, earned its name when railroad workers threw down their tools and headed out for the Alaska gold strikes in 1898. The town of Ella owes its naming to a bribe. In order to stop his young daughter from crying over an

and lawlessness of the times, not to mention the oddities, eccentricities, and prejudices of the pioneer settlers.

Silica, east of Arlington, is a station barren of most everything but sand, and Devil's Canyon in Gilliam County is a basin so treacherous, say locals, that only Satan himself could have carved such stonework. During the fur-trapping era, unhappy travelers cursed the switchbacks of Crooked River many times in their journeys through present-day Crook, Jefferson, and Deschutes counties. It was not nostalgic southerners who named Gumbo, but frustrated immigrants who invariably got their wagon wheels stuck in the mud. On the other hand, Dry River in Crook and Deschutes counties yielded water only when immigrants dug in the gravelly channel. Klamath County's Bug Butte is an unhappy reminder of the periodic devastation of the forests by the western pine beetle.

A number of place-names in Central Oregon pay tribute to the rough-and-ready times of pioneer settlement. The Jefferson County town of Axehandle became known as Donnybrook after a group of Irish immigrants staged a battle-royal at a local fair. Today, Donnybrook is known as Kilts, retaining at least the Celtic flavor in its name. A bit to the north, Dukes Valley is known as the place where Hood River County pugilists met in the 1860s to "put up their dukes." Sometimes the fighting was more than just with fists. Wasco County has both a Deadman Spring and a Deadman Valley, each location notable for the discovery of a body, one white and one Indian. Lonerock, southwest of injury, Postmaster Frank Oviatt promised to name the town after her. Gilliam County's Olex is an enduring tribute to bad handwriting. In 1874, locals petitioned to name the town after a respected citizen, Alex Smith. Unfortunately, the petition was unreadable in Washington, and the bureaucrats offered Olex as their best guess. Hood River County's Sonny has a curious etymology. Mr. and Mrs. Charles Parker, nearby residents of this way station, proposed Little Boy, the name of their ranch, but settled on Sonny when telegraph operators complained.

Locals in Willow Creek thought their town name was bland, so they chose Madras instead, apparently naming the city after a colorful bolt of cloth sitting prominently in the window of the general store. In earlier times Contention was a stage stop fourteen miles north of Mitchell in Wheeler County. Returning home from finishing school, Miss Frankie Parsons objected to the unsophisticated name and proposed Twickenham, after a popular poem read at school. Residents of Kent put suggestions in a hat to name their town. When the winner was drawn, the contributor simply said that he liked Kent because the name was "nice and short." Brothers was not named to complement Sisters, as many people have supposed, but because six sets of brothers brought their families to settle there.

Some Big Bend country names derive from frontier politics. Sherman County was first proposed as Fulton County, after a well-known Eastern Oregon politician. But after two readings of the bill in the state house of representatives, disgruntled "wet siders" removed Fulton's

name and slipped in that of William Tecumseh Sherman, the Civil War hero whom Fulton had once slighted. Terrebone was once called Hillman, a blended name recalling the two principals in the Great Rail Race of Deschutes County (see Bend, p. 101), James J. Hill and E. H. Harriman. Unfortunately, shortly after the town was named, a real-estate swindler actually named Hillman was arrested in town. In an apparent attempt to keep others from thinking Hillman had been named for a crook, the townsfolk started stamping Terrebone, meaning "good earth," on the outgoing mail. Richmond was named by R. N. Donnelly to gall a political adversary. Donnelly argued with pioneer resident William Walters about the location of a school, and when Walters became contentious, Donnelly named the town after the home of Jefferson Davis, another rebellious fellow. Arlington on the Columbia River was probably named by southern sympathizers after the hometown of Robert E. Lee.

Of course, Central Oregon has its fair share of locations bearing Native American or Chinook Jargon names. Ketchketch Butte near Crane Prairie is named for Fox of Native American mythology, and Talapus Butte, near Sparks Lake, is the home of the trickster Coyote. In Deschutes County is Lemish Butte, the abode of the Thunderers, five powerful deities of the Klamath nation. Hehe Butte in Wasco County is just one of many sacred locations in Oregon where the *hehes*, or fun-loving wood spirits, congregated. The *skookums*, evil and powerful forest gods, gathered at queer places such as Cultus Lake, the name implying "bad" in Chinook Jargon. Wampus in Klamath County is another such place, the word meaning "forest demon," a solitary beast not unlike the far-ranging Sasquatch. Memaloose Island in the Columbia River was a sacred burial ground near The Dalles, at least until settler Vic Trevitt was buried there in 1883 under an expensive granite monolith, defiling the ground for the Native Americans.

Needless to say, Central Oregon place-name legends are sometimes pleasant and positive reminders of the reasons people immigrated to the middle regions of Oregon. Horse Heaven was a land of tall grasses and pure waters, the perfect grazing meadow. Early, a town in the John Day Valley, was named for its long growing season and warm, windless climate, while Mt. Defiance in Hood River County was noted as the last promontory to give up its winter snows. Central Oregon vistas are breathtaking, and the sights include such natural monuments as Cathedral Ridge in Hood River County, Courthouse Rock in Grant County, and, of course, world-famous Crater Lake in Klamath County.

Belknap Springs

Lane County. These springs, located on the old route to the McKenzie Pass—now Highway 126—were discovered in 1869 by R. S. Belknap, who planned a resort there. The post was originally called Salt Springs, but changed to Belknap's Springs in 1875 and to its current name in 1891.

In the previous century, when the settlers were less prepared for harsh weather, there were some infamous winters, such as the "Double Winter" of 1881. At Rail Creek Ranch in the upper McKenzie Valley, fish guide and storyteller Prince Helfrich remembered the Belknap family's strange experience in one of those unbelievable winters, a time when even the wild animals feared the elements more than they feared humans.

THE UNUSUAL BARN CATS AT BELKNAP SPRINGS

The Belknaps were some of the earliest settlers, and a lot of places around here were named for the Belknaps. You know, Belknap Springs, the Belknap Bridge, Belknap Ranch, and the Belknap Crater up in the High Country were all named after them. The last of the Belknaps just died a little while ago [during the 1960s]. Arthur Belknap, he was the oldest, and he was the one with a very clear memory. He could tell stories about this country in the very early days. He said that they used to have at least four or five feet of snow up here in this High Country. Much more snow then. And he said that it would chase all the game down here into the valley. The elk would come down here and the wolves and the cougar—and all the game, they would have quite a time. He said that they would have to lock their barns every night.

Arthur Belknap told me a story about the old Belknap place. He said that he was just a young fellow, and he went out to milk one morning when the snow was about five feet deep. When he went out to the barn and opened the door, why he said the old cow was just acting crazy. He shut the door again, and she wanted to get out. He couldn't imagine what was wrong. And so he opened the door again and peeked in. Right up in the hay-mow sat a cougar. So he shut the door again and ran back to the house and got a gun. He killed that cougar. But there were three cougars in the hay. That's what scared the cows so bad. The other two cougars escaped—they jumped out and ran.

Bend

Deschutes County. Population 19,724. This city on the banks of the Deschutes River was first called Farewell Bend because it was the location where travelers caught their last view of the river. Farewell Bend was also the only available ford for many miles.

Although the city of Bend itself is a pleasant and lush place, Big Bend land is a cold, dry, and rocky land. Some suggest that the small rocks of the countryside are the best available fertilizer. Commonly sung in pioneer days was this folk song, a reflection on the disappointing climate at the End of the Trail. Like the prominent Willamette Valley versions, "Big Bend Land" is a parody of the Christian hymn "Beulah Land" (see Blodgett, p. 37).

BIG BEND LAND

I've reached the land of dust and heat
Where nothing grows for man to eat;
The sun would blister both our feet,
This old land is hard to beat.

Chorus:
Oh, Big Bend Land, poor Big Bend Land,
As on your sandy soil I stand,
I look away across the plain
And wonder why it never rains.
Then Gabriel blows the trumpet sound
And says the rain has passed around.

Bend made the news in the years 1908 to 1911 when James J. Hill and E. H. Harriman scrambled to build rail lines from Wishram to Bend. Harriman's competition with Hill created the Great Rail Race of Deschutes County, with both men attempting to secure rights for lines through Central Oregon to California. During the fervor to reach Bend first, Harriman's Union Pacific workers and Hill's Great Northern employees continuously engaged in sabotage and gang warfare as the ribbons of rails stretched down opposite sides of the Deschutes River. Nearly 5,000 men labored in the Great Race, and officers of the law were unable to quell daily outbreaks of violence. The Wishram-to-Bend segment was finally completed by Hill in

1911, after he agreed to deed Harriman a different section of the line. The completed project became known as the Oregon Trunk Railway because portions of track were eventually owned by Southern Pacific, Union Pacific, Great Northern, and the Spokane, Portland, and Seattle railways.

In 1911, when Hill completed the Deschutes line, Bend became an important rail center. According to Claude Vandevert, the first train into town attracted a huge crowd; people from all over the Deschutes region came to see the arrival. Of course, they crowded right up against the tracks on both sides. The engineer, deciding to play a little joke, slowed to a crawl, leaned out of his cab, and motioned the crowd away from the tracks. "Back out of the way," he yelled. "We need room to turn the train around." Immediately, everyone stepped back from the tracks.

From the early 1900s, railroad workers shared a common jargon and a series of gestures particular to their work, many of these incomprehensible to the outsider. Here is a typical version of railroaders' talk, with a glossary of terms still in use today. The terms were collected in 1974 from a Union Pacific agent.

HOGMASTERS AND BAKEHEADS

It was a bright Tuesday morning. The hogmaster *had a* call figure *for 8 a.m. at the Bend Branch line. So he went for* beans *in downtown Bend. When he arrived at the yard house, the* brass pounder *was busy at his desk, copying a* consist *for the next train arrival.*

"This incoming arrival—is it a hotshot *or a* drag?" *asked the hogmaster.*

"I don't know," said the brass pounder, "but here comes the bakehead. *Ask him."*

The bakehead walked in with the new man, Jones, who had just bumped *his way onto the Bend run. Jones was a* deadhead *with lots of experience, and he chewed his tobacco with a determined look.*

"Jonesy," said the hogmaster. "I thought you were dog-catching *up at The Dalles."*

"Naw, I went up there last night, but they sent me back with the outlaws. *Those guys are still asleep, but Sawyer was snoring so loud that I took off."*

"Where did you leave the outlaws?" asked the hogmaster. Jones just scratched his side *in a deliberate motion, and the bakehead said, "I don't blame you. Trying to sleep in a* crib *full of rail hands ain't easy."*

"Well," said the brass pounder, "here comes the load from Shaniko. It looks like a manifest."

"Right," said the yardmaster. "We're gonna need some help. I'll go get those boomers *that rode into town yesterday." And so he walked out of the yard house and caught a ride on the* goat.

RAILROADIN' GLOSSARY

The fireman is the **bakehead**, so called because he had his head over the fire so much. Bakeheads were also called **bell-ringers** or **blackies**.

Beans is any meal taken during working hours. The term derives from Depression days, when beans were a frequent staple.

Boomers are transient rail workers, drifters who "boom" from one job to another, staying only a short while. In pioneer days, the best rail workers were in great demand and "boomed" from one job to a better one with short notice [probably from German **Bummer**, pronounced "boomer"].

The **brass pounder** in earlier times was a telegraph operator. The telegraph keys were made of brass so that the current wouldn't burn them. Today the brass pounder handles train-line communications with modern conveniences.

To **bump** someone is to use seniority to secure a position or a desirable run.

A **consist** is a list of the cars on a train.

A **call figure** is the scheduled time for a new crew to report at the yard, usually one hour after the train's arrival, allowing time for switching of cars.

A heavy train or slow freight is a **drag**.

The **deadhead** is the brakeman. The term also refers to riding free on a pass: "They **deadheaded** the bakehead home to Bend."

Dog-catching occurs when a fresh crew relieves one that has already worked the legal twelve-hour shift.

The **goat** is the yard engine that switches cars in the yard, perhaps deriving from an earlier time when engines "butted" cars rather than pulling them.

The **hogmaster** is an engineer, also known as a **hoghead**, **hogger**, or **hogineer**. The term derives from the locomotive, known as the **hog**, probably dating back to steam engine days. The opposite of a drag is a **hotshot**, a fast-moving freight.

Manifest is another term for a fast-freight, or hotshot.

Outlaws are the crew replaced by the dog-catchers.

Scratching one's side (gesture) indicates the caboose, a blatant reference to the fleas that inevitably occupied the caboose, also called the **crib** or the **crummy**.

Sometimes it is best not to intrude upon the esoteric lore of a working group. One young woman on The Dalles line tried to borrow the gestures of the rail workers and learned an embarrassing lesson, according to a story collected by Nancy Anderson in June 1974 for the Mills Archives.

There used to be a girl working at Messner. The train was supposed to drop off ice there. So when the crew stopped, she asked what sign to give for ice. So they gave her the sign for sexual intercourse and told her the train would respond when it went by. So the train comes by, and the girl goes and gives 'em this sign, and the whole crew gave it back to her.

Condon

Gilliam County. Population 635. The town, also the county seat, was perhaps named for Dr. Thomas Condon, a nationally renowned geologist from the University of Oregon and a frequent visitor to the local fossil beds, or for his nephew, Judge J. B. Condon. However, William H. McNeal says that both theories are wrong; the town was named for another relative, Harry Condon, an Alkali lawyer, who was willing to draw up the town papers in 1884 for no charge.

In most parts of Oregon—in fact, throughout most of the world—the insiders tell jokes about the outsiders. Naturally, people from big cities or from the sophisticated East Coast are easy targets in rural Oregon. In this sense, "Pig Farming, Eastern Style" has similarities to "The Portland Hunter" (see Baker City, p. 126) and "The 'Horned Coon' Hunt" (see Lakeview, p. 158); all these tales are told at the expense of outsiders, who have failed to learn common sense and folk wisdom from the land. A Central Oregon farmhand in the summer of 1971 told the story that inspired this description of newcomers to Condon.

PIG FARMING, EASTERN STYLE

There was this guy who came in from the East in the pioneer days, and he didn't know much about farm life. But somebody convinced him to go into the pig business. So he bought a little place down near Condon and settled into an old shack on the property with his wife.

So the next morning a neighbor came by and said, "What are you raisin'?"

"Pigs," came the reply from the Easterner, pointing to an old sow he had bought in Salem.

"Where's the boar?" said the neighbor. But the Easterner just looked puzzled. All he had was the one old sow.

So the neighbor said that a man four miles up the holler had a fine boar that he might lend for service. And the next morning the Easterner said goodbye to his wife and drove the sow off in the direction of the next farm. But he couldn't get her to walk up that long hill. So he tied on a rope and tried to lead her, but she wouldn't budge.

Finally the Easterner borrowed an old iron wheelbarrow and hauled her up the hill, the man sweating and cursing the whole way. When he arrived, the man with the boar was agreeable to a deal. So the two men sat and drank coffee for a few hours while the pigs got acquainted.

Well, the next morning the Easterner went out to the pigsty and found no piglets, just the sow. So he rigged up the wheelbarrow and hauled the sow back up the hill. The neighbor didn't say much, but he poured the Easterner some more coffee, and they jawed away the afternoon while the pigs made friends again.

Dawn came on the third morning, but the Easterner was so sore from hauling that sow around that he couldn't get out of bed. He called down to his wife, however, saying, "Honey, go check to see if that sow has any little pigs this morning." So she did.

After a few minutes, the wife returned, and the husband asked about the piglets.

"Nope," said the woman. "She ain't got no piglets yet, but she is sittin' in the wheelbarrow."

Crater Lake

Klamath County. In 1853 a prospector, John Hillman, was searching out the Lost Cabin Mine, when he became the first pioneer to see majestic Crater Lake. Sixteen years later a group of picnickers from Jacksonville gave the lake its name. In 1902, through the efforts of Judge William Gladstone Steel, the lake and its surroundings were made Crater Lake National Park.

Crater Lake held some mystery for the Klamaths and other Native Americans in the area. Some of the tribes considered it the abode of evil *skookums*; others considered the lake sacred and went to the rim to mark "marriage trees." A young fir was split at its top; if, after a year, the tree had grown back together, the planned marriage would be harmonious. Crater Lake, for a long time rumored bottomless, has been measured at over 2,000 feet deep. Two eerie eruptions through the deep blue lake surface are Wizard Island and the Phantom Ship. The Phantom Ship, having the appearance of a craggy sea craft, protrudes sixty-five feet above the waterline.

Crater Lake was formed about 6,600 years ago at the eruption of Mount Mazama, which was approximately 12,000 feet high. After the huge mountain exploded, the remaining base and the caldera filled gradually with rainwater and snow, forming the pristine blue lake that remains today. Of course, the Klamath Indians have another version of the beginnings of Crater Lake.

THE CHIEF OF THE UNDER WORLD

Before the white man came, the spirits of the world talked more directly to the people. At that time, there was no lake—just the opening to the world below, which stood high on the top of The Mountain. On special days the Chief of the Under World came from his hole in the earth to talk to the elders.

One day the Chief of the Under World came forth to see Loha, a beautiful young girl with long, dark braids and fiery eyes. He was smitten with her, and he made an offer of marriage to her father, the Chief of the Upper World. But Loha convinced her father to say "no," and the Chief of the Under World returned to his home in The Mountain in great anger.

The spirit chief thought of a way to win Loha. He called forth his greatest warrior and sent him as messenger to the Klamath land with offers of horses and skins, more than a man could count in a day. But the Chief of the Upper World listened again to his daughter and turned away the messenger shamed and empty-handed. This rebuke enraged the Chief of the Under World, and he began to spit forth fire and flames.

Finally the Chief of the Under World vowed to destroy the world above. He climbed to the top of his mountain, stood at the peak, and hurled liquid fire across the entire Klamath land. But the Chief of the Upper World fought back, standing atop Mount Shasta in full battle dress. As the two chiefs blackened the land with their battle, the Klamath people ran to Klamath Lake and jumped in. As they shivered there in the waters, the elders said to each other, "We can only save ourselves with a sacrifice to the Chief of the Upper World. Who will do so?" But the young warriors of the tribe remained in the water, some breathing through tule reeds.

So the two oldest medicine men of the Klamath tribe stepped from the water and walked toward the mountain home of the Chief of the Under World. They carefully moved up the east side of the ancient mountain, with fire raining all around them. For a moment they stood at the end of the opening. Then, at once, they jumped into the fiery hole.

The brave deed of the medicine men was favored by the great Chief of the Upper World. He raised his powerful hand above his head and threw an immense bolt of fire at the Chief of the Under World. The earth trembled, and The Mountain collapsed around the spirit chief. When the morning came, the mountain was gone, and only a huge hole remained.

In the years that followed, the snows came, and the rains fell. The home of the Chief of the Under World filled with water and became silent. But it is a fearful place for the Klamaths. They will not go there and look into the blue waters, for it is sure that they would see the face of the Chief of the Under World staring back.

The Dalles

Wasco County. Population 10,900. *Dalle*, meaning flat stone, was the term used by French traders to describe a river rapids. A French trapper, Joseph Lavendure, was the first settler in the Wasco area, and the French gave The Dalles its distinctive name. Before dams appeared on the Columbia, the Indians found these rapids one of the most abundant fishing areas in the Northwest. Also, The Dalles location served as the most important trade center in the precontact period, perhaps for 9,000 years before white settlement.

In the earliest period of trading, the area was known as La Grande Dalle de la Columbia; later, the name Dalles City was used; in 1853, this post became Wascopam (small bowl of horn); by 1860 the name Dalles dominated. The Dalles is the parent town of Central Oregon, an important intersection of the Columbia River and established Indian trails. In 1854 The Dalles became the seat of "Old Wasco" County.

Just downstream, "one sleep" below The Dalles, is the place known as the Bridge of the Gods, long celebrated in Native American lore as a natural land mass spanning the Great River of the West. It is an oft-told tale, perhaps appearing in as many versions as there are tellers. The existence of such a natural bridge was supposedly known by all the Indian tribes west of the Mississippi. In 1890 Frederick Homer Balch wrote, "One can see submerged the trees beneath the waters of the river, still standing upright, as they stood before the bridge fell in and the waters rose over them. It is a strange, weird sight, this forest beneath the river, the waters washing above the tree tops, fish swimming among the leafless branches; it is desolate, specter-like, beyond all words." Poetry aside, geologists today doubt the existence of such a land bridge. Nonetheless, the story of "The Bridge of the Gods" is one of the most pervasive in Oregon lore. The following version of "Tahmahnawis" builds on details provided by Medford's Greg Culver, who heard the myth-legend from a member of the Klickitat tribe.

TAHMAHNAWIS

A long time ago when the world was still young, all the people were happy. The Great Spirit gave the people food in plenty, and the sun shone to keep them warm. At this time the Great Indian god Sahale had two powerful sons, Wy'East and Klickitat, who quarreled constantly over who would rule the most land.

Soon the Great Spirit Sahale became impatient. While the brothers were asleep, he took them to a new land—one with many mountains and forests and a mighty river flowing between the mountains. On both sides of the river, the land was rich and beautiful. To connect the banks of the river, the Great Spirit built a bridge of stone.

Sahale called the brothers to the middle of the bridge. "Now," said the Great Spirit, "you will each shoot an arrow. Where your feathers fall will be your homeland." Wy'East shot his arrow south and became chief of the Multnomah people; his brother shot his arrow north and became chief of the Klickitat people.

"You will both become great chiefs," said Sahale. The river will separate your lands, but your people can travel this bridge as long as you remain friendly and peaceful."

Many years passed, and the brothers were at peace. The people crossed the bridge with their many ponies to visit family and friends. But one day the brothers became selfish and greedy; they began to quarrel again. These arguments made the Great Spirit angry, and he punished them by taking away the sun. The people had no fire and soon became very cold. They prayed to the Great Spirit to give them back the sun. Once again Sahale decided to help his people. He went to the old woman, Loo-wit, who had not joined in the selfish quarreling of her people. She still had a fine fire in her lodge.

"Share your fire with your people, and I will grant you what you want most," promised the Great Spirit.

"I am old. I wish to be young and beautiful again," she answered.

"After one sleep," said the Great Spirit, "you will be young and beautiful. Then you must take your fire to the bridge so that people from both sides may share it. And you must keep it burning as a reminder to the people of the kindness of Sahale."

The next morning, the sun rose again on now-beautiful Loo-wit, who was sitting beside her fire on the Bridge of the Gods. The people saw the fire, and soon their lodges were warm again. All was peaceful. The brothers also saw the fire and came often to visit the beautiful maiden who tended it. Loo-wit was fond of both brothers, but she couldn't decide which she liked better.

Soon the brothers became jealous over Loo-wit. They began to fight with each other, and the people on both sides of the bridge began to fight as well. Many warriors died.

The Great Spirit was very angry. He shook Tahmahnawis, *the Bridge of Peace, causing the great rock formation to fall into the river. Then he changed Wy'East and Klickitat to mountains towering above the river and Loo-wit to a beautiful peak nearby. But the brothers did not stop fighting. They still competed for Loo-wit's affections. Soon fire spewed from their tops, and they hurled hot stones at each other. Some of the stones fell into the river, where the Columbia River is now narrow and swift at The Dalles.*

Still today you can see Wy'East, Klickitat, and Loo-wit. Wy'East became Mt. Hood, and Klickitat became Mt. Adams. To the west is Loo-wit, the beautiful snow-capped Mt. St. Helens.

Fort Rock

Lake County. In 1938, Oregon anthropologist L. W. Cressman discovered sagebrush sandals in a caldera cave near Fort Rock, the natural amphitheater cut by prehistoric lake waves. The sandals, found on property owned by Fort Rock yarn-spinner Reub Long, were carbon-dated to an age of about 9,000 years and are among the oldest artifacts ever found west of the Rocky Mountains. Fort Rock, famous for its geology and its folksy native son, is one of the driest spots in all of Oregon, receiving rainfall of less than ten inches each year. As Reub Long says, "There was a Fort Rock cowboy up on my spread who had never seen rain. One day he heard a clatter on the tin roof, so the damn fool stepped out of the bunkhouse and got hit smack in the forehead with a big raindrop. Why, it took six buckets of sand in his face to revive him."

A former resident, LaDessa Walter, offers a musical complaint about the unforgiving Fort Rock climate, set to the tune of the traditional hymn "Beulah Land."

Oh, Fort Rock hot and Fremont dry,
As in the rimrock vale we lie
And when I go to view my rye
I almost wish that I might die.

For the average citizen, early-day entertainment in Central Oregon usually meant box-socials, Sunday School picnics, and community dances. Nearly every town had a dance hall, and on Saturday night people would ride for hours to visit friends in Bend, The Dalles, or Klamath Falls. Locals scratched out tunes on the guitar, fiddle, accordion, and (in rare instances) the piano. At four o'clock in the morning, the women would fry up breakfast; then the dancers would gather their sleeping children and head for home. On Sunday afternoons in hot weather, Big Bend residents would meet at the ice caves, bringing along jars full of fruits and vegetables, sharing their bounty and trading foodstuffs in preparation for the long winters ahead. Near Fort Rock are a series of ice caves, beautiful and refreshing places for a Sunday picnic. Within the ice caves are a number of miniature volcanoes, thirty-foot cones created by leaking gases long ago in the time when the lava beds were cooling.

Reub Long described a humorous incident at the ice caves in *The Oregon Desert*. Two boys, knowing the favorite picnic spot for Fort Rock families, chose one of the volcanic cones at the back of that particular cave. Then they labored for several days to pack the cone with sticks, dry grass, juniper branches, wood chips, and any other refuse they could find. Finally the boys poured kerosene into the cone and waited anxiously for Sunday.

On that lovely afternoon a great many of Fort Rock's finest were gathered in the favorite ice cave. Married couples spread the picnic blankets and sent the children scurrying for ice to make ice cream, while young lovers flirted and whispered in the cool, crisp air of the cave.

Suddenly, "all hell broke loose!" The boys had slipped unnoticed to the rear of the cave and climbed up the back side of the cone. When one of them dropped a lighted match into the opening, the miniature volcano began to smoke and belch flames. Within minutes, the entire cave was in mayhem.

Children screamed, women fainted, and—to the horror of everyone—a number of husbands and gallant boyfriends leaped onto their horses, leaving their wives and children to face the catastrophe alone. Later, when the smoke had cleared and the excitement was over, several of these husbands and lovers returned to the caves to face the accusing eyes of those left behind. As Long observed, the incident in the ice caves at Fort Rock raised the status of some and lowered the reputations of others.

For most long-term citizens of Central Oregon, the mere mention of "Bend" and "Fort Rock" calls to mind Central Oregon's best-known storyteller. Along with Hathaway Jones in Southern Oregon and "Huckleberry" Finn in the Willamette Valley, Reub Long is one of Oregon's favorite yarn-spinners. Not only was Long an outrageous storyteller, he was a kind of high desert sage as well. In many ways, Long's reflective thoughts embody the folk wisdom of Central Oregon.

Proverbs, such as these from *The Oregon Desert*, are collective wisdom, truths passed from generation to generation. The proverb is a traditional statement—a memorable phrase, sometimes characterized by poetic language, such as antithesis, metaphor, and paradox. The proverb, usually only a single sentence, functions in one of several ways: to preserve the values of a community, to educate youngsters, or to exclude outsiders. Reub Long's proverbs lean a different direction; they remind us of the values of the

past, when most of America was rural and life, as it remains today in much of Big Bend land, was far less complicated.

CENTRAL OREGON WISDOM

☐ *If you have a long, hard ride, a trot is the best gait.*
☐ *The nicest time in all the day is tomorrow morning about sunup.*
☐ *When there was only one man camped at the water hole, democracy was easy.*
☐ *A man should be judged by what he stands for—also by what he falls for.*
☐ *A man was digging a ditch. A passerby asked him what he was digging it for. He said, thoughtfully, "So far as I know, it's to get money to buy food to give me strength to dig the ditch."*
☐ *It's lots better to get home with a light load than to be stuck out on the road with a heavy one.*
☐ *Don't build a reputation when young that will be hard to keep when old.*
☐ *Of all the persons I've known, personally, who tried to be great, the only time they were the most important persons present was at their own funerals.*
☐ *Lazy people work the hardest.*
☐ *Conduct yourself in such a manner that you are in good company when you are alone.*
☐ *Nothing gets a man into such hot water so quickly as good credit. A lot of my troubles have come upon me because my credit was too good. Be careful not to acquire too much of it. It has ruined more people than bad credit ever did.*
☐ *Most people camp too close to the creek to make good coffee.*
☐ *I was never too good a horse trader because, if I had a nice horse, it was hard for me to find anyone who liked him better than I did.*
☐ *If you take care of your cows, your cows will take care of you.*

Fossil

Wheeler County. Population 399. In 1876, while clearing land at his ranch, Postmaster Thomas B. Hoover discovered some well-preserved fossils. This archeological find prompted Hoover to stamp Fossil on the mail that went west from his post office.

Fossil is surrounded by some large ranching operations, including those run by the competing families, the Steirwalds and the Rattrays. At both ranches, the riders are tough and rugged. Terry Logan and Glen Shearer collected this story in 1971 from a Rattray ranch hand. According to the fieldworkers, it is a common tale around the Condon-Fossil area. The collectors speculated—probably correctly—that the Steirwalds have their own version of this whopper.

THE STEIRWALDS AND THE RATTRAYS

Well, seems several years ago there was a Steirwald cowboy comes bustin' through the brush up there in the top of the mountains—back of Kinzua somewhere. He's ridin' a bear, usin' a log-chain for a bridle, and whippin' him with a rattlesnake. He's a Steirwald rider. There's a sheepherder sittin' there in the camp, and he busted out of the timber, and the sheepherder yelled at him and says, "Come on over and have a cup of coffee."

This old cowboy, he slid his bear to a halt, wrapped his log-chain around a tree, tied the bear up, throwed the rattle snake on the ground, and put a rock on him to hold him down. He went over and the sheepherder had a fire goin' there and a coffee pot sittin' in the fire. And [the sheepherder] says, "Have a cup of coffee."

This Steirwald cowboy, he just reached down and picked up this boiling pot of hot coffee, jerked the lid off of her and drank her right down, right from there. Man, that sheepherder thought, that's quite a thing goin' on, you know. He says, "Sit down and we'll josh awhile."

And this Steirwald rider, he walked back over to the bear and stepped on, grabbed his rattlesnake, and says, "I'd sure like to, but there's a Rattray man after me."

Gilchrist

Klamath County. Gilchrist, between Lapine and Chemult on Highway 97, is a company town, developed in 1938 by the Gilchrist Timber Company. In 1970 Sally Lillis visited Gilchrist and interviewed several longtime residents, including descendants of the founder.

Gilchrist is a stratified community, consisting of "this side of town," where the upper class lives, "the other side of town," where the millworkers live, and the village center. According to Lillis, "This is a distinction understood and accepted by all those living in Gilchrist." Furthermore, every building in Gilchrist [1970] is painted the same color, with all the dwellings on "the other side" trimmed in intricate stenciling that resembles Swedish designs. Until recently, the Gilchrist mill employed most of the people in town, and logger stories are common to the community.

In 1950 Richard M. Dorson coined the term "fakelore" to describe stories that mimic the folk tradition but do not circulate in the oral tradition. When the word "folklore" is mentioned, many people think of Paul Bunyan tales. However, Paul Bunyan is largely the creation of James Stevens and his imitators. In fact, Paul Bunyan tales have rarely been told in the woods, and most versions exist in literature such as Stevens's *Paul Bunyan Comes West* or Virginia Tunney's *Ol' Paul, The Mighty Logger.* Occasionally, however, contrived tales have found their way into the oral tradition, where the creative process reinvents them as folklore. The following Paul Bunyan anecdotes from *Oregon Oddities* illustrate both folklore and fakelore.

PAUL BUNYAN IN OREGON

Paul was never a slouch when it came to work. Realizing that he was not accomplishing as much as he was capable of doing, he invented the double-bladed ax with the flexible handle. He was thus able to chop down two trees at once. The grindstone was so large that when it made one revolution it was payday again.

In spite of his industriousness, Paul did get behind with his work. It was then that he invented the "day stretcher," which really was not a happy contrivance. With this, he stretched a lot of days to twice their length. He found, however, that if he had gone behind in his work on short days, he went behind twice as much on the long days. He abandoned the day stretcher and the Eskimos got hold of it. The lads under the northern lights did not know how to use it, and they stretched a day until it was six months long. Naturally, the night as well became six months long. Some of the days Paul did not use were lost, and whenever there is an extra-long day anyplace, it is one of Paul's. Some people come across these long days just before payday. . . .

One of the tragedies in Paul's life came when he fell in love with three sisters in Oregon. Paul always did things in an expansive way. The three sisters all died, and he buried them together. The earth he heaped over their graves as monuments are the Three Sisters Mountains of the Cascades. Long ago as Paul hurried into Oregon across the Oregon-California border, the Blue Ox was traveling so fast that a

swamphook jerked from the sled and stuck in the Cascade Mountains. When the ox pulled out the swamphook, the hole formed Crater Lake. . . .

Paul found Babe, the blue ox, during the winter of the blue snow, when she was a calf, half starved and nearly frozen. Paul took her home and fed her on moose moss. As a calf, she was big as four full-grown Texas steers, and Paul had to carry her in his arms. During babyhood Babe grew so fast she doubled in size every two hours. When full-grown, she measured seven of Paul's ax-handles, a plug of tobacco, and two small tomato cans. She was so long in the body that Paul carried field glasses so he could see from one end to the other.

In Paul's camp was a road so crooked that loggers met themselves several times while traveling it. Paul got a log-chain, wrapped it around the end of the road, had the blue ox pull at it, and made the road straight. There were many miles left over, and Paul sold them to the state of Oregon for the Pacific Highway.

Babe also helped Paul solve the problem of the Crooked River. He hitched her to one end. When she pulled it straight, it was too long. Paul went to the North Pole and caught a blizzard in a bag. He brought the blizzard south and froze the river, cut off what he didn't need, hauled it out on the prairie, and left it. When it thawed, it made Malheur Lake. . . .

Paul and Babe still live on in the Oregon woods and may be found in any logging camp where Knights of the Caulked Boots and Stagged Pants are gathered about the

fires of an evening, yarning of this and that. Wayfarers along the dark aisles under the pines plainly hear the thud of Babe's hooves and the rumble of Paul's voice as he talks to her. When the chinook wind rushes through the pine and fir, the swish of Paul's great double-bladed ax can be heard. As long as there are mighty forests to test their strength, Paul and Babe will live.

Heppner

Morrow County. Population 1,408. The first settlement in this area was originally called Butter Creek, after a stream far to the east, a location where, during the Cayuse War, some enlisted men raided the officers' mess for butter to put on flapjacks. However, in 1873, the location was named Heppner, after merchant Henry Heppner opened the first store there. Heppner was one of many pioneer store owners who had a simple method for deciding how much to charge his customers for bringing supplies to the wilderness: "Keep raising prices until the customers scream like hell. If no one complains, you're not charging enough."

Heppner was nearly destroyed on June 14, 1903, when a dam on Willow Creek above the city broke, endangering most of the residents. Even though more than 250 people drowned, swift action by the "Paul Revere of Oregon" saved hundreds more. Leslie Matlock, observing the collapse of the dam, rode ahead into town and galloped full speed through Heppner, Lexington, and Ione, shouting "Get to the hills! Get to the hills!" Until his death in 1958, Matlock continued to carry a gold-headed cane, given him in grateful thanks by the survivors of the Heppner Flood.

Not everyone involved in the flood was as heroic as Matlock. Consider, for example, the experience of Hood River's stuttering coroner, Charles "Binks" Burget, called east to help bury the dead. This "Binks" story was told by Hal Fancher, who arrived in The Dalles in 1914, and the narrative was collected by his grandson, Peter Gay. Fancher is a master storyteller, says Gay: "He builds his stories, including always just the proper amount of facts to keep the listener informed, but curious—so that once the punch line of a joke or the conclusion of a story rolls around, you are usually so anxious to hear how the story comes out, you can hardly sit still." Using no gestures, but a broad variety of facial expressions, Fancher told one of two "Binks" stories (see Mosier, p. 113). Binks seems to represent a segment of the American working class from an earlier era—fruitful and productive, but not always respectful of others' customs, in this case the Chinese community.

BINKS AND THE HEPPNER FLOOD

Speaking of Binks reminds me of a story Binks used to tell about an experience he had during the Heppner Flood.

This terrible catastrophe occurred in 1903, when a sudden cloudburst on Willow Creek swept down on the town of Heppner, leaving 225 Heppner inhabitants drowned. They sent out a call for all available undertakers and embalmers to come and help get the bodies in shape for burial.

Binks went up there with a group, and one of the bodies he had to take care of was a well known and wealthy Chinaman. There were lots of Chinamen in the Heppner area, as there were around The Dalles in those days. Binks said that one of the Chinese customs that was always observed was to put a coin in the dead person's mouth so that they would have enough money to pay their ferry charges across the River Styx, when they reached "the other side."

While he was working on this Chinaman, a couple of his friends came up and put a ten-dollar gold piece in his mouth, and Binks figured that was entirely too much for anyone to have to pay for ferry charges. So he watched for the opportunity to take the ten dollars out and slip in a 25- or 50-cent piece instead.

But the Chinamen watched the body so carefully that, when Binks finally got a chance to get the ten dollars, he couldn't pry the Chinaman's mouth open far enough to get it out.

Binks said he lost the ten dollars, and "the Chinaman had f-f-f-far too much much to pay his f-f-f-fare."

Hood River

Hood River County. Population 4,490. According to Joanne Kment, speaking to folklore collector LaVada Barber, the naming of this community dates to the pioneer era: "It was during the time of the explorers. They were following the Columbia Gorge east from Portland. They had gone past Multnomah Falls when they started running out of supplies, so they named the creek that they stopped at Starvation Creek. They continued on, and by the time they got to the next river or creek, they were eating their dogs to stay alive, so they called it Dog Creek. A community sprang up there, and they named it Dog Creek also. However, the first mail mistress, Mildred Coe, refused to accept mail there addressed to Dog Creek. She changed the name to Hood River and would accept mail only to that address."

About the turn of the century, Oregon became home to thousands of Japanese immigrants. Some came to work on the railroads, others to labor in the orchards or truck farms. In 1904 the initial *issei* (first generation) workers arrived in Hood River, where they cleared stumps in exchange for brushland to farm. By 1910, seven farms in Hood River were owned and operated by Japanese.

According to Wendy Ng, Japanese women arrived in Hood River during the next ten years, most having entered contractual marriages. By 1930 the Japanese in Hood River County totaled 5.8 percent of the population, but the numbers gradually declined before the war, largely due to legal restrictions on land ownership by Asian noncitizens. *Nisei* (second generation), since they were born in the United States, were citizens and could legally hold property.

In time, Hood River's Japanese community established its own identity. Japanese Halls flourished in Hood River County towns such as Oak Grove, Parkdale, Odell, and Dee Flat; the cultural center and trade post, however, remained Hood River.

At first, says Ng, "the Japanese worked in areas which posed no economic competition with white Oregonians." In many cases, the Japanese simply filled the same hard-labor roles that had belonged to the Chinese in pioneer times. With economic success, however, the Japanese were considered "serpents" on the American land. In 1919 the Anti-Alien League formed in Hood River, an organization whose members believed the Japanese would eventually purchase all the land in Hood River Valley. In 1923, Governor Walter M. Pierce, who had campaigned on an anti-Japanese platform, pushed the Alien Land Bill through the legislature, barring land ownership to Japanese, Chinese, or Filipinos. Nonetheless, the Hood River Japanese discovered that local lawyers were willing to circumvent these laws—for a price—and, says Ng, "prior to World War II, the Japanese believed themselves to be fairly well integrated into the Hood River economy as successful orchardists and merchants."

On December 7, 1941, as the bombs fell on Hawaii, the Japanese of Hood River were preparing a variety show at the Hood River Recreation Hall. Says Ng, word spread in the community that the Japanese, armed with advanced knowledge of Pearl Harbor, were meeting to celebrate the attack. From that moment, Hood River became a nightmare. Officials imposed a curfew on Japanese residents, and several local civic leaders went to jail without formal charges. On May 13, 1942, the Japanese residents of Hood River were loaded onto trains heading for the Pinedale Assembly Center, near Fresno.

After the war, many Japanese returned to Hood River, only to be met by anti-Japanese advertisements in local newspapers, many placed by the American Legion. Although most landowners were able to reclaim their property, the "Japanization of Hood River" became a topic for newspaper editorials and barber shop diatribes. In the next few years, the nisei and *sansei* (third generation) of Hood River carved out a different sense of community, building social networks and kinship ties that helped to buffer the Japanese against lingering prejudices of the *hakujin* (whites). As Ng notes, the Japanese community is not outwardly in evidence today in the Hood River Valley; nonetheless, the careful observer can easily find evidence of Japanese residence. For example, the sign on Nobi's grocery store reads: "Groceries, gasoline, bait, and tofu."

In her 1989 study of the Hood River Japanese community, Wendy Ng discovered that, despite being sansei, she was considered an outsider in Hood River. Gradually, Ng gained access to many Japanese orchardists in the area; in the process, she encountered some long-standing customs and practices.

At Christmas every year, there would be a Japanese Santa Claus, but also families would gather to make *mochi*, rice cakes made from steamed and pounded rice. Mochi is generally made around New Year's and stored for the ensuing year. The father usually decides how much mochi will be required before the family begins the day-long effort. According to Suzi Jones, writing in *Oregon Folklore*, "Mochi is supposed to revitalize the mind and body, and mochi meals are served at times when someone in the family is under stress. Being strong enough to lift and swing the mochi hammer is a sign of coming of age for the males in the family, and this usually happens when a boy is about fifteen. At this time he is also supposed to have the maturity to remember important family matters such as stories of his heritage."

Nisei and sansei cling to the notions of *on*, an ascribed obligation, or *giri*, a contractual obligation, often owed to the parents. As a result, many older children return to Hood River, especially when their parents reach advanced age, to help with the orchards or to honor their father and mother in other ways. One of Ng's informants, discussing why he returned to Hood River after the war, gives the following reasons.

THE FAMILY OBLIGATIONS OF ON AND GIRI

I owed my parents. I think it was all a part of coming back to the farm—obligation to parents, getting married. Then we had a place, we had the farm. My father thought schooling [an education would be better for him], and it wasn't possible. . . . Even then you're going to have to make a living, right? I owe it to my parents. . . . Because they shared their lives. You just can't watch your folks work so hard and not help.

Sometimes the gullibility of Anglos leads to humorous incidents, especially when they try to emulate their Japanese neighbors. In spring, the issei would go to the Hood River forests to seek *matsutake* (a wood mushroom), wood sorrel, lambs quarter, dandelion, and *warabe* (young bracken ferns). The following is a story told among the nisei.

WHAT TO DO WITH WARABE

So they were gathering this warabe, *in the spring, when it first comes up before the fronds open. And the Caucasian people said, "What do you do with that?"*

They were too embarrassed to say that we eat it. Because you know, after all, the lowly bracken! And they didn't want to tell people they were eating it. So they said, "Well, we take a hot bath with them. Good for health."

They said, "Well, you know the Japanese are pretty healthy." So they tried it. And I guess they just itched so bad! And they said, "What do you do? You take a bath and you don't itch?"

And they had to confess and say, "We were just too embarrassed to say we eat it. We don't take a bath in it, we eat it." You do! But you know, that's a true story.

Izee

Grant County. A post office was established at Izee in 1899, the settlement taking its name from the cattle brand (I Z) of local rancher M. N. Bonham. At the height of the range wars near the turn of the century, the Izee Sheep Shooters Association was a vigilante group responsible for the slaughter of several thousand sheep and a handful of sheep ranchers.

Here are superstitions and beliefs from Central Oregon sheep country, some of them found in *Sheepherders: Men Alone*, a photographic essay and oral history by Michael Mathers.

SHEEP COUNTRY CUSTOMS AND BELIEFS

☐ *Raw wool is a good cure for corns. Get some wool from a fence that sheep have passed and place it on the corns.*

☐ *Sheep lice, collected from the wool of a healthy animal, can cure liver problems. Swallow the lice, and they will "eat the poison" in the liver.*

☐ *The day of the month of the first snowfall indicates the number of snow days that winter. (First snow on November 8 would indicate eight snow days that winter.) But there has to be enough snow for a rabbit to leave tracks.*

☐ *When sheepherders have a party in town, and somebody hollers "Timber!" it means "drinks for the house!"*

☐ *A "granny" is a dry ewe that can't give birth but wants a lamb. When a lamb is born, a granny will often circle the birthplace and try to shove the mother away, in hopes of getting the lamb.*

☐ *A "bum" is a lamb rejected by its mother. When a sheepherder finds a bum, he covers the lamb with the coat of a stillborn lamb. Then, to assure that the "bum" will be accepted by his foster mother, the sheepherder winds the liver and intestines of the dead lamb around the rear end of the orphan.*

☐ *If you see the horns of the moon pointing down, it will rain within three days.*

☐ *It is bad luck to walk a few feet into a cabin with one shoe off.*

☐ *One herder left several pairs of worn underwear in the trees around his flock of sheep because he knew there were coyotes around. The smell kept the coyotes away.*

☐ *To cure rheumatism, dissolve some earthworms in a glass of whiskey and drink it down.*

☐ *If you're sleeping out on the range, put a rope made out of hair around your bedroll. A snake will not crawl over anything rough.*

☐ *For a sore throat, fill a long sock with earthworms and tie it around your neck. When the worms are dead, they have drawn out all the poisons, and your sore throat should be gone.*

☐ *A "sheepherder's monument" is a rock-pile at the top of a hill. Most sheepherders build such an obelisk as they're watching the sheep.*

☐ *If you step on a nail, grease the nail carefully with sheep fat so that the wound won't get infected.*

☐ *For an earache, pour pee in it. A wonderful remedy.*

☐ *Some sheepherders won't go into town on the seventh or fourteenth day of a month, considering it bad luck.*

☐ *If you see a snake in a tree, it will rain within three days.*

☐ *"Brrrrr! Brrrrr!" is the salt call. Sheep will come when the sheepherder makes this sound.*

Klamath Falls

Klamath County. Population 17,430. In the era before settlers arrived, the river between Upper Klamath Lake and Lake Ewauna was named *Yulalona,* meaning "to move back and forth." Apparently during strong southern winds, the river waters backed up, leaving the stream and its falls partly dry. Immigrants called this stream the Link River, and the town nearby was dubbed Linkville. In 1867 George Nurse founded Linkville; to commemorate the founding of the town, pioneers placed a memorial plaque on a standard of the Link River Bridge. Other events, less memorable, have also occurred at that bridge, as recorded in the December 9, 1881, edition of the *Ashland Daily Tidings.*

OCCURRENCE AT LINK RIVER BRIDGE

A most ludicrous incident occurred at Linkville some time ago. As reported to us, it seems too amusing to keep. One citizen of the place sold another a cook stove, but had not been paid for it. They met in a saloon, one or both of them somewhat "corned." The first citizen said, "When are you going to pay me for that cook stove?"

The second citizen replied, "The *%#$@* old stove is not worth paying for, and I'll never give you a cent. It's all burned up and cracked."

"Well, I'll have the money or the stove."

"No, you won't neither. You cheated me with the old iron, and before I'll let you have it, I'll heave it into the Link River."

"I'll bet you five dollars you don't dare do it."

"I've got no cash, but here's a five dollar hat, and I'll put this up against five dollars that I dare to do it."

"Done."

The stakes were put up. And the hatless man hitched up his team, drove to his house, put out the fire in the stove, loaded it onto the wagon, drove to the bridge, and in the presence of a large number of amused spectators, picked up the stove in his arms (he was a large, strong man) and heaved it over into the turgid waters of the Link River.

Ida Spangler was a teenager when her parents died in Idaho. Because the state threatened to take charge of her nine brothers and sisters, she moved to Klamath Falls. From family, from friends, and from the folk wisdom of the community, Ida Spangler learned marvelous cures and treatments for the variety of ills suffered by the younger children. Folk cures often employ either contagious magic or homeopathic magic, terms coined by James G. Fraser in his folklore compendium *The Golden Bough.* People using homeopathic magic treat disease by analogy: "Place a sharp knife under the bed to cut pain." Mrs. Spangler's methods, however, use contagious magic, where some curative actually touches the wound or diseased limb.

☐ *For pink eye, boil tea leaves, make them into a poultice, and bind it over the eyes.*

☐ *To take out infection, use fresh cow chips as a poultice. (They were used on my mother's breasts when my brother Albert was born.)*

☐ *For head lice, rub coal oil and lard on your scalp.*

☐ *For coughs, mix the juice from an onion with an equal amount of honey and drink it.*

☐ *For styes on the eyes, my mother used her gold wedding ring to rub on them. In a few days, they were gone.*

□ *For corns, put a slice of lemon on the corn, then wrap your foot so that the lemon stays over the corn.*

□ *To cure a chest cold, use an onion poultice. Put a whole onion in a pan and warm it in an oven 'til it swells great big. Slice it and place it between flannel cloth pieces and put it on your chest.*

□ *For colds, rub goose grease directly onto your chest and throat. Mother always had a jar of goose grease on the shelf, and she used it like we use Vick's today.*

□ *For chapped hands, wash them in your own urine before going to bed. My father was a blacksmith, and his hands would get so chapped and sore, with big cracks in his knuckles. He would cure them up in a few days' time by using his own urine to wash his hands before going to bed at night. (This remedy was told to Mrs. Spangler's folks in 1908 by an eighty-year-old Indian woman in Glenns Ferry, Idaho.)*

□ *To soothe and heal burns, rub vanilla on them.*

□ *For bee stings and deep slivers, use a bread-and-milk poultice to bring the sliver or stinger to the surface.*

□ *For stomach aches, take peppermint in warm water.*

□ *To prevent colds in the winter, wear a little sack of asafetida around your neck. It smells like skunk oil.*

□ *To prevent colds in the spring, drink saffron.*

□ *For boils or rashes, take molasses and sulphur to purify the blood.*

□ *To cure burns, rub axle grease on them.*

□ *To get rid of warts, rub a chicken bone (leg is best) over them and throw it over your left shoulder. When I was a young girl, I had seed warts on my hand. Mother told me to rub a chicken bone on them and throw it over my left shoulder. That weekend the family went to Aunt Mabe's for dinner, and we had chicken, so I grabbed a few bones (cause I had so many), took 'em home, rubbed them all over the warts, and threw them over my left shoulder. Within a week the warts were all gone.*

La Pine

Deschutes County. In 1910, the Deschutes Gorge Railroad Race created new communities in the area, and Lapine was so named because of the heavy pine forests nearby. John Uhlman of Scappoose, who had won a medal for butter making at the 1905 Lewis and Clark Fair, chose the site for a new dairy. In 1951, the name was altered to La Pine. Perhaps using cream and butter from Uhlman's dairy, Fern Rametes of La Pine baked cream pies for the men of a La Pine logging camp. Unfortunately, there was no refrigeration in those days, so Mrs. Rametes used the pioneers' method of cooling perishable foods.

HOW TO COOL CREAM PIES

We took an orange crate, nailed it to a tree, and added shelves—just separated enough so the top of the cream pie would not touch the shelf above. Then we put a hinged door with mesh screen on the front of the crate. I then added a pan of water on the top of the crate and hung burlap sacks down the sides. The sacks hung down into another pan of water at the bottom.

Well, air would pass through these wet sacks. You know, the burlap sacks would siphon water out of the pans. Then the air currents blowing through the crate would cool the pies. We used a lot of cream pies because they were a favorite of the men. And nobody ever died from them in the logging camp.

Mrs. Rametes also used salt sacks to make another camp staple, cottage cheese.

HOW TO MAKE COTTAGE CHEESE

Just let the milk sour and put it on the back of the stove. This wood stove business today is a problem. You couldn't do it now because you don't have a place where you sit it on the back of the stove. Anyway, the curds will stay warm there.

So you save salt sacks. That's where you'd pour this fibered milk after it curdled. And then you'd just hang up the sack on the clothesline. It would drip on the ground, and when it quit dripping, you'd bring it in and mix some cream with it. The ones that wanted sugar would put sugar in it, and the ones that wanted salt and pepper would put salt and pepper in it. But we ate cottage cheese as a staple almost every day of our lives. And fed the leftovers to the chickens.

EGG GLASS

The following recipe will preserve eggs from August until springtime: Take a piece of quick-lime as large as a good-sized lemon and two teacups full of salt; put it into a large vessel and slack it with a gallon of boiling water. The mixture will boil and bubble until it gets as thick as cream. When it is cold, pour off the top, which will be perfectly clear. Drain off this clear liquor and pour it over the eggs. See that the liquor more than covers them. A stone jar is most convenient—one that holds about six quarts.

HOMEMADE SOAP

One can of lye
2 heaping teaspoons of borax
2 1/2 pints of water
6 pints of fat

Render and clarify the fat. Then strain it through a cheesecloth. Pour the water into a large granite dish or crock. Then add the lye and borax. Stir the mixture with a wooden spoon. As the lye dissolves, the mixture becomes hot. Let it cool to lukewarm. Then melt the fat and cool it again to lukewarm. Add the fat to the lye mixture, stirring gently until it has the consistency of thin honey. Pour this liquid into waxed paper-lined boxes or milk cartons. Cut the soap after twenty-four hours. Keep it at room temperature for two or three days. Let the soap ripen for two weeks before using it.

PANTRY CURES

In 1858 and 1859 *The Oregon Farmer* published these cures from the pantry and cupboard, the cures employing simple household products and staples.

☐ *For a bee sting, bind onto the place a thick plaster of moistened salt.*

☐ *To cure boils (if they are very painful), apply a plaster of bread and milk.*

☐ *For hoarseness, take a white of two eggs, beat it well with a spoonful of white sugar, grate in a little nutmeg, and add a pint of lukewarm water. Stir it well and drink it often. Repeat this cure if necessary. It will cure the most obstinate case in a short time.*

☐ *For burns, a simple remedy is the white of an egg. It excludes the air and has healing properties.*

☐ *For a rattlesnake bite, stir salt with the yolk of a good egg until it is thick enough to spread and plaster. Then apply it to the wound as soon as possible.*

Malin

Klamath County. Population 725. Malin, named for a town in Czechoslovakia, means "wonderful country," a place where crops never fail. The community was settled in 1909 by Bohemian Czechs who first landed in Omaha, Chicago, and St. Louis. Sixty-six families, eager for open land and a community of their own, bought tracts for $35.00 an acre in the Tule Lake region, most of them trusting only the advice of an advance scout. Then they crowded into a rented rail car and traveled across country to their new farmlands.

When they arrived, the Czechs found their purchases partly covered by Tule Lake. They also found themselves poorly equipped to deal with the harsh elements in lower Klamath County. According to Agnes Drazil, one of the original settlers, "We came here bare-handed." Indeed, the Czechs of Malin survived only because they got much-needed help from two local ranchers. J. Frank Adams lent the new settlers money and farm equipment, keeping his accounts on the back of his barn door. A plaque in Malin Park commemorates Adams's contributions to the Czechs' survival. But there was more than generosity behind the Czechs' success. Despite winds, floods, ice storms, and plagues of pests, there was never a foreclosure on their properties, and every colonist eventually paid off the loan (and 8 percent interest) in full.

The Czechs largely thrived by growing potatoes. One of the ranchers who first encountered these Europeans said, "I know you can't raise potatoes here. The Bureau of Reclamation knows you can't raise potatoes here, but those Czechs don't know you can't raise potatoes here." After successfully cultivating potatoes and some grain

crops in the Tule Lake region, the Czechs found time to celebrate their heritage. Today, they share those customs in song, ritual, and ethnic foodways.

Traditions are carried on through dance and music and through the communal making of *jaternice* sausage and *strudl*. The Czechs produce sausage as they have for hundreds of years, using the same recipe and method that has been handed down through generations. All the Czechs in Malin take part. Similarly, the *strudl* is a community project, involving time-honored recipes. Other traditional foods include *kolace*, a Czech pastry. The recipe here was contributed in 1983 by Ellen Rajnus, a longtime resident, while researchers were preparing "The Czechs of Malin," a presentation sponsored by the Oregon Committee for the Humanities.

KOLACE

1 cake yeast	1 teaspoon salt
1¼ cup water	4 to 5 cups flour
1½ cups scalded milk	½ teaspoon mace
½ cup shortening (half butter)	rind of half a lemon
¾ cup sugar	2 egg yolks or whole egg

Dissolve yeast in warm water. Measure into a large bowl four cups of flour. Add the egg, sugar, salt, mace, lemon rind, melted shortening, and dissolved yeast. Beat the mixture very hard until the dough is smooth, soft, and a little bit sticky. Add flour only if it is necessary. For excellent eating, the dough should be soft—just so you are able to handle it. Cover the dough with a sheet and let it rise in a warm place until it doubles in bulk.

Then pour the dough onto a floured board and roll it out to one-quarter inch thickness. Then cut out rounds or make rounds and flatten them, making indentations in each center. Place one-half teaspoon of fruit filling in each indentation. These fillings are available in most grocery stores. The rounds should be placed on a well-greased pan and then allowed to raise for one-half hour. Bake at 400 degrees for 20 minutes.

Mosier

Wasco County. Population 244. In the mid-1850s, J. H. Mosier originated this landing, located about fifteen miles downriver from The Dalles. Mosier, son of German immigrants, actually held a law degree, but in pioneer Wasco County, legal matters were handled with pistols and ropes, so Mosier tried his hand at several jobs. First he built a sawmill, but by 1858 the mill had burned down twice and been washed away by flood, so Mosier tried ranching, mining, carpentry, and real estate. In his spare time he was the local blacksmith and eventually the hostler at the Mosier Inn. An interesting feature of the Mosier Inn was an extensive bookcase in the study, filled with hundreds of wooden books.

In 1975 Dalles resident Hal Fancher told this story to his grandson, Peter Gay, using Binks's typical stutter as part of the storytelling style.

BINKS AND THE BODY

Speaking of Judge Fred Wilson, that reminds me of one of my favorite stories about him. He came here in 1914 and was the district attorney. He had been promoted from deputy district attorney, and he had a ranch down near Mosier. He had a farmhand that had been working for him all summer. The farmhand suddenly disappeared one day and not only left his clothes but a considerable amount of unpaid wages.

The judge had been very much worried, but he couldn't for the life of him figure out what had happened. The judge made a lot of inquiries, and one day he was coming downtown, and somebody told him they had picked up a body down at the ferry landing. That was in the days when ferries still operated twenty-four hours a day across the river. Somebody had picked up this body down there and had come up and placed it in the morgue. The coroner at that time—and also the undertaker—was a character by the name of Binks Burget. Binks had a lot of funny habits, and one of them was the fact that, when he got excited, he stuttered. He said one day to me that he never stuttered when he was talking long distance because it was "t-t-t-too expensive."

Anyway, the judge met Binks and said, "Binks, I hear you picked up a body last night down at the ferry landing."

Binks said, "Y-y-y-yes, Judge."

The judge said, "You know, Binks, it occurs to me that might be my long lost farmhand. Do you mind if I look at the body?"

"N-n-n-no, Judge. Of course not," answered Binks.

So Binks took him into the back room of the undertaking parlor, where the body was laid out on a slab and covered with a sheet. Binks turned the sheet back so that the judge could look at the features of the dead man, and the judge put his hands behind his back, and he strolled around the body slowly, looking at it from all angles. Finally he stopped and said, "Binks, I don't believe I know this man."

Binks said, "Well, by God, judge, it's t-t-t-too late to introduce you now."

Redmond

Deschutes County. Population 7,136. Two North Dakota schoolteachers, Mr. and Mrs. Frank Redmond, founded this community by pitching a tent on open ground. Redmond grew up a wild and wooly town. Even Governor Oswald West got into the act in 1912, urging Redmond to raise "less hell and more hogs." West's words went unheeded, however. In 1915, the *Redmond Spokesman* complained, "There is too much promiscuous shooting in the outer edges of the city limits." In that same year, a

citizen told a *Spokesman* reporter that he had loaded some sticks of his firewood with dynamite and expected to see a house "not far distant from him" blown to pieces in the near future. Reacting to reported lawlessness and corruption, West eventually sent a deputy to Redmond, and the man arrested both the mayor and the town marshal for irregularities involving a poker game in the back room of the Redmond Hotel.

Rex Putnam, a noted Oregon educator, had an interesting experience on the streets of Redmond, one that he often described when he spoke to an audience. A frontiersman accosted Putnam on the streets, the man carrying a shotgun and a jug of moonshine. The man pointed the shotgun at Putnam and said, "Have a drink." So Putnam pulled on the jug, stood dazed for a moment, and then vomited into the street. With a sympathetic smile, the moonshiner said, "God, ain't it awful? Now you hold the gun on me."

In recent years, another group of rough-and-ready men landed in Redmond at Roberts Air Field to work for the United States Forest Service. Flying out in renovated B-17s, the Forest Service's smokejumpers trained for many years, bringing a new jargon and folk speech to the town of Redmond, here described by folklorist Bob McCarl, an expert in occupational lore, who spent some time working with the Redmond crews.

SMOKEJUMPERS' INITIATIONS

One of the most interesting areas of folklore and folk practice among smokejumpers is the initiation of rookies and the whole treatment of returning smokejumpers (or older

smokejumpers) toward the rookies. The main thrust of the whole treatment is degradation—a sort of rite-of-passage for the smokejumper.

A lot of the older jumpers, specifically those from Winthrop [Washington], where the first smokejumping took place in 1939–40, see smokejumpers as a tremendously elitist group of men. They therefore feel that initiation is in order. When I first came to Redmond, there were four or five of these guys from Winthrop, Washington, the smokejumper base up there. You make seven practice jumps seven days in a row, the last two being in timber and the first five in an open field. So, the night before the first jump, which is probably the night when everyone is the most nervous, is the one picked by the older jumpers as initiation night.

Initiation for me consisted of being pulled out of my bed at about ten o'clock in the evening and tied with plastic tape, which is impossible to break because it has a test of about 150 pounds, I think, and I had all my clothes taken off. Then they took me out on the front lawn and poured soap and I-don't-know-what-else on me and hosed me down. There were twenty-five of us that this happened to. Then we turned around and did the same thing to the guys who had done it to us. And that was more or less it, except that we were kept up all night by people pounding on the door and by firecrackers, and being squirted. Our rooms were torn apart—all our beds dumped over and stuff like this.

This is the kind of rite of passage for the morning of your first jump. Having experienced it, I don't know that it does more than keep your mind away from jumping in the morning. But in the morning, you're so tired that it sort of dulls your senses, I think; and I can't even remember the first jump that I made. It goes beyond this point, though. As the rookies make more jumps, you're considered a rookie until your first summer when you get a smokejumper pin. If you return, then you're a returning man the summer after that.

But in the morning, all the older jumpers, at breakfast, will talk about guys they used to jump with: "Don't you remember good old Sam Jones up at Winthrop and what a nice guy he was? It's really too bad that the capewells broke when he made his first jump, and they had to scrape him off the field." Or they would make dummy chutes, which are just flap containers with no chute—just wadded nylon that is used for patching chutes. It's exactly like the nylon in a parachute. They'll strap one of these things on the back of a rookie before he gets on the plane, and there will be a tiny section of nylon sticking out underneath the flap container. One of the older guys will come up and say, "Boy, someone sure didn't pack this chute too well. There's some nylon sticking out here." Of course, he'll pull about a foot out and cut it off, then pull out another foot and cut it off. The poor guy, who hasn't made a jump yet, is standing there watching someone destroy the "parachute" that he's supposed to use. . . .

Because of the hazards of smokejumping, there are lots of rules that have to be followed by jumpers, both in training and in actual fire-jumping. A lot of these things have turned into folklore because of their specific uses in jumping. For instance, when I first started jumping, there were a lot of stories going around about the lower guy turning right underneath the guy above him. Because the parachute creates a vacuum above it, the upper jumper's chute would deflate, and he would end up walking across the top of your chute. Then, all of a sudden, the lower guy would see a body go hurtling by, and the chute would open below.

I've heard stories about good smokejumpers—guys who have been doing it for a number of years—doing this on purpose to rookies.

SMOKEJUMPER JARGON

The **playground** is the training area, and it consists of the jump tower, the practice tower, the let-down tower, and the obstacle course.

The **torture rack** is a device invented by Marines to strengthen the leg muscles. It's a knee-high bar with stirrups. The jumper straps himself into the stirrups, wraps them around his ankles, and bends backward, touching his forehead to the ground. The torture rack is used extensively in training.

A **barnburner** is a fire that's raging out of control, burning in slash, in dry timber, or in flash fuel (salal and sagebrush), which simply explodes when torched.

An easy jump with a moderate fire is a **candy-ass blaze**. In the plane, everyone says, "What a candy-ass jump these guys have." In some ways, it's an indication of jumpers being jealous about an easy job, maybe one that can be prolonged for days with some overtime hours.

A drop into rocks or over steep terrain is a **hairy-ass jump**. Sometimes this term refers to a dangerous jump over water hazards.

A **hang-up** occurs when a smokejumper gets caught in a tree. There are divided opinions about whether a hang-up is beneficial. Some people would much rather hang up in a tree because it's a featherbed landing, compared to landing on rocks or steep hillsides. But at the same time, the jumper must eventually retrieve his gear, which sometimes means returning to the site to climb a pretty good-sized tree after the fire has been contained.

A **stick** is the number of men going out on one jump. You can either have two men jumping at a time, which is a two-man stick, or three. I've jumped in five-man sticks, but they never do that in a fire; that's just on practice jumps.

To **plane** is to turn the chute into a strong head-wind. For example, the forward speed on a Forest Service FS-5A chute is about seven miles per hour. If you are bucking a nine-mile-an-hour wind, you turn and ''plane,'' keeping almost equal footing to the wind. Thus, you'd be going nearly straight down. To pull a ''plane,'' grab the front risers and do a chin-up, pulling down on the shroud lines. That gives you more forward speed.

To write a **fat diary** is to come home with a lot of hours of overtime on the payroll sheets.

In a forest fire, a **widow-maker** is a snag in a tree. These snags can burn out almost hollow at the bottom and either be held up by the limb of another tree or by a tiny bit of solid wood left inside the core. Any kind of jarring movement can send these widow-makers crashing down. Particularly in a fire, they're dangerous because you don't know how strong the branches are in the center.

Hot doggers are men who move their chutes around, trying to manipulate toward a good landing position. The term may be positive or negative, depending on the jumper.

To **exit** is to get out of the plane. No one says he's going to ''jump'' from a plane. He says he will ''exit'' the plane.

There's a bug that bothers all fire-fighters. It is a bee with a long stinger, usually about an inch-and-a-half long. It's called a **stumpfucker**. At any given fire in the Northwest you can see the jumpers chasing these things around with a shovel, but they are almost impossible to kill.

After fifty jumps, the smokejumper gets a **lawn-party**, an initiation function. At the lawn-party, the smokejumper gets taped up and thrown into the irrigation ditch or into the sinks at the smokejumpers' dormitory.

Santiam Pass

Jefferson and Linn counties. The pass, like many landmarks in the Cascades, was named for a nearby Kalapooian tribe, the Santiams. The pass was first used as a toll road in 1868 and named Hogg Pass, after an early railroader who surveyed here.

In 1970 mountain climber Michael Ehrlich interviewed fellow climbers, gathering mountaineers' jargon. While climbing the South Sister, Mt. Hood, and slopes near Santiam Pass, Ehrlich concentrated on the terms exchanged by experienced climbers, looking especially for argot he had never seen printed in manuals or magazines, therefore excluding terms such as belay and rappel. By now, however, some of the terms have no doubt been widely adopted, while others have slipped into obscurity. One complication added particular stress to Ehrlich's fieldwork. As he says, ''Gathering information while in the process of executing various climbing maneuvers was obviously problematical.'' No doubt, it was dangerous as well.

MOUNTAINEERS' JARGON

apron: an ice sheet covering rocks, making them smooth and slippery

'biner: a shortening of the word carabiner, an oval snap-link used to connect ropes

chicken point: a place on a mountain where inexperienced climbers usually get frightened and turn around. Says Ehrlich, ''On quite a few occasions, I have run across the term scrawled on some rock near some precipice.''

devil's kitchen: cracks or caves in the snow, spouting steam or sulphur fumes. These are found on nearly every high volcano in the Northwest.

end run: a tactic for moving around large crevasses or cracks in a glacier. The climber finds the terminus, instead of attempting to cross the glacier by jumping. The term comes from football.

glazed: to get caught in an avalanche, perhaps deriving from the fact that bodies recovered from avalanches have an ice glaze over the face

gut plunge: a face-in *glissade*, a controlled downhill slide on the stomach, to speed up descent of a snow slope

heartily: a signal to climb after the climber has been outfitted with a rope to stop a fall (adapted from sailing): ''Heartily!''

hogsback: any sort of sloping ridge, a roughness in topography

jive: to throw or heave the end of a rope. ''Jive it over the rock.''

moat: a trough, as much as two or three feet deep, dug in a circle in the snow. Climbers lay rope in the trough, winding it around a central mound of snow, creating an anchor. A moat is also a long downhill gully.

'schrund: a shortening of the word *berschrund*, used to describe
a crevasse where one lip is higher than the other
scoop: an ice ax, which has a curved end
scoop steps: footholds in the ice, cut by the ax
scooper: the lead climber who is cutting footholds
scooping: chopping footholds in the ice

Sisters

Deschutes County. Population 679. The current town of
Sisters is just east of the summit of the Cascade Range and
is named for Faith, Hope, and Charity, the glacier-filled
mountains that provide such distinctive Oregon landmarks
from either Eastern or Western Oregon.

THE "FAMILY" OF CENTRAL OREGON MOUNTAINS

"This is not the first family which grew too large for
its house."

—WPA Federal Writers' Program

Around 1840 several members of the Methodist mission at Salem ventured into mountainous Central Oregon to
survey the countryside. Finding three majestic mountain-
tops together in the Cascade Range, the Methodists christened the north peak as Faith (10,085 feet), the middle
crest as Hope (10,047), and the south peak as Charity
(10,358). Later they came to be known simply as The
Three Sisters. In 1910 the Mazama Indians, borrowing
from the established theme, named their sacred peak The
Little Brother (7,822).

Several mountains lie on the jagged foundation of
ancient Mt. Multnomah, which centuries ago rose approximately a mile above the Sisters. Nearly 10 million years
ago the top of Mt. Multnomah was blown away in a gigantic
eruption, leaving a rim of peaks that includes The North
Sister, Little Brother, The Husband (7,520), The Wife
(7,045), and Broken Top (9,152), all resting on the under-
pinnings of the original Mt. Multnomah and formed by
subsequent volcanic activity. Ironically, the stream that
flows between The Husband and The Wife is called Separation Creek, perhaps an omen of domestic strife in the
family. Other Cascade peaks born from the demise of Mt.
Multnomah include The Aunt (*Kwolh* Butte) and The
Uncle (Tot Mountain), Maiden Peak (7,818) and Bachelor
Butte (9,060). All these relatives, of course, have a common ancestral home, House Rock (6,737).

The Indian tribes east of the Cascades helped name
many of the peaks, and most of the bands have stories
about the origins of the various mountains. "The Legend
of the Three Sisters" is a sweathouse story told by Gilbert
E. Conner, a Nez Perce tribesman.

THE LEGEND OF THE THREE SISTERS

*A long time ago when Coyote was acting foolish, as
young men sometimes do about women, he did something
very bad. He saw three beautiful young women washing
berries in a stream, and he thought he would like to have one
of them for his woman. But he couldn't decide which one he
wanted because they were all so lovely and young. So Coyote
crossed the stream to talk to the women to see if that would
help him make his choice.*

*In talking to the young women, he learned that they were
all sisters and that they were newly married and had strong
young husbands. So they told Coyote that they were already
taken and that he could have none of them. This angered
Coyote because he always has to have what he wants. Coyote
thought, as he usually does, that no one should tell him what
he can't have and what he can't do.*

*So Coyote captured the three sisters and kept them.
Eventually they all became pregnant. Coyote was very happy
with the fact that these beautiful young women were his and
were going to have his children.*

*One day while Coyote was gone, the husbands who had
been searching for their lovely wives found the sisters tied up
in a rock cave crying. The men freed the sisters, and they all
hurried home together.*

*When the husbands found out that Coyote had impreg-
nated their beautiful wives, however, they became very sad.
In their misery they went to talk to the Old Man, who was
very wise. In the sweathouse the Old Man told the men it was
not possible for a human to bear a four-legged. He said that*

the babies inside would create a poison in the women. The Old Man said that the Great Father would know what Coyote had done was wrong and that he would punish Coyote by killing the children and women at birth-time.

The grieving husbands left the Old Man, and on their way home they decided that they would kill their wives and save them from many days of unhappiness, rather than prolonging their lives to when the Great Father would cause them to die.

So the next day, when the sisters were again at the stream, lying there with their pregnant bellies in the air, the husbands killed them. They died with their big stomachs protruding up into the skyline as they still do today. You see, The Three Sisters in the mountains near Redmond are the big stomachs of the three sisters that Coyote stole. They are there as a reminder—always—of Coyote's wrongdoing.

Sunriver

Deschutes County. Sunriver, sixteen miles southwest of Bend, stands at the former site of Camp Abbot, named for Brigadier General Henry Larcom Abbot, who camped at this meadow in 1855 while surveying for the railroad. After World War II, the U.S. Army training center was closed and the land sold. Sunriver is a planned resort community, the name chosen by its developers. Sunriver activities include fishing, boating, golfing, and horseback riding. Along with the newer developments, a large log lodge remains from the Civilian Conservation Corps' efforts in the 1930s.

Buck Davis is a Bend farrier who has provided shoes for the horses at Sunriver's resorts during past summers. Horses grow entirely new hooves in a year, and shoes need to be changed "every six weeks to two months." According to Davis, horseshoeing is both a family business and a traditional art requiring special skills.

My dad and brother and I, if we're working alone, it takes us each about forty-five minutes to shoe a horse. All three of us together can do three in an hour. What we do is start out trimming by tacking the shoes on with one or two nails, and my brother will come around and finish the nails. We have three horses with maybe two shoes apiece, but they'll all be finished up about the same time. It's kind of like running through an assembly line—Dad does a part, I do a part, and Joe does a part. We carry two sets of tools and share them.

My dad started shoeing at about age thirteen for about $2 a horse; he was still making money. Now we charge $16. . . . During the summer we do from ten to fourteen horses a day on the average. We've done as many as twenty-five a day together, the three of us. One day we shod twenty-five horses for Sunriver and trimmed thirteen or fourteen. That's a pretty good day's work.

Working as a farrier is hard work and an exacting art, each step requiring strength and skill. Davis says that assessing a horse's particular needs is perhaps the most important part of the job.

A good horseshoer will always watch to see how the horse travels. He'll look to see if he's pigeon-toed or toes out. He can shoe him to correct for these kinds of problems. The first thing you do is trim the horse's foot as far as it'll possibly go, leaving as much heel as you can. Another thing to be careful of is the triangle-shaped area on the bottom of the foot; you want to leave as much of that as you can. This is called the frog. You want to leave as much as you can and not whittle on it too much.

The frog is sometimes called the horse's "second heart" because when the blood goes all the way down to the bottom of the foot, it needs something to kind of push it back up. The frog, every time the horse steps down, absorbs some of the shock and acts as a cushion and a heart that's pushin' the blood back and forth. . . .

If you get a pigeon-toed horse, a lot of people think that to break him of it you have to take the inside heel and raise it up. This is the worst thing you can do because whatever side is high is the side the horse's foot will favor. So, if the horse is pigeon-toed, you should have more heel on the outside than on the inside. That way, when the horse is stepping, heel-first as he does, he'll drop down to his toe, and the outside wall will then touch first.

As a general rule of thumb, the front foot is a little more rounded than the hind foot, and the hind foot is a little more pointed. On most horses, the front foot is a little bigger than the hind foot. If you've got a horse with a size 6 foot in front, he'll wear a size 5 in back. Shoes run size 2 to size 9.

My dad and brother and I, when we nail on a back shoe, we put only seven nails in—all four on the outside, an inside heel nail, an x-2, and leave the heel nail, inside-out on both feet. It's for good luck—and part of the reason is that everyone does it. But also it's because it's the worst nail to finish, the hardest nail to finish.

After talking at length about the art of shoeing, Davis remembered a legend, "The Devil and the Blacksmith." The story explains why the horseshoe is lucky and why farriers use only seven nails. Bend resident Tom Mittendorf recorded this material in 1976 while meeting with Davis and two other friends.

THE DEVIL AND THE BLACKSMITH
(Why the Horseshoe is Lucky)

Anyway, the Devil was traveling the Earth in disguise as a horse around the 15th or 16th Century, and he'd done quite a bit of traveling around. One day he came up lame and was pretty sore.

So he went to the nearest town and looked up the local blacksmith and asked if he could fix his feet. The blacksmith, being a good, upstanding Christian, recognized the Devil for

Well, it was during huntin' season years ago, this Rube Barnes and—I can't remember the other fella's name now—had a foot race for their clothes, article by article. They were backed up by a bunch of hunters, who were all boozed quite thoroughly, and everybody had a good time over it.

They ran down and back—point a to the turn and then back. Whoever won the heat won the round, and the other guy lost an article of clothes. Anyway, they call that place Rube's Ridge.

One of the most colorful characters in Suplee history was Wild Gus DeLore. Sometimes Gus would follow a young ranch hand who was heading off to see his girl after work. After dark, Gus and his pals would find the young man's horse, take off the saddle, and run the horse off. Then Gus and the ranch hands would tie the saddle in the limbs of a tall tree. If none was available, they would ride to a willow grove, bend down a tall willow, tie the saddle to the top limbs, and let it go. Many a young man ended his evening of courting by having to walk home and get the axe.

Wild Gus DeLore could break any bronc alive, according to "Spikes" Kuhn: "He usually did it by just wearing the horse out, letting him buck until he was too tired to buck anymore. He would ride a wild horse with one end of his rope tied around the horse's neck. If the horse stampeded, Gus would take the other end of the rope and lasso a sturdy fence post, a tree, or whatever else was handy. Then he would slip off the horse while the horse would continue to run at a full gallop. When the horse came to the end of the rope, sometimes he would break his neck and sometimes he wouldn't. But he wouldn't ever stampede again—if he survived."

what he was and tied him up in the shop and started nailing all the nails into the quick. The Devil was screaming and hollering and trying to get away, but [the smith] had tied him down too solid. So finally, the blacksmith was on the last foot, the hind foot, and he had one more nail to go. And the Devil, who was screaming and hollering, said to him, "I'll do anything if you don't drive that last nail."

And the blacksmith says, "OK." He says, "If you'll promise me never to enter a home with a horseshoe above the door, then I'll let you go."

And the Devil agreed, and the blacksmith let him go. And in order for this horseshoe to be lucky, then it has to be a hindshoe, and it has to be one with only seven nails in it, and if you hang it above the door, you should always hang it with the heels up, so that the luck doesn't run out, 'cause if you turn it around, all the luck will pour out.

If you have a bar shoe, that's a shoe where the heels curve around and meet each other so it's more like a circle, you have never-ending luck. A bar shoe is one that looks like a heart. So if you can get one with seven nails in it that's off a hind foot, then you're a pretty lucky "sum-bitch."

WILD GUS DeLORE

One time, Wild Gus DeLore faced a special challenge. He came across a little blue pony—one of the meanest, orneriest animals ever born. Wild Gus had no corral, so he snubbed the pony to the nearest tree, saddled it up, and jumped on. Bang! That pony started jumping and spinning, and before Gus could catch his breath, the horse was blazing across the mesa, jumping over boulders taller than a man, running full out. Finally, he came to a gulch with straight sides—about twenty feet deep and forty feet across. Neither Gus nor the horse flinched. That little blue pony hit the edge in full stride and jumped way out across that ravine. But, just as Gus and the pony neared the far side, Gus saw that they weren't going to make it. So he turned that horse around right there and went back to the other side.

Suplee

Crook County. Population 0. East of Bend, the now-forgotten community was named Suplee by Charles Dorling, Suplee being his mother's maiden name. The town always had its share of eccentric characters. One of the enduring landmarks around the original site of Suplee is Rube's Ridge, named for such a character. Bill Weberg, a cattle rancher from Suplee, tells about the naming of this crest.

Wild Gus DeLore, in his best days, might have had trouble with "The Strawberry Roan," a horse deceivingly tough to ride. Here is the Central Oregon version of the bronc-buster's favorite folk song, as sung by Ralph Christensen.

THE STRAWBERRY ROAN

I was hang-in' 'round town and just spen-din' my time, Out of a job and not ma-kin' a dime When a fel-la stepped up and he says "I sup-pose You're a bronc-bus-tin' man, I can tell by your clothes." Straw-berry 'til he makes his high dive.

I was hangin' 'round town and just spendin' my time,
Out of a job and not makin' a dime
When a fella stepped up and he says,
''I suppose you're a bronc-bustin' man,
I can tell by your clothes.''

He says this old pony ain't never been rode,
And the guys that gets on him is bound to be throwed,
So I gets up all excited and I asks what he pays
If I ride this old goat for a couple of days.

He offers a ten-spot and I says, ''I'm your man.
For the bronc never lived that I couldn't fan.
No the bronc never lived, or he never drew breath
That I couldn't ride 'til he starved plumb to death.''

So he says, ''Get your saddle, I'll give you a chance.''
So we got in the buckboard and drove to the ranch.
Until morning we stayed and then right after chuck,
I goes down to see if this outlaw can buck.

Down in the horse corral standing alone,
This old caballo, this strawberry roan.
His legs are all spavined, he's got pigeon-toes,
Little pig eyes and a big Roman nose.

Little tin ears that slit at the tip,
With a big 44 stamped on his right hip,
With a big ''U'' neck and all, with a long underjaw.
You can see with one look he's a regular outlaw.

Well, I put on my spurs, I was sure feelin' fine,
Pulled down my hat and I coiled up my twine,
And I tossed the loop on him and a'well I knew then
Before he gets rode, I'll sure earn that ten.

First comes the blinds, it sure was a fight,
Next came the saddle and I screwed her down tight.
Then I stepped upon him and I raises the blind,
I'm a'ridin' his middle to watch him unwind.

Well, he bowed his old neck and I guess he unwound,
For he seemed to quit livin' down there on the ground.
He went up toward the east, came down toward the west,
And to stay in his middle I'm a'doin' my best.

He sure is provokin', he heaved a big sigh,
He only needs wings to be on the fly.
He fanned his old belly right up to the sun,
He sure is a sunfishin' son-of-a-gun.

He's about the worst bucker I've seen on the range,
He can turn on a nickel and give you back change.
And when he's a'buckin' he squeals like a shoat,
I'll tell you this pony has sure got my goat.

I'll tell you, no foolin', this pony can step,
But I'm still in his middle and a'buildin' a rep.
He goes up on all fours, came down on his side,
Don't see how he keeps from a'losin' his hide.

Well, I loses my stirrup and also my hat,
And I'm pullin' the leather as blind as a bat.
With one more big plunge, he goes up on high
And leaves me sittin' on nothin' way up in the sky.

Well, I turned over twice and I came back to earth,
And I laid there a'cussin' the day of his birth.
Then I know there's some ponies, impossible to ride,
There's some of 'em left, they haven't all died

But I'll bet all my money that man ain't alive
That can stay with old Strawberry
'Til he makes that high dive.

Warm Springs

Native American Territory. Population 3,047. The Warm Springs Reservation is home to a confederation of tribes, including the Wascos, Paiutes, Teninos, Umatillas, and others.

Myths and legends are important aspects of tribal culture in any Native American society, and explanations of natural phenomena are among the most popular themes, as featured in legends such as ''How Coyote Made the Columbia River,'' ''How the Bluejay Got His Topknot,'' or ''The Origin of Crater Lake.'' Most sacred stories are told in lodges during the chill of winter, with the men and women gathered separately.

Coyote stories are especially restricted to the colder months and should not be told out of season. ''My grandmother used to tell us,'' said a Warm Springs woman, ''that a rattlesnake would bite us if she told stories in summer.'' Her neighbor added, ''My grandfather always said that he would get bald and yellowjackets would sting us.'' According to Pat Lewis, when the storytellers give a tale to an out-

HOW COYOTE AND WOLF GOT THEIR COLORING

One day Coyote came to a ridge and spotted three wolves on the flat below him, the wolves preparing to eat eggs. The animals put the eggs into a pit in the ground surrounded by fire, and they left a "test hole" to pour water into the pit. Coyote grew very hungry and watched with interest.

Eventually the wolves went to sleep. Coyote sneaked into their camp, went to the pit, took an egg from the test hole, and ate it. Before long, he had finished all three eggs, even though they were runny. Fearing discovery, however, he rubbed some of the yolk on the wolves' chins and paws, hoping to make each of the wolves think the others had consumed the dinner. Sure enough, when they awoke, the wolves began quarreling over the lost eggs and were nearly to blows when they realized that only Coyote could be responsible for such a trick.

In the meantime, Coyote had gone to the river for a drink. While there, he noticed salmon swimming in the water and wanted some. Finally he devised a net and caught some salmon, putting them on the fire to cook while settling down for a short nap. At that moment, the wolves ate the wonderful salmon. Then to mislead Coyote, the wolves rubbed the oily charcoal remnants onto his nose, over his paws, and under his chin.

Coyote awoke surprised. He knew he had an empty stomach, but the salmon were gone. He went to a quiet pool for a drink and saw his frightening color in the reflection. Soon Coyote's sister arrived, telling him and the wolves that they would wear their badges of shame forever, signs of their mutual bad deeds.

sider, who writes it down and carries it away, the story no longer belongs to the tribe. To counteract this loss, Warm Springs storytellers will occasionally tell Coyote tales but leave out or change an essential detail. "How Coyote and Wolf Got Their Coloring" was told by a white minister who lived for several years on the Warm Springs Reservation.

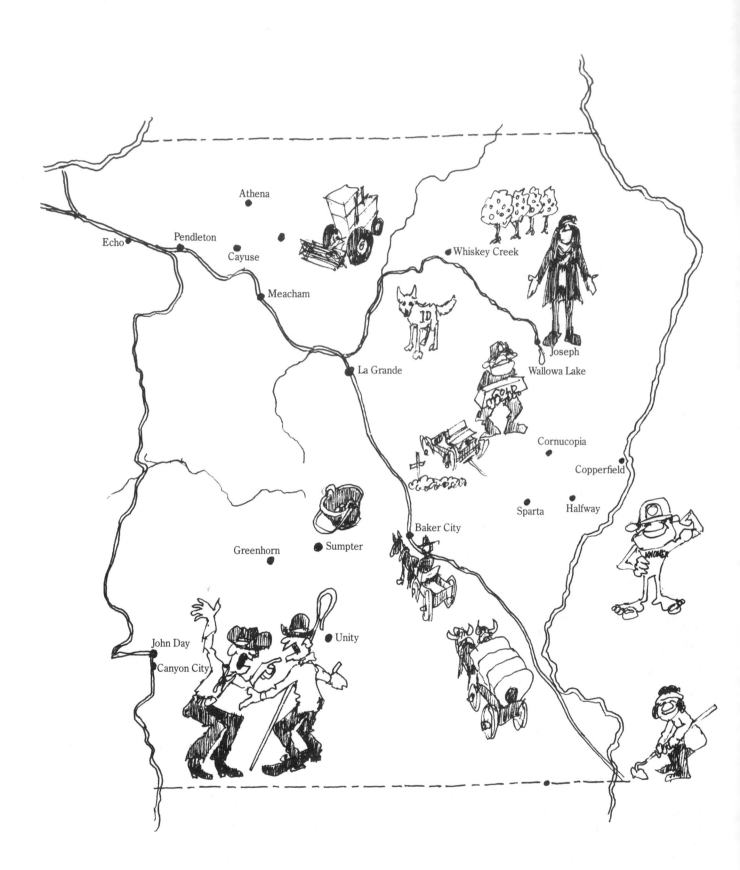

Athena

Echo

Pendleton

Cayuse

Meacham

Whiskey Creek

Joseph

Wallowa Lake

La Grande

Cornucopia

Copperfield

Sparta

Halfway

Greenhorn

Sumpter

Baker City

John Day

Unity

Canyon City

Northeastern Oregon

Swinging across the northeastern corner of the state, the Old Oregon Trail bisects the two most significant geologic formations of the Northeast, the Blue Mountains and the Wallowa Mountains.

The Oregon spurs of the Blue Mountains are Strawberry Range, the Ochoco Mountains, Greenhorn Ridge, Elkhorn Range, and the Eagle Creek Mountains, all ranging in elevation from 4,000 to 9,000 feet. Above the 4,000-foot level, pine forests cover the slopes. The higher peaks, often snowcapped, are barren. The Blues are drained by streams that have cut deep, narrow canyons on their routes to the Columbia and Snake rivers, leaving, among others, Hell's Canyon, the deepest gorge in America.

In the canyons, valleys, and watersheds of the Northeast, early drifters found gold, a mineral that in the 1860s transformed the country to a series of rough-and-ready boomtowns and gold camps. In 1861, Henry Griffin hired a guide named Adams to help him find the Blue Bucket Mine, a stream full of nuggets along the route of the Lost Wagon Train of 1845. After some days of circling, Adams admitted he was lost and was driven from camp without food or a horse. The next day, however, Griffin stumbled upon gold dust in the Powder River. Soon Griffin's Gulch was crawling with miners; even the discredited Adams was allowed to stake a claim. Later this place was called Poker Creek and finally Auburn. At some claims in Auburn, gold ran from one to four ounces per pan. The men were shoulder to shoulder when they panned, with the average claim running only twenty-five feet in length along the creeks.

In 1862 the first Eastern Oregon mining district was formed, just four miles south of Griffin's claim. E. C. Brainard, elected recorder, was also probably the first Union County resident to earn a living from gold without using his back. Brainard, charging a dollar per claim, earned the tidy sum of $30 a day. Brainard was not the last Oregonian to benefit handsomely from other men's back-breaking labor in the mines.

After these earliest strikes in Union and Baker counties, thousands of miners rushed into the Blue Mountains, followed by the usual cast of supporting players—saloonkeepers, dance hall girls, card sharps, and businessmen. Overnight, new towns appeared: Bourne, Granite, Greenhorn, Sumpter, Gem. Many were abandoned with similar quickness when the lodes played out. But while it lasted, the gold rush invigorated Northeastern Oregon, and the luck was sometimes fantastic. John Potter, a miner with a rich claim, got into a poker game and lost his poke. Potter borrowed a lantern from the bartender and walked to his claim. An hour later he returned with $300 worth of gold dust and proceeded to win $3,700 that night in the game.

In 1863 the Reverend T. F. Scott reported his opinion of working as a missionary in the Oregon goldfields: "It is evident that the only services of any real value in this country are those of hardy, self-denying itinerants, going where the people go, and preaching where they congregate, sharing their toils, their tents, and their grub, visiting the sick and burying the dead, of whom most are murdered." In fact, some of the shepherds were not even hardy enough to *find* the goldfields. By 1864 Auburn miners decided they needed religion, so they sent a group to Canyon City to hire a French preacher. After two days he hadn't arrived, so the men sent out a search party. When they found him, the preacher was lost, having walked through the hills for two days, living on huckleberries.

Preachers had a big job in the mining camps, according to the collections filed by Chris Grissom and Candy Anderson. In Sumpter, Billy Rawlins hired a line of chorus girls, who came to his saloon wearing appropriately short skirts. The miners' favorite pastime was to throw gold nuggets on the floor, so that the girls would have to bend over to pick them up. In Butte, a miner told this story on himself: ''I went home one day after having been drunk for two days, and on the porch was this suitcase and a lunch pail. There was a sign left by my wife that said, *Take one or the other.*''

Not only the miners lived wild and wooly lives in Northeastern Oregon. The citizens of Adams in Umatilla County once robbed an O. R. and N. train headed for Walla Walla with a load of coal. To the citizens of Adams, hijacking the train seemed a practical solution to the problem of finding winter fuel; however, most thievery occurred on a more modest scale. Folklorists Chris Grissom and Candy Anderson discovered that petty theft was the cause of some negligent driving on the road to Sumpter Valley.

They'd bring [whiskey] from Umatilla Landing in 50 gallon oak barrels. The teamsters—freighters—would always carry a brace and bit. These were used to make a hole in a barrel by carefully knocking up one of the hoops on the barrel so they could put it back in place when they were through. They would then bore the hole under [the hoop] so they couldn't be seen and then replace the hoop. Nearing the end of the journey, they would carefully refill the portion they had drunk with water, plug the hole, tap the hoop back into place, and they drank at the miners' expense.

Wherever there was a gold town, there was also a Chinatown. Large numbers of Chinese established themselves in John Day, Sparta, Baker, Canyon City, and elsewhere. Some mined abandoned claims or tailings of larger operations. Others established businesses, often stores, cafes, or laundries. But life was not easy for the Chinese. Indians sometimes worked the mines as laborers, and they disliked competition from the Chinese. Perhaps in response to these feelings, Paiute-Bannock Chief Egan attacked a group of forty Chinese workers on their way to the Silver City mines, killing them all after promising safe passage. Nor was life in the mining towns safe for the Chinese either. They were often the victims of slander, cruel jokes, thefts, and violence. Robbing or killing a Chinaman was rarely considered a crime in Northeastern Oregon.

Nonetheless, many Chinese were widely respected by their Anglo neighbors. In Sumpter, Loc Mun raised vegetables and sold them to the housewives in town. He operated on a credit basis, leaving the vegetables needed by the housewife and writing down the debt somewhere on the side of each house. Now and then he would read the clap-board accounts and collect. Sadly for Loc Mun, the fire that destroyed Sumpter also wiped out his bookkeeping system.

North and east of the goldfields lie the Wallowa Mountains, home of the Nez Perce Indians. Wallowa, often called the ''land of winding waters,'' features spectacular lakes and mountain peaks that feed those lakes. Eagle Cap, Sacajawea, Aneroid Peak, Glacier, Twin Peaks, and the Matterhorn are some of the fifteen mountains that range over 9,000 feet in elevation. Aneroid Lake at 7,600 feet may be the most beautiful lake in Oregon, and the Wallowas have eight snow-filled lakes at elevations above 8,000 feet. From the top of the loftiest peaks to the canyons of the Snake River, the Wallowas display five distinct growing regions, different in foliage and vegetation.

Because these mountains are inaccessible, settlers avoided the Wallowa country until the 1870s. From the earliest times, the whites began to divide land inhabited traditionally by the Nez Perce tribe. In 1877 young Chief Joseph, having tried unsuccessfully to share his valleys with the settlers, found his people increasingly embroiled in hostilities, leading finally to his retreat toward the Canadian border, his classical strategies of defense, his defeat by the army forces, and his eventual exile from the beautiful lands of the Wallowas.

Place-names in Northeastern Oregon fancifully record the history of the region and its people. California Gulch near Baker had a population of transplanted '49ers, called ''Tarheads'' by the Oregonians, who in turn were labeled ''Webfooters.'' Farther south, Salt Lake City miners established a settlement at Mormon Basin. In the Wallowas, a stream panned mainly by Cantonese miners was called China Creek. Mining areas where hopes ran high picked up appellations such as Eureka, Cornucopia, and Blue Bucket Creek.

Other Northeastern Oregon place-names suggest the realities of pioneer life. Union County's Thief Valley recalls the hanging of a horse thief in 1864, and Cash Hollow between Tollgate and Milton-Freewater is where a pack-train drover, having won a huge stake in a poker game, buried his fortune before being attacked and killed. The two towns of Milton and Freewater were once separated only by railroad tracks; drunks and gamblers thrown out of Milton simply stepped across the tracks into Freewater and continued their roughnecking. In order to clean up their streets, the town councils decided to merge the towns, creating Milton-Freewater. Battle Creek was named by Wallowa County residents who watched with dismay as two old-timers continued a nasty dispute over mining rights on the stream. And Shirttail Gulch observes the flight of a Baker County settler who ran so fast from a band of Snake Indians that his shirttail flapped in the wind behind. The name of Freezeout Creek reflects the harshness of winter in the Wallowas, and Boneyard Creek records the winter of 1898 when a Wallowa rancher lost an entire herd of cattle to snow and cold.

Certain ironies show up in a scan of Northeastern place-names. The boys at Temperance Creek, for example, were not Prohibitionists; they just ran out of supplies and were reduced to drinking water. The towns of Utopia, Paradise, and Promise (''The Promised Land'') probably were examples of wishful thinking by homesteaders, and Virtue Flat, although named for a Baker City settler and not a descriptive term, no doubt seemed an odd title for a town in the middle of mining country.

Other place-names in the Wallowas and the Blues are simply colorful remembrances of the past. Top was named for a popular brand of chewing tobacco, and both Maiden Gulch and Old Maid's Canyon signified hollows where single women built cabins. Buttercreek, north of Hermiston, was named by Oregon Trail voyagers. According to Jim

McDole, some travelers put their butter tubs in the creek to cool and were attacked by Indians. Quickly they left, leaving the butter to wash down the creek, where other settlers saw it. Wingville in Baker County was founded by John Blue from Wing, Minnesota, a Confederate sympathizer who moved west to avoid bearing arms against the Confederacy. On the other hand, Coyote Brown's Mountain was the hiding place of a Baker County man who wanted to avoid being drafted by the Union Army. Catched Two Lake in Wallowa County probably derives its name from a fisherman's understatement, while Thirty-two Point Creek in the same county suggests a hunter's exaggeration.

Athena

Umatilla County. Population 991. Approximately halfway between Pendleton and Walla Walla, this community was first known as Centerville. The current name was offered in 1889 by the local school principal, who attempted to instill an interest in learning by choosing Athena, Greek patron of the arts.

Athena has a rich Scottish heritage. A favorite holiday in Athena is the birthday of Robert Burns, Scotland's national poet. Every year in July, Athena sponsors the Caledonian Picnic and Highland Games. Local Scots celebrate their homeland with bagpipes, Scottish reels, coats of arms, colorful tartans, and traditional games, such as the caber throw. At the turn of the century, the Caledonian Society was only open to ''Scotchmen, sons of Scotchmen and their descendants, or the husband or wife of a Scotchman, all of good moral character, possessed of some visible means of support, and over 18 years of age.'' In 1914 there were 119 members who met these qualifications in Athena. Today the Caledonian Society is more inclusive.

Scots often arrived in Oregon by a long and difficult route, landing in Philadelphia or points south, pouring through the Cumberland Gap and overland to Missouri, where they joined the wagon trains for the Oregon Trail. In their vast travels from Scottish lowlands or highlands, these adventurers carried with them a wealth of cures, charms, and folk belief. In 1974 folklorist Karin Smith collected a number of typical Scots beliefs and superstitions, reminiscent of the Scottish countryside, and found often in places such as Lake County's Paisley and Caledonian Athena. Smith's collection in the Mills Archives draws from interviews with Janet D. Lauener from Paisley, Scotland, and Frank Gilmour of Coltbridge. Both informants offered traditional beliefs and superstitions, many of them concerning birth, marriage, weather, and folk cures.

SCOTTISH FOLK BELIEFS

☐ *In Scotland we put a piece of white heather in our bouquets and a six-pence in our shoe. I had a piece of white heather sent to me from Scotland when I was married here,* for good luck. You keep the six-pence and the heather after marriage where I come from.

☐ There are very few weddings in May. There's much against marriage in May; you'll ruin the day.

☐ I had a friend one time. An owl came into the house one time down the chimney—a young one—and she was expecting a baby. And she was so upset the baby died.

☐ We never would buy anything but the bare necessities for the baby. You know here they have the crown, the bassinet. Oh, you would not buy anything until the baby came, because they would say, "That was tempting providence." Not until the baby came. Then you went and bought for it.

☐ At New Year's time we would not let anyone in the house after midnight unless they were a dark-haired person. They never come with empty hands. They always bring a piece of coal or salt, tea—any of these. They would put the coal on the fire and say, "Hope your fire burns all year." This is good luck.

☐ If you visit a new home, take a gift and say, "That's to hansel your new home." You'd never go and visit someone in a new home without taking a little minding.

☐ For the whole month of January after New Year's, at home you'd never go to anyone's home without taking something—even if it was just a little package of tea or some candies.

☐ I know an Irish lady at home (Scotland), and every time she had company that was Protestant, she would bring the priest to bless her house and drive those Protestant spirits from her home.

☐ When a cat [washes] right over its ears, it's going to rain.

☐ In Scotland, a spider's good luck because a spider saved Scotland at one of the battles. They were going to have to retreat the next day, and the Bruce was laying and watching a spider. Seven times it was trying to make its web, and it succeeded on the seventh time. So he tried again the next day and won the battle. No one would kill a spider in Scotland at all.

☐ In Britain or Scotland, thunder turns milk sour.

☐ If you take your fasting spittle in the morning and spit on a wart, it is supposed to make the wart go away.

☐ If anybody got hit in the head or face and it raised a bump, we used to put a penny on it and hold it there. A big penny, you know, a British one.

☐ A black cat following you is good luck.

☐ You'd never pass a penny on the road. That was good luck, a half penny.

☐ A safety pin on the ground: You'd pick it up and spit on it three times and keep it. That's good luck.

☐ If we saw a white horse, a pure white horse, we'd come [turn] around three times.

☐ One crow, sorrow;
Two crows, joy;
Three crows, a letter;
Four crows, a boy.

☐ In Scotland, if a dog howls at night (and they couldn't stop her) very soon somebody would die.

☐ We have a superstition about green. It's a very unlucky color to wear. I had one sister wore green constantly, and she died. And I had a sister-in-law that in her house everything was green. She couldn't get enough green; everything was green. And she is gone.

☐ When you went and bought new shoes, we didn't dare put the new shoes on the table.

☐ Sing before breakfast; cry before bedtime.

☐ To dream of water is trouble.

☐ If you give anyone a pin or knives, you always get a penny or coin of some kind in return. Even when I sent knives over to my girl friend there, I told her "You have to send me back a coin." And she did.

JANET LAUENER'S NEW YEAR'S PREPARATIONS

You scrub your doorstep and you polish your name plates because you will not open that door again til after midnight. And about fifteen minutes before midnight, you hang your drapes, you take the ashes out, but you leave a little of last year's ashes; it means good luck. And everything is spotless. The table is set with the wine and the shortbread and the pig and dumplings.

Then you just sit and wait for midnight and for your company, your "first-footer" to come. They must be a dark person. They come in, and they bring a piece of coal, some tea, or a bottle. And they'll wish you "Happy New Year," and then go from one house to another, all night until about 8 o'clock in the morning.

Baker City

Baker County. Population 9,114. Both Baker County and its largest city are named for Edward Dickinson Baker, a U.S. senator from Oregon. Before the incursions of settlers, the location of Baker City was "safe ground" for Native Americans of all tribes; members of warring bands recognized the sanctity of the place and would not disturb even the most hated enemy. Baker City was a central location on the Old Oregon Trail, and after 1861, the hub of mining country, an area approximately 200 miles square.

Today a common story in Baker County is "The Portland Hunter," an insider's tale that makes fun of big-city folk. Like many stories told in rural Oregon, the Portland hunter lacks common sense, but makes up for it with an extra portion of gall. In 1971, Melissa Oestreich collected this well-known legend on the streets of Baker City.

THE PORTLAND HUNTER

This guy comes over from Portland hunting around here. Never been hunting before in his life. "Portland hunters" is what they call 'em. And he doesn't know what *an elk looks like, so he's asking everybody what an elk looks like. And they tell him. They give him a pretty good description of what an elk looks like.*

And he goes tromping out through the woods, and he comes back several hours later. He's bragging to everybody about this big elk he's shot. And he gets everybody out there to the trunk of his car to see the elk that he shot, and what is it? It's a bull. He shot a bull; the thing even had a brand on it . . . skinned the thing out, brought it all the way back to the town before somebody that saw the thing told him that he had shot a bull.

Bingham Springs

Umatilla County. In 1864 a large building was erected at this site, called Warm Springs, by William "Tip" Parrent. At various times in Oregon history, Bingham Springs has been a popular Blue Mountains resort.

Nearby on the Umatilla River stands Elephant Rock, a powerful reminder of the time when the gods walked on the earth. From the Cayuse tribe comes the ancient legend of Bingham Springs' curious rock formation. Thought to derive from memory of mammoths, it is a story that proves Coyote's power among the great natural deities of the land. The Cayuse tale bears some structural similarities to the Siletz story of "Elephant Rock" (see Otter Crest, p. 28), also an etiological legend.

THE LEGEND OF ELEPHANT ROCK

A long time ago, the Cayuse lived along the Umatilla River. They were happy and peaceful. There was much food from fish and deer. One day, as the hunters were searching for game, they heard a great commotion. The animals were running to the south in great flight. The earth began to tremble. The trees started to fall. Great strange creatures, making terrible noises, came crashing through the forest, ripping out pines and hurling them to the canyons below. The Cayuse warriors were brave, but the huge monsters could not be overcome. The warriors fled to the high points of the mountains.

Soon the monsters came to the Umatilla River and plunged in. They churned the water and splashed it over the banks with their huge feet. The salmon were frightened, and many were trampled on the bed of the stream. Many salmon threw themselves onto the bank of the river to die.

Fleeing to the River of the North, the Cayuse people talked about the monsters who had destroyed the land and turned the Umatilla River to mud. The deer were gone, and the berries and roots had been trampled. The Cayuse could find no food.

Now, Coyote was all-powerful and saw everything that had happened. He was watching from high on his mountaintop. Coyote could see what the monsters had done, and he

knew they had been sent by skookums, *evil spirits who made trouble for the Cayuse. When he heard his people crying for help, he hurried quickly to the Umatilla River.*

Reaching the river, Coyote called the great creatures before him. Then he said, "Look at me, elephants. I am the great god Coyote! I am all-powerful. I am all-seeing. I am angry. You have been sent by the evil spirits to destroy my people. The Cayuse are my people. They are brave, gentle, and peace-loving. They have done you no harm. But you have destroyed their homeland and driven them from the river. Now you must return to your own country in the North. You must never return, or you will be punished. Much evil will befall you. Now go, and you will not be punished. I have spoken."

The elephants knew Coyote was the more powerful, so they did as commanded. Then the Cayuse returned to the Umatilla River. The salmon began to run up the stream; game returned to the forest; and berries took root once again. The Cayuse people learned again to smile.

But in the North the leader of the elephant herd was not content. He was angry at being told what to do, and he remembered the green hills, the forests, and the feel of the water as he bathed in the Umatilla River. One dark night he left the herd and returned to the river, where he bathed in the comforting pools and roamed through the forest. He felt good. The elephant thought, "Coyote is not such a strong god. I am not afraid."

One day while the elephant was standing in the river, letting the cool water flow onto his belly, he looked up and saw Coyote coming down from the mountaintop. Fear went through his body, and he tried to slip quietly away. But Coyote had seen him in the river. He said, "Well, my friend, you did not heed my words when I told you never to return to the land of the Cayuse. Why did you come back in spite of my warning?"

Coyote's gentle manner gave the elephant courage. He thought, "Why should I fear such a small creature? He is not nearly so powerful as he pretends. Coyote is afraid of my great size. I will show him I don't take orders from anyone."

So the elephant said, "I am the leader of the elephants. You are nothing but a small god. You are miserable and weak. What makes you think you can tell me where to go and what to do? I am not going to leave, and I will bring back the other elephants from the North. We will see what you can do about that."

Now Coyote was a gentle god and very wise, but he could not allow such impudence. "You are an arrogant, stubborn bull," he said, and immediately put a curse on the elephant. "From this day you will never return to your homeland. You will stand on this spot forever, through winter's ice and snow, through summer's sun and heat. You will serve as a warning to all other evil-doers. I have spoken."

That was a long time ago. The elephant still stands there today, looking toward the Northland.

Canyon City

Grant County. Population 647. Canyon City, on the south side of the John Day River, was first called "Lower Town," with John Day City the "Upper Town." The name Canyon City is purely descriptive. The town sprang up overnight, as many boomtowns did, when gold was discovered in Whiskey Gulch in 1862.

The town was established on the banks of Canyon Creek. Nearly 5,000 miners camped at Whiskey Gulch and Whiskey Creek, mining either side of the streams, shoulder to shoulder. At the peak of the rush, 10,000 miners and camp followers made up the population of the bustling town. Millions of dollars in nuggets and gold dust were taken from the streams during the 1860s, bringing the usual collection of snake-oil salesmen, gamblers, and fast-buck schemers. Tempers were short in the gold towns, and times were precarious. William Kane earned the rope for shooting a man who had the audacity to pay Kane's salary in greenbacks instead of gold.

After the ore played out in the creeks and rivers, hydraulic mining began on the canyon walls. Prospectors still visit this area with sluice box or gold pan to try their luck in the streams. Some think the nuggets of the famous Blue Bucket Mine came from the tributaries of the John Day River.

Joaquin Miller, the "poet of the Sierras," settled in Canyon City after the gold strike. When Grant County was formed in 1864, Miller was elected the first judge. The jail building, much used in those early times, still stands.

In 1910 ranch hand Charlie McKay was walking toward Canyon City along the old stage route from Bear Valley. About three miles out of town, he looked down and saw a big chunk of high-grade ore, a nugget about as big as a man's head. Unable to haul the nugget all the way to Canyon City, he broke off some pieces, rolled the main chunk into the creek, hiding the fortune where he could find it later. Unfortunately, McKay's mind was on Nora, the little dance-hall girl at the Whiskey Gulch Saloon, who held more glitter for Charlie than the gold he had just found.

The next morning, holding his head in his hands, Charlie staggered back down the stage road toward his fortune. For the next six days, Charlie searched the bend in the river where he knew he had left the nugget, but to no avail.

Early in March 1915, Chuck McCorkle rented a horse and lit out for Miller Mountain, south of Canyon City, at a time when the snow was melting fast. McCorkle sat down on a big quartz boulder to eat lunch. As he sat there, more by instinct than design, he broke off several pieces of the quartz rock and pocketed them. Days later, McCorkle got the chunks from his pocket, washed them off, and found rich gold ore embedded in the quartz. Unable to retrace his trail, McCorkle spent several frustrating seasons trying to retrace his steps and to recover the fantastic boulder.

Cayuse

Native American land in Umatilla County. South and east of Pendleton, the Umatilla Reservation, with a population of 2,495, is the home of Umatilla, Cayuse, and Walla Walla Indians. The Cayuse Indians, who had a reputation for bravery, were known as the monarchs of the Pacific Northwest after their acquisition of horses. Cayuse, a synonym for horse, is evidence of the tribe's adaption to life on horseback.

The Confederated Tribes were drastically reduced by settlers' diseases in the 1800s—especially smallpox and diphtheria, for which they had no immunity. These ravages, plus the encroachment of settlers onto Indian lands, gradually led to Indian wars and to the erosion of Native American life-styles. Nonetheless, Indian cultures have retained much of their rich folklore, as shown in the symbolism of the feather. In 1982, Beatrice Rubio attended a powwow in Eugene, a meeting of Native Americans from tribes all over the Northwest. Although being outside the ethnic group no doubt served as a barrier to collecting, Rubio's Mexican-American heritage gave her a slight advantage over Anglo interviewers, as she suggests.

Rubio noted both dynamism and conservatism (Toelken's terms) in the style of the feather. "The majority of my informants," says Rubio, "knew something traditional about the feather, which they combined with their personal philosophy." For the Confederated Tribes, the feather is a significant symbol of culture. The color, number, and patterns of worn feathers reveal much about Indian society, as incorporated in traditional dress. Although the lore of the feather is complex, some generalities hold.

FEATHERS AND FOLKLORE

☐ *A single feather is the sign of purity, especially the eagle feather. Women in the Umatilla tribe indicate that they are unmarried by wearing a single feather.*
☐ *Two feathers signifies a marriage or relationship, especially when a woman wears them in her hair.*
☐ *Plumes are more sacred than tail feathers, worn for religious or ritual occasions.*
☐ *When a young woman wears a headband and a feather, that means she is single and a princess.*
☐ *Eagle feathers connote strength and wisdom. They must be earned, however. Not just anyone can wear the eagle's feathers.*
☐ *Colors have special significance. White is for the north and the cold, the enduring winds that purify the earth. Red is for the east, where the Morning Star dwells to give man wisdom. Yellow is for the south, country of heat and sun, signifying birth and growth. Black is for the west, where the thunder beam dwells to bring rain upon the earth.*

□ *Owl feathers are not good medicine because, for most tribes, the owl is the harbinger of death (see Siletz, p. 30).*

In 1974, Roberta Conner contributed the "Legend of the Eagle and the Skunk" to the Randall V. Mills Archives. Conner collected the story from her grandmother Elsie, a speaker of the Umatilla language and a member of the Confederated Tribes. The storytelling took place on a trip to Walla Walla where the family would buy Christmas gifts. Because the car had no radio, Grandmother Elsie stretched out this story for almost forty miles, entertaining Roberta and her younger brother. "She animated the Skunk's walk with movements of her fingers across the dashboard," says Conner, "and the swoop of the Eagle the same way, with her hands."

THE LEGEND OF THE EAGLE AND THE SKUNK

Well, the Eagle had just made a trade for a beautiful young human woman to become his wife. When the Skunk heard of this, he got jealous and, being that he was one of the least respected animals and the Eagle was very respected, he began to think that he should take the Eagle's new bride. Besides, he had heard that this woman was very, very lovely, so he thought he would like to have her for himself.

So when the bride's family came to the Eagle's camp to deliver her, Eagle was not there, but Skunk was hiding in the brush behind the camp. The family left the bride and went home. Then Skunk went into the camp and told the bride

that he was her new husband because he had made a deal with Eagle. She cried and cried that morning; she didn't want to be the bride of a skunk.

That same afternoon Eagle came back to camp to meet his new bride, but he found Skunk had taken over his camp and his beautiful new wife, too. When he tried to chase the skunk away, Skunk would raise his tail and threaten to fire "stink" at the Eagle. The Eagle knew how bad Skunk's stink smelled, and he knew if Skunk aimed at him, the stink would make his wife and his camp stink for a long, long time. So Eagle left.

A few days later Skunk became confident that he'd beaten Eagle, and so he let the beautiful woman go out to dig roots, yet she was still within his view. The Eagle was watching the camp the whole time. So when the woman was out digging roots, Eagle flew very fast into a tree near her. He flew so fast that Skunk did not see him. Eagle called to the woman, and she moved toward him, all the time doing digging movements so Skunk wouldn't suspect anything.

Eagle told her that he had a plan to rescue them both from their unhappiness. He told her that she and Skunk were to go to the hilltop tomorrow, and she would pick berries while Skunk lounged on the top of the hill watching her. She said she would convince Skunk that she wanted to pick berries the next day, and she knew he would go with her.

The next day, as she was picking huckleberries, she saw the Eagle approach the hill. Skunk saw him, too. Eagle yelled to the woman to come to him. The woman did this, and at the same time, Skunk began to holler threats at them. She and Eagle just kept walking closer toward Skunk, and Skunk kept on yelling, all the time thinking, "I'll wait 'til they get real close, and then I can do them in for good." Eagle had a plan, too. He had a small, round stone hidden in his feathers.

So when they were real close, Skunk raised his tail, turned around, and started backing toward them, laughing all the time. So when he was just about to fire stink at them, Eagle, who has a deadly aim at all that he does—like how he swoops down and snatches the tiniest, scurrying creatures from the ground—threw the small stone at Skunk's itits, and it fit perfect and stuck there. With Skunk all plugged up and mad, the Eagle went back to his camp with his lovely bride, never to fear that Skunk again, for he had taken the only power that Skunk had.

Copperfield

Baker County. Population 0. The name Copperfield recalls the ore mined in this once-flourishing boomtown. Copperfield disappeared from Baker County maps after three fires wiped out the town's wood-frame buildings. But no amount of flame is likely to purify the rampaging reputation of Wild West Copperfield.

Copperfield was a rough-and-ready place during the gold rush. Lewiston, Idaho—just downriver from Copperfield—has one of the largest cemeteries in the world with unmarked gravesites. Apparently it was common practice for desperate men to dump their victims in the Snake River and let them float down the canyons to Lewiston.

Governor Oswald West acquired a reputation as a fearless politician and will always be remembered by Oregonians for saving the coastal beaches from private ownership. However, West's reputation for political daring suffers a bit when the topic of conversation turns to events at Copperfield. On January 2, 1915, in response to the news of shameless indecencies, public drunkenness, and unrestricted thievery, Governor West sent his personal emissary to Copperfield to close down the saloons and clean up the town. Miss Fern Hobbs, the governor's secretary, arrived with a small contingent of military men, only to find the streets of Copperfield decked with flowers in honor of her arrival. Unbowed by this show of affection, Miss Hobbs carried out the governor's orders and beat a hasty retreat by the next train.

While Miss Hobbs was retreating, others were arriving. According to two skilled folklore collectors, Bert W. Bennehoff and Diane C. Brooks, Jim Mulino came to America from Ireland, heading for New Zealand. When he got to Huntington, Mulino had a long layover, and a fellow traveler suggested that the two men go down to Copperfield, a town grown large by the activities of the Red Ledge Mine. Mulino agreed, and soon found himself chugging into this wild and wooly place. When the men arrived, the "working girls" were walking across the main street in only their high-heeled shoes—stark naked otherwise—to get their mail.

The Irishman said, "Oh, God. What kind of place is this? Man I ain't seen nothin' like that in my life." Well, Mulino stuck around Copperfield for thirty days, went to Seattle to cancel his ticket to New Zealand, and returned to Copperfield. He spent his whole life there and died in Eagle Valley, just down the road.

Bennehoff and Brooks also collected a story about Eagle Valley, just west of Halfway. One day, Ernest Anderson, Dave D'Oliva, John Crocker, Joe Matson, Dutch Hollins, and Alvin Johnston [names changed] were "stompin' wool" in Homestead with the three Barnes boys on a twelve-man sheep-shearing crew. In a short time, however, three Copperfield girls arrived and shut down the operation.

IN THE SACK

Barney Hollins (he still lives in Eagle Valley), he was stompin' wool. And there was three girls, the oldest one was seventeen, lived right across the canyon. Their old man sold moonshine whiskey. And they come over, and they said, "Less' have a party."

And Joe says, "Well, we gonna start shearin' sheep. It's the noon; we can start in right after dinner and shear sheep, we're not gonna party." And he's jacked up a Model T Ford, an' leave one wheel on the ground. It left the other one runnin'—it did the pullin'—for power. And the girls got in the boat and went back across the river and went up to the old man's still and come back with twelve gallons of moonshine, and they walked around and set one by every shearer.

Well now that moonshine, I don't know what percentage alcohol, but it's pretty stout. But anyway it ain't long 'till John comes in and Ernest Anderson—that's the one that died, that was the barber—was givin' Alvin over here a haircut with the sheep shears. And Old Barney Hollins has one of them girls in the wool sack with him. You know how big a wool sack is, and she's down inside the wool sack.

And they wonder what's goin' on and one of the guys says, "Well, let's look and see," and grabs a jack-knife and just cut the wool sack length[wise]. That's what was goin' on, 'cuz he never even quit right out on the floor.

And Dave says, "Well, shut off the plant 'cuz they're gonna tear it up." And they had a party. And the oldest girl was seventeen.

Cornucopia

Baker County. Cornucopia, meaning "horn of plenty," is a mining town. It lies in the Wallowa Mountains northeast of Baker City.

In 1938, Walker Winslow of the Federal Writers' Project interviewed Hank Simms at a nursing home in Portland. Simms was a miner who had spent several years in the Cornucopia-Baker area, holding every job from blaster to mine superintendent. When asked about his mining career, Simms said, "I have followed it for 50 or 60 years and dug a shaft straight into this poorhouse. You can't call that very good mining." An interesting gloss on Northeastern Oregon mining days is Simms's oral history of Wild West Cornucopia.

BLIND PIGS AND COUSIN JACKS

I drifted into Cornucopia one night on the late stage—just out shaking the smell of Portland off myself—and I dropped into a blind pig *to warm up a little. I am not a drinking man, but the bartender there could see I was an old* overlander, *and he grinned at the sight of me. We didn't talk much and when I was leaving to go to the hotel to bed, he asked me, "Looking for a job, old-timer?" I told him that was the idea. He says, "Well, you go see So-and-So in the morning; he wants a man. What's your name?" I told him and went to bed.*

The next morning I went around to see the guy he told me about, and [the foreman] asked me a lot of questions about who I knew and where I worked, and I told him as much as he wanted to know. I could see that the job was in highgrade *and that he wanted to know who he was hiring. Well, he was just about to* paint my check *for me, when here comes that bartender, and he says, ''Say, So-and-So, aren't you hiring this man? This is Hank Simms. He don't amount to nothing and never will, but he's a* hard rock *from way back and so tight* you'd have to take a ten-pound sledge to drive a drill up his ass.''

''You're hired,'' So-and-So says. Well, I handled some of the steepest highgrade you ever seen for that man. I have seen the time we pulled down a stand of highgrade that would run 600 ounces of silver to the ton, and maybe 300 gold. I don't think the man ever watched me. He trusted me and that was the kind of highgrade you handle in canvas so none of it will leak out. That bartender's word was better than a deacon's.

I had a Swede working with me that couldn't leave that highgrade alone. He was an honest man, I guess, but there was just too damned much highgrade there for him to stand up under. The shaft ran straight back in the mountain, and this highgrade ore came in clumps ever so often. The way you do with it is leave it hanging—work around it till you get ordinary dirt again. That way the super can see it and know you aren't highgrading him. (Highgrading is stealing ore when it pays to cart it off). One day we ran around a hanging of rich stuff and finished it off at quitting time. I always came out of the tunnel, but Ole couldn't seem to drag himself away and about the time I got outside, I knew that he had weakened. I heard a crash, and the Swede had brought down the hanging.

When he came out, he said, ''We can pick it up first thing in the morning and we won't have to knock it down.'' An hour later the super came around and said, ''Ole, I am going to have to lay you off. You're a good man, but I got to lay someone off, and it might as well be you. I am going down the hill tonight, and you can go with me for company.'' You couldn't leave that Swede and that highgrade in the same county, and the super knew it. He didn't blame the Swede, and he walked down to town with him to keep him honest. I have been too god-damned honest. People used to call me Honest Hank Simms. They ought to have said, ''There goes Honest Hank Simms on the way to the poorhouse.''

Besides highgrading there was a lot of salting *and crooked assaying went on in the early days—still does. I saw a lot of it. Some of those* highbinders *brought ore samples clean from Mexico to salt an Oregon mine with, and a man that had worked this country would know it was foreign ore, but people are prone to be fools. That's why we got places like* [the Odd Fellows' Old Folks Home]. *I didn't open my mouth about it many times for the chances are that the man who was mining on a salted claim had just as much chance as he would anyplace else. If he had to be digging a tunnel, it didn't make much difference where, just so it was in mining country.*

What was worse was the crooked assayers. You'd take your samples to them, and they'd pitch them out the back door and tell you what they had been paid to tell you—that your ore was worth, say, 70 or 80 dollars a ton. You take them a piece of highgrade, and they'd tell you the same thing. There was a way to get around that, though, and I showed more than one man how to do it. You'd take a half dozen samples and put them in six numbered envelopes and then take a half dozen envelopes that were empty, and when you got in the office of the assayer, you split the samples between envelopes and told him you were going to have the Government check on him, but that you wanted a hurry-up assay. You'd scare the Jesus out of him that way, and he would be as honest as he was able. Most assayers were drunkards and had the jimmies so bad that they didn't know what they were doing. I saved one man—I won't give you his name—a lot of money that way. When I tell you about him, you'll wonder why I did it. He was as big a fool as I am. He railroaded forty years in this state, starved his family, and spent every cent he made on mines. The only thing that ever paid him was the pension he had spent forty years staking a claim on. Miners are fools, boy—all of them.

I saw one poor galoot of a Cousin Jack—that's a Cornishman—come into a place with not enough clothes on him to flag a handcar. He put his last dollar on the Double 0 on the wheel in the gambling hall, and it hit. He was drunk, and so the dealer said, ''Let it lay.'' Double 0 pays 36–1. He did and, by God, he hit her. The house didn't have enough money to pay him more than $800. In three days, all Cousin Jack had was the jimmies and no breakfast, and the next

time I saw he was a bull cook *in a Mormon camp. Happy, he said as soon as he made a stake he was going prospecting.*

MINERS' JARGON

blind pig: a saloon, usually on the wrong side of the tracks
ball mill: a large steel hopper with balls of steel that rotate inside, breaking up the ore
bull cook: a chore boy or cook's ''gofer''
come along: a chain and pulley device for lifting heavy objects. It fits over a timber or girder.
cut shot: to drill straight into the face of a rock to break it
cyanide tanks: a chemical bath to separate the gold from the ore
drag line: a shovel and bucket that pulls forward and removes the topsoil
highbinder: a cheat
highgrade: the richest kind of ore
Jim Crow: an implement to straighten and lay mine track
left shot: to drill at an angle, so that the rock will shear off rather than break
overlander: a transient or hobo
paint a check: to fire a man, to pay him off, or to choose not to hire him
powder headache: a headache caused by inhaling fumes from blasting. As a cure, ''suck on a piece of dynamite.''
retort: to melt down gold and turn it into bars
salting: using a shotgun to implant gold pieces in the wall of a mine shaft, often done by someone wishing to sell his played-out claim.
stamp mill: a machine that stamps and crushes the gold ore
tight: honest, trustworthy

Echo

Umatilla County. Population 499. Echo was named for Echo Koontz, daughter of Mr. and Mrs. J. H. Koontz, who settled there around 1880. Echo's claim to fame was a down-on-his-luck hungry kid who rolled from the rods of a slow-moving freight train. He was the ninth child in an Irish-Cherokee-Jewish family, whose friends called him Harry. Broke and looking for work, he found the hobo jungle on the bend of the Umatilla River, where men without work shared food and company. Soon he was working the irrigation canals and worked weekends as a bouncer in a Pendleton saloon. In the bars, his fighting earned him the title of Jack, the Giant Killer. Instead of Harry, the young man soon was known as Jack.

Every now and then, Jack would visit Logsdon's Butcher Shop, order twenty-five cents' worth of meat, and hand the merchant a $100 bill. Of course, the butcher could not change the bill, so he inevitably gave Jack the meat and said, ''We'll square up next time.'' After several repetitions, Logsdon got wise. When Jack once again appeared, the butcher said, ''Sure, I can change that bill.'' Quickly young Jack withdrew the money, saying, ''I have lived for several months on this bill,'' before giving Logsdon the right change for the meat.

Young Jack spent many years in Eastern Oregon—enough time to marry and divorce a girl from Echo; he also found time to hone his fighting skills on the chins of many local ruffians. After leaving Echo, the young man entered the professional fight game, eventually becoming heavyweight champion of the world in 1919 when he beat Jess Willard in four rounds. Since the Roaring Twenties, residents of Echo have proudly claimed Jack Dempsey as one of their own.

Manerva Mendenhall was the daughter of British settlers who moved to Oregon in 1865. After her birth in Lane County in 1869, young Manerva traveled with her family to Umatilla County, where they established a homestead on the outskirts of Echo. In her scrapbooks and diaries, Manerva Mendenhall left this fascinating cupboard of folk medicines, some of them not nearly as dangerous as the offending disease. The notebooks were discovered by Beverly Berry in 1970 and excerpted for the Mills Archives.

TRADITIONAL CURES AND FOLK MEDICINES FROM ECHO

☐ *Remedy for summer diseases. Mix and sift through a fine cloth one-half ounce of gunpowder, one-half ounce of alum, one-half ounce of saltpeter, one-half ounce cream-of-tartar, and one-half ounce of sulphur. Take three-quarters teaspoonful for a dose. It may be mixed with a little vinegar and water.*

☐ *Rattlesnake bites. Moisten fresh earth with water or saliva and bind on the wound immediately, changing it every quarter of an hour. Tie a handkerchief tightly above the wound to prevent the poison from spreading. Keep the patient quiet and send for whiskey to completely stupefy him as quickly as possible. Recovery is usually sure.*

☐ *For poison ivy. Rub garden mold on the infected area; the mold will neutralize the poison.*

☐ *Remedies for rheumatism. (1) Serving asparagus as the chief article of diet (and avoiding all acids in food and drink) will effect great relief in a few days. (2) Celery, boiled in milk or water and eaten is helpful in the same disease. (3) Put six large onions in a pint of molasses and steep the mixture until a thick syrup is formed. Take some every two or three hours. Persevere and success will follow. A tea of burdock roots or burdock leaves may be taken at the same time with good effect. For an outward application, a flannel bag with arnica blossoms heated in a steamer may be applied to the spot. (4) Rheumatic pains in the face and teeth may be greatly alleviated by adopting the following course: Take two teaspoonsful of flour, the same quantity of grated ginger, and incorporate them well together with sufficient spirits to make a thin paste. Spread this paste on a linen rag and apply it to the affected part on going to bed. Wrap a piece of flannel over all, and it will effect a cure.*

□ *For bad blood. Mix one ounce of saltpeter and one ounce of rum. Use one teaspoonful three times a day before eating. Very good. Cooling to the blood.*

□ *For scalds and burns. Nothing in the world is better for a burn, however severe, or a scald, however deep, than a preparation as for a pie crust, omitting the salt. Everyone knows that lard and flour rubbed together is good, but it rubs off. If water be mixed with these two ingredients and the whole rolled out thin and placed over the burn as quickly as possible—and allowed to remain until it drops off—neither inflammation nor scar will remain.*

□ *Remedies for neuralgia. (1) Heat a flat-iron or brick and cover it with two or three thicknesses of flannel wrung out of strong vinegar. Apply to the painful spot. (2) Neuralgia of the face has been cured by applying a mustard plaster to the elbow. For neuralgia in the head, apply the plaster to the back of the neck.*

□ *For headache. A foot-bath, provided a handful of common soda is added to the water, will often relieve a severe headache, especially if followed by a brisk rub.*

□ *For diphtheria. Put one teaspoonful of flour of brimstone into a wine glass full of water. Stir it with the finger and use as a gargle, swallowing some of it, if possible. If a patient cannot gargle, take a live coal, put it on a shovel, and sprinkle a spoonful or two of the flour of brimstone on it. Let the patient inhale the fumes, and the fungus will die. In extreme cases, blow the sulphur through a quill into the throat and, after the fungus has shrunk, give the gargle.*

□ *Remedy for removing suntan. Mix one cup of buttermilk and one tablespoonful of freshly grated horseradish. Let it stand twelve hours, strain it, and apply the mixture to the face.*

□ *To prevent hair from falling off. Mix two ounces of* eau de Cologne, *two drachms of tincture of cantharides, ten drops of oil of lavender, and ten drops of oil of rosemary. Use once or twice a day.*

□ *For toothache. Add one ounce of alcohol (33 degrees), four grains of camphor, twenty grains of opium in powder, and eighty drops of oil of cloves.*

□ *Dental care. Mix equal parts of Castile soap (grated fine) and prepared chalk (precipitated). Mix and use as a tooth powder.*

Greenhorn

Baker County. Population 0. Greenhorn, once a lively mining community, lies quiet and undisturbed, west of Sumpter and east of Vinegar Hill, below Greenhorn Mountain. Known originally as The Green Horn, this 7,700-foot promontory was named for the bright green color of its serpentine rock. During the gold rush of the 1860s, when the hills were full of city boys looking to make a strike, the name of the mountain and the town were changed to Greenhorn by the arrival and subsequent good luck of a fresh kid from the city. According to Carl Hentz, interviewed by WPA folklorists in 1939, the new man in town stretched good luck to its limits.

ONE OPHIR HOLE IS AS GOOD AS ANOTHER

A greenhorn came into the small mining town looking for a mine. The boys, after giving him the "once over," decided he was looking for shade. They told him that under a large tree near the camp would be a good place to start digging. The most pleasant part of the digging would be all the nice shade he would have from the tree. I'll be damned! The greenhorn dug there, went down about seven or eight feet, and struck it rich. He took the odd-looking stuff that he had found and asked a fellow in the camp if that wasn't gold. Poor guy, he didn't know gold from brass. To him, rock was rock. Well, the boys told him it was gold. Hell, there wasn't anything else to do. He sold the mine for $70,000.

In Greenhorn it was not unusual to get fifteen feet of snow, and Baldy, one of the locals, was fond of an occasional glass of whiskey to "warm the bones." Despite his impecunious state, old Baldy was a smart businessman. Whenever he was feeling chilled, Baldy would sell his dog, Spike, for enough cash to buy a bottle. It wasn't that Baldy didn't like his dog, but the old man knew that Spike would take the first opportunity and run home. Baldy sold that dog many times.

In Greenhorn the miners were often Cousin Jacks, men from Cornwall. The Cornishmen ate miner's grub that was not elegant, but nourishing and filling, usually carrying their fare in a scoured-out lard bucket. Besides the usual lunch of beans, bacon, biscuits and gravy, the Cousin Jacks often carried "pasties" to work—little meat pies, made of meat and potatoes wrapped in a pastry blanket.

PASTIES

4 cups of flour
1½ teaspoons of salt
1½ cups of lard or shortening
½ cup of water

Add the salt to the flour and cut in the shortening. Work the mixture with your hands until it is like cornmeal. Add the water and continue to mix. Roll the dough into eight-inch circles.

¼ cup of butter
1½ to 2 pounds of beef (Lean round steak is best.)
3 or 4 medium potatoes
2 medium onions
3 or 4 carrots
pinch of garlic
dash of pepper

Chop the meat and vegetables into small pieces and mix with the melted butter, garlic, and pepper. Spread this mixture over half the pastry round; wet the edges of the circle and press the halves together with the tines of a fork. Cut slits in the top crust of the pastie. Bake the pasties on a cookie sheet at 425 degrees for one hour.

Halfway

Baker County. Population 311. Ironically, Halfway is no longer halfway between any two towns or noteworthy stations, although perhaps at one time the post office lay somewhere near the midpoint between Pine and Cornucopia. Halfway was a wide-open town in earlier years when the Cornucopia Mine was in full operation. In an account gathered by Chris Grissom and Candy Anderson, Baker resident Jack Nash tells about a typical night's recreation in Halfway around 1935.

A SMALL DISPUTE OVER CARDS

Tex—he hauled freight for the mine—had just got paid off from his freight contract, and he had about 4,000 bucks. He went into this saloon, and they were playing cards in there, so he got into the card game. Well, anyway, Tex caught Rhoner cheating, so they got into a fist fight. Everybody else around got up from their tables and moved them against the wall and made an arena for these guys to fight in. So they fit and they fit. This went on for a good half hour. Both of them were a real mess.

In their fighting they had got over against the wall where a doctor was standing that had been playing poker. So the doctor got up and was trying to stop them, and Tex was on top of Rhoner, and both of them were about done for. So the doctor grabbed Tex by the hair and banged his head a couple of times under the card table. Rhoner got loose, and everybody picked up their card tables, with their hands and drinks still laid out, and moved them back to their original places. Everybody started playing again, Tex and Rhoner together.

Joe Samples was a famous Halfway-area resident. Old Joe couldn't go very long without a drink of whiskey, a fact that didn't sit too well with his employers. But Joe was a practical man, a fellow who found easy solutions to vexing problems. A version of this story, here slightly revised, comes from a man who knew Joe Samples in Baker. Speaking without gestures, the informant describes the ''Old S,'' meaning the Snake River Highway before the Brownlee Dam was built, and Pine Valley, the land surrounding Halfway. A ''horse on me'' refers to a disadvantage in a dice game; a ''horse'' is a negative score.

THAT THERE'S A HORSE ON ME

Old Joe Samples believed you couldn't live without a little whiskey. Well, Joe drove the stage line for Cooper out of Pine Valley down to Robinette—down the Old S, down the crooked grade on the old side. There's a water pump at the

top of the canyon, and when he stopped by, the bosses said, *''Joe, by God, we're gonna fire ya if you don't quit drinkin'. No more drinkin' on the job.''*

''Awright, awright,'' he said. So, every time he wanted a drink, he'd just stop the stage, get off, and take a big drink. But he never stopped drinking.

One time Joe was in the stage office in Halfway. All stage offices had pot-bellied stoves, and underneath lots of them was a metal grate that the stove sat on. Well, old Josiah, he said, ''Joe, you've drank whiskey so long, why don't you quit?''

Joe said, ''I'll tell you what I'll do. I'll just flip this silver dollar.'' He took one out of his pocket. ''If it lands on edge, I'll quit, and if it lands flat, I'm gonna keep right on a drinkin'.'' So Joe flipped the silver dollar, and it bounced a few times and rolled right up alongside the metal stove bracket. The dollar teetered a little bit and stood right up on edge.

Well now, that chance wouldn't happen more than once in a million times—that a dollar would stand right up on edge. Maybe never, who knows. But it did. Old Joe looked down and said, ''Best two out of three.'' ''But,'' he added with a wry smile, ''That there's a horse *on me!''*

Irrigon

Morrow County. Population 731. The area where Irrigon now stands was originally called *Ronde Landing* and later named *Stokes.* The name *Irrigon* was coined by Postmaster Addison Bennett in 1903, who noted the area's immense investment in irrigation projects. *Irrigon* is actually a blend of the words Irrigation and Oregon. Addison, a newspaperman by trade, later quit the post office and began a regional newspaper he called the *Oregon Irrigator.*

From the folklore collections of the Federal Writers' Project comes a light-hearted account of the Yakima Indians' joke on the settlers.

THE BRANDED COYOTES

Livestock brands originated in the early 1800s, a necessity when little homesteads and ranches began to blossom on the open range. Even then, there were constant conflicts over cattle ownership, and Northeastern Oregon, like every other Western region, was plagued with stories of gun-fights settling the matter of which cow belonged to which rancher at round-up time.

The Indians of the Irrigon area looked on these range conflicts—and on the curious practice of branding—with a skeptical eye. After all, to the Native Americans, putting a stamp of ownership on a cow's rump made about as much sense as trying to buy or sell 100 acres of land.

By the late 1890s, there was not a steer, sheep, or ox in Indian territory that did not bear the white man's brand. The Yakima Indians, who at that time occupied a reserva-

tion on the Oregon side of the Columbia, found the prolifera-tion of brands particularly amusing, and the elders made jokes among themselves about the industrious folly of the ranchers.

Soon the youngsters of the tribe began mimicking the whites in a quiet but ironic way. The young Yakimas began to rope the reservation coyotes, pressing the hot brand of ID (Indian Department) into their flanks. Soon the people of the Irrigon region noticed great numbers of coyotes slinking around the reservation with the logo of the Yakimas etched into their sides. Some old-timers even claim that the sport become entirely too popular; before long, coyotes were being born with the ID brand etched neatly into their rumps.

John Day

Grant County. Population 1,816. John Day is the old Upper Town, north of Canyon City and across the river. John Day is well represented in Oregon place-names, lending his name to a town, two rivers, and a dam. Coming west with the Astor expedition in 1810, Day was described by Washington Irving in *Astoria* as "about forty years of age, six feet two inches high, straight as an Indian; with an elastic step as if he trod on springs and a handsome, open, manly countenance." Irving's description of Day in his "salad days" would not hold for later years, however.

Day became an "accidental explorer" when, along with Ramsey Crooks, he fell behind other expedition members. In the years since meeting Washington Irving, Day

had embraced a less healthy life-style. On the trail, he found himself unable to keep pace with the Astor scouts. Crooks stayed to help him. They were attacked by Indians, who took their weapons, clothes, and food, leaving the explorers naked near the banks of the Columbia River in an early spring chill. Lost and suffering from exposure, they finally found an Indian who fed them and gave them skins. Soon after, Day and Crooks ran into a small party from the Astor company traveling upriver and returned to Astoria.

The town of John Day is a crossroads for major roads in the area, standing as it does in the center of Grant County. It is a supply center for valley ranchers. Annually the town turns into an Old West town, as cowboys drive cattle down Main Street on the way to winter pastures.

Thousands of Chinese lived in John Day in the gold-mining era. The Kam Wah Chung Company, a Chinese grocery, is all that remains of the large Chinatown. A queer old structure with thick stone walls, this historic building on Canton Street is being preserved as a museum. "Doc" Hay, an herbalist and the last owner of the store which closed in 1952, left an interesting collection of Chinese objects. The Kam Wah Chung Company papers give us a picture of how the Chinese lived during the gold-mining days. Lung-On, the man who owned the company prior to Doc Hay, was an intelligent man who kept records both in Chinese and English. His establishment served as a meeting place and home away from home for the Chinese laborers, who gathered to speak their own language, cook traditional foods, worship their gods, and smoke opium.

When the Kam Wah Chung store in John Day was opened to historians in 1968, the findings were fascinating. Among the relics were firsthand records of Chinese workers living in this country, as well as letters and diaries. In addition, the archivists found English-Chinese dictionaries, Buddhist statuettes, Chinese novels, fireworks, Korean ginseng, swallows' nests, texts of Cantonese opera, wooden fans, and opium pipes. Of special interest are the boxes of writings in Chinese.

CHINESE CUSTOMS FOR WEDDINGS AND BURIALS

☐ *At a wedding, the bride and groom go from table to table to be toasted by each guest in turn.*
☐ *The cousins of the bride line the chambers of the couple's bedroom with paper chains. Each cousin must receive money; then the cousin cuts the chain link, allowing the couple to pass closer toward the bed.*
☐ *At a wedding the bride and groom must each wear something made of jade, for good luck.*
☐ *It is bad luck for any family member to wash their hair on the day of a wedding. Breaking this custom can bring bad luck or even death.*
☐ *Mothers would never let their daughters wear blue, red, or white scarves; these colors on the head cause bad luck.*

□ *After a wedding, the traditional Chinese meal includes chicken soup, birds' nest soup, or shark-fin soup. The birds' nests were actually imported to this country from an island off the Chinese coast, and the contents include regurgitated food eaten by the birds.*

□ *Red is a sign of good fortune. Most Chinese brides wear red for their wedding costumes.*

□ *Someone who marries must give a gift to all unmarried family members—a money-filled envelope called* lichee. *The envelope should be red for good fortune.*

□ *At a burial, a Chinese riding in the horse-drawn hearse would throw out hundreds of small tissue papers with holes punched through them. The holes were to confuse the devil, who had to pass through each opening before approaching the soul.*

□ *At a cemetery, each person attending the funeral received a piece of Chinese candy and a coin.*

□ *Whites in John Day were often buried with their heads to the west, awaiting the Second Coming, but Chinese always lay with their heads to the east, looking homeward.*

□ *On the Chinese graves people would put food and valued objects for the departed: apples, bread, and sometimes tobacco.*

□ *The burial of any respected Chinese in John Day was temporary. When a suitable time had passed, the bones of the dead—or at least the arm bones—would be sent to China for permanent burial.*

Joseph

Wallowa County. Population 1,073. Joseph is named for Old Chief Joseph, who was the leader of the Nez Perce people in the Wallowa area. Old Chief Joseph, who claimed this land as the Nez Perce ancestral home, refused to force his people to leave. Old Chief Joseph—not to be confused with his son, who led the Nez Perce exodus of 1877—is buried in the Wallowas by the shore of his beloved Wallowa Lake.

CHIEF JOSEPH

We took away their country and their means of support, broke up their mode of living, their habits of life, introduced disease and decay among them, and it was for this and against this that they made war. Could anyone expect less?

—William Tecumseh Sherman, 1878

The culture of the Northeastern Oregon tribes had undergone a definite change a few decades before the invasion of the settlers. Through the introduction of the horse, these Native Americans had become nomadic. The Snakes, Nez Perce, and Cayuse counted their wealth in horses, and because they were thus free to move about

their culture was largely based on the chase and warfare. The Cayuse developed the breed known today as the Appaloosa.

Most Indians wore buckskin ornaments decorated with dyed porcupine quills. Quilling was found on moccasins as well. For robes, blankets, and shelters, the Northeastern Indians used skins dressed with fur intact. Wild game, roots, and berries were their staple foods. The Wallowa Mountains provided a home for the Nez Perce Indians. During the time of early settlement, the Nez Perce flourished, first under the wise leadership of Old Chief Joseph and then under Young Chief Joseph. By 1877, however, he led his people in a final desperate fight with the invaders. Young Chief Joseph had agreed that each family of white settlers could occupy 160 acres of land, leaving room enough for all. But that agreement was not enough for the settlers.

The Nez Perce watched angrily as the settlers drew artificial lines across traditional hunting and camping grounds, often cutting through their villages and holy places. Soon the old treaty agreements were broken, and the immigrants offered new treaties. But Young Chief Joseph refused to sign; his people continued to live in Wallowa country. Thereafter, Young Chief Joseph became the symbol of honesty, courage, and nobility, not only to his own people but to the settlers as well.

In 1876 the Nez Perce were ordered to leave the Wallowas. Stockmen needed the land for their cattle. Chief Joseph knew that more fighting would bring only bloodshed and no peaceful solution. Sadly his people prepared to depart; but the Indians did not move quickly. The military therefore issued harsh orders to the Nez Perce, telling them to be on their way to the reservation in Lapwai within thirty days or suffer the consequences.

Chief Joseph talked to the army generals, saying his young men were angry and would not be harassed. He told them that if his people were left alone, they would go peaceably. So the Nez Perce began their journey, but some army officers ignored Chief Joseph's warning and harassed the warriors. Subsequently, three Nez Perce men left the band and killed the three settlers who had been most insolent and hateful, providing the opportunity that the army had been waiting for; immediately, they grouped to attack. Outnumbered, knowing his people would be massacred, Chief Joseph ordered the Nez Perce to follow him as quickly as possible into Canada, where they would be free to find new land.

The army would not allow them to go in peace but pursued them, striking at White Bird Creek. Forced to fight, Chief Joseph employed a brilliant military strategy and defeated the army. Again the Indians traveled on, with the army in unrelenting pursuit. Slowed by their families and badly outnumbered, the Nez Perce lost more lives at every encounter. Finally, just short of the Canadian border, after a winding journey of nearly 1,000 miles, Chief Joseph had to surrender in order to save the lives of the women and children. The band had been reduced to 200 men and 600 women and children. On October 5, 1877, Chief Joseph sent this now-famous message to General Howard:

Tell General Howard I know his heart. What he told me before I have in my heart. I am tired of fighting. Our chiefs are killed. It is the young men who say yes or no. He who led the young men is dead. It is cold and we have no blankets. The little children are freezing to death. I want time to look for my children and see how many of them I can find. Maybe I shall find them among the dead. Hear me, my chiefs, I am tired; my heart is sick and sad. From where the sun now stands, I will fight no more forever.

That afternoon Chief Joseph walked toward General Howard and offered the general his rifle. Joseph's people gave up their weapons. Seven years later, after seeing his people suffer at Fort Leavenworth and moved to Lapwai, Chief Joseph returned to the Pacific Northwest, where he lived on a reservation at Colville, Washington, until his death in 1904.

In 1966 Roberta Conner listened to sweathouse stories told by her great aunt, Blanche Conner Hung. Among them was a narrative explaining the origins of the tribes, including the *Nimipu*, or Nez Perce. Roberta and her cousin, both age twelve at the time, sat in the sweathouse listening to the tale of Coyote and the monster. The sweathouse, says Conner, was a place so dark "we felt as though we could be inside the monster's stomach." Many tribes tell a similar story, said Conner's great aunt, but "only the Nez Perce version is true."

CREATED FROM THE HEART

A long time ago there was a great monster who was eating up all the animals. There were no people then. Well, this monster was so big he didn't even chew up the animals, he'd just swallow them whole. Coyote was worried about all his brother and sister animals, so he devised a plan to save them all.

After the monster had swallowed all the animals, Coyote let the monster swallow him, too. So when Coyote was in the monster's stomach with all the other animals, he held a meeting. He told the animals, "I have a knife, and I'm going to crawl up the monster's stomach, up close to his heart, and I'm going to stab him 'til he dies. When he begins to die, all the openings of his body will open up as his muscles relax. When this happens, I'll give the signal, and you all run out through his tsitsit."

Then Coyote went to work stabbing and cutting at the monster's heart. When the monster began to get weak, he said to Coyote, "Let's make a deal, you stop stabbing me and trying to kill me and I'll let you go." Coyote refused and just kept right on cutting deeper into the heart of the monster until

the monster died. All the animals escaped through the tsitsit *as Coyote hollered to them to go. Then Coyote crawled out too.*

Then he ordered all the animals to help him cut up the monster. So they cut off the feet and threw them up to the northwestern area of what's now Montana, and there grew the Blackfoot *people. Then they cut out the brain and the head and threw them out, and that became the* Flathead *tribe. So they kept right on cutting off all the parts of the body, including the intestines, and threw each part to a different section of land, at each place creating a new Indian nation.*

When they had thrown all the parts away except the heart, the animals asked what Coyote would do with the heart, and he told them that he was going to make a very special people from the heart, and he was going to put them in the most beautiful country of all. Coyote placed the heart halfway between what is now Lewiston, Idaho, and Wallowa, Oregon. There the Nez Perce people were created from the heart.

La Grande

Union County. Population 11,709. The name of this city was suggested by a French Canadian trapper in recognition of the near-perfect roundness of the Grande Ronde Valley. The city took root around the pleasant tavern of Ben Brown and was first called Brown Town and later Brownsville.

Not far from the Umatilla Reservation, home of the Confederated Tribes, the college town of La Grande has a number of storytellers who retell the etiological legends of the Umatillas and Cayuse. "How Raccoon Got His Dark Eyes" is a Umatilla tale that Twilo Scofield collected at a 1982 La Grande folklore conference. The tale came from a woman who wanted to be identified only as an "Umatilla storyteller."

HOW RACCOON GOT HIS DARK EYES

A long time ago, when the animals were part of one big family, they took care of each other like brothers and sisters. It was a time when Cougar was very strong and Raccoon, very mischievous. Raccoon was always playing and dancing. He didn't pay attention and would never concentrate on his work.

One day, when Cougar and Raccoon were together, they needed food. Cougar decided to go hunting. He was strong and a better hunter than the little raccoon. So when he went to hunt, Cougar left Raccoon behind. He said, "You stay and take care of the fire and keep your mind on what you are doing. The old devil-woman lives just across the river, and she has four big sons. Stay out of trouble."

So Cougar went off hunting, and Raccoon watched the fire. Soon Raccoon became tired of doing nothing, and he began to sing and dance around the fire. He was having such

137

a good time that he let the fire go out. "Oh, oh," the Raccoon thought, "Cougar is going to scold me and beat me for letting the fire go out. I must find some fire."

Raccoon looked across the river and saw the old devil-woman getting ready to cook at her fire. So he thought, "Maybe I can get some of her fire and bring it over here. Then Cougar won't know what happened."

So Raccoon swam across the river. He watched carefully, and when the old woman turned her back, Raccoon grabbed a burning stick from the fire and carried it in his paws back to the river.

He began to swim across, but without his front paws, he began to drift downstream. Raccoon knew that the water would put out the fire if he wasn't careful, so he put the stick on his nose to keep it dry. He kept swimming, but the water kept touching the burning stick. Raccoon pushed the fire stick higher and higher up the bridge of his nose and kept swimming. Finally he made it across, but the fire had burned the fur high on his nose, leaving charred spots around his eyes.

Meacham

Umatilla County. Brothers Harvey and Alfred B. Meacham bought this station, originally known as Lee's Encampment, in the 1860s. Alfred became sole owner of the toll road and hostelry in 1872 when he felled a tree that struck and killed his brother. According to Lornel Tweedy Morton, editor of *Papa Was A. B. Meacham*, Alfred Meacham is best known for his part in the Modoc War (1872–73); he was the peace commissioner who was partially scalped by Captain Jack's men in the Lava Beds near Klamath Falls, escaping perhaps because his bald pate made such a worthless trophy. After the sad conclusion of the Modoc Wars, A. B. Meacham devoted his life to publicizing the indignities faced by the Indians. Traveling throughout the East with, among others, the man who had tried to scalp him, Meacham lectured until his death on the need for reforming U.S. policies toward the Native Americans.

Meacham, at the top of the Blue Mountains, was a welcome station on the Oregon Trail. When the O. R. and N. Railroad was routed through Meacham, the company built a log-cabin restaurant in 1895. Katherine L. "Grandma" Munra was the proprietor, a woman famous for her fried chicken, salad, cakes, and pastries—an entire meal, plus generous second portions, for only seventy-five cents. Grandma Munra also introduced the world to the "free refill." Grandma never charged for a second cup of coffee, an act well received in the chill wintry days of Meacham's flowering.

The railroad was a new experience for most Blue Mountain residents in the 1890s, and yet some treated the iron horse like a large metal stagecoach. As reported in the *Times-Mountaineer* for September 27, 1893, a fifteen-year-old Meacham Creek boy stopped an O. R. and N.

train, stepped on board, and asked the passengers, "Got any tobaccy?" When no one pulled out a chaw, the boy left the train in disgust, saying, "It must be a hell of a train what's got no tobaccy aboard."

According to the folklorists of the Federal Writers' Project, J. G. "Whispering" Thompson was an Umatilla County legend whose ordinary conversational voice had a unique volume. It is said that when he actually yelled at his mule team, Thompson's voice carried across two counties. The best mule skinner east of the Cascades, "Whispering" Thompson worked in the Blue Mountains as a freighter in the 1870s and 1880s. Each of the fourteen mules in his team understood his every word and responded immediately, not only to the jerkline, but to the profusion of pebbles that Thompson carried in a blue bucket on the seat next to him. His familiar cry, "Gee-e-e-e, Nig!" signaled that "Whispering" Thompson was nearby, at least within a three-mile radius.

"When Thompson was leaving Meacham at the top of the Blue Mountains, you could hear his voice calling to that mule team clear in La Grande," said Fred Andrews of Echo. Others said that when Thompson was gently urging his mule-drawn caravan to leave Umatilla Landing, his voice, louder than a steamboat whistle, could be heard in Pendleton. "Whispering" Thompson was opposed to monopolies, detested the O. R. and N. Railroad, and often held protracted discussions on these topics—with himself. When asked to explain why he talked mostly to himself, Thompson said, "I like to talk to a smart man once in a while."

The *East Oregonian*, reporting in the spring of 1881, observed, "Last Wednesday the flue-like voice of Whispering Thompson could be heard about two miles; we went to see what was the matter and found his fourteen-mule team in front of a pretty good house, which was moved about a fourth of a mile in about four hours—Thompson gently encouraging the mules."

Pendleton

Umatilla County. Population 14,841. Pendleton is another town with a name deriving from Civil War-era politics. George Hunt Pendleton was the Democratic nominee for president in 1864, and, in 1868, the Oregon Democratic Convention agreed on Pendleton as their choice for president. In 1868 the town of Pendleton was named, reflecting the political sentiment of the area.

In the early days there was no wilder town anywhere in the West. Pendleton was called the "sin and six-gun capital" of the country. C. S. "Sam" Jackson, an early editor of the *East Oregonian*, wrote in the 1880s, "Our principal street is lined with saloons in front of which congregate drunkards and gamblers so thickly that it's very difficult to walk along the sidewalk, and ladies can never go the length of Main Street without being compelled to hear vile and profane language from these loafers.'' In its wildest era, Pendleton was a town where men shot first, and the survivors talked it over later.

The first Pendleton Roundup occurred in 1910. After some negotiations, Major Lee Moorhouse and Roy Bishop met with Chief No Shirt of the Walla Wallas, Chief Umapine of the Cayuse, and Amos Pond of the Walla Wallas; all endorsed the frontier show. Even Poker Jim, the well-known Walla Walla horseman, agreed to bring his string of race horses if ''suitable prizes were offered.''

President Teddy Roosevelt received a personal invitation, and every citizen in Pendleton was dunned for a contribution to the $3,000 kitty. The first show featured a Westward Ho Twilight Parade, led by military and cowboy bands, Indians in paint, cowgirls on horseback, and full-dress soldiers. Tournament Film Company of Detroit, the largest picture company in America, sent six men to record the events.

For the rodeo events, the best ropers and riders in the country were secured, including Buffalo Vernon, famous for throwing a rampaging steer with his hands and holding it down with his teeth, and George Fletcher, a black bronc-rider who had won in his event many times. The prize for the bronco-busting championship was a $250 saddle, the finest ever made, trimmed with silver and studded with silver dollars. First-year events included the Fancy Shooting Exhibition, the Indian Race, Fancy Riding and Trick Roping, the Barrel Race, the Ladies' Cowpony Race, and the Slow Mule Race, among others.

Seven thousand people filed into the Pendleton stadium for the first day's events and, at nightfall, workers bent to the task of building 2,000 extra seats for the expected crowds at the next performance. In both 1911 and 1912, more than 40,000 spectators ventured through the Blue Mountains and the Wallowas to watch the roundup.

In the early days, women often competed against men. Dressed in cowboy hats and fringed leather skirts, they rode wild bucking broncs, their stirrups hobbled beneath the horse's belly to keep them in the saddle. In those years, there were no chutes in the arena; horses were roped, tied to a saddle horn, blindfolded, and eared-down so that the cowpokes could get a saddle on them.

Cowgirl competition was discouraged in 1929 after a tragic accident. Bonnie McCarroll of Boise was thrown from her bucking bronc and, trapped by the hobbled stirrups, dragged across the arena. Ten days later she died in a Pendleton hospital. After that, women could no longer join the open bronco-busting competition.

Sparta

Baker County. Population 0. Visiting the Powder River area in 1871, William Packwood named this settlement

after a town in Illinois. Previously the town had been known as Eagle City. Sparta was heavily undermined by gold-mining shafts and irrigation ditches.

Like most mining towns, Sparta had a large number of Chinese residents who had traveled to the Land of the Golden Mountain hoping to profit enough to return to China with money for land. Most of these men did not plan to establish permanent residence. The Chinese residents of Sparta, who kept to themselves, lived in a separate section of town. They were hard-working, patient people who were often mistreated and maligned; regularly they were robbed and beaten. A favorite sport among Sparta residents was to cut off the long braid of local Chinese. According to Sparta resident Harley Derrik, who lived in Sparta all his life, ''They'd work, those Chinese.'' For the most part, the Chinese miners had drifted into Oregon from California after the completion of the railroad, migrating toward the richest gold strikes. Shortly afterward, says Derrik, gold was discovered in Griffin's Gulch outside of Baker in 1869. For a time, approximately 7,000 to 10,000 people lived there. ''Now,'' says Derrik, ''you have to look real hard to find the cemetery.''

According to Derrik, the Chinese miners, newly arrived in Sparta, worked hard until it was time to be paid. Then the bosses would kill them. At Chinese Gulch near Sparta, several Chinese dug extensive ditches. Reportedly, ''there was a bunch of Chinese that were doing some diggin' and [the Sparta miners] thought they had a lot of gold.'' With no apparent regrets, the Sparta miners killed the entire community of Chinese. The men looked all over for the gold, but never could find it. Of course, says Derrik, they always thought that the Chinese had hidden it in cans in the ground.

Besides having no peace or respect from the townsfolk, the Chinese of Baker County were handy to have around when somebody needed a scapegoat. ''Judge Martin Duffy,'' a song circulated widely in the mining towns of Oregon and Idaho, relates the story of ''practical'' Judge Duffy and frontier justice, as it was too often practiced.

JUDGE MARTIN DUFFY

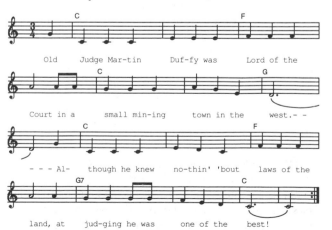

Old Judge Martin Duffy was Lord of the Court in a small mining town in the west. — Although he knew nothin' 'bout laws of the land, at judging he was one of the best!

*Old Judge Martin Duffy was Lord of the Court
In a small mining town in the West.
Although he knew nothing about laws of the land,
At judging, he was one of the best.*

*One night in our town a murder occurred,
And the blacksmith was accused of the crime.
We caught him red-handed and gave him three trials,
But the verdict was "Guilty!" each time.*

*Now he was the only good blacksmith we had,
And we wanted to spare him his life.
So Duffy stood up in the court like a lord
And with these words, he ended the strife:*

*"I move we dismiss him; he's needed in town."
Then he spoke out these words, which have gained him
        renown.
"We've got two Chinese laundrymen, everyone knows.
Why not save the poor blacksmith and hang one of those?"*

Sumpter

Baker County. Population 119. Settled during the early days of the Civil War, the mining town of Sumpter was named for Ft. Sumter, South Carolina, a place prominent in the news of that time. When the postmaster applied for the name, however, he was told it was illegal to name a post office after a military installation. So the postmaster added the letter *p* to Sumpter.

Because the Sumpter area stands at more than 4,300 feet, there is much snow. In the early days, children often went to school on skis. When the snow was crusty, they could step over eight-foot-high fences without so much as

a break in stride. But in the dead of winter, according to Sumpter resident Woody Woodall, the snow really covered the houses, and only the stove pipes remained, in melted troughs called *gopher holes*: "The only way kids could tell which house was theirs was to find the *gopher hole* and count how many it was from the school."

According to Fred Young, who grew up in Sumpter, such towns were "lively—very lively." In fact, some of Young's fondest memories involve going into post-gold-rush saloons on the shoulders of his liberal-minded father. In its heyday, Sumpter boasted four churches and perhaps two dozen saloons, the number of bars varying from one account to another. Because saloons sprang up quickly and closed down as fast, it was impossible to keep an accurate census. The saloons of Sumpter were class-conscious. Some catered only to business and professional men; the "bucket stiffs," working men who stopped for a beer on their way home, were advised to take their business elsewhere. Women, of course, were welcome in neither the businessman's bar nor the working man's tavern. The red-light district welcomed all comers, day or night, in any condition.

For many years the Sumpter Valley Days Celebration was the social event of the year. One of the celebrated competitions held yearly was the Mucking Contest, an event in which miners shoveled one ton of rock and dirt from one box to another. The winner received a case of whiskey from the Omega Mines in Bourne, Oregon. More often than not, that champion was one of Sumpter's many *Cousin Jacks*, English immigrants from the mines at Cornwall. From Cornwall came some of the stories of *Tommyknockers*, the little men of the mines. This version builds on stories collected in 1969 by two of Eastern Oregon's most productive folklore collectors, Chris Grissom and Candy Anderson.

THE TOMMYKNOCKERS AT BALD MOUNTAIN MINE

In the Sumpter mines, the little people who live underground are called Tommyknockers. *They are mischievous and mysterious. Tommyknockers like to throw rocks down on miners' heads, blow out their gaslights, and steal their lunch boxes. They live in Tommyknocker nests made of rock-eggs. If you are quiet, you can hear the Tommyknockers laughing, talking to themselves, and tapping out messages from mine shaft to mine shaft. Miners, who are naturally superstitious because they work in dangerous surroundings, often leave a bit of their lunch for the pesky Tommyknockers.*

John Powell was a miner in the Bald Mountain Mine. One day, old John came tramping down the hill with a 150-pound pack of his belongings and said to the others, "Hell, there's ore up there, but there's also Tommyknockers."

"You been drinkin' too much," said one miner.

"No way," said John. "The only time I do drink is when the Tommyknockers quit!"

So the foreman tried to talk Powell into returning to the mine, but John said, "No. Not unless you get me a new section wagon."

"What's wrong with the old one?" asked the boss.

"There's a Tommyknocker in it."

"I'll tell you what," said the foreman. "Every night when you get ready to quit, leave a quarter for the Tommyknocker, right up there on the tongue of that section wagon." And John Powell, because he couldn't really afford to give up his job, agreed to the plan. Whether the Tom-

myknockers bothered John Powell again is not clear. But every Friday night, for many years, the foreman went to the Sumpter Bar, ordered a glass of the best whiskey, raised his cup, and said with a huge smile, "Here's to the Tommyknockers!"

Union

Union County. Population 1,829. During the Civil War, some Oregonians showed their colors when they chose names for their hamlets. While Arlington honored the home of Robert E. Lee and Wingville was the garrison for the "left wing" of the Confederate Army, Union boasted a large group of northern supporters.

Long after the disputes of the Civil War, Eastern Oregonians had unique ways of expressing their political opinions. In many locations such as Union, it was not practical for a dozen ranch hands to pack up and head for a polling booth. So the cattle hands devised a clever plan, one practiced all over the plains and high plateaus, rolling hills and deserts of the "dry side."

A week before an election, every male adult on the ranch would go to a meeting. There would be political speeches, rabid campaigning, and the usual amount of arm-twisting. Then, after all the wind was out of the bag, they would hold their own election.

Let's say there were fifteen hands on a ranch near Union, and nine wanted to vote Democratic, while six cast ballots for the Republicans. Rather than sending all fifteen to the Union County Courthouse, they followed this procedure: Because there was a three-vote margin for the Democrats, the group would choose three Democratic enthusiasts to go to town and vote. At the next election, when the Republicans prevailed by two votes, the ranch would send two GOP voters to the county seat. It was a practical solution to a serious problem—keeping the ranch hands on the job while completing their civic duties as voters.

Unity

Baker County. Population 87. Unity was a prosperous town during the Baker County gold rush of the 1860s. Now Unity is primarily an agricultural and mining area, but also known for its scenery, particularly as a hub to the beautiful Malheur Forest, home of two rare Northeastern Oregon animals.

In the Malheur Forest around Unity are two rare creatures, the "wizzensnifter" and the "beaver cat," animals seldom seen, but no less a part of Oregon's past and present. Joan Aschim of Unity collected the legends of the wizzensnifter and the beaver cat in 1975 from her informants, Joe and Wayne.

The wizzensnifter is a shy creature that leaves its mark on the Malheur landscape. It is short and squat, but very fast—too large to miss, but too small to see. The wizzensnifter is known mainly by its eating habits. It chews off trees in the national forest, leaving uneven stumps on hillsides and clearings. The wizzensnifter has an overbite, so the trees he eats are cut off not cleanly, but with an irregular notch. The name wizzensnifter comes from the sound the animal makes when it chews down a pine tree or a Douglas fir: "*wizzen . . . snift!*" According to Wayne,

Wizzensnifters used to be quite common, you see. They were, they were here before the white man invaded North America, you see. They lived with the Indians quite happily. The Indians didn't bother them too much. They respected the Wizzensnifters. But the white man came around, and they started cutting down the forest, so Wizzensnifters had to retreat with the forest, you know. They're just kind of scattered around in the national forest.

Beaver cats are equally rare, but more dangerous than wizzensnifters. Sometimes called beaver panthers, these animals are a cross between the flat-tailed beaver and the sleek mountain cat. Beaver cats lurk in trees at night waiting for prey to cross their trails. They make a sound like a cat: "*wrowrr!*" But they also have flat, flexible tails like a beaver. They are dark-colored and virtually invisible at night. If you walk under a beaver cat perched in a tree on a dark night, that great big tail will whack you right across the face. Few people ever survive a beaver cat attack.

Wallowa Lake

Wallowa County. The Nez Perce word *Wallowa* describes a series of tripods used in fish traps; however, the more popular and poetic meaning is "land of winding waters." The lake lies at the base of the Wallowa Mountains, sometimes called the Switzerland of America. The Wallowas are the largest alpine area in Oregon, featuring mile-high lakes and fifteen peaks over 9,000 feet in elevation.

Wallowa Lake is one of Oregon's most beautiful bodies of water. Standing at 4,550 feet, the lake covers an area five miles long and a half mile wide—surrounded by towering mountains. In this remarkable setting, the Nez Perce tell stories suggesting that Wallowa Lake is inhabited by a huge prehistoric creature. Those stories were furthered in pioneer times by a series of drownings in the lake. Soon people began to say, "Well, the monster has claimed this year's victim." In recent times, visitors to the lake have noticed a strange wavelike action in the middle of the lake—no doubt the surfacing of the Wallowa Lake monster.

THE WALLOWA LAKE MONSTER

Long ago the Blackfeet and the Nez Perce were at war. For many years they fought. Summer after summer, Red Wolf, chief of the Nez Perce, fought bravely and took many scalps from the men from east of the Shining Mountain.

Every summer the tribes would meet in battle. Red Wolf's warriors were strong and wise, but the Blackfeet began to grow more powerful under the leadership of Bloody Chief, a fierce fighter. Finally the Blackfeet pursued the Nez Perce into Wallowa country and killed many men. Red Wolf's band grew small, and they knew the Blackfeet would soon kill all the men and take as prisoners the women and children.

Red Wolf's daughter was named Wahluna. She was beautiful and loved by all her people. When she saw that Red Wolf's warriors were too few to defend against the Blackfeet, she made a plan. That night, she went across Wallowa Lake in her canoe and walked into the camp of the Blackfeet. Bloody Chief and his son Tlesca were sitting by the fire when she appeared. Tlesca had never seen anyone so lovely.

"I am Wahluna, daughter of Red Wolf. I come to plead for my people. Our warriors are few. Our children are sick and weary. My father says you will defeat us in the morning."

Bloody Chief became angry. He said, "Your men are cowards. They deserve to die. We will take your women and children as slaves. Go back to your camp and await your fate."

But Tlesca's heart was moved. He said, "You are brave, and you love your people." He left his father's side and placed his robe over Wahluna's shoulders. When the old chief saw his son's compassion, he softened and said, "Yes, the daughter of Red Wolf is brave. I will spare her people."

So Tlesca led Wahluna back to the water's edge and to her canoe. As she prepared to return across the lake, he said, ''Wahluna, you are beautiful and brave. My heart is with you. I want you to be my wife.''

Wahluna was moved, but she also knew that the men of Red Wolf and the men of Bloody Chief would never stand for such a union. She said, ''It can never be. My father's warriors would kill you and scatter your bones, and your father's warriors would do the same to me.''

But they agreed to meet again. When Wahluna heard the cry of the gray wolf at night, she would leave her tepee and go down to the lakeside. When Tlesca heard the call of the owl, he would leave the fire and seek out Red Wolf's daughter at the shore. For many moons they met and soon pledged to one another.

But they knew the elders would not allow them to marry. So, one night Tlesca and Wahluna gathered supplies and packed them into a sturdy canoe. They went out onto the lake and headed down the length of the water, facing directly into the rising moon. As Tlesca paddled away, Red Wolf saw the two shadows moving on the lake. He rushed to the shore, calling for his daughter.

Just then, ripples came over the lake and huge waves. A creature rose from the water—at least thirty feet long, with a serpent's head and a long, scaly body. The serpent rose up in the water, swam around the canoe, and raised his great tail. Then, with a sharp twist of his body, he thrashed against the canoe.

Wahluna and Tlesca were lost forever. Both Red Wolf and Bloody Chief searched the lake for days, but no trace could be found of daughter or son. The Blackfeet went back to their land in the east, certain that the Great Spirit had punished them for relenting in the battle against their ancient enemies. And the Nez Perce, always fearful of the Wallowa Lake monster, never returned to the shores of their ancestral lake.

Whiskey Creek

Wallowa County. In 1872, some entrepreneurs brought kegs of whiskey to the area to sell to the local Indians. Alarmed, the Wallowa settlers interrupted the transaction, busting the kegs apart with axes and hammers, and the whiskey flowed into a nearby stream, which soon came to be called Whiskey Creek—one of many in the Pacific Northwest. In 1985 Harry Tackett gathered this Whiskey Creek story from an Eastern Oregon miner who had moved to Southern Oregon and staked a claim near Gold Hill. According to Tackett, the miner was actually a church-going teetotaler, who nevertheless told the story as though he never went fishing without a little ''mountain lightning.''

A GOOD DAY OF FISHING ON WHISKEY CREEK

When that wagonload of whiskey got dumped into Whiskey Creek back in '72, the animals in the area were drunk for days, especially the rattlesnakes. Old-timers say some of them rattlers acquired a taste for the sauce.

I went out there one day lookin' to catch a few trout for dinner. Brought my best flies, a whole box full. But Umatilla County is full of rattlers, so I also packed a little snake-bite medicine, just in case. It's always a good idea to take a fifth of whiskey into rattler county. A great snake-bite remedy.

Well, it was just one of those days. I tried my brown spackled fly and the black gnat, the yellow-jacket and the grub-hatch. Nothing worked. So I was getting depressed, and I poured myself a little snake-bite medicine in my coffee cup. As I was sitting there on a rock, contemplatin' my lack of success, I started turnin' over stones and pebbles, tryin' to find some worms or grubs. Then, right in the middle of digging up the creekside, I heard a rattlin' sound. I looked around, and there was a huge rattler with a toad in his mouth.

Suddenly I remembered the old story about the load of whiskey that got dumped in the creek. So I found an indentation in a rock, and I poured a good-sized shot of whiskey into the pocket. Well, as soon as that old rattler smelled that whiskey, he dropped that toad and slithered up to that booze.

While that snake was drinkin', I put the toad on my hook and tossed it into a nice stretch of water. Before long I had a nice cutthroat trout about sixteen inches long. Well now, that was a lot of fun, but it just set me to wonderin' where I was gonna' find another toad. So I sat there for a minute on that rock. Pretty soon I felt a tap on my pants leg, and here was that rattler again with another toad in his mouth.

I walked over to that same rock, poured in a healthy dram of whiskey, and that rattler dropped that toad right at my feet. Before that day was over, I went home with a nice limit of cutthroat trout, but not a drop of whiskey.

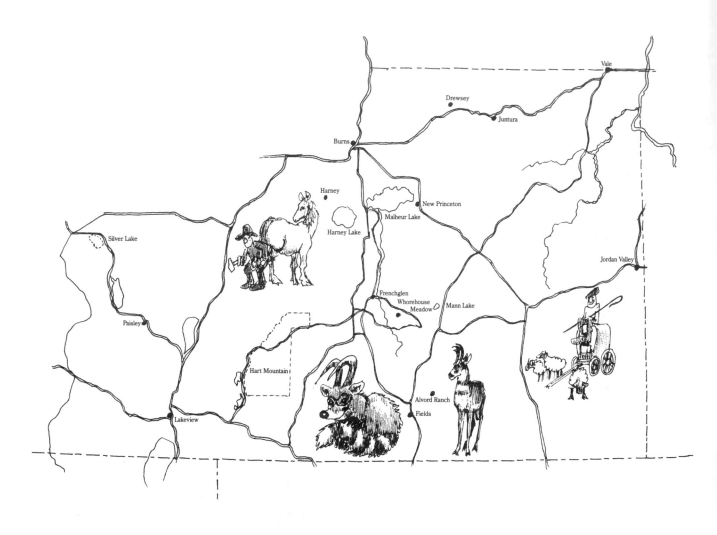

Silver Lake

Paisley

Lakeview

Hart Mountain

Burns

Harney

Harney Lake

Malheur Lake

New Princeton

Frenchglen

Whorehouse
Meadow

Mann Lake

Alvord Ranch

Fields

Drewsey

Juntura

Vale

Jordan Valley

Southeastern Oregon

Why, if all you wanted was sagebrush and jackrabbits, I guess you'd call this heaven.
—*Burns homesteader, 1888*

Southeastern Oregon is called the Inland Basin. It is part of the great American desert and covers most of Malheur, Lake, and Harney counties. The Southeastern region stretches from the Gearhart Mountains in the west to the Idaho border and from the Blue-Wallowa Mountains in the north to the California line. The region is sparsely populated except where irrigated, with Burns and Lakeview the principal towns.

High and dry, the Southeast has an annual precipitation of about ten inches. A Vale cowboy once put this detail into perspective: "You remember the time it rained 40 days and 40 nights? We got an inch-and-a-half." The region is generally treeless, although in the Deschutes and Fremont national forests, there are some fine stands of pine. Some of the place-names here suggest the conditions. Barren Valley, near the south fork of the Malheur River, is not far from the deserted outpost of Windy. Harney and Lake counties share Venator Canyon, named for a rancher who died of thirst when his saddle horse ran away. Malheur County has one town with the simple but descriptive name of Arock (a rock), suggestive of the harsh landscape. In eastern Harney County, one homesteader with a sense of irony called his place Follyfarm, a name that stuck for the entire settlement.

Along the Snake River at Oregon's eastern border is a majestic plateau at an elevation of 3,000 to 4,000 feet. In this section are low ranges of mountains; narrow, deeply cut river valleys; buttes and rimrock; and sagebrush plains. Although semiarid, Southeastern Oregon has some fertile farms, the result of energetic irrigation projects. Large herds of sheep, cattle, and horses range here.

Alkali hollows mark the dry ancient lake beds, which sparkle in the morning dew as the sun strikes the small grains of salty sand. Some brine-filled pools remain, such as Alkali Lake, near Juniper Mountain, a reminder of the time when Southeastern Oregon was covered by a vast inland sea. Despite its dry climate, geographers have avoided calling this land a desert. In fact, the land is generally level, with ridges here and there—extinct craters and small volcanic buttes, surrounded by a scattered growth of juniper. Sagebrush and dry grasses grow in profusion, lining the natural wells and hot springs at the base of the hills. When it rains in the Southeast—a rare but lively occasion—the drops are usually accompanied by a violent thunderstorm. In Pete French country, the Donner and Blitzen River was named after the "thunder and lightning" encountered by General George Curry's troops as they rode toward a battle in the Snake War of 1864.

Southeastern Oregon is home to the Paiute Indians, as well as the Snake and Bannock tribes, renowned for their fierceness in battle. In 1878 the Southeast was consumed by the Bannock Wars, and despite the efforts of people such as Paiute Princess Sarah Winnemucca, who traveled to Washington to ask President Rutherford B. Hayes to intercede, the Bannocks remained hostile, spreading destruction from the Snake River across much of Eastern Oregon, burning farms, strangling horses, and shooting ranchers. Pete French and his *vaqueros* were attacked near the P Ranch; French rode for his life—sixteen miles to shelter. But the Chinese cook, who feared horses, fell from his mount and was scalped. Near Wagontire the Bannocks killed a herd of cattle, leaving them to rot in a place now known as the Bone Corral.

After the Bannock uprising was quelled, more than 500 Indians, hostile and friendly alike, were exiled north to the Yakima Indian Reservation in subfreezing weather, causing many deaths, especially among the men, who walked the entire distance. The settlers, recognizing their allies in the Bannock Wars, named several locations after friendly leaders among the Paiutes and Walla Wallas, including Homly in Umatilla County, Ochoco Creek in Wheeler County, and Winnemucca in northwest Nevada.

Perhaps the most tenacious memory of the settlement era involved the Lost Wagon Train of 1845, also called the Blue Bucket Wagon Train. Looking for a shortcut through the last difficult stages of the Oregon Trail, one train followed the lead of Stephen Meek, crossing the Snake River and heading southeast. It is an often-told tale. According to the version told by W. H. Herron, whose parents were part of the 1845 company,

[Meek] planned to guide them over a route which was shorter and which he knew from trapping over the Blue Mountains to the Deschutes and north along the west bank of that river to the Dalles. Traveling over these mountains with a pack horse or saddle horse was much different than traveling with wagons, and many tributaries of the south Malheur were tried without success. Provisions were getting low and faith in Meek even lower. Finally the immigrants told Meek unless he could find their way out of there in a certain length of time, his life would be in danger. Meek became alarmed and skipped out and left them to their fate. Left on their own, several young men scouted the country until they had found a ridge that led to the summit of the mountains. By hitching ten and sometimes twelve yoke of oxen at a time to a wagon, they finally succeeded in getting them onto the divide.

There was no water on the divide, so they had to make dry camp. The captain told all the young people who had saddle horses to take buckets and go hunt for water. My father [Dan], then 23, and his sister took their old blue bucket and started out to find water. They finally found a dry creek-bed, which they followed until they found a place where a little water was seeping through the gravel, and while my father was digging for water, his sister saw something bright and picked it up. . . .

That something, unrecognized at the time, was gold. The Herrons picked up two good-sized clumps and threw them into the blue buckets. Men in camp said that gold

nuggets would be malleable, and in fact a man named Martin helped the brother and sister pound the metal into saucer-shaped pieces against a wagon rim. Unconvinced by their own experiment, the Herrons finally threw the rocks into a tool chest, where they stayed until 1849 when—ironically—the gold nuggets provided Dan Herron a grubstake for his trip to the Sacramento goldfields.

But the stories of Blue Bucket gold have persisted, and the many versions of this legend have dispersed gold seekers across much of Eastern Oregon—into such widely separated places as Vale, the Malheur River, Crane, Juntura, Canyon City, Ochoco, and Stinkingwater Pass. No one has found the Blue Bucket bonanza, but many have discovered a land of subtle surprises.

The Southeast, while prey to both extreme cold and extreme heat, is not all barren. On the windward sides of the hills, where scattered rains fall, juniper grows in profusion. Occasionally rimrocks and buttes create a landscape that seems to reach to infinity, where at night the stars shine brilliantly and seem close enough to touch. Harney Valley, said pioneer Jesse Harret, was "one of the most sublime places I ever saw. . . . The soil is rich and beautifully set with fine grass intermingled with patches of sage."

Perhaps the most beautiful spot in the Southeast is the Steens Mountain, the highest point in Southeastern Oregon, dominating the landscape to an elevation of 9,733 feet. Steens Mountain is the world's largest "fault block," reaching thirty miles in length. The east face, an escarpment one mile high, looks down on the Alvord Desert—so far down, some say, that "it takes two looks to get there."

The spectacular beauty of the Steens appears in four different vegetation belts determined by elevation, soil, and topography. The Sagebrush Belt is found at elevations below 5,500 feet. The Juniper Belt stands between 5,500 and 6,500 feet, has rocky terrain, and is cut with a myriad of canyons. At the 6,500- to 8,000-foot range is the Aspen Belt, rich with beautiful stands of quaking aspen and mountain mahogany, interspersed with small meadows. The Alpine Belt above 8,000 feet has high-country wild flowers, valleys, lakes, and rich meadows. Even in summer, the mountain is subject to sudden, short-lived, but ferocious storms.

In the valleys surrounding the Steens, early settlers built huge cattle ranches. Even though these ranch buildings are no longer standing today, some of the place-names are reminders of this abundant era, when cattlemen lived like frontier lords: Gap Ranch, the Whitehorse Ranch, Alvord Ranch, Roaring Springs Ranch. Peter French's famous P Ranch, the greatest empire of them all, today comprises much of the Malheur National Wildlife Refuge.

Harry Telford worked seven years on Frenchglen's P Ranch, and when interviewed in 1972 by folklorist Linda Lorene Miller, he described life on the Southeastern range.

We didn't dress fancy like you think of cowboys. We just dressed in ordinary work clothes. And we didn't carry six-shooters. But we did take a notion one time to all send and get us a gun. We'll just carry them along and we'll see lots of deer and antelopes and stuff, you know, and we can shoot an antelope or a deer and get a little change from eating beef all the time. So we all sent and got us these revolvers, Colts, and Smith and Wesson; we got good guns although it took half a month's salary in those days. I got thirty-five or forty after I started breaking horses. That included your beans and beef—that's about all you got to eat—and sourdough biscuits. But we all got these guns, you know, and the first week we had 'em they was three cowboys had to walk home. They shot off their guns and the horses bucked them off way out on the range. They had to walk home—walkin' eight or ten miles in a pair of high-heeled boots, ya know. Well, we wore them for about a week and threw them on the beds and just forgot about them.

There was a fella worked on the ranch that was quite a character. He never did get to be much of a cowboy or roper but the darn fool; there was lotsa rattlesnakes on the range where we rode, and he would see a rattlesnake go under a rock and he'd jump off his horse and grab that snake and pull it out and whirl it around by the tail and snap its head off. I wouldn't have done that for $10,000.

Most of the food we ate was beans, biscuits, and beef. Most everything was cooked in Dutch ovens and you just filled your plate out of these Dutch ovens and then found a comfortable place to sit down by a sagebrush or against a wagon wheel and eat your dinner. Sometimes we'd have dried prunes. Leftovers was just dumped in the fire, extra steaks and all. We weren't allowed to kill any steers but we picked a good fat heifer and they made very good steaks. Sometimes the cook would make some suet pudding and a sauce we called panther sauce and that was a big treat.

Not all the trail food was palatable, however, and some cooks never quite got the hang of it, as Telford explains in an anecdote about driving the cattle past the town of Drewsey.

Our buckaroo cook had got drunk and the boss fired him. Old John Robison, the Double-O Ranch, was our trail boss that trip. He hired a guy there in Drewsey who said he was a cook. Well, the first day out, why, the guy tried to make some sourdough biscuits in the Dutch oven. I don't know what he did or didn't do, but I've never seen any biscuits like the ones he turned out before or since. They didn't have any raise to 'em—they didn't raise any—and they were covered with little brown spots. And they were harder than any hardtack I'd seen in my life. Well, Old John, he looked at 'em and he never even tried to eat one. He just took the Dutch oven and dumped them all out, then mixed up a batch of bread himself and fired the cook. Well, those biscuits were laying out there along side camp, and we got to playing with them. We could sail one all the way across the Malheur River right next to our camp. Then some of the boys got a bright idea, an' they drilled two holes in 'em and tied 'em on their bridles for conchos. And those things stayed on there for weeks in all kinds of weather, so you can imagine about how solid they were.

The P Ranch *vaqueros* left more than sourdough *conchos* on the plains of Southeastern Oregon. The Spanish-speaking immigrants, in creating the unique ''cow-culture'' of the Southeast basin, also contributed many of the place-names, landmarks such as Llano (Flat Plain) and Fangollano (Mud Flat) in Malheur County; Diablo (Devil) Mountain and Latigo (Whip) Creek in Lake and Harney counties; and Berdugo, an outpost named for one of Pete French's workers, Joaquin ''Chino'' Berdugo. These place-names are part of the color of Southeastern Oregon, as are appellations such as Plush, an Indian's mispronunciation of his poker hand, and Poker Jim Ridge, named for a Bannock scout who regularly lost his pay at the tables. But none of these names can hold a candle to Voltage, a way station near the Donner and Blitzen River, so called because the postmaster was convinced that a dam on the creek could generate abundant electricity for the town.

Alvord Ranch

Harney County. Population: a few cowboys and several hundred thousand head of cattle. In the high desert country, far from any incorporated town, lies the Alvord Ranch, started sometime after 1871 by John Devine, who rode into Southeastern Oregon on a proud stallion and called his first spread the Whitehorse Ranch. After great success, Devine moved to a location on the eastern side of the Steens Mountain, at the base of the long escarpment. Alvord Ranch eventually grew to 25,000 acres and is one of the few green spots in all of Southeastern Oregon. Jagged snowcapped mountains on one side and the Alvord Desert on the other give Alvord Ranch complete isolation.

Alvord Ranch is also windblown, lying as it does between the natural extremes of mountain and desert. ''You can always tell the Alvord cows,'' says rancher Constance Wilson, ''because they stand on their hay.'' In the Alvord area, one rancher had to put hinges on his house so that, when a huge blow came along, the house, which had flattened out on the ground, could be raised back into place. The wind is also hard on the farm animals. Most Alvord residents put buckshot in the chicken feed so that the hens won't blow away. Even at that, Alvord chickens are easy to butcher because the winds leave them plucked clean. One ranch hand claimed he witnessed a hen laying the same egg five times during a blow. A stranger once asked, ''Does the wind always blow this way?'' ''No,'' came the answer. ''About half the time it blows the other way.''

Naturally, Alvord residents have different ideas of what constitutes a windstorm. Outside the main bunkhouse is a heavy log chain fastened to a post. If the chain hangs at a forty-five-degree angle, that's a ''slight breeze.'' If the chain stands straight out, that means ''a real *blow* is building up.'' If the chain is gone, ''that's a *storm*!''

The weather is changeable in Alvord. On a hot day, one cowboy jumped out of his clothes for a swim in a nearby stream. As he jumped toward the water, a flash flood roared down the creek bed. But he was in luck. When he was coming up for air the last time, a hailstorm came up, and the freezing wind froze the creek solid. Then, just as the cowboy thought he was going to freeze to death in that chunk of ice, the sun came out scorching hot and melted the ice. All he got was a sunburn.

One winter day, a couple of fence riders were sent out to dig holes for some heavy fence posts. But while they were carrying the wire out to the right section, the cow-punchers came across a great mound of frozen rattlesnakes. Deciding to save themselves some work, the men pounded the snakes into the ground for fence posts. They were pretty proud of themselves, but not for long. Overnight a warm spell hit, and the foreman came around with the bad news. ''Them snakes crawled off with nine miles of barbed wire,'' said the boss. ''You boys is fired.''

Early cattlemen were adventurous and colorful. Soon after John Devine arrived from Virginia, everyone in Southeastern Oregon knew that he loved ''fast horses, fast women, and a fast buck.'' He also enjoyed spending money. Once he journeyed to San Francisco for a few weeks and, said the locals, every time he put in an appearance at the Barbary Coast or on Market Street, Devine had a woman or two hanging on each arm. In short order, John Devine spent all his money, supposedly $100,000.

When he came back to the ranch, the hands joked that the only thing of value he returned with was his white horse.

ANYTHING WORTH DOING IS WORTH DOING WELL

"There's all kinds of stories about how he was quite the gentleman," said one of the White Horse hands. "But one involved a traveling troupe—you know, those groups they have that came around to entertain. Well, when one came through once, he propositioned one of the pretty girls in the show, and she said to him, 'Why, Mr. Devine, would you ruin a young girl's life for just twenty minutes of pleasure?' And he answered, 'Why, young lady, if it's done well, it will take at least an hour and a half.'"

Burns

Harney County. Population 2,907. In the early 1880s, George McGowan and Peter Stenger hired a cowhand to circulate a petition calling for the establishment of a post office at the present site of Burns. The cowboy, seeing no need for riding all over Harney County just to get a few John Hancocks on paper, signed the names himself. Stenger, a rancher, wanted the town named after himself, but McGowan argued that people would call the town Stingerville, putting a note of suspicion in the minds of folks heading for the mercantile. McGowan therefore suggested naming the community after Robert Burns, the Scottish poet, and in 1884 Burns was established.

Burns was once Oregon's unofficial capital of the nineteenth-century cattle empires. Henry Miller, who acquired a million acres and more than a million head of cattle, was typical of cattle barons of the Burns region. Although life on a spread like Miller's has been romanticized in literature and film for years, the ranch life was a hard way to make a living, and lots of men who sought a glamorous life "breakin' broncs" soon discovered that sodbusting or laying rails was easier work.

The term *cowboy* is familiar to most people, but was rarely used in Southeastern Oregon. Instead, cowhands were generally called buckaroos (from the Spanish *vaquero*, "cowboy"), although the term varied with the job. In Southeastern Oregon a buckaroo could ride, rope in open country, shoe a horse, and understand the whims and notions of cattle and horses. The lingo of the buckaroos, always rich in slang, denoted the kind of work they were doing: *leather-pounders, waddies, cowpokes, saddle-warmers,* or *cowpunchers* (but never *horsepunchers*). A cowpuncher usually carried a "prod pole," a stick about six feet long, used to prod cattle into stock cars. For the cowhand, the range was open land, while *fenced range* was the ranch. The *big house*, home for a cattle baron, stood some

ways away from the bunkhouse and the cook shack, where the *old woman* prepared the *feed bag* or the *swaller-and-get-out trough*.

The owner of the ranch was called the *ramrod* or *the old man*. The *foreman* was accepted as the range boss, and the new man was described as a *tenderfoot*. When a tenderfoot rode in wearing store-bought cowboy clothes, he was called a *mail-order* cowboy. An experienced cowhand wise in the ways of the West was called a *rawhide* and said to be *alkalied* or *bone-seasoned*.

The ranch hands also had special terms for buckaroo clothing. Chaps went over pants or britches, never trousers. When made of goatskin with the hair out, the chaps were called *angoras*; with sheepskin, they were called *woolies*; with bearskin they were called *grizzlies*. Depending on the style, chaps might also be called *bat-wings* or *buzzard-wings*. The cowpokes called plain leather chaps *shotguns*.

On the trail the old woman fed and cared for the cowhands. Often the old woman was an elderly cowpoke who could no longer endure long hours in the saddle. Nevertheless, his years of experience made him trail-wise, a man who could be counted on for food and philosophy. The old woman knew cures for a steer's diseases and for a buckaroos's complaints. The trail cook always drove the chuck wagon ahead of the cattle, choosing a campsite for the night, then starting a fire and setting up the ever-present coffee pot. Most cowhands liked their coffee strong:

COWBOY COFFEE

Boil the coffee and throw in a horseshoe. If it floats, the coffee's not done. When the horseshoe dissolves, the coffee is ready.

In the fall after roundup time, the Burns cowhands drove the steers to market, usually at Winnemucca, Nevada, in bunches of 1,000 each drive. The trip, nearly 150 miles, took eight to ten days on the trail. In camp the cook was in charge. It is said only two kinds of animal will cross a cook: a skunk and a fool. The fare was not fancy but filling and substantial, and typical meals included beans, steaks, stews, sourdough flapjacks, and biscuits. Now and then the cook treated the crew to pie for dessert, often made from dried apples.

Collected from many sources, here are traditional recipes of Southeastern Oregon, beginning, of course, with sourdough, the staple of the buckaroo's diet. Sourdough "starter" is a fermented mixture that produces gas bubbles and serves as a substitute for yeast. The trail cook might keep the "starter" brewing for many years, adding more flour, water, and salt as necessary.

SOURDOUGH FLAPJACKS

⅓ cup of milk
1 cup of warm sourdough starter
1 teaspoon of baking soda
1 tablespoon of bacon fat
2 eggs
2 cups of flour
1 tablespoon of sugar
2 cups of warm water

Stir together the starter, the water, and the flour. Let the mixture stand for 6 to 10 hours. Then stir in the rest of the ingredients. Let it stand a few more minutes. Then cook the flapjacks on a well greased grill.

SOURDOUGH BISCUITS

½ cup of butter
½ teaspoon of salt
1 tablespoon of sugar
1½ cups of warm starter
2 teaspoons of baking powder
2 cups of flour (some whole wheat)

Sift the salt, sugar, baking powder, and flour into a bowl. Then cut in the butter and stir in the starter until everything is well mixed. Knead the dough lightly. Then roll it out to a thickness of one-half inch. Cut out the biscuits and cook them in a Dutch oven for about 10 minutes.

BEEF STEW

This recipe, easily altered to feed any number of hungry range-riders, will generously serve four. Stew, of course, is never the same twice because the taste depends on what kinds of vegetables are on hand to throw into the pot.

2 pounds of stew meat, cut into one-inch pieces
1½ cups of tomato sauce or juice
2 large onions, chopped
2 stalks of celery, chopped
2 large carrots, chopped

Dredge the meat in flour and brown it in hot fat, using a heavy kettle or Dutch oven. Season the meat with salt, pepper, and garlic. Then add the remaining ingredients. Cover the kettle and simmer the stew for 2 hours.

RANCH OR GRUBSTAKE BEANS

This recipe serves six but can be expanded, if necessary, to accommodate scores.

2 pounds of navy or pinto beans
1 large onion, chopped
2 cups mashed tomatoes (optional)
1 cup tomato sauce (optional)
1 clove of garlic
1 bay leaf (optional)
salt and pepper to taste.
1 pound of beef cut into one-inch pieces or
1 hambone or 2 hamhocks

Put the onions and garlic into the Dutch oven and brown the meat. Then place the remaining ingredients into the oven and cook until the beans are tender.

A memorable character was Tom Stevens, a gambler who lived in Burns during the Roaring Twenties. After gathering stories from a lifelong area resident, Carol Peterson contributed a number of Tom Stevens anecdotes to the Mills Archives in 1972. Many of those moments are recorded in the narrative below.

"FATHER, NONE OF THIS COUNTS IF I LIVE"

Stevens had a crush on one of the girls at the bank. One day he would go in and get change for a twenty; then the next day he'd exchange it for a bill. This foolishness went on for quite a while, so finally one day the banker, Mr. Brown, walked over and asked him why. So Stevens says, "Well, Mr. Brown, someday someone's going to make a mistake, and it's not gonna be me."

In the late 1920s, Tom Stevens spent a lot of time working and gambling in the local saloons. There were three saloons in Burns—Tish and Donegan's, the Red Front, and Burns Hotel Saloon. When the cowhands came into town, they would tear these places apart, the cowboys' way of having a good time. Things were pretty wild. One of them, a foreman at the Island Ranch, Tex Long, came to town one night and played cards and drank all night and pretty well did himself under. Next morning he woke up with a hangover and no money, so he strapped on his gun and made the rounds to where he'd been the night before. Long went into the first saloon, Tish and Donegan's, and the bartender, Caldwell, saw him and knew right away what he was after. He wasn't about to tangle with big Tex Long. So Caldwell reached under the counter real quick and give him some money, sayin' "Ya know, Tex, you were in here last night, and I could see you were pretty far along, and the boys knew you were, so they held back most of the money ya lost."

Tex took the money and went over to the saloon in the hotel, where Stevens was behind the bar. Tex saw Stevens reaching under the bar and pulled out his gun and killed him, just like that. Then he went up the street to the hardware and bought some bullets. He took out the empties and put in new shells. *Then he started across toward the Red Front Saloon. It was right across the street from the Burns Hotel.*

Well, what he didn't know after he shot Stevens was that the bullet had gone through the bar and hit Stevens right in the belt buckle. It didn't kill him, but it knocked him out, knocked the wind out of him. So Stevens got a shotgun and raised the window that looked on the street and laid the gun across the sill and waited for Tex to cross the street. While Tex was crossing, a guy in the Red Front yelled just as Stevens fired. Tex dodged the shot and just started firin' all the time he was walkin' back to the window 'til he got up to it. He fired inside, and there was Stevens, runnin' up the staircase. He hid under the bed for a while, then ran out of town and up north, the John Day way. They didn't see him in town for quite some time after that.

One day when Stevens was heading back to Burns from the John Day area, he rolled his car over and down a pretty steep grade just outside Canyon City. He was banged up pretty bad and it didn't look like he'd last. Nobody thought he would live, so they called in a preacher to take his confession. Stevens went on relating all of his sins, telling about all the questionable things he'd done in his life. He was lyin' there so banged up, everybody thinking he was dying. . . . Then he looked up at the preacher and says, "Ya understand, Father, none of this counts if I live." He pulled through all right.

Drewsey

Harney County. Perhaps the most appropriate place-name in Oregon has been lost. In 1883 Abner Robbins started a store in this location and called it Gouge Eye, a reference to the frontier brawls that passed for recreation in this cow town. Robbins formed a partnership with Elmer Perrington, a Maine native, who left behind a sweetheart named Drewsey. Reluctantly, Robbins accepted Perrington's suggestion for a name change when post office authorities chafed at the more colorful selection.

In 1972 Linda Lorene Miller met with Harry Telford, a cowboy born in 1887, and a man who told countless stories about the ranch life in Southeastern Oregon during the cattle baron era. With his wife occasionally encouraging him, Telford brought out his photo albums and memorabilia and operated the tape recorder himself. For Miller's amusement, he played the "bones" on a cow's ribs, an art taught him by Tebo, the famous storyteller from the P Ranch. Miller told Telford that she "did not want a whitewashed, romanticized picture of the Old West." And, indeed, Telford revealed western traditions never seen in a John Wayne movie. According to Miller, Telford showed great admiration for French's Mexican cowhands and for Chino, the black cow-boss, but contempt for every "rich man's son from New York" who couldn't pull his weight on the ranch.

Telford described a Southeastern Oregon where people looked to men of strength and character to enforce justice. Every ranch had one or two buckaroos who gained everyone's respect with quick fists and noble actions. One day, Telford's crew got a pointed lesson in how crimes were handled in the Wild West.

WELL, THEY DID A FINE JOB

One spring there were two outfits that was camped within riding distance to go, in the evening, to the little town of Drewsey over on the Malheur River. And so all the boys that were off duty went into the town that evening to kind of celebrate a little bit and quench their thirst; and a few days before this, there had been a half-witted or retarded girl in the town there that had been raped by kind of a no-good hanger-on around the town, Lars.

And people were quite upset about it, but nothing had been done, and while we were in there at the bar, this guy came in and bellied up to the bar real important like and started to brag about raping this girl. And there was a big tall fellow named Charlie Ward in the White Horse outfit or Miller Lux outfit, and he said, "Why, you unprincipled S.O.B.! We'll teach you how to ravish our young womanhood. Grab 'im, boys!" And so we grabbed him and took him right out into the Main Street of Drewsey, and operated on him just like you would a bull calf, and boy did he holler, but it didn't do him any good. Well, after it was over, some of the citizens thought, well, maybe they'll kill the guy, and so they took him up to the local doctor, an 'ol fella, and he looked him over, and he says, "Well, they did a fine job." He says, "Just as good as I could've done myself. He got just what was coming to him!"

Fields

Harney County. The homestead at Fields was named for early settler Charles Fields. In this station horses and rattlesnakes are serious concerns, and there are buckets full of superstitions and beliefs about both. In 1971 Mardi Wilson collected folk beliefs from several sources, including a Montana cowboy working at the Alvord Ranch. Typical of a body of folk beliefs, some Southeastern Oregon superstitions seem contradictory. For instance, it is common belief that white horses are ''lucky''; however, most buckaroos think that white hooves are soft, so a horse with four white shoes is considered unlucky.

HORSELORE AND SNAKELORE

☐ *Blessed are you if you can mount over white.*

☐ *One white sock, buy it.*
Two white socks, try it.
Three white socks, deny it.
Four white socks, cut off its head
and feed it to the crows.

☐ *Four white feet, it's a horse for a thief;*
Three white feet, it's a horse for a fool;
Two white feet, it's a horse for a king;
One white foot, I'll give him to none.

☐ *One white foot, buy a horse;*
Two white feet, try a horse;
Three white feet, look well about him;
Four white feet, do without him.

☐ *One white sock, buy it;*
Two white socks, try it;
Three white socks, deny it;
Four white socks, leave it alone—
It won't carry you home.

☐ *A rattlesnake sheds its skin in August, and at that time it is blind. Therefore, you must be extra careful because in August a snake will strike without warning.*

☐ *If you kill a rattlesnake, watch out; the mate will return to the same place.*

☐ *If you circle your bedroll with a horsehair rope, you will be safe from rattlesnakes. Rattlesnakes won't crawl over horsehair.*

☐ *If you make a horsehair rope, make it from the hair of a gelding; horsehair from a gelding will not disturb a mare or a stud horse.*

☐ *If you have seven coils in your rope when you go to rope a cow, then you won't miss.*

☐ *In a snowstorm at high elevations, a cow will come down home, whereas a horse will climb higher.*

☐ *When water is frozen, a cow will go thirsty; a horse will break the ice to drink.*

☐ *Cows won't eat where sheep have grazed, and sheep won't drink where cows have drunk.*

☐ *Coyote soup will make you smart, give you strength, and cure colds.*

☐ *If a mountain lion comes anywhere near a pregnant mare, she will sluff her colt.*

☐ *Each time a horse rolls over, that means he's worth $50.*

☐ *Whatever horse the mare sees first after it's been bred, that's what the foal will look like.*

☐ *For worms in horses, have the horse eat a cigar.*

☐ *A wheat mark—a mark in the shape of a head of wheat—is a good luck sign; it grows right at the base of the horse's neck.*

☐ *The way to figure a horse's age is to pull out a hair from its tail, tie the hair to a nut (as in nut-and-bolt), hold the hair very still, and let the nut hang inside a tin can. It will swing back and forth; the number of times it hits the side of the can is the age of the horse.*

Frenchglen

Harney County. Frenchglen was named for pioneer rancher Pete French and his partner, Dr. Hugh Glenn. French's P Ranch, seventy-five miles long and thirty miles wide, was one of the great cattle empires in Old West history, and Pete French, a character larger than life, was known to fight with his fists to protect his land from squatters and poachers. Although on the one hand kind and generous, Pete French was also powerful and self-confident. His imperious ways angered many, and French was shot in cold blood by a man who was later cleared of wrongdoing by a Harney County jury.

Many people thought that the P Ranch was named for French's first initial; actually Pete French bought his first piece of land from an old prospector named Porter, who used the P brand, a practice continued by French. Normally French had about fifteen to twenty buckaroos working the ranch and a similar number riding the ranges.

With the help of six Mexican *vaqueros*, Pete French drove 1,200 head of cattle from Sacramento to Oregon in 1872. French and Glenn bought cheap swamp land under the provisions of the Swamp Land Act but had to spend hundreds of thousands of dollars to drain and reclaim the land. Ironically, fifty years after French's death, the U.S. government spent similar amounts converting the land to its original condition.

According to Mimi Bell, when French began his empire at Frenchglen, the grass grew so high that "a man on horseback could get lost from view." Bit by bit, French used Glenn's money to buy out local ranchers and, with the help of his *vaqueros*, kept newcomers from the *meanderlands*, sometimes by persuasion and sometimes by intimidation.

People who knew or worked for Pete French usually admired him and his way of getting things done. He was a strong leader and an innovative rancher. Channeling water from the Blitzen River over parts of the valley where only sagebrush grew, French cleared the land of sagebrush, a plant that cannot survive if its roots are under water. This irrigation project dropped the water level at Malheur Lake, creating more dry land between the water and the meander line, a surveyed border tracing the shoreline of a given body of water. Strangely, this innovative act contributed to French's death. Homesteaders began to claim part of the newly created meander land. On the day after Christmas in 1897, Ed Oliver, one of those homesteaders disputing with French, rode out to the present location of Sodhouse, where French's men were working. Oliver suddenly galloped in a rush toward French, trying to knock the cattle baron from his horse, but French defended himself with a hazel switch. After a few threatening words, Oliver pulled his gun. Pete French, unarmed, fell dead, a bullet through his head. Oliver rode past the body and sped away at a gallop.

It was an emotion-packed trial. Locals spread the rumor that three or four of the homesteaders had agreed that French must be killed, drawing straws for the duty. Despite the evidence, including the eyewitness testimony of French's men, Oliver was acquitted, perhaps because sentiment was running strongly against French's method of empire building.

By far, the most colorful *vaquero* at Frenchglen was Prim Ortego, better known as *Tebo*. Tebo was one of the best storytellers in Southeastern Oregon, known everywhere from the Steens to the Blues, and he always ended a tall tale by saying, "If Pete French was here, I'd prove it." Luckily for Tebo, Pete French was usually somewhere else on the immense expanse of the P Ranch. Like other Oregon storytellers—Hathaway Jones, "Huck" Finn, and Reub Long—Tebo served as a "folklore magnet." Whenever a good story passed through the county, it was attached to Tebo's reputation. From many sources, including the WPA files and Linda Lorene Miller's interviews with Harry Telford, here are some tall tales associated with the Southeast's premier yarn-spinner, Tebo.

TEBO'S PET TROUT

Tebo went fishing in the Donner and Blitzen River, with a large iron hook at the end of a rope, the hook baited with a beefsteak. A huge trout bit, but as Tebo pulled it onto the bank, the fish shook out the hook and shredded the lasso that held it. And as the trout bounced around on the bank, it flipped its tail and knocked Tebo out, killing his mule in the process. So instead of trying to fry up that monster, Tebo made a pet out of the trout. He trained that fish, and for years it followed him around like a puppy.

But a terrible accident took the life of Tebo's pet trout. One Sunday the fish was out for a stroll with Pete French and some ranch hands, and it fell into the creek. Before Tebo could fish it out, the poor fish drowned. "And if Pete French was here," Tebo was heard to say after the sad event, "I'd prove it."

TEBO DRESSES HIS HORSE FOR WINTER

One winter day Tebo was out riding by the Kiger Gorge, looking for strays. Kiger Gorge, on the Steens, is a deep-walled canyon, both sides high and steep. Well, just as he rode by a tight spot, his horse bumped into a precarious boulder and sent it crashing down into Kiger Gorge. "That boulder," said Tebo, "rolled down one side of the gorge and up the other. The horse and I sat watching that boulder for half an hour, and when we left it was still rolling up one side and down the other. The next spring when I passed that way again, there was a medium-sized rock still in motion. And that summer, when I returned to the same spot, there was just a cloud of dust rolling up one side of Kiger Gorge and down the other."

Another cold winter day, Tebo got his wagon mired in the mud after one of the Southeast's infrequent rainstorms. But Tebo trusted his horse, and he knew the strong animal could pull the wagon out. Tebo tied one end of a rope to the tail of that horse and the other to the wagon. The horse struggled and strained, trying mightily to recover the wagon from the mire.

"That was some horse," Tebo said. "He pulled so hard that he pulled himself right out of his skin. I worked and worked, but I couldn't get the skin back on him. Well, I couldn't let him go around that way, so I got a bunch of sheep pelts and made him a new suit of clothes. The following spring I sheared 500 pounds of wool from that horse, and I got top prices for it on the market. And if Pete French were here, I'd prove it."

Harney

Harney County. Population 0. Harney was once the seat of Harney County, but lost its position and eventually its population as Burns grew in importance. In the 1880s, Harney County held an election to determine the location of the county seat. The city of Harney won the election, but undaunted Burns businessmen rode into Harney at night and stole the county records. From that point on, Harney's influence and population declined rapidly.

In Southeastern Oregon the pioneers were rugged. Naomi Johnson grew up in Harney and traveled once a year with her mother to Burns to see the Chautauqua show. At the end of a performance of *East Lynne*, there was supposed to be a shooting. "Just when it was supposed to occur," says Johnson, "there were shots outside. The play stopped, the men ran outside, and there really had been a shooting."

Harry Loggan, who also spent his youth in Harney, found plenty of excitement in town, as he explained in 1969 to Kate Loggan.

A PLAY WITHIN A PLAY

One summer afternoon when I was playing in the yard—I was about ten years old—across the street from one saloon with my sister and Chester Irving and his sister, all of a sudden the air was filled with gunfire, and that was followed by the screaming of a woman. We, of course, were scared out of our wits and ran for home.

Later, I learned in detail what had happened. The city marshal ran the saloon on Main Street, and two brothers ran the one around the corner next to the post office. There was jealousy and hard feelings between the owners. The brothers thought the marshal was using his authority to pick on them.

Finally, on this summer afternoon, encouraged by several drinks of whiskey, the two brothers with three friends plotted a gun fight with the marshal. They knew that the marshal always went to the post office for his mail at precisely 2:00 P.M., so they arranged to pick a quarrel. The two brothers stood at the front door of their saloon armed with automatic pistols; two newcomers were at the back door with 30–30 rifles; and the fifth friend was in the middle of the street.

The one in the street started cursing the marshal and calling him a "coward." Then all started shooting at once. The marshal was killed, and the man in the street wounded. The screaming came from the aged mother of the marshal, who lived nearby, when she discovered her son dying.

Hart Mountain

Lake County. Elevation 8,022 feet. At one time this mountain was known as Warner Mountain, but the name change was influenced by ranchers on the valley floor who used the heart as a cattle brand.

Hart Mountain is a refuge for pronghorn, mule deer, golden eagles, sage grouse, bobcat, and other species of wildlife, including the unsociable badger and the ever-present prairie dog. Hart Mountain is also a refuge from the weary human condition: the quietest place with the clearest nights and the biggest sky.

Also of unusual dimensions are record-breaking Hart Mountain mosquitoes, insects so big that one can whip a dog, two can overcome a man, and four can fly off with a cow. A man camping on Hart Mountain was asleep in his tent when awakened by a terrifically loud buzzing sound, followed by unusual voices. "He looks mighty tasty," said one of the voices. "Should we take him home?"

"Naw," said the other. "Let's eat him here. If we take him home, the big guys will grab him."

Carole Hunt of Klamath Falls says that a trip to Southeastern Oregon presents a wonderful opportunity to see some of Oregon's rarest creatures. In fact, the hard-to-catch "side-hill gougers" are native to Hart Mountain.

SIDE-HILL GOUGERS

You may have noticed that Hart Mountain has many curious ridges. There is a reason for this phenomenon. The ridges are caused by animals that resemble badgers, but are called side-hill gougers. *The gougers have shorter legs on one side, so they can run around easily on the slopes. By the way, there are right-sided gougers and left-sided gougers. A right-sider can go only in one direction, and a left-sider can go only the opposite way. If they meet on a ridge, they're stuck forever. Side-hill gougers cannot turn around to face the same direction. They meet head-on and remain that way.*

Jordan Valley

Malheur County. Population 450. Jordan Valley, a hamlet on the western border of Idaho, was named for Michael Jordan, a miner who discovered gold here in the 1860s. Nearby Jordan Crater is one of the youngest volcanoes in the United States, having appeared just 500 years ago. Jordan Valley is a Basque community, featuring a *pelote* (jaialai) fronton in the center of town, and the town is surrounded by prime sheep-grazing land.

—Gu Amerikarentzat eta America, Jaungukoarentzat. ("We are for America, and America is for God.")
—Basque proverb

GOD BLESS AMERICA

Gora America gure echea poses beterik
Serguin dago emengo esiskal elum gentia
Viochetik Maitedegu gueure nasino berria
Gora America gure echea
Gora America maite maitea. . . .

The Basque homeland is the Pyrenees Mountains on the border between France and Spain, an area called *Euzkadi* by the people themselves. Basques are fiercely

independent people who resisted colonization attempts by both the French and Spanish, remaining autonomous until 1839. Under the twentieth-century dictatorship of Spanish Generalissimo Franco, Basques could not openly speak their language, write literature in Basque, or perform traditional dances. Many Basques, tired of oppression, left their homeland and traveled to America.

No one is quite sure what caused the Basques to settle in Southeastern Oregon. According to WPA Federal Writers' Project authors, "a Basque sea captain came to San Francisco in the 1880s and found his way up through Winnemucca to the grazing region. He remained to make a fortune and then returned to his native home in Spain to tell of the great sheep country in Oregon." Whatever the cause, Basque shepherds range widely throughout this region, and their culture and language have left their marks in places such as Basque Station and Jordan Valley.

According to folklorist Reba Bruner, the Basques were not always sheepherders, but in the old country often fished for a living. "Not until coming to this country did a majority begin herding," says Bruner. In Jordan Valley, the Basques are evident in their traditional dress, including a waist sash, which provides support for heavy lifting, and bindings around the pants legs, to keep the trousers from catching on rocks and brush. Women wear traditional aprons and head scarfs and, on the feet, rope sandals. Basques, deeply religious people, often wear religious medals and enjoy colorful jewelry.

The Basque language is unique. Although probably Indo-European in origin, Basque bears little similarity to any other language of the world. Basques sometimes explain that Tubal, the grandson of Noah, left for Europe before the Tower of Babel separated the tongues. As a result, Basque descendants speak "the pure language of Eden, the tongue of Adam and Eve." At any rate, Basque is a difficult language to learn. In the summer of 1990, Mark Erro, a Basque descendant, explained to members of the Oregon Writing Project the remarkable complexity of the Basque tongue.

THE DEVIL TRIES TO SPEAK BASQUE

God told the Devil that he would have a chance to be delivered from hell if, after seven years, he could learn to speak Basque. The Devil agreed and went down to earth among the Basques. After seven years the Devil had succeeded in learning only two words, "yes" and "no." A huge storm came up, lightning struck, and the Devil was thrown to the ground. When he got up, he realized he had forgotten the two words that he had learned. He told God he would rather go back to hell than to spend another seven years learning Basque. There is now a saying among the Basque that, because of the Devil's frustrations with the language, Basque people cannot go to hell.

Because the Basques are far from their homeland and isolated in remote regions of Southeastern Oregon, they tend to cling tightly to old traditions, including costume, folk speech, and foodways. Folklorists call this phenomenon marginal distribution, suggesting that great distance usually strengthens folk custom and belief, rather than diminishing it. In the Basque settlements of Southeastern Oregon, the locals play *muz,* a complex card game; dance the *jota* and *porrusalda* at Christmas time; and wager huge amounts on *pelota* games—perhaps with more enthusiasm and dedication than even in the homeland provinces.

In Jordan Valley, Basque customs and proverbs reflect a philosophical approach to life and a skeptical wisdom. Basques are spiritual people with strong family ties and well-defined moral codes. Much of Basque philosophy can be found in these proverbial sayings, collected mostly from the Wasil family in 1972.

BASQUE LORE

☐ *"Its own nest is lovely to every bird."*
☐ *"There is no small quantity that will not reach all; nor is there any large quantity that will not terminate."*
☐ *"A home without a fire is a body without blood."*
☐ *"The salesman needs only one eye. But not even one hundred are enough for the buyer."*
☐ *"As turbulent and muddy that his water is, never say, 'Of it I shall not drink.' "*
☐ *"While herding sheep, I give orders to my dog . . . and he to his tail."*
☐ *Basque women should not have their pictures taken during pregnancy; it damages the spirit of the baby.*
☐ *When ill, a Basque woman puts medication on the soles of her feet because nerve endings in the feet carry the solution to the rest of the body.*
☐ *A true Basque wears his beret even at meals. He removes it only in church, in bed, and sometimes when playing pelota.*
☐ *The Basque house is always open to any of its children. All must share in its goods as well as in its labors.*
☐ *Herders make thick bread in dutch ovens on the range. Always they scratch each loaf with the sign of the cross before cutting the bread.*
☐ *When drinking wine from a* bota, *a goatskin bag, Basques sometimes have a contest to see who can most skillfully direct a stream of wine to his forehead, allowing the wine to trickle down the nose and into his mouth.*
☐ *During any excitement, the Basque war cry* Irrintzi! *can be heard. It begins like a laugh, changes to a horse-neigh, alters to a wolf's howl, then ends like the bray of a jackass. When invading Spain, Napoleon's soldiers shuddered to hear the Basque war cry; Basques are fierce fighters.*

Good Basque cooks use lots of olive oil and garlic; some say these ingredients are the secret to the delicious flavors of Basque dishes. Few can duplicate the traditional Basque ways of cooking goat, mutton, and lamb.

If you are fortunate enough to be asked to a Basque dinner, be prepared to stay awhile. The procession of food seems never to stop: big bowls of soup with a meat, chicken, or lentil base, followed by several side dishes. At a Basque dinner, expect bowls of lettuce with a vinegarlike dressing, string beans or peas, mashed potatoes and gravy, or platters of spaghetti and gravy sauce. Veal is usually cooked in a highly seasoned sauce. Basque cooks fry chicken until the skin is crisp; then they simmer the chicken in wine and herbs. And, of course, the table always overflows with wonderful round loaves of bread and a plentiful supply of dark wine.

BASQUE LAMB CHOPS

8–10 lamb chops
salt and pepper
small amount of flour (4 tablespoons)
2 tablespoons of butter
2 tablespoons of olive oil
1 clove of garlic, sliced
1 medium onion, sliced
½ pound of mushrooms
1 cup of chicken stock
½ cup of tomato juice
dash of nutmeg
¼ cup grated parmesan cheese

Mix the salt and pepper with flour and dredge the chops in this mixture. Mix the butter and olive oil in a heavy skillet; then saute the garlic and onion. Remove the ingredients from the pan. Then brown the chops in the skillet. Next return the onions and garlic to the pan. Add the mushrooms, tomato juice, broth, and nutmeg. Cover this combination and cook over a low heat for 30 minutes, stirring occasionally. Finally sprinkle the chops with a little cheese. Let stand a few minutes before serving.

BASQUE BIG-LOAF SOURDOUGH BREAD

This bread can be baked in a kitchen or in a Dutch oven over a fire pit. The old-fashioned recipe would not include commercial yeast, just the starter.

1 packet of dry yeast
2 cups of lukewarm water
⅓ cup of sugar
1 teaspoon of salt
1 cup of sourdough starter
5 cups of flour
shortening for greasing the pan

In a mixing bowl, dissolve the yeast in the warm water. When it is dissolved, stir the contents and add sugar, salt, and sourdough starter. Mix the ingredients. Then add flour and mix everything well. Grease the Dutch oven liberally on the bottom and the sides and turn the dough into the oven to rise. Place the bread in a warm spot and allow the dough to rise until it is double in volume. Cover the contents with a lid and bake it in the fire pit for an hour.

Juntura

Malheur County. Juntura is a quiet little town nestled in the bunchgrass hills at the junction of the north and middle forks of the Malheur River. Juntura is Latin for "junction." As was often the case, a Southeastern Oregon pioneer schoolteacher was responsible for this classical reference.

The Blue Bucket legend exists in conflicting versions, and during the 1920s and 1930s, descendants of the Lost Wagon Train of 1845 debated the place and details in the "Letters to the Editor" columns of the *Morning Oregonian*, *The Dalles Optimist*, and the *Ontario Argus*. According to Captain W. H. Hembree, interviewed by the WPA in 1938, each of the blue-painted wagons also carried a blue tar bucket, used to lubricate the axle. When the train made "dry camp," many people carrying the blue buckets went looking for water. Then, "[o]ne member came upon a wet, oozy spot where it appeared water was near the surface of the ground. He dug down, using the bucket as a spade, and upon raising the bucket found it filled with wet dirt containing nuggets of gold. And that was how the Blue Bucket mine was discovered."

According to other traditions, travelers who had camped for the evening stumbled upon shiny rocks but failed to recognize the mineral as gold. In most versions, the pioneers were lost, cold and hungry, or desperate. Whatever the case, the children of the wagon train found shiny rocks and put the nuggets into buckets painted with a blue antioxidant, where they remained until the party had reached Bend, The Dalles, or the Willamette Valley. Only then did the sojourners discover that their blue buckets were filled with gold. As folklorist Jan Frederickson discovered, some people feel that the lost Blue Bucket gold cache was uncovered somewhere near Juntura. In the winter of 1969, Frederickson's informant heard this Blue Bucket story from Mrs. Stitz, a businesswoman from Fort Rock.

THE BLUE BUCKET MINE

The story of the Blue Bucket Mine is a familiar one in Oregon. When Mrs. Stitz first started talking about it, I was prepared to hear the same story I had read about, but her version was altered somewhat and made much more interesting because she thinks she has found the mine.

In approximately 1850 a wagon train from Missouri was en route to the Pacific Coast of Oregon. When they reached Juntura, Oregon, they had a feud over which route to take. They couldn't come to a compromise and, as a result, the train was split in three—one following the Columbia River, one going south along the Applegate Trail, and one going through the center of Oregon. The train going through the center of Oregon ran out of water somewhere between Glass Mountain and Wagontire Mountain and made camp. Members of the train, even the children, spiraled out in search of water. Two brothers, their sister, and her boyfriend went north of the camp and found many animal bones within a small area. They thought there may have been a water hole that had dried up, so they began digging. The boys dug about ten feet into the earth and found a small spring. While they were digging, the girl sat at the top of the dirt pile playing in the dirt and found small golden nuggets. She thought they were pretty, so she stuck them in her pocket. They had carried with them a small blue bucket and had left it on a tree above the spring as a marker. Then they went back to the train.

Other members of the train had found a larger spring by the time they had returned, so the children's spring was forgotten. The train then went northwest to Bear Creek and up to the Astoria area, where they reunited with the members of the original train. By this time, they had discovered that the nuggets the girl was carrying were gold. But they had also heard of the abundant amount of gold in California, so they set out to make their fortunes.

Several years later the brothers decided to come back to Oregon to find the Blue Bucket Mine. They found the general vicinity but were unable to find the exact area because of land slides. Up until this time there have been many searches for the mine, but none has been successful.

In 1930, while Mrs. Stitz was the owner of The Horse Ranch (a gas station and several cabins on Highway 31 about five miles from Fort Rock), a man and wife stayed in one of her cabins while touring Oregon. He pointed out three areas in Oregon that a psychic in California had told him would be points of interest. They had already been to two of the areas but told Mrs. Stitz that the third one was "clear to hell and back." They wouldn't go into that wild area for anything.

Mrs. Stitz went into the kitchen to get some coffee, and while she was away a voice told her the third point was the Blue Bucket Mine. She told her visitors about the mine and said that the third point of interest on their map was this mine. It made no difference to them so she looked for it herself.

She found the exact area but didn't have the money or help to dig for it until this year [1970] after she sold The Horse Ranch. She is now in the process of blasting with dynamite and says she has only six feet left.

Lakeview

Lake County. Population 2,518. Lakeview, a descriptive term, comes from the city's 4,800-foot elevation and its position overlooking Goose Lake, a body of water that seems to be receding from the town's limits. From its days as a cow town, Lakeview has continued its role as a business center for the Southeastern region. For years Lakeview residents have celebrated Labor Day Round-Up, one of the Northwest's oldest amateur rodeos.

Stories about the hazing of outsiders are often told to the delight of locals. Two favorites feature the ubiquitous "jackalope" (descended from the German/Austrian/Swiss *Hasenback*) and the "horned coon." Adapted from a tale by Chester Stevenson, "The 'Horned Coon' Hunt" recaptures a moment of hilarity when the eastern editor of *Archery* magazine met his match in the area around Lakeview.

THE "HORNED COON" HUNT

Some years ago Oregon was visited by the editor of Archery *magazine, who often wrote uncomplimentary articles about bow hunters in the Wild West, saying they were a lawless bunch, ignoring game laws, bag limits, and posted seasons. Finally, the editor accepted an invitation from a bow-hunting group, the Western Archers, and came out from New York for a special raccoon-hunting trip.*

The local hunters loaned him a bow and arrows and took him out to tromp through the bushes at night, the best time to hunt raccoons. In the meantime they had arranged for Benny Barnes to mount some small deer horns on a stuffed raccoon that had been gathering dust in his basement for twenty years. Benny hid in the bushes with a string tied to the "horned coon," while the locals paraded the editor around in the woods, telling him outrageous "whoppers" about the exotic animals of Oregon.

With great satisfaction, the hunters prodded the editor through one thicket after another for three quarters of an hour, until they came to the spot where Benny was hiding with the moldy old trophy. All at once, the Western Archers waved their flashlights toward a single spot, and the "horned coon" jumped into full view. Benny yanked on the string a few times, and one of the guys yelled, "Hey, it's one of them horned coons!"

Immediately everybody turned to George, the editor, who was fumbling around with his gear, and said, "Shoot, George! Get that horned coon!"

Sure enough, the Easterner pulled out an arrow and plugged the coon right in the chest. But just at that moment, a whistle blew, and out stepped a uniformed Oregon State Trooper. The trooper said, "This here horned coon is an endangered species, and you are in some kinda trouble now, mister. They're extremely rare. Don't you know better than to kill a horned coon?" So the trooper read George his rights and started to march him through the woods toward his car, which the editor thought was miles away—but was actually just a few hundred yards over the next hill. Meanwhile, the editor tried to explain that he was from New York and had never even heard of a horned coon.

After fifteen minutes of walking, the locals couldn't stand it any more and began to break up with laughter. The editor was humiliated, but the Western Archers had made their point. From that time on, there were no more negative articles about Western bowmen in Archery *magazine.*

Mann Lake

Harney County. Named for a local rancher, Mann Lake lies at the north end of Alvord Valley. Mann Lake is cattle country.

In 1971, Mardi Wilson called on her experience as a Southeastern Oregon resident and contributed an extensive collection of ranching terms to the Mills Archives at the University of Oregon. Wilson picked up the buckaroo jargon at the Mann Lake Ranch. Many of the terms are Spanish in origin, suggesting the pervasive Hispanic color of ranch life. Words such as *caviata*, *concha*, *honda*, *mecate*, and *tapadero* chronicle the ongoing influence of Pete French's Mexican *vaqueros* on Southeastern Oregon cow culture.

RANCHING TERMS

borrow pit: the gulley on the sides of a dirt road from which dirt is borrowed to fill and level the center of the road

bosal: a nose band usually made of braided rawhide, worn under a horse's bridle and held in place by a leather strap which runs behind the horse's ears

breakdown: when a horse stops to go to the bathroom, causing the impatient rider to wait for a few minutes: "I was just about to chase that calf when my horse had a breakdown."

broke to lead: a cow which ceases to struggle after being roped and allows herself to be pulled behind a horse: "Hey, I got this old cow broke to lead. She won't be so ornery now."

bronco faced: a cow with a speckled face

buckaroo: the term used in the Southeast part of Oregon instead of "cowboy"

bulldog taps: Taps are a leather covering on the forward part of the stirrup, which protect the rider's foot from the brush. Bulldog taps are those which have no leathers hanging down, which are often used for decoration. [Tap is short for *tapadera*.]

burn 'em up: an expression frequently used to describe a horse which can keep up with a cow, steer, or calf when the rider is attempting to rope it: "Old Smokey really burned 'em up out there this afternoon."

caviata: the horses used for riding purposes, generally referred to as the "cavvy"

centerfire: a western saddle with only one cinch (part of the saddle which goes around the horse's belly and keeps the saddle in place)

Cheyenne roll: a cantle (the rear part of the seat on a western saddle) which rolls under

chinks: leather-fringed coverings worn over a buckaroo's pants to protect him from the brush and weather. They reach just below the knee and are kept in place by a buckle around the waist and metal clips which attach behind the leg.

choke cherries: red berries which grow on bushes in the region of the Steens Mountain and probably in many other localities. When eaten, they make the mouth so dry that it is extremely difficult to swallow.

concha: silver ornaments which are often used to decorate a bridle or saddle

coyote: a term sometimes used to describe a cunning person or animal: "You have to be a real coyote if you want to catch stream trout."

crow hop: When a horse humps his back and jumps around in a stiff-legged manner, he is said to be "crow hopping."

cull a cow: to get rid of an old or sick cow which can no longer be used for breeding purposes

cut her an' can her: a phrase used to describe a cow which will be shipped out and butchered for dog food

dally: after a cowboy has roped a calf, he wraps the rope remaining in his hand about three or four times around the saddle horn to hold the calf fast. This is called "dallying."

dock tailed: a cow's tail which has had the very end cut off. This is done so that the cow can be more easily recognized.

dry cow: a cow which is not nursing a calf and is therefore dried up, or not producing milk

earin' down a horse: It is possible to control a horse from the ground by holding his ear very tightly.

fiador: a type of knot which is used to tie the *mecate* around the upper part of the horse's neck

fistful of coils: the coiled rope which is held by the hand that does not throw the loop in calf roping

ganted up: describes the flanks and belly of a horse when it is drawn and shrunken after hard work

goose 'em: to kick or spur a horse in order to make him move quickly forward

gummer: a cow with no teeth

gut-hooks: spurs

had his old ass buried in the ground: refers to a horse that slides on its haunches when it pulls to a halt

hard in the mush: a horse that has an insensitive mouth and does not respond to the pressure of the bit

heading a cow: throwing the loop of the rope around the cow's neck when roping

heeling a cow: throwing the loop of the rope around the cow's hind legs when roping

hobbles: a leather strap which is wrapped around both front legs of the horse to keep him from wandering off

honda: a small brass or rope loop on one end of a *lass rope*

honkin' on: This refers to geese which honk when they fly overhead.

humpy: a horse which raises its back as though it were about to buck

jerk your slack: pulling the slack out of the rope after a calf has been caught and before "dallying" around the horn

lass rope: a rope used to rope cattle or lasso them

latigo: the leather strap on a western saddle, which is used to tighten the cinch

leppy: a calf which has no mother and is generally in poor condition

Let your turns slide: when you allow the rope which is "dallied" around the horn to loosen

line back: a cow that has a natural line down her back

loving cup: a heavy metal pounder which is used to drive steel fence posts into the ground. It is grasped by two side handles.

maguey: hemp rope

marker cow: a cow that has unusual coloring or any other marked characteristics which make it easy to recognize her

mecate: usually pronounced "McCarty," a pliable rope which is run through a ring on the bosal, tied in a knot around the upper part of the horse's head, with the remainder tied to the saddle

mothered up: when a cow and her calf are together: "The calves have stopped bawling now that they're all mothered up."

mountain oysters: the testicles of a calf which are cut off when he is castrated. They are often roasted and eaten.

nurse cow: a cow which is being used as a wet nurse for motherless calves

old bag: an uncooperative cow

oreana: a large calf which has not been branded

pigging string: a short piece of rope used to tie three of a calf's legs together after it has been roped, so that it will not get away

push the cattle: drive them from one location to another

put a kink in her tail: When cows are moving through a chute, they often get jammed up. Sometimes it is necessary to pull a few tails in order to get them moving again.

riata: a braided leather rope. A buckaroo who uses one is often referred to as a *"riata man."*

riggin'—saddle, saddle blankets, bridle, and bosal

rimfire: a western saddle with a back and a front cinch

ringy: ornery or acting crazy. Can be used to describe an animal or a person.

rodire: cattle which are bunched together in an open space: "We held the rodire while the calves were roped and branded."

romal: a heavy leather strap attached to the ends of the reins. "Romal 'em over and under" or "Romal 'em down where the colt sucks" are expressions used to describe whipping a horse with the romal.

rough string: the horses which are generally more difficult to ride

slick calf: a calf which has not been branded

shitters: wild horses which run loose on the desert

shotguns: leather chaps worn over Levi pants to protect the legs from the brush, rain, and cold when riding

steep as a cow's face: A cow's face is very straight. This is self-explanatory.

straight bellied: a cow that is not pregnant

stretch her neck: roping a cow around the neck and dragging her behind a horse

take the drag: riding behind the cattle on a cattle drive

take the lead: riding in front of the cattle on a cattle drive

take your turns: the same as "dallying"

tapidero: taps which have leather hangings for ornamentation

tight bag: a cow with a swollen udder because she is producing milk and the calf has not sucked. This will often occur if a cow has lost her calf.

turnover shot: a sloop which is thrown over the opposite shoulder when roping cattle

twine: the same as a *lass rope*

two halked: when a cow is roped by both hind legs

wad: a hunk of chewing tobacco which is held between the lower lip and gum

wattle: a piece of skin which has been cut away from a cow or steer's hide. It remains attached to the animal when the cut heals and serves as a mark of identification. [The wattle in a cow or steer is like a double chin in humans; handmade notches in the wattles serve the same purpose as brands.]

wax up: A waxy substance appears on a mare's udder just prior to foaling. When this happens, she is said to be "waxing up."

weaner: a calf that has been weaned from its mother

wet cow: a cow that is producing milk and is being sucked by a calf

wrangle: to gather the riding horses and bring them into the corral so that they can be caught more easily

wreck: when the horse falls down, the rider falls off, or both: "If you get that rope caught under that horse's tail, you're bound to have a wreck."

Paisley

Lake County. Population 348. The town of Paisley got its name from a Scot who fondly remembered a town in Scotland and wished to live once again in Paisley.

Paisley had a sheriff who might not have had a lot of knowledge about the law, but he had some common sense and certainly knew how to make the best of a bad situation. One day a trapper and a cowboy got into a big argument in a Paisley saloon about whether rattlesnakes could jump. The trapper won the argument by filling the cowboy with lead, and somebody went for the sheriff.

The sheriff came into the bar, stepped over the body, and went right up to the trapper, who was over six feet tall and 250 pounds—a rugged lookin' cuss wearing a Bowie knife on his belt. The sheriff took a good look at the trapper and then a good long look at the expired cowpoke and declared, "Any man crazy enough to call a long-haired, whiskey-drinking trapper a liar surely must have died of ignorance."

Harry Telford, the ranch hand who spent most of his young life at Frenchglen's P Ranch, also worked for the Z-X ranch near Paisley. One September, after the crew had brought in the hay, Telford rode into town for a drink; he brought back a story about the typical wild-and-wooly nightlife in Paisley.

A SHORT FUSE

There was a little saloon and place where they played cards in this little town of Paisley, and these cowboys and the hay men and all would gather up there, and they'd have poker games in this little saloon place. And there was kind of a goofy guy, a cowboy that worked for the Z-X Company, named Joe Bush. Joe had been in the poker game and they'd cleaned him out. He didn't have any more money, and so he left. And he thought he'd have some fun with the other guys, so he got a piece of a broomstick and wrapped some brown paper around it. Then he put a dynamite fuse on it—and he didn't leave it very long, either. But he went up there into the saloon, and he lit this fuse and threw it down on the floor of the saloon. It looked, of course, just like a stick of dynamite, and there was the grandest rush to get out of that saloon that you ever saw in your life. One fellow dove right through the window and come out with a part of the window sash hanging around his neck. Of course, the thing was a dud. It didn't blow up. But it sure caused a big commotion there for quite a long time. There was probably twenty people in the saloon, and they all tried to get outta one door and, of course, some of them got out through the windows. But nobody got seriously hurt. I was workin' in the lead gettin' out the door. I didn't get any window sash on my neck. It was quite a lot of fun, and that's one of the ways they played in those days.

Princeton

Harney County. Princeton was named for Princeton, Massachusetts, birthplace of early settler C. B. Smith. Princeton is the Saturday night station for cowpunchers from nearby Mann Ranch.

One day a couple of cowhands went out to dig some postholes. It got dark before they finished, so they went home and left their tools behind, hoping to finish early the next day. It blew so hard that night that, when they returned, they found both the tools and the postholes had blown clear to Winnemucca.

The chuck wagon cook, or "old woman," is usually a seasoned cowhand who is too old to ride all day in the saddle. The old woman can be counted on for a variety of needs. Not only can he prepare food and keep the coffee simmering, he can also cure minor ills with his snake oils and herbs. Most can even set broken bones and doctor the usual trailside ills. Crossing the old woman is never a good idea, as shown in this story related by a Mann Ranch cowhand.

THE TRAIL COOK'S CURE-ALL: THE LIVER-REGULATOR

One day on the trail, after the trail crew had been eating the same diet of beans and fatback for about a week, a shorthorn, just new to the outfit, started complaining. He turned to an old-timer in the outfit and said, "The chow here is

killin' me. I got permanent heartburn and my stomach feels terrible."

The old-timer gave the tenderfoot a serious look and said, "What you need is some of that liver-regulator. Go to the old woman. He'll set you straight."

So the cowpuncher went over to the feed-trough and found the ranch cook out behind his wagon stirring up a big pot of beans.

"Hey, cookie," said the shorthorn, "Them beans is gettin' to me. I think I need a shot of that liver-regulator."

"Aw-right, cowboy," said the cook. He went over to the chuck wagon, pulled back the flap, and pulled out a Colt .45 hanging from a wagon rail. Then he fired a shot into the dust beneath the cowpoke's feet. "How many shots do ya think it'll take?" Funny thing, that shorthorn cowboy never seemed to have any more stomach trouble.

Silver Lake

Lake County. The Indian name for Silver Lake was *Kalpshi*, meaning "decayed wood." Silver Lake is surrounded by groves of petrified logs. Silver Lake lies on the open range, a place divided between timber land and dry sage land. "The town couldn't help but grow," said one Silver Lake resident. "Yer see, it was such a durn fierce trip that, after a feller tried it once he never wanted ta repeat the trek . . . so he stayed with us."

On December 24, 1894, the frontier town of Silver Lake suffered a tragic fire, a blaze that took the lives of forty-three people. Everyone in town was touched, losing either family members or friends. A monument in memory of those who perished stands in the town cemetery.

The whole town had turned out for the Christmas Eve program held in the upstairs hall of the Chrisman Store. The building was a typical western structure with a raised wooden porch under a sloping roof. Outside, one staircase led to the hall, which was used for dances, celebrations, school programs, and the rare traveling shows that happened through town. As the choir was singing the last Christmas song, a man in the audience stood up, apparently to get a better view, and bumped an oil lamp with his shoulder. Flames leaped up. Many people tried to smother the flames, but they spread quickly. As people crowded toward the stairway, panic prevailed. When scores of people climbed out the window onto the porch roof, it collapsed under their weight, causing most of the deaths.

Vale

Malheur County. Population 1,490. This town on the Malheur River was an important stopover on cattle drives, and Vale is a good place to learn about horses and "horse sense."

Buckaroos knew a great deal about the behavior of cattle on the home ranch as well as on the trail. Two cattle ailments that were accepted without scientific explanation were *holler horn* and *wolf in the tail*, both suspected when cattle began to act "loco." The cow might shake its head or run in a wild manner. For holler horn, the cowhand drilled a hole in the horn—yes, it is hollow—and poured salt inside. When afflicted by wolf in the tail, a steer would run and switch its tail wildly; the cowpoke split the bulb of the tail and applied a mixture of salt and turpentine. Out on the trail, cows got a malady for which there was no cure except time; the cowboys called it *hot ass*, an affliction that occurred after cattle grazed through plants similar to peppers.

Doctoring cattle was hard enough in spring and fall, but in winter it was downright unpleasant. One week the boys in the bunkhouse faced a really nasty spell of cold weather. A buckaroo from Vale reported that the cold air froze his candle; he had to wait until noon the next day to put out the flame. "But," he said, "that was nothin' compared to the coldest night of the year. The foreman came out to give us some orders, and the words just kinda froze as they came outen his mouth. We had to break 'em off one at a time just to hear what he was sayin'."

A man's horse was perhaps his most important possession, as chronicled in numerous Southeastern Oregon stories about the sudden justice afforded horse thieves. Nonetheless, a good mount all too often walked away from the hitching rail at the local saloon. This story, told by former Klamath Falls resident Carole Hunt in 1984, describes what often happened next.

CLEAR TITLE ON A HORSE

Horse thieving was pretty much the worst kind of crime in cattle country. Generally speaking, horse thieves were hanged first and tried later. It saved a lot of time and trouble.

One day a fancy cowboy rode into Vale on a particularly handsome mount. One of the locals went up to the stranger and offered him a good price for the horse. After thinking a while, the man accepted the offer. But the local man, always a careful sort, asked, "Is the title clear on this here horse?"

The cowboy, who was stuffing the money into his shirt pocket, gave a thoughtful look and said, "Yep, as long as you go east the title's free and clear. I wouldn't go west, though. It ain't quite as good in that direction."

Whorehouse Meadow

Harney County. East of Fish Lake, wood and canvas houses provided temporary quarters for a group of female entrepreneurs from Vale and Boise, the women traveling by wagon for prearranged meetings with cattle hands and Basque sheepherders. Righteous map makers once

attempted to change the name of this pasture to Naughty Girl Meadow, but old Southeastern logic prevailed and in 1981 the Bureau of Land Management gave up trying to whitewash this particular place-name.

The inveterate Harry Telford describes both the rationale for such a place as Whorehouse Meadow and some of the consequences for the trail hands.

A ROUGH DAY IN THE SADDLE

[A]nother kind of medicine we used out there—thankfully I never had to use any of it, but some of the boys did—there was a traveling sporting house came by and there were a couple of girls there, middle-aged women; they weren't very fancy whore ladies. But, however, women were mighty scarce in that country in those days. I know one time I went for seven months without speaking to a woman; there just weren't any to speak to. But anyway, these girls did quite a business with the buckaroo outfit, and then they pulled out, went on to the next camp I 'spose, or next buckaroo outfit they could find or whatever. And come to find out that they'd been pretty well inflicted with venereal disease, and so a lotta the boys they got in pretty bad shape, and there's one thing that you don't do when you have that—is to ride horseback if you can possibly help it. But somebody knew about this sage-rabbit brush, we called it—it was a small kind of a sage brush that grew in alkali, heavy alkali soil; and they made tea out of that sage brush, that rabbit brush, and it seemed to work probably just as good as some of their high-priced drugs they put out nowadays.

A Folklore History

There is no history, only fictions of varying degrees of plausibility.

—Voltaire

Most people believe that history is truth and folklore is fiction. Sometimes that distinction holds, but usually it is misleading. In reality, folklore is often an imaginative combination of fact and fiction. As William A. Wilson explains in "Folklore and History," some narratives have a theme or symbolism that makes a story plausible, perhaps even compelling, despite obvious elements of fiction. Narratives that are not historically accurate, says Wilson, may be called culturally factual if they express ideas that are significant to a folk group. Many of the items in a folklore history fit Wilson's definition.

In *The Well-Traveled Casket* one culturally valid story is the place-name legend for Noti. A white man and an Indian were "riding and tying" from Florence to Eugene, a strategy that called for each man to ride twenty miles, tie the horse, then walk twenty miles while the second man rode the horse ahead. But when the white man reached the final exchange point west of Eugene, he broke the bargain and continued on horseback into town. Arriving at the "tying tree," the Indian searched for the horse and finally had to admit reluctantly, "Him *no tie*." Despite its improbability, the "ride and tie" legend endures, not only because it is colorful, but because it has cultural validity. After helping and trusting many of the initial white settlers, most Native Americans found themselves burdened with a series of broken promises, contracts, agreements, and treaties. The Noti story, like so many of the tales and legends in *The Well-Traveled Casket*, is culturally valid, if not historically true.

From Astoria to Vale, Oregon folklore reveals much about Oregon history—good and bad, noble and savage—in ways that often transcend fact. For instance, historians admit that Oregon's past includes lengthy periods of racial prejudice, intolerance, and xenophobia. But those attitudes may best be expressed in folklore. "Binks and the Heppner Flood," for example, hints at white intolerance for the Chinese population of Oregon. Astoria's "Ben Gun" legend suggests the collective paranoia that led to

World War II internment camps for Japanese citizens. The Siletz legend of Toemannah, the "owl man," symbolizes the decline of Native American traditions and the displacement of Indian values after government attempts to decertify the tribe around 1925. These narratives, which do not appear in history texts, nonetheless capture attitudes that are historically accurate. Such orally transmitted stories are part of Oregon's folklore history.

Of course, Oregon's folklore history is more than a fanciful record of injustice. It is also a chronicle of diligence, cooperation, ethnic pride, and cultural tradition. "The Last Needle" (Lebanon) is an oft-told tale dramatizing the virtues of responsibility and cooperation, values that spelled the difference between survival and disaster in the 1850s. Loggers' initiation rites from Oakridge and Wolf Creek underscore the importance of good humor, patience, and competence; sending a greenhorn for a "board stretcher" or a "choker hole" serves to test the character of the new logger, as well as the greenhorn's capacity to learn the ways of the woods. Apocryphal on the surface, Yoncalla's "Hooker and the Whistle Punk" shows on a deeper level that a hospital stay is not uncommon when loggers get their messages garbled. Ethnic pride surfaces in "Created from the Heart" (Joseph), a Nez Perce myth-legend shared after the exile of Chief Joseph by survivors of the 1877 massacre. Echoing the voice of tradition, "The Log Truck Driver and the Bikers" (King's Valley) recaptures the Wild West notion that native Oregonians' actions speak louder than their words. From Riddle, "Here Lies a Bum Steer" demonstrates that traditional ways of doing things (in this case, barbecuing venison) are preferable to newfangled notions.

In Oregon, history and folklore are marvelously intertwined. Historians sometimes characterize the rigors of the Oregon Trail by describing the Lost Wagon Train of 1845; folklorists study the incidental "Blue Bucket Mine" legends of the Lost Train as an appropriate metaphor for pioneers' frustrations, delusions, and tragedies. In the same way, historians examine Fred Lockley's *Conversations with Pioneer Women* for information about the harshness of settlement life; folklorists find the Lockley diaries no more ''factual'' than lines from ''The Housewife's Lament,'' a song based on the diary of Sara Price.

It's sweeping at six, and it's dusting at seven;
It's victuals at eight, and it's dishes at nine;
It's potting and panning from ten to eleven;
We scarce break our fast till we plan how to dine.

Likewise, historians talk about settlements at Union, Arlington, and Wingville in order to explain divided loyalties in Civil War-era Oregon, but folklorists retell ''Auntie Ganung Casts Her Ballot'' (Jacksonville) for the same purpose. Phil Brogan's history of dry country law and order in *East of the Cascades* is fascinating, but carries the same weight as ''Well, They Did a Fine Job,'' a grisly tale of frontier justice from Old West Drewsey.

Seeing history as no more than a list of dates and names is a serious (but common) mistake. Gouge Eye, Crazyman Creek, and Spanish Charlie Basin are pockets of Oregon history, but these place-names also evoke the image of storytellers gathered around campfires. Intrinsically we know that behind every date and name is a tale; behind every landmark is a story. In the spring of 1991 the authors discovered that even youngsters understand the relationship between folklore and history. At the Oregon Writing Festival in Portland, groups of middle schoolers were given lists of Oregon towns, creeks, and mountains and asked to ''speculate about the origins of these names.'' After ten minutes of talking it over with friends, Catherine penned this explanation for the naming of Tillamook County's Idiot Creek.

Before the white people came, the Indians called this place Higheyeque Creek. *But a bunch of pioneers settled there on the banks, and the children wouldn't do their homework. Gradually they got dumber and dumber, until everyone started calling this place* Idiot Creek.

Catherine seemed to understand that history is a series of stories about the land, its inhabitants, and cultural change. Like the Noti legend, Catherine's explanation was colorful, imaginative, and unimpeded by fact. History often takes such turns. In dealing with the past, it is not always wise to insist on a respectful distance between fact and fiction. The cultural truths of Oregon history extend well beyond the pages of Lewis and Clark's *Journal* or Hubert Bancroft's *History of Oregon*. They often lie in the tales, legends, and proverbs of oral tradition.

Works Consulted

Abrams, Elizabeth. Randall V. Mills Folklore Archives #060076021. June 1976.

Agee, Bill. Randall V. Mills Folklore Archives #060176093. June 1976.

Alanis, Yolanda. Randall V. Mills Folklore Archives #070073258. July 1973.

Allen, Barbara. *Homesteading the High Desert.* Salt Lake City: University of Utah Press, 1987.

_____. "The Story of the Christmas Eve Fire." *Northwest Folklore* 4.2 (1986): 3–17.

Allison, Mildred. "Annual Event Comes Long Way." *Pioneer Trails* 4.1 (1979): 3–7.

Altman, Sandra. Randall V. Mills Folklore Archives #030868012. 1970.

Anderson, Eva Greenslit, and Dean Collins. *Stories of Oregon.* Lincoln: University of Nebraska Publishing Co., 1949.

Anderson, Nancy. Randall V. Mills Folklore Archives #060074052. June 1974.

Anonymous. "How to Dress Ducks." *Tillamook Memories.* Tillamook: Tillamook Pioneer Association, 1972.

Armstrong, A. N. *History of Oregon.* 1857. Fairfield, Washington: Ye Galleon Press, 1969.

Aschim, Joan. Randall V. Mills Folklore Archives #030075001. March 1975.

Asla, Besse E. Randall V. Mills Folklore Archives #080076115. August 1976.

Atlas of Oregon. Ed. William G. Loy *et al.* Eugene: University of Oregon Press, 1976.

Baker, James C. "Echoes of Tommy Knockers in Bohemia, Oregon, Mines." *Western Folklore* 30.2 (1971): 119–22.

_____. Randall V. Mills Folklore Archives #121569076. December 1969.

_____. Randall V. Mills Folklore Archives #050070038. May 1970.

_____. Randall V. Mills Folklore Archives #121569076. December 1970.

Baker Record-Courier. Centennial Edition. 22 July 1982.

Balch, Frederic Homer. *The Bridge of the Gods: A Romance of Indian Origin.* Chicago: A. C. McClung and Co., 1890.

Barber, LaVada. Randall V. Mills Folklore Archives #030773105. July 1973.

Barker, Linda. Randall V. Mills Folklore Archives #000069002. May 1969.

Barry, Sheramy. Randall V. Mills Folklore Archives #060075079. June 1975.

Bartlett, Grace. *Wallowa: The Land of Winding Waters.* Grace Bartlett, publisher, 1967.

Beach, Janice. Randall V. Mills Folklore Archives #120070146. December 1970.

Beck, Horace P. "Sea Lore." *Northwest Folklore* 2.1 (1967): 1–13.

Beckham, Steven Dow, ed. *Tall Tales from the Rogue River: The Yarns of Hathaway Jones.* Bloomington: Indiana University Press, 1974.

Beers, Robert. "The Logger's Sweetheart" (traditional). Eugene, 1971.

Bell, Mimi. *Off-Beat Oregon.* San Francisco: Chronicle Books, 1983.

Bellomo, Andy. "Pioneer Park Served First as Burial Place." *Pioneer Trails* 5.1 (1980): 20–24.

Bennehoff, Bert W., and Diane C. Brooks. Randall V. Mills Folklore Archives #060071173. June 1971.

Berry, Beverly A. Randall V. Mills Folklore Archives 000000007. 1970.

Bisbee, Mark, *et al. Celebrating: Lane County Residents Remember Their Heritage.* Eugene: Lane County Summer Youth Employment Program, 1978.

Bolden, Bob. Personal interview. Eugene, October 1990.

Bolton, Walter A. "Brownsville Mountain" (traditional). Eugene, 1970.

Braddock, George. Randall V. Mills Folklore Archives #040076004. April 1976.

Braly, David. *Juniper Empire: Early Days in Eastern and Central Oregon.* Prineville: American Media Co., 1976.

Bright, Verne. "Sailors' Diggings in the Siskiyous." *Western Folklore* 11 (1952): 65–173.

Brimlow, George Francis. *Harney County, Oregon.* Portland: Binfords & Mort, 1951.

Brogan, Phil F. *East of the Cascades.* Portland: Binfords & Mort, 1977.

Bruner, Reba. Randall V. Mills Folklore Archives #060170195. June 1970.

Calderon, Brian, and Michelle Woosley. "Living Off the Land." *Kingfisher* 4.1 (1981): 1–5.

Campbell, Jean. Randall V. Mills Folklore Archives #080074128. August 1974.

Carey, Charles H. "First Man to Write *Oregon.*" *Junior Historical Journal* 5.3 (1945): 91–95.

Cheatham, Thayer. Randall V. Mills Folklore Archives #060073163. June 1973.

Christensen, Ralph. "The Strawberry Roan" (traditional). Burns, 1982.

Clark, Ella E. *Indians of the Pacific Northwest.* Berkeley: University of California Press, 1953.

Clark, Keith. *Redmond: Where the Desert Blooms.* Western Imprints Series. Portland: Oregon Historical Society, 1985.

Clark, Keith, and Donna Clark. "William McKay's Journal, 1866–67: Indian Scouts, Part II." *Oregon Historical Quarterly* 79.3 (1978): 269–333.

Clarke, Dwight L. Randall V. Mills Folklore Archives #030072001. March 1972.

_____. Randall V. Mills Folklore Archives #060072027. June 1972.

Clason, Leslie D. Randall V. Mills Folklore Archives #000084143. April 1984.

Cloutier, James. *This Day in Oregon*. Eugene: Image West Press, 1982.

Coleman, Charmaine. Personal interview. Eugene, October 1990.

Coleman, Edwin. Personal interview. Eugene, October 1990.

Colvin, Penny. Randall V. Mills Folklore Archives #080075123. August 1975.

Conner, Roberta. Randall V. Mills Folklore Archives #060076030. December 1975.

Cooper, Trudy. Randall V. Mills Folklore Archives #070073273. July 1973.

Cornett, Jack. Personal interview. Azalea, August 1990.

Culver, Greg. Presentation at South Medford High School. Medford, 7 March 1990.

Davenport, Marge. *Fabulous Folks of the Old Northwest*. Tigard: Paddlewheel Press, 1980.

Davis, Wilbur A. "Logger and Splinter-Picker Talk." *Western Folklore* 9 (1950): 111–23.

Day, Donna. Randall V. Mills Folklore Archives #030073030. March 1973.

Dean, Kathryn. Randall V. Mills Folklore Archives #060072028. June 1972.

Dean, Kevin. Randall V. Mills Folklore Archives #061580049. June 1980.

DeCourcey, Jeanne. Randall V. Mills Folklore Archives #080070101. August 1970.

Degh, Linda. "The Hook." *Indiana Folklore* 1 (1968): 92–100.

Dicken, Samuel, and Emily F. Dicken. *The Making of Oregon: A Study in Historical Geography*. Portland: Oregon Historical Society, 1979.

Donegan, James J. *Historical Sketch of Harney County, Oregon*. Burns, 1936.

Dorson, Richard M. "Folklore and Fakelore." *American Mercury* 70 (1950): 335–43.

Douglas, Dennis. Randall V. Mills Folklore Archives #080071329. August 1971.

Douthit, Nathan. *A Guide to Oregon South Coast History*. Coos Bay, Oregon: River West Books, 1986.

Drawson, Maynard C. *Treasures of the Oregon Country*. Salem: Dee Publishing Co., 1975.

Duhaime, Mary. Randall V. Mills Folklore Archives #081375163. August 1975.

Dundes, Alan. "Texture, Text, and Context." *Southern Folklore Quarterly* 28 (1964): 251–65.

East Oregonian. New Year's Edition. 1 January 1892: 7–8, 9, 10–11, 15, 17.

Edson, Christopher H. *The Chinese in Eastern Oregon: 1860–1890*. San Francisco: R. and E. Research Associates, 1974.

Ehrlich, Michael. Randall V. Mills Folklore Archives #120770182. December 1970.

Erro, Mark. Oregon Writing Project presentation. Ashland, Oregon. June 1990.

Esherick, Judy. Randall V. Mills Folklore Archives #080074136. August 1974.

Fee, Chester A. "Oregon's Historical Esperanto—the Chinook Jargon." *Oregon Historical Quarterly* 42 (1941): 176–85.

"Folklore." Federal Writers' Project of the Work Projects Administration. State of Oregon Archives, Salem. Series 1. Box 66.

Fitch, Leslie. Randall V. Mills Folklore Archives #080072113. August 1972.

Florin, Lambert. *Oregon Ghost Towns*. Seattle: Superior Publishing Co., 1970.

Forester, Mike. "Saloons: A Natural Basic Part of Life." *Pioneer Trails* 1.2 (1976): 19.

Frederickson, Jan. Randall V. Mills Folklore Archives #052069054. Winter 1969.

French, Giles. *Cattle Country of Peter French*. Portland: Binfords & Mort, 1964.

Friedman, Ralph. *Tracking Down Oregon*. Caldwell, Idaho: Caxton Printers, 1978.

Frink, Jayne. "The 1910 Round-Up." *Pioneer Trails* 12.3 (1988): 1–14.

Gambell, Cara. Randall V. Mills Folklore Archives #060371285. June 1971.

Gant, Morris. Randall V. Mills Folklore Archives #000000019. 1970.

Gay, Peter. Randall V. Mills Folklore Archives #120075173. December 1975.

Grant, Rena V. "The Chinook Jargon, Past and Present." *California Folklore Quarterly* 3 (1944): 259–76.

Grants Pass Daily Courier. Centennial Edition. 2 April 1960.

Grissom, Chris, and Candy Anderson. Randall V. Mills Folklore Archives #030569019. March 1969.

Grobe, Valerie. Randall V. Mills Folklore Archives #030071017. March 1971.

Guthrie, Woody. "Roll on, Columbia." The Woody Guthrie Foundation. Composed ca. 1941. New York: Ludlow Music, Inc., 1957.

Haines, Francis. "Goldilocks on the Oregon Trail." *Idaho Yesterdays* 9 (1965–66): 26–30.

Hamilton, Greg. Randall V. Mills Folklore Archives #000069003. 1969.

Harkins, John. "Oregon Vortex Lore." State of Jefferson Folklore Archives, Southern Oregon State College, 1985.

Harrison, Russell M. "Folk Songs from Oregon." *Western Folklore* 11 (1952): 174–84.

Helm, Mike. *Oregon's Ghosts and Monsters*. Eugene: Rainy Day Press, 1983.

Henry, Francis. "The Song of the Old Settler." *Washington Pioneer Association Transactions 1883–89*. Compiled by Charles Prosch. Seattle, 1894: 150.

Herring, Kathleen. Randall V. Mills Folklore Archives #030182020. March 1982.

Highsmith, Gerry. Personal interview. Tillamook, July 1983.

Hildenbrand, Donald Gerald. Randall V. Mills Folklore Archives #120075178. December 1975.

Hill, Bonnie. Randall V. Mills Folklore Archives #080075130. August 1975.

Hill, Carolyn. State of Jefferson Folklore Archives, Southern Oregon State College. March 1990.

Hill, Geoff, ed. *Little Known Tales from Oregon History*. Vol. I. Bend: Sun Publishing, 1988.

Hilton, Peter B. Randall V. Mills Folklore Archives #050076010. May 1976.

History of Hood River, Oregon. Vol. II. Hood River: Hood River Historical Society, 1987.

Hobbs, Gregory. Randall V. Mills Folklore Archives #120070155. December 1970.

Hockema, Bess Finley Wasson. "Old Mr. Fox" (traditional). Pistol River, Oregon. 1969.

Hoig, Stan. *Humor of the American Cowboy*. Lincoln: University of Nebraska Press, 1958.

Holbrook, Stewart H. *The Far Corner: A Personal View of the Pacific Northwest*. New York: Macmillan, 1952.

_____. Review of *Oregon, End of the Trail*. *New York Times* 22 September 1940.

Holman, Frederick V. "Oregon Counties, Their Creations and

the Origins of Their Names." *Oregon Historical Society Quarterly* 11 (1910): 1–81.

Holt, Arlie. Personal interview. Monmouth, 1982.

Howay, F. H. "Origin of the Chinook Jargon on the Northwest Coast." *Oregon Historical Quarterly* 44 (1943): 26–55.

Hubbard, Anne. Randall V. Mills Folklore Archives #031171117. March 1971.

Hunt, Carole. Personal interview. Portland, 1987.

Hysmith, Gerry. Personal interview. Tillamook, 1983.

Jackman, E. R., and R. A. Long. *The Oregon Desert*. Caldwell, Idaho: Caxton Printers, 1973.

Jansen, William Hugh. "The Esoteric-Exoteric Factor in Folklore." *Fabula* 2 (1959): 205–11.

Januik, Michael. Randall V. Mills Folklore Archives #060074066. June 1974.

———. Randall V. Mills Folklore Archives #030075025. March 1975.

Johansen, Dorothy. *Empire of the Columbia*. 2d ed. New York: Harper and Row, 1967.

Johnson, Cynthia. Randall V. Mills Folklore Archives #000070005. May 1970.

Johnson, Harriet. Randall V. Mills Folklore Archives #052375068. May 1975.

Johnson, Sidona V. *A Short History of Oregon*. 1904.

Johnston, Jeri. Randall V. Mills Folklore Archives #080075133. August 1975.

Jones, Ginger. Randall V. Mills Folklore Archives #011267013. August 1975.

Jones, Pamela. "*La Llorona* in Southern Oregon." State of Jefferson Folklore Archives, Southern Oregon State College. 1987.

———. "There Was a Woman: *La Llorona* in Oregon." *Western Folklore* 47 (July 1988): 195–211.

Jones, Janice Suzanne (Suzi). *Oregon Folklore*. Eugene: University of Oregon Press and the Oregon Arts Commission, 1977.

———. "Regionalization in Oregon Folklore." Unpublished dissertation, University of Oregon, 1978.

Justus, Debra. Randall V. Mills Folklore Archives #031975062. March 1975.

Knight, Tanis. Randall V. Mills Folklore Archives #080075135. August 1975.

Knox, Carol. Randall V. Mills Folklore Archives #060077036. June 1977.

Kropf, Rosemary. Randall V. Mills Folklore Archives #030074026. March 1974.

Kyle, Ellen. Randall V. Mills Folklore Archives #052474046. May 1974.

LaLande, Jeffry M. *Prehistory and History of the Rogue River National Forest*. Medford, 1980.

Larson, Karen. Randall V. Mills Folklore Archives #060170082. June 1970.

Lee, Deborah, *et al.* "Early Days in Hermiston." *Pioneer Trails* 13.1 (1989): 20–21.

Lewis, Marvin. "Humor of the Western Mining Regions." *Western Folklore* 14 (1955): 92–97.

Lewis, Pat. Randall V. Mills Folklore Archives #000068003. 1968.

Lickteig, Mary J. Randall V. Mills Folklore Archives #060070067. June 1970.

Lindsay, Robert J. Randall V. Mills Folklore Archives #030074029. March 1974.

Lindsey, Peter. Randall V. Mills Folklore Archives #120070159. December 1970.

Livermore, Annamae. "1878 Merchant." *Pioneer Trails* 2.2 (1977): 28–30.

Llewellyn, Diane. Randall V. Mills Folklore Archives #080072129B. August 1972.

Lockley, Fred. *Conversations with Bullwhackers and Muleskinners*. Ed. Mike Helm. Eugene: Rainy Day Press, 1981.

———. *Conversations with Pioneer Women*. Ed. Mike Helm. Eugene: Rainy Day Press, 1981.

Loggan, Kate. Randall V. Mills Folklore Archives #060069048. June 1969.

Lonergan, Lori. Randall V. Mills Folklore Archives, n. n. July 1982.

Loomis, C. Grant. "A Tall Tale Miscellany." *Western Folklore* 6 (1947): 28–41.

Lord, Lydia. Randall V. Mills Folklore Archives #050077004. May 1977.

Lord, Tracy. Randall V. Mills Folklore Archives #120075181. December 1975.

Low, Joann. Randall V. Mills Folklore Archives #050074041. May 1974.

Lowe, Judge D. J. "Chowder from the Storm." *Junior Historical Journal* 6.3 (1946): 116.

Lubert, Arbrella, and Henry. Personal interview. Eugene, October 1990.

McArthur, Lewis A. *Oregon Geographic Names*. 5th ed. Ed. Lewis L. McArthur. Western Imprints Series. Portland: Oregon Historical Society, 1982.

McCarl, Robert S., Jr. Randall V. Mills Folklore Archives #060269062. June 1969.

———. "Smokejumper Initiation: Ritualized Communication in a Modern Occupation." *Journal of American Folklore* 89 (1976): 49–66

McDole, Jim. Randall V. Mills Folklore Archives #060071237. June 1971.

McKaughan, Nancy J. Randall V. Mills Folklore Archives, n. n. June 1981.

McLagan, Elizabeth. *A Peculiar Paradise: A History of Blacks in Oregon, 1788–1940*. The Oregon Black History Project. Portland: The Georgian Press, 1980.

McNeal, William H. *History of Wasco County, Oregon*. The Dalles, ca. 1953.

Mainwaring, William L. *Exploring the Oregon Coast*. Salem: Westridge Press, 1977.

Martin, Larry. Randall V. Mills Folklore Archives #030071067. March 1971.

Mathers, Michael. *Sheepherders: Men Alone*. Boston: Houghton-Mifflin, 1975.

Miller, Eleanor. "Joe Meek, Frontier Marshal." *Junior Historical Journal* 5.3 (1945): 100–101.

Miller, Linda Lorene. Randall V. Mills Folklore Archives #080072134. August 1972.

Mills, Hazel E. "The Constant Webfoot." *Western Folklore* 11 (1952): 153–64.

Mills, Randall V. "Notes on Oregon Place-Names." *Western Folklore* 10 (1951): 316–17.

———. "Oregon Speechways." *American Speech* (1950): 81–90.

———. "Place-Name Notes from *The Oregon Spectator*." *Western Folklore* 9 (1950): 60–63.

Mittendorf, Tom. Randall V. Mills Folklore Archives #060176105. June 1976.

Moore, T. Randall V. Mills Folklore Archives #060076060. June 1976.

Morris, Richard Artells. "Three Russian Groups in Oregon: A Comparison of Boundaries in a Pluralistic Environment." 2 vols. Unpublished Dissertation, University of Oregon, 1981.

Morrison, Jean. Randall V. Mills Folklore Archives #120074272. December 1974.

Morton, Lornel Tweedy. "Papa Was A. B. Meacham." Unpublished thesis, Southern Oregon State College, 1989.

Mullin, Susan. "Oregon's Huckleberry Finn: A *Munchhausen* Enters Tradition." *Northwest Folklore* 2.1 (1967): 19–25.

Munro, Sarah Baker. "Basque Folklore in Southeastern Oregon." *Oregon Historical Quarterly* 76 (1975): 153–74.

The Name "Oregon," Its Origin and Significance, Compiled from Various Articles. Eugene: University of Oregon Library, 1921.

Ng, Wendy Lee. "Collective Memory, Social Networks, and Generations: The Japanese American Community in Hood River, Oregon." Unpublished dissertation, University of Oregon, 1989.

Noble, Iris. *Notes from Oregon*. States of the Nation Series. Toronto: Longman's Canada, Limited, 1966.

O'Brien, Kathleen Joy. "Nettie Connett: A Mountain Legend." *Mountain Magazine*. February 1971: 15–21.

O'Dell, Michael. Randall V. Mills Folklore Archives #080078007. August 1978.

Oestreich, Melissa. Randall V. Mills Folklore Archives #080071357. August 1971.

Old Believers. Portland: Northwest Media Project, 1981.

Olson, Grace G. "Indian Wars." *Pioneer Trails* 3.3 (1979): 24–30.

Olson, Joan, and Gene Olson. *Oregon Times and Trails*. Merlin, Oregon: Windyridge Press, 1980.

Orcutt, Ada M. *Tillamook: Land of Many Waters*. Tillamook County Pioneer Commission. Portland: Binfords & Mort, 1951.

An Oregon Almanac for 1940. Oregon Writers' Program of the Work Projects Administration. State of Oregon.

Oregon Blue Book 1989–90. Salem: State of Oregon, 1990–91.

Oregon, End of the Trail. Ed. Writers' Program of the Work Projects Administration. American Guide Series. Portland: Binfords & Mort, 1940.

Oregon Oddities. Oregon Writers' Program of the Work Projects Administration. Vols. I–IV (1938–41).

Oregon Shakespeare Festival. Personal interviews. Le Hook, Joe Vincent, Skip Greer, Mary Turner, and Shirley Patton. November 1985.

Patrick, Isaac. "Mountain Journey Offers Adventures." *Pioneer Trails* 3.3 (1979): 12–15.

Patton, Waible E. "Loo, A Chinese Friend." *Pioneer Trails* 4.2 (1980): 20–23.

Pearce, Helen. "Folk Sayings in a Pioneer Family of Western Oregon." *California Folklore Quarterly* 5.3 (1946): 229–42.

Peterson, Carol. Randall V. Mills Folklore Archives #080772173. August 1972.

Peterson's Magazine. Tillamook County, 1858.

Phillips, Bonnie, and Roy Phillips. Randall V. Mills Folklore Archives #080070112. August 1970.

Phillips, Cheryl Lynn. Randall V. Mills Folklore Archives #031478001. March 1978.

Pitney, Clarence A. *Eighty-Seven Years on a Century Farm*. Ed. Alice Pitney Norris. Junction City, 1976.

Port, Lee. *Notes on Historic Events*. Medford: Southern Oregon Historical Society, 1945.

Price, Sara. "The Housewife's Lament." Ca. 1865. *Sing Out*. Vol. VI. New York: People's Songs, 1956.

Rajnus, Ellen. Personal interview. Malin, Oregon, 1983.

Ramsey, Jarold, ed. *Coyote Was Going There: Indian Literature of the Oregon Country*. Seattle: University of Washington Press, 1977.

"Rattlesnake Mountain" (traditional). Collected by Wayne Tabler in Brownsville, ca. 1945.

Riddle, Claude A. *In the Happy Hills*. Roseburg: M M Printers, 1954.

Robe, Stanley L. "Basque Tales from Eastern Oregon." *Western Folklore* 12 (1953): 153–57.

Roeser, Donna. Randall V. Mills Folklore Archives #060071257. June 1971.

Rubio, Beatrice L. Randall V. Mills Folklore Archives #061082095. June 1982.

Scofield, Twilo J. "The Czechs of Malin." Oregon Committee for the Humanities. Malin, 1984.

———. "Logtown Rose" (song), 1989.

———. "Oregon Folks" (song), 1980.

———. "The Timber Beast" (song), 1966.

Scott, H. W. "Not Marjoram." *The Quarterly of the Oregon Historical Society* 1 (1900): 165–68.

Searcey, Mildred. "Athena Revives Caledonian Fling." *Pioneer Trails* 1.1 (1976): 5–7.

———. "Elephant Rock: A Legend." *Pioneer Trails* 10.2 (1986): 3–6.

Shearer, Glen, and Terry Logan. Randall V. Mills Folklore Archives #060071224. June 1971.

Shelton, Cuyla Saum. Randall V. Mills Folklore Archives #060071265. June 1971.

Shepherd, John. Randall V. Mills Folklore Archives #031580008. March 1980.

Smith, Fern M. Randall V. Mills Folklore Archives #031469025. March 1969.

Smith, Karin. Randall V. Mills Folklore Archives #006074089. June 1974.

Smithson, Michael James. "Of Icons and Motorcycles: A Sociological Study of Acculturation among Russian Old Believers in Central Oregon and Alaska." 2 vols. Unpublished dissertation, University of Oregon, 1976.

Stafford, Kim. "Wake Up, It's Rainin'" (song). Portland, 1980.

Steel, William Gladstone. "Oregon Place Names." *Steel Points* 2.1 (March 1917).

Stewart, Jennifer. Randall V. Mills Folklore Archives, n. n. February 1987.

Street, Willard, and Elsie Street. *Sailors' Diggings*. Wilderville, Oregon: Wilderville Press, 1976.

Stumbo, Allison. Randall V. Mills Folklore Archives #123079020. December 1979.

Sullivan, William. "Colorful Chinook Jargon Graces Oregon 'Sticks'." *Eugene Register-Guard* 11 January 1987: 3E.

Sunset Oregon Travel Guide. Ed. *Sunset Books* and *Sunset Magazine*. Menlo Park, California: Lane Publishing Co., 1987.

Susac, Cathryn. Randall V. Mills Folklore Archives #030071087. March 1971.

A Taste of Oregon. Eugene: Junior League of Eugene, Inc., 1980.

Tabler, Wayne. "Rattlesnake Mountain" (traditional), 1946.

Tackett, Harry. Personal interview. Ashland, 1985.

Tepfer, Gary. Randall V. Mills Folklore Archives #060070071. June 1970.

Thomas, Edward Harper. *Chinook: A History and Dictionary*. Portland: Binfords & Mort, 1954.

Thomas, John. Randall V. Mills Folklore Archives #030071090. March 1971.

Tillman, B. J. Randall V. Mills Folklore Archives #060076084. June 1976.

Toelken, J. Barre. "Alsea Girls" (traditional), 1968.

———. *The Dynamics of Folklore*. Boston: Houghton-Mifflin, 1979.

———. "Rollin' Cross the Bar" (song). Coos Bay, 1975.

Tolar, Bennie Lee. "Jack Dempsey." *Pioneer Trails* 10.1 (1986): 3–5.

Umatilla County: A Backward Glance. Pendleton: Umatilla County Historical Society, 1980.

Undermining the Great Depression (Jacksonville). Eugene: Rainlight Films, 1983.

Walker, Charlene. Randall V. Mills Folklore Archives #060070075. June 1970.

Wasil, Rita. Randall V. Mills Folklore Archives #060170091. June 1970.

"Webfoot Land" (song), ca. 1920.

Wegelin, Tina. Randall V. Mills Folklore Archives #120070176. December 1970.

"Will the North Rise Again?" *This World* Magazine. *San Francisco Chronicle* 6 December 1987: 11, 14.

Williams, Gladys. Personal interview. Ruch, 1983.

Williams, Sandra. Randall V. Mills Folklore Archives #012369006. December 1969.

Wilson, Larry. Randall V. Mills Folklore Archives #120070179. December 1970.

Wilson, Mardi. Randall V. Mills Folklore Archives #031571132. March 1971.

Wilson, William A. "Folklore and History." *Readings in American Folklore*. Ed. Jan Harold Brunvand. New York: Norton, 1979: 449–66.

With Her Own Wings. Ed. Helen Krebs Smith. Portland: Beattie and Co., 1948.

Woodcock, Richard. Randall V. Mills Folklore Archives #060071281. June 1971.

Woolley, Betty Ann. Randall V. Mills Folklore Archives #080071383. August 1971.

Wright, Tina, and Valerie Soll. Randall V. Mills Folklore Archives #081375164. August 1975.

Young, Frederick. "Early Resident Remembers Those Sumpter Saloons." *Baker Democrat-Herald* 23 July 1982.

_____. *Home in the Blues: A Collection*. Baker, Oregon: Record-Courier Printers, 1988.

Index

A

Abbot, Henry Larcom (brig. gen.), 118
Abernathy, George (gov.), 35–36, 55
Abernathy Rock (money), 55
Abraham, Solomon (railroad planning engineer), 78
Abrams, Elizabeth (folklore collector), 26–27
Adams (guide), and Henry Griffin, 123
Adams (town), 124
Adventures of Captain Bonneville, The (Irving), 41
Advertisements for wives, 46
African Americans (blacks), 15, 36, 41, 59–60; role in Neahkanie Treasure legend, 22, 23–24
Agee, Bill (folklore collector), 93–94
Aguilar, Martin de (Spanish explorer), 11
Albany (city), 9, 33, 36, 37–38
Albino monsters, legends of, 9, 38
Alert (ship), "Rollin', Rollin', Cross the Bar" based on, 19
Alien Land Bill of 1923, 109
Alien visitors from space, Gold Hill's reputation for, 81, 82
Alkali Lake, 145
Almanac signs, in folk beliefs, 45
Alpine Belt, Steens vegetation belt, 147
Alsea (town), 13–14, 51
"Alsea Girls" (song), 13–14
Alsi Indians, Alsea named for, 13
Althouse (town), 72, 87
Alvord Desert, 5, 146
Alvord Ranch, 147, 148–49
Alvord Valley, 159
American Legion, anti-Japanese advertisements, 109
Anderson, Candy (folklore collector), 8, 124, 134, 141
Anderson, Nancy (folklore collector), 102
Andrew, Fred (Echo resident), on "Whispering" Thompson, 138
Antelope (town), 97, 99
Anti-Alien League, in Hood River County, 109
Anti-Japanese sentiments, in Hood River, 109–10
Appaloosa (breed of horse), 136
Applegate, Jesse (settler), 35, 69
Applegate Trail, 29, 71, 72, 87
Archery (magazine), 158
Arlington (town), 100, 141
Arnold brothers (miners), 71
Arock (town), 145
Aschim, Joan (folklore collector), 141–42
Ashland (city), 71, 72, 74–75
Ashland Mills, original name for Ashland, 71, 74
Aspen Belt, Steens vegetation belt, 147

Assayers, crookedness, 131
Astor, John Jacob, 3, 12, 15
Astor Column (monument), 15
Astoria (city), 5, 12, 14–16
Athena (city), 125–26
Auburn (town), 123
Aunt, The (Kwohl Butte), 117
Aura agua, as Oregon name source, 3
Aurora (Aurora Mills), (town), 38–39
Automobiles, legend about early, 50
Axehandle, original name for Kilts, 99
Azalea (town), 75–76, 77

B

Babe, the Blue Ox, 107–8
Bachelor Butte, 117
Bachelor Flat (town), 37
Baghwan Shree Rajneesh, 97
Bakeheads (railroad term), 102
Bakeoven (town), 99
Baker, Edward Dickinson (U.S. sen.), 126
Baker, James C. (folklorist), 44
Baker City, 124, 125, 126–27
Baker County, 9, 129–30, 134, 141–42; Cornucopia, 125, 130–32, 134; Greenhorn, 123, 133–34; Sparta, 124, 139–40; Sumpter, 8, 123, 124, 140–41
Balch, Frederick Homer, 104
Bald Mountain, 90
Bald Mountain Mine, 141
Baltimore Rock, 13
Ban (town), 37
Bandon (city), 5, 12, 72
Bannock Indians, 99, 145–46
Barber, LaVada (folklorist), 109
Barker, Berta K. (Salem resident), recipes, 62
Barker, Joel L. (folklore collector), 79
Barlow, Samuel (pioneer), 97
Barlow Road, 97
Barnes, Benny (Lake County resident), 158
Barnes, Jane (settler), 4
Barnes, Rube (Crook County resident), 119
Barren Valley, 145
Barter and exchange, use by the Bethelites, 38
Barton, H. L., on Bohemian miners, 44
Baseball, folk beliefs, 8
Basque Station, 155
Basques, ix, 9, 155–57
Battle Creek, 99, 125
Battle Rock, Battle of, 71, 79, 90
Bauman, Rick (state legislator), 61
Bean Gulch (town), 71
Beans, ranch or grubstake, 150
Bear(s), legends about, 25, 45, 78, 80, 85
Beaver cats (Beaver panthers), 37, 141, 142

Beaver Creek(s), 97
Beaver Money, 4, 55
"Beaver State, The" (Oregon nickname), 3
Beavers, 95
Beck, Horace (folklorist), 28
Beckham, Steven Dow, *Tall Tales from the Rogue River*, 79
Beef stew, recipe for, 150
Beekman, C. C. (Jacksonville banker), 83
Beer, 87–88
Beers, Bob, version of "The Logger's Sweetheart," 66
Beeswax spill, 11, 23
Beet juice, as folk remedy, 53
Belknap, Arthur (Lane County resident), 101
Belknap, R. S. (settler), 101
Belknap (Belknap's) Springs, 100–101
Bell, Mimi, on Pete French and the P Ranch, 153
"Ben Gun" legend, 15–16, 163
Bend (city), 101–2, 105
Bender, Edward (settler), 25
Bennehoff, Bert W. (folklorist), 130
Bennett, Addison (postmaster), 134
Benton County, 13–14, 37, 39–40, 50–51
Berdugo, Joaquin "Chino," 148
Berdugo (outpost), 148
Berlin (town), 37
Berry, Beverly, Mendenhall's notebooks found by, 132
Bethelites (religious commune), 38–39
"Beulah Land" (hymn), 39; parodies, 39–40, 101, 105
Big Bend land, 99–100, 101–2, 105–6
"Big Bend Land" (song), 101–2
Big Eddy, in Portland, 57–58
Billiard table, role in founding of Kerby, 84
Bingham Springs (town), 127
"Binks" stories, 108–9, 114, 163
Bird(s): Merlin named for, 71; role in Clatsop legend, 11. *See also* Owl(s)
Biscuits, sourdough, 147–48, 150
Bishop, Roy (Umatilla County resident), 139
Black Butte, 5
Black powder, Hathaway Jones story about, 80
Blackfoot Indians, 137, 142–43
Blacks. *See* African Americans
Blacksmiths, 97, 118–19
Blanchet, Archbishop, Oregon name theory, 3
Blind pigs, 130, 132
Blodgett (town), 39–40
Bloody Chief (Blackfoot leader), 142–43
Bloody Run, near Grant's Pass, 71
Blooming (town), 37
Blue, John (Wingville founder), 125
Blue Bucket Creek, 125

Blue Bucket Mine, 128, 146; search for, 97, 123, 157–58, 163
Blue Bucket (Lost) Wagon Train of 1845, 97, 123, 128, 146, 157–58, 163
Blue Mountains, 123–24, 138, 145
Blue River (and village), 40–41
Board stretcher, 54
Boggs, Walt (logger), 75
Bohemia (town), 37
Bohemia mines, 43–44
Bohemians, 44, 113
Bolton, Walter (singer), 42
Bone Corral, 146
''Bone Express,'' Oregon Trail known as, 97
''Bones,'' playing the, 151
Boneyard Creek, 125
Bonham, M. N. (rancher), 110
Bonneville, Benjamin Louis (explorer), 41
Bonneville (town), 41
Bonneville Dam, 5, 41
Boston Mills, original name for Shedd, 65
Bouncers, at Erickson's Bar, 58
Bounty hunts, 35
Bourbon (town), 99
Bourne (town), 123
Bowmer, Angus (theatre founder), 74, 75
Bowmer Theatre (Ashland), 75
Bracken ferns (*Warabe*), 110
Braddock, George (folklore collector), 8, 76, 92, 93
Brainard, E. C. (mining district recorder), 123
Braly, David, on Central Oregon, 95, 98
Branding, 134–35
Brandy Bar, 13
Bread pudding, recipe for, 62–63
Bridal Chamber (chamber of the Oregon Caves), 77
Bridge of the Gods (Tahmahnawis), ix, 104–5
Bristow, Elijah (settler), 44, 56
British, the: exploration of Oregon Coast, 11; in Oregon Territory, 12, 35
British immigrants, domestic folk beliefs, 47–48
Brogan, Phil, *East of the Cascades*, 164
Broken Top Mountain, 117
Bronco-busting, 119–20, 139, 149
Brookings (city), 5, 12, 72
Brooks, Diane C. (folklorist), 130
Brothers (town), 100
Brown, Ben (settler), 137
Brown, John (settler), 41
Brown, Olive, source for ''Goldilocks on the Oregon Trail story,'' 87
Brown Town (Union County city), original name for La Grande, 137
Brownsville (Linn County city), 41–43
Brownsville (Union County city), former name for La Grande, 137
''Brownsville Mountain'' (song), 42
Browntown (Josephine County town), 87, 88
Bruces Bones Creek, 13
Brujas, evil done by, counteracted by the *curandera*, 60
Bruner, Reba (folklorist), 155
Bryant, William Cullen, 3
Buckaroos (cowboys; *vaqueros*), 148–53, 159–62; derivation of name, 149; jargon, 149, 159–60; of Pete French's P Ranch, 146, 147–48, 151, 153
Buckhead, original name for Sweet Home, 67
Buckskin, worn by Native Americans, 136
Bug Butte, in Klamath County, 99
''Bunchgrassers'' (nickname), 73
Burget, Charles ''Binks.'' *See* ''Binks'' stories

Burial, Chinese customs for, 136
Burial grounds, Native American, 18, 81, 100
Buried fortune/treasure. *See* Treasure legends
Burnett, Peter H. (settler), 4
Burns, Robert, 125, 149
Burns (city), 5, 145, 149–51, 154
Burnside Street area, in Portland, 57–58
Bush, Joe (cowboy), 160
Butte, 124
Butte Disappointment, original name for Dexter, 44
Butter Creek (Morrow County city), original name for Heppner, 108
Buttercreek (town on the Oregon Trail), 125
Buttermilk Creek, 37

C

Calapooia Mountains, 72
Caledonian Society, in Athena, 125
California, 35; gold discovery effects on Oregonians, 36, 71, 72; Northern, 72, 73–74
California Gulch (town), 124
California laurel (myrtle) trees, 25, 87
Camp Abbot, 118–19
Canby, Edward (major gen.), 43
Canby (city), 43
Cannon Beach (city), 13, 16, 21
Canton Creek (stream), 76–77
Canyon City, 97, 124, 128, 146
Canyon Creek, 128
Canyonville (town), 9, 77
Cape Disappointment, 11, 14–15
Cape Meares, 13
Captain Cook Point, 13
Card game(s), 123, 134; Basque, 156
Carroll, Ann-Mari, source for domestic folk beliefs, 47–48
Carson, Kit, 97
Carver, Jonathan (explorer), 3
Cascade glaciers, 95
Cascade Range, ix, 72, 95, 97, 116–17; Paul Bunyan's feats in, 107–8
Cash Hollow, 125
Catched Two Lake, 125
Cathedral Ridge, in Hood River County, 100
Catholic rituals, mix with Hispanic folk rituals, 60–61
Cattle and cattle ranching, 113, 145, 147–54, 161–62; conflict with sheep ranchers, 98, 99, 110; Fossil area legend, 106–7; jargon, 149, 159–60; John Day as center, 135; lost herd in Wallowa Mountains, 125; need for Nez Perce land, 136; Yakima Indians' joke, 134–35
Cave Junction (town), 77–78
Cavett, Dick, 74
Cayuse Indians, 36, 108, 128–29, 139; etiological legends, 127, 137; importance of horses, 128, 136
Centerville, original name for Athena, 125
Central Oregon, ix, 18, *map* 96; geography and history, 95–100; local place-names and folklore, 98–121
Champoeg (town), 37
Charity Mountain, 117. *See also* Three Sisters Mountains
Charleston (city), 16–17
Chehalem Valley, wolf meetings, 35
Chemeketa, original name for Salem, 61
Chickens: Basque cooking method, 157; wind's effects on, 148

Chief of the Underworld (Native American), role in creation of Crater Lake, 103–4
Chief of the Upperworld (Native American), role in creation of Crater Lake, 104
Chilblains, Coast region folk cures, 16–17
Childbirth, folk beliefs on, 82. *See also* Pregnancy, folk beliefs on
Childs, John L. (State of Jefferson gov.), 73–74
China Creek, 125
Chinese, ix, 13, 109, 146; ''Binks'' story treatment, 109, 163; in Northeastern Oregon, 124, 135–36, 139; in Southern Oregon, 71–72, 78, 88
Chinese Gulch, 139
Chinook, Billy, as guide for Frémont, 97
Chinook: A History and Dictionary (Thomas), 18
Chinook Jargon, 12, 17–18, 18, 23; as source for Oregon place-names, 37, 43, 60, 100
Choker hole, 54, 163
Choker setters, 54–55, 65
Christensen, Ralph, ''The Strawberry Roan,'' 119
Chuck wagon (trail) cooks (old women), 147–48, 149–50, 161
Civil War era, 138, 140; divided loyalties, 36, 71, 84, 100, 125, 141, 164
Clackamas County, 18, 37, 43, 63–64; Lake Oswego, 5, 51–52; Oregon City, 5, 36, 55–56
Claim jumping, in Southern Oregon, 72
Clams. *See* Seafood
Clapping games, 59
Clark, James (settler), 95
Clark, William (explorer), 11–12, 15. *See also* Lewis and Clark expedition
Clarke, Dwight L. (folklorist), 79
Clarno, Andrew (settler), 95
Clason, Leslie (folklore collector), 92
Clatskanie (city), 17–18
Clatsop County, 13, 21–22; Astoria, 5, 12, 14–16; Seaside, 5, 12, 30
Clatsop Indians, 11, 18, 23
Clinica Azteca, in Phoenix, 88–89
Clothing: Basques, 155; buckaroos, 147, 149; Native Americans, 136; Russian Old Believers, 9, 68
Coast. *See* Oregon Coast
Coast Fork, of the Willamette River, 43
Coast Highway (Highway 101), 11
Coburg (city), 37
Coe, Mildred (postmaster), 109
Coffee, for buckaroos, 149
Coleman, Charmaine (Eugene resident), source for Southern folklore, 59–60
Collins, Mattie, gold nugget found by, 87
Colors, 47; in Chinese customs, 135–36; in Native American feather symbolism, 128
Columbia, The (film), 41
Columbia County, 17–18, 37
Columbia River, 5, 97; Bonneville Dam, 41; The Dalles, 104–5; search for, 11, 12–13, 14
Colvin, Penny (folklore collector), 79
Company towns: Gilchrist, 107. *See also* Timber communities
Condon, Harry (lawyer), 103
Condon, J. B. (judge), 103
Condon, Thomas (geologist), 95, 102–3
Condon (town), 9, 102–3
Confederacy, sympathy for, 36, 71, 84, 100, 125, 141
Confederated Tribes, 128–29, 137. *See also*

Cayuse Indians; Umatilla Indians; Walla Walla Indians
Conn, J. C. (merchant), murder, 98
Conner, Gilbert E., source for the ''Three Sisters'' legend, 117–18
Conner, Roberta (folklore collector), 129, 137
Connett, Nettie (mountain woman), legends on, 63–64
Conser Lake monster, 9, 38
Conservatism, in Native American folklore, 128
Contagious magic, in folk cures, 111–12
Contention (stage stop), 100
Conversations with Pioneer Women (Lockley), 46, 163–64
Cook, James (naval capt.), 11, 13
Cooking. *See* Foodways
Cook-koo-oose, meaning, 18
Cookstove, Dexter named for, 44
Cooper, Ernie (House of Mystery owner), 82
Cooper, Trudy (folklorist), 69, 81, 82, 84
Cooper's Island, 53
Coos Bay (city), 8, 12, 18–19
Coos County, 8, 12, 13, 16–17, 18–19, 25
Copperfield (town), 129–30
Coquille Indians, Battle of Battle Rock, 90
Coquille River, 25
Cornett, Jack (postmaster), 77
Cornishmen (Cousin Jacks), 44, 131–32, 133–34, 140–41
Cornstarch, recipe for, 62
Cornucopia (town), 125, 130–32, 134
Corpse, Scottsburg legend of, 29–30
Corvallis (city), 36
Cottage cheese, recipes for, 62, 112
Cottage Grove (city), 5, 43–44, 61
Cougar(s), legends about, 101, 137–38
Counting-out rhymes, 59
Courthouse Rock, in Grant County, 100
Cousin Jacks. *See* Cornishmen
Cowboys. *See* Buckaroos
Coyote Brown's Mountain, 125
Coyote (*Talapus*) (trickster-god) legends, 11, 100, 120–21, 127; on the creation of The Three Sisters, 117–18; on origins of the tribes, 137
Coyotes, branded by the Yakima Indians, 134–35
Craig, James C. (folklore collector), 48
Cranberry juice, as folk cure, 17
Crane Prairie (town), 18, 100
Crater Lake, 18, 100, 103–4
——— creation of, 95, 103; Native American legends on, ix, 103–4; by Paul Bunyan, 108
Crater Lake National Park, 29, 103
Craze, Billy (hotel owner), 90
Crazyman Creek, 164
''Creaking mantel'' story, 92
Cream pies, cooling method, 112
Crescent City (town), 87
Cressman, L. W. (anthropologist), 105
Crime(s), 4, 124, 151, 160; murders, 4, 98. *See also* Law and justice
Crook County, 18, 99, 119–20
Crook County Sheep Shooters Association, 98
Crooked River, 97, 99, 108
Crooks, Ramsey (pioneer), 135
Crowley, Martha Leland (pioneer), 71
Crowley, Polly (settler), 64–65
Cultural geography, ix
Cultural validity, of folk legends, 163
Cultus Lake, 100

Culver, Greg, source of details on Bridge of the Gods legend, 104
Cupid's Knoll (mountain), 52–53
Curandera (healers), spells cast by, 60–61
Cures, folk. *See* Remedies and cures, folk
Curry, George (gen.), 145
Curry County, 13, 18, 89–90; Gold Beach, 71, 72, 79–81; Port Orford, 71, 72, 73, 90–91
''Curse of the Spanish Boots, The,'' as illustration of the folktale, 76–77
Cuts, folk remedies for, 17, 53
Czechs, 43–44, 113

D
D River, 12
Dale, William, and the *Tomonos* rock, 51
Dalles, The (Dalles City). *See* The Dalles
Dalles Indians, 95
Dams: Bonneville, 5, 41; Heppner flood, 108–9
Dance: Basque, 156; Czech tradition, 113
Dandelion wine, recipe for, 63
Danebo (town), 37
Danish settlers, 37
Davidson, Elijah (settler), 77 78
Davis, Buck (farrier), 118–19
Davis, H. L., ''The Frozen Logger,'' 65–66
Davis, Jefferson, 100
Davis, Wilbur A., source for loggers' folklore, 65, 69
Day, John (pioneer), 135
Dead Indian Road, 71
Deadman Spring, 99
Deadman Valley, 99
Dean, Kevin (folklorist), 68
Death, folk beliefs on, 46, 48, 86
Deathball Rock, 37
Deception Bay, 14
Deer Creek (city), original name for Roseburg, 92
Deer Creek (stream), 92
Degh, Linda (folklorist), 53
Delake, 13
Delaplane, Stanton (journalist), 73
DeLore, Wild Gus, legends about, 119
Democrat Gulch (town), 71
Dempsey, Jack (Harry), 132
Denmark (town), 13
Dental care, folk remedies, 133
Depoe, ''Old Charlie,'' 19
Depoe Bay (city), 12, 19–20
Derebaum, Madame (hotel owner), 83
Derrik, Harley (Sparta resident), on Chinese workers, 139
Deschutes County, 18, 99, 100, 112–13, 117–19; Bend, 101–2, 105; Redmond, 98, 114–16
Deschutes Gorge Railroad Race, 100, 101–2, 112
Deschutes National Forest, 145
Deschutes River, 97, 99
Devil, the, legends about, 118–19, 156
Devil's Canyon, in Gilliam County, 99
Devil's Lake (*Neotsu*), 12, 13
Devine, John (rancher), 148–49
Dexter (town), 44–45
Diablo Mountain, 148
Diarrhea, folk cures for, 16, 17
Dice game, in Halfway area, 134
Diphtheria, 128; remedies for, 133
Disease: brought by the settlers, 128. *See also* Remedies and cures, folk
Dixie, former name for Rickreall, 60
Dock-Spu Indians, 95

Dog Creek/River, original names for Hood River, 99, 109
Dog River Indians, 95
Dogs: hunting, story about, 56–57; reaction to the Oregon Vortex, 82
Donation Land Act of 1850, 4
Donation Land Grants, and settlement of Scio, 64
Donkey engine, naming of, 54
Donnelly, R. N., Richmond named by, 100
Donner and Blitzen River, 145, 148, 153
Donnybrook, former name for Kilts, 99
Dorling, Charles, Suplee named by, 119
Dorson, Richard M. (folklorist), 107
Douglas County, 9, 18, 69, 72, 75–77, 91; Glendale, 77, 78–79; Myrtle Creek, 25, 77, 87; Reedsport, 28–29; Roseburg, 8, 71, 72, 73, 77, 92–93; Scottsburg, 5, 29–30
Drake, Sir Francis, 11
Drazil, Agnes (Malin settler), 113
Drewsey (town), 147, 151
Dry River, in Crook and Deschutes County, 99
Duckworth, original name for Elmira, 45
Duffy, Martin (judge), 139–40
Dukes Valley, 99
Dummy Box, theatre tradition, 75
Dundes, Alan (folklorist), 27
Dynamism, in Native American folklore, 128

E
''Eagle and the Skunk'' legend, 129
Eagle City, former name of Sparta, 139
Eagle Creek Mountains, 123
Eagle Valley, 130
Eagles, Native American symbolism of feathers, 128
Early (town), 100
Earthquake fault line, Cave Junction on, 78
East of the Cascades (Brogan), 164
East Oregonian, on ''Whispering'' Thompson, 138
Eastern Oregon. *See* Central Oregon; Northeastern Oregon; Southeastern Oregon
Echo (town), 132–33
Eddy, Israel, legends concerning, 20–21
Eddyville (city), 20–21
Education, Methodist missionaries' contribution to, 33, 35
Edwards, Cecil (state legislator), 61
Eero, Mark, on the Basque language, 156
Egan (Paiute-Bannock chief), 124
Egg(s): preservation, 112; role in exorcism of the ''evil eye,'' 60–61
Ehrlich, Michael (mountain climber), 116–17
Eight Dollar Mountain, 72
Elderberry tea, as folk cure, 17
Elections: for county seat of Harney County, 154; ranch hands' method of voting, 141
Elephant Rock: Lincoln County, 28; Umatilla County, 28, 127
Elkhorn Range, 123
Ella (town), 99–100
Ellensburg, original name for Gold Beach, 79
Elmira (town), 45–46
''Emerald State, The'' (Oregon nickname), 3
Empacho, Hispanic folk cures for, 60
Empire of the Columbia (Johansen), 35
Emrick, former name of Blodgett, 39
Enchanted Prairie, 12

"End of the Trail State, The" (Oregon nickname), 3
Enola (town), 37
Erickson, August, bar in Portland, 58
Esoteric knowledge. *See* Insiders
Espanto, Hispanic folk cures for, 60
Ethnic communities, 13, 47–48; Czech, 8, 43–44, 113; Japanese, 8, 37, 109–10; Scots, 125–26; Swiss, 37, 44. *See also* Chinese; Cornishmen; Germans; Spanish-speaking people
Etiological legends
_____ Native American, ix, 104–5, 117–18, 137; Coyote tales, 11, 117–18, 127, 137; on Crater Lake, 103–4; Elephant Rock tales, 28, 127
_____ Paul Bunyan in Oregon tales, 107–8
Eugene (Eugene City), 5, 36, 37, 46–48
Eureka (town), 125
Evans, Dr. John (geologist), 90
Evil eye (*mal ojo*), belief in, 60–61
Evil spirits. See *Skookums*
Exclusion laws, in Portland, 59
Exorcism of the "evil eye," 60–61
Exoteric knowledge. *See* Outsiders

F

Faith Mountain, 117. *See also* Three Sisters Mountains
"Fakelore," 107
Family obligations, for Japanese Americans, 110
Fancher, Hal, source for "Binks" stories, 108–9, 114
Fangollano (landmark), 148
Farewell Bend, original name for Bend, 101–2
Farmers and farming, ix, 33, 145; Canby zucchini squash story, 43; effects of wind on animals, 148
Farriers, 97, 118–19
Fashion Reef, Willamette River, 37
Fault block, Steens Mountain world's largest, 146
Feather, symbolism of, in Native American folklore, 128–29
Fern Ridge (waterfowl habitat), 45
Fern Ridge Reservoir area, 53
Ferree, D. J. (capt.), 99
Filipinos, landownership banned, 109
Finn, Benjamin Franklin "Huckleberry," 48–49
Finn Rock (landmark), 48–49
Finns, origin of Delake name, 13
Fire, Silver Lake (1894), 161
Fireplaces, Hathaway Jones story on, 79
Fish as friend/pet, tales of, 40–41, 153
Fishermen and fishing, ix, 8, 26–29, 125, 143; Coast customs, 19–20, 21–22; jargon, 21–22; Judge Lowe's expedition, 90–91; Tebo's pet trout story, 153; Willamette Valley legends and beliefs, 40–41, 45, 67. *See also* Seamen
Fishing communities: Depoe Bay, 19–20; Hammond, 21–22; Newport, 26–28; Reedsport, 28–29; Yaquina Bay, 32
"Fishspeak" (fishing industry jargon), 21–22
Flathead (Salish) Indians, 30, 31, 137
Fleet of Flowers, at Depoe Bay, 19
Fletcher, George (bronc-rider), 139
Floods: Willamette River, 57; Willow Creek, 108–9
Florence (city), 12
Flour mill, at King's Valley, 50–51
Folk songs. *See* Songs

Folklore: defined, 8; relationship to history, 163–64
"Folklore and History" (Wilson), 163
Folklore geography, 9
Follyfarm (homestead), 145
Foodways, 22, 52, 61–63, 99, 112, 113; African American, 59–60; Basque, 156–57; Chinese, 136; Cornish, 133–34; Czech, 113; hardtack recipe, 44; Japanese American, 110; Native American, 22, 31, 91, 136; Russian Old Believers, 68; Southeastern Oregon buckaroos, 147–48, 149–50
Forbidden Ground, at Gold Hill, 81, 82
Ford, Nathaniel (colonel), 36
Forest (Jackass) Creek, 86
Forest Service, U.S., smokejumpers, 114–16
Fort Clatsop, 12, 13, 15
Fort George, Astoria under the British, 12
Fort Grant, 88
Fort Hall, 35
Fort Kearney, 38–39
Fort Rock (town), 105–6
Fort Stevens State Park, 15–16
Fossil (town), 95, 106–7
Fossils, found in Central Oregon, 95, 106
Foster (town), 49–50
Fraser, James G., 111
Frazer River gold strike, 93
Frederickson, Jan (folklorist), 157–58
Free blacks, provisional legislature's law on, 36
Freewater (town), 125
Freezeout Creek, 125
"Freezing up" ("going north"), in theatre parlance, 74–75
Frémont, John C., 97
Fremont National Forest, 145
French, Pete, 146, 152, 153; P Ranch, 147–48, 151, 152–53
French, the, The Dalles named by, 104
French (language): place-name source, 60
French Canadians, 33, 35, 37, 137
French Hotel, at Jacksonville, 83
French Prairie, (settlement), 33
Frenchglen (town), 152–54
"Frenchman, The" (gambler), 4
"Frozen Logger, The" (song), 65–66
Fu Sang (Oregon Coast kingdom), legend of, 11
Fulton (Eastern Oregon politician), 100
Fulton County, name proposed for Sherman County, 100
Further (psychedelic bus), 56
Fur trade, 12, 15, 95

G

Gable, Gilbert (State of Jefferson gov.), 73
Gale, Joseph (seaman), 37
Gales Creek, 37
Galice (town), 72
Gambell, Cara (folklore collector), 26
Gambling, 91, 131, 134, 150, 156
Ganung, "Auntie," and the Confederate flagpole, 71, 84, 164
Gap Ranch, 147
Gasberg, original name for Phoenix, 88
Gay, Peter (folklore collector), 108–9, 114
Gearhart Mountains, 145
Geese, Hathaway Jones story about, 81
Gem (town), 123
George, Earl of Orford, Port Orford named for, 90
Germans, 16, 17, 37, 38–39, 47–48

Gervais, Joseph (settler), 35, 37
Gestures, of railroad workers, 102
Ghost legends, 15–16, 32, 75, 78
Gilchrist (town), 107–8
Gilchrist Timber Company, 107
Gilliam County, 9, 95, 99, 100, 102–3
Gilmour, Ethel, source for domestic folk beliefs, 47–48
Gilmour, Frank, source for Scottish folk beliefs, 125
Giri (contractual family obligation), for Japanese Americans, 110
"Girl with the Striped Stockings" (song), 58–59
Gladstone (city), 33
Glendale (town), 77, 78–79
Glenn, Hugh (doctor), 152
"God Bless America," Basque words, 155
Gods Valley, 12
"Going north" ("freezing up"), in theatre parlance, 74–75
Gold, 23, 25
_____ burial at Fort Grant, 88
_____ discovery in California, 36, 71, 72
_____ discovery in Oregon, 9, 36, 97, 155; by members of the Blue Bucket Wagon Train, 97, 123, 128, 146, 157–58; in Southern Oregon, 71, 72, 81, 83
_____ miners and mining, ix, 5, 8, 99, 123; Bohemia mines, 43–44; jargon, 130–32; legends about, 57, 93; Mucking Contest, 140; in Northeastern Oregon, 123–25, 126, 128, 129–32, 133, 139, 140–41; in Southern Oregon, 71, 72, 83, 93
Gold Beach (city), 71, 72, 79–81
"Gold brick" story, 57
Gold Hill (town), 81–83
Gold Hill Cemetery legend, 82–83
Golden Bough, The (Fraser), 111
Golden Rule whiskey, 38–39
Gone Creek, 37
"Good Ole Boys" string band, 7
Goose Lake, 158
Gopher holes (stove pipe troughs), 140
Gouge Eye, original name for Drewsey, 151, 164
Gougers, side-hill, 155
Government, provisional, 35–36
"Grab ist Tief und Stille, Das" (song), 38
Grande Dalle de la Columbia, La, original name for The Dalles, 104
Grande Ronde Valley, 137
Granite (town), 123
Grant, Rena V., examples of Chinook Jargon, 18
Grant County, 95, 99, 100; Canyon City, 97, 124, 127, 146; Izee, 98, 110–11
Grants Pass (city), 71–72
Grass Flat (town), 72
Grave Creek, 71
Gray, Robert (capt.), 11, 15
Gray Eagle Bar, Willamette River, 37
Great Northern railroad, 101–2
Great Rail Race of Deschutes County, 100, 101–2, 112
Great Spirit (Sahale), role in the Bridge of the Gods legend, 104–5
Great White Eagle (nickname for John McLoughlin), 33
Greenhorn (town), 123, 133–34
Greenhorn Mountain (The Green Horn), 133
Greenhorn Ridge, 123
Greenhorns, 133; in fishing, 20; in logging, 54, 163; in mining, 88

Griffin, Henry (miner), 123
Griffin's Gulch (original name for Auburn), 123, 139
Grisly Gulch, ghost of, 78
Grissom, Chris (folklore collector), 8, 124, 134, 141
Grouse (Louse) Creek, 71–72
Gumbo (town), 99
Guthrie, Woody, songs on the Bonneville Dam, 41
Gyppo logging outfit, 69

H

Haines, Francis (historian), 87
Halfway (town), 134
Hammond, Andrew B. (merchant and railroad builder), 21
Hammond (town), 21–22
Hand, Wayland (folklorist), 82
Handsaker, John, on origin of Dexter's name, 44
Handsaker, Samuel (postmaster), 44
Hanging Bridge, over the Crooked River, 99
Hangings, 92, 93
Hardtack, recipe for, 44
Harney (town), 154
Harney County, 5, 145, 147, 148–54, 161; Mann Lake, 159–60; Whorehouse Meadow, 162
Harney Valley, 146
Harret, Jesse (pioneer), 146
Harriman, E. H. (railroader), 100, 101–2
Harrisburg (city), 33
Harry and David Company, 88
Hart Mountain, 5, 154–55
Haskell, Charles (settler), 16
Hathaway Jones stories, 72, 79–81
Hawaiians, in Southern Oregon, 71
Hay, "Doc" (owner of Kam Wah Chung Co.), 135
Hay wagon, legend of Israel Eddy and, 20–21
Hayes, Rutherford B., 83, 146
Hazeldell (early name for Oakridge), 54
Headache, remedies for, 133
Healers (*curanderas*), 60–61
Heart of a monster, Nez Perce created from, 137
Heceta, Bruno (naval capt.), 11, 13
Heceta Head, 13
Hehe Butte, 100
Hehes (Native American wood spirits), 100
Helfrich, Prince (fish guide and storyteller), 101
Hellman, Abel (settler), 74
Hell's Canyon, 123
Helm, Mike (folklorist), *Oregon's Ghosts and Monsters*, 38
Helvetia (town), 5, 37
Hembree, W. H. (capt.), 157
Hentz, Carl, source for Baker County greenhorn story, 133
Hepner, Henry (merchant), 108
Heppner (city), 5, 99; flood, 108–9
Hermann, Binger (settler), 25
Hermann, Frankie (La Grande resident), recipe, 62–63
Herron, Dan (Lost Wagon Train member), 146
Herron, W. H., source for Lost Wagon Train story, 146
Hess, Rebecca Heater (pioneer), 46
Highballin' logging outfit, 69
Highgrade (ore), 131, 132
Highsmith, Gerry, source for traditional Tillamook recipes, 31

Highway 101 (Coast Highway), 11
Hill, Carolyn S. (folklore collector), 19–20
Hill, James J. (railroader), 100, 101–2
Hill, Tony (Alsea resident), on the log truck driver and the bikers, 51
Hillman, John (prospector), 103
Hillman, original name for Terrebone, 100
Hills Creek, 37
Hilton, Peter B. (folklore collector), 30–31
Hispanics. *See* Spanish-speaking people
History, 4, 9; relationship to folklore, 163–64
Hiyu Mountain, 18
Hobbs, Fern (governor's secretary), Copperfield clean-up attempt, 130
Hobson, Murilla Greenstreet (Sublimity resident), legend about, 67
Hockema, Bess Finley Wasson, source for "Old Mr. Fox," 89–90
Hogg Pass, original name for Santiam Pass, 116
Hogmasters (railroad jargon term), 102
Holbrook, Stewart, "The Frozen Logger," 65–66
Holladay, Ben (railroader), 30, 50
Holt, Arlie, source for "The Hook" story, 53
Holt, Vintie (Bridgeport resident), recipe, 63
Homeopathic magic, in folk cures, 111
Homly (town), 146
Hood River (city), 99; Japanese Americans, 8, 109–10
Hood River County, 18, 99, 100, 109–10
Hook, Le (scenery engineer), 74
"Hook, The" (story). *See* "Man with the Hook" story
"Hooker," in loggers' jargon, 69, 163
Hoover, Thomas B. (postmaster), fossils found by, 106
Hop beer, 87–88
Hope Mountain, 117. *See also* Three Sisters Mountains
"Horned coon" hunt, in outsider-insider jokes, 9, 158
Horse Heaven, 100
Horse Ranch, The, owned by Mrs. Stitz, 158
Horse Thief Meadows, 37
Horselore, 55–56
Horses, 55 56, 145, 151–52, 161, 162; acquisition by Native Americans, 128, 136; Tebo's winter story about, 154; thieving, 162
Horseshoeing, 97, 118–19
Hot ass (cattle ailment), 162
House of Mystery, on the Oregon Vortex, 81–82
House Rock, in the Cascades, 117
"Housewife's Lament, The" (song), 46–47, 164
Howard, Oliver O. (gen.), 137
Hubbard, Anne (folklore collector), 45, 53
"Huck Finn" stories, 48–49
Hucka, Bill, source for "Pappy" Hucka stories, 45
Hucka, Vern "Pappy" (storyteller), 45
Hudson's Bay Company, 12, 23, 33, 35, 95
Hughes, Elias G. (farmer), and the *Tomonos* rock, 51–52
Humbug Mountain (Tichenor's Humbug), 72
Hung, Blanche Conner, source for tribe origin legends, 137
Hunt, Carole (Klamath Falls resident), 155, 162
Hunting, 125; Hathaway Jones stories, 80, 81; legends, 30, 49, 63–64
Hunting dog, story about, 56–57

Hurt, William, 74
Husband, The (mountain), 117
Huss, Dwight B. (early motorist), 50
Hyak chuck (Chinook Jargon), possible origin of Rickreall name, 60

I

Ice caves, near Fort Rock, 105–6
Idiot Creek, 13, 164
Illinois River and Valley, 5, 87, 88
In the Happy Hills (riddle), 91
Incantation rituals, 60–61
Inch Creek, 37
Indians. *See* Native Americans; individual tribes
Initiations: for fishermen, 19–20; in logging camps, 54, 163; for smokejumpers, 114–15
Inland Basin, name for Southeastern Oregon, 145
Inland ocean, Oregon partially covered by, 95, 145
Insiders, 9; jokes about outsiders, 103, 126–27, 158; for Russian Old Believers, 68
Integration, racial, 59
Internment camps, Japanese Americans in, 8, 109
Irrigation project, on P Ranch, 153
Irrigon (town), 134–35
Irving, Washington, 41, 135
Isolationism, foreshadowed in 1838, 35
Issei (first-generation Japanese Americans), 8, 109–10
Izee (settlement), 110–11
Izee Sheep Shooters Association, 98, 110

J

Jack, Captain (Modoc leader), 43, 138
"Jack" tales, third son's role in, 76
Jackalopes, jokes about, 158
Jackass (Forest) Creek, 86
Jackson, C. S. "Sam" (Journalist), 138–39
Jackson County, 8, 36, 81–83, 85–87, 88–89, 93; Ashland, 71, 72, 74–75; Jacksonville, 71, 72, 73, 83–84; Rogue River (city), 5, 92
Jackson Creek, Jacksonville named for, 83
Jackson Territory, proposal for, 73
Jacksonville (city), 71, 72, 73, 83–84
Jai alai (*pelota*), as Basque tradition, 9, 155, 156
Jails, nineteenth-century, 98
Japanese, 8, 37, 109–10; Alien Land Bill of 1923, 109; and the "Ben Gun" legend, 15–16, 163
Jargon: buckaroos, 149, 159–60; fishing industry, 20, 21–22, 26; loggers, 69; miners, 130–32; mountaineers, 116–17; railroad workers, 102; smokejumpers, 114, 115–16. *See also* Chinook Jargon
Jefferson, State of, ix, 72, 73–74
Jefferson County, 99, 116–17
Jenson, Mrs. Lawrence (Corvallis resident), recipe, 63
Joaquin Miller Chapel, in the Oregon Caves, 78
Johansen, Dorothy (historian), 35
John Day (city), 124, 128, 135–36
John Day Fossil Beds, 95
John Day River, 95, 99, 128, 135
John Day Valley, 100
"John F. Adams" story, Hathaway Jones story told as a, 79

Johnson, Naomi, Chautauqua recollections, 154
Johnston, Jeri (folklore collector), 54–55, 79
Jones, Hathaway, stories, 72, 79–81
Jones, Pamela (folklorist), 88–89
Jones, Suzi, source for Japanese-American customs, 110
Jordan, Michael (miner), 155
Jordan Crater, 155
Jordan Valley (town), 9, 155–57
Joseph, Old Chief, 136
Joseph, Young Chief, 124, 136–37
Joseph (city), 136–37
Josephine County, 71, 77–78, 87–88, 93–94
Josephine Junction, Kerby, 84–85
"Judge Martin Duffy" (song), 139–40
Julia, original name for Glendale, 78
Jumbo (bouncer at Erickson's Bar), 58
Jumpoff Joe Creek, 72
Junction City, 5, 50
Juniper Belt, Steens vegetation belt, 147
Juniper Empire (Braly), 95
Juniper Mountain, 145
Juntura (town), 146, 157–58
Justice. *See* Law and justice
Justus, Debra (folklore student), 8

K

Kalarup guns, 49
Kalpshi, Indian name for Silver Lake, 161
Kam Wah Chung Company (grocery), 135
Kanaka Flat (town), 71
Kanakas (local name for Hawaiians), 71
Kane, William (Canyon City resident), 128
Keach, Stacy, 74
Kees Precinct, early name for Lebanon, 52
Keil, William (doctor), Bethelite religious commune, 38–39
Keil, Willie, journey from Missouri to Oregon, 38–39
Kelley, Hal J., Oregon name theory, 3
Keno (town), 99
Kent (town), 100
Kerby, James (settler), 84
Kerby (Kerbyville) (town), 71, 84–85
Kerosene, use in folk cures, 16–17
Kesey, Ken, 56
Kester, Gene (miner), 78
Ketchketch Butte, 100
Kidney problems, folk cures for, 17, 53
Ki-gal-twal-la Indians, 95
Kilchis (man), in Neahkahnie Treasure legend, 22, 24
Kilchis (town), 22
Kilts (town), 99
King, Nahum (settler), 50
King's Valley (town), 50–51
Klamath Basin, 97
Klamath County, 99, 100, 105, 107–8, 111–12; Malin, 8, 113. *See also* Crater Lake
Klamath Falls (city), 105, 111–12
Klamath Indians, 95, 100, 103–4
Klamath Lake, 5
Klamath Reservation, 97
Klamath River, 5, 99
Klickitat Indians, 5, 51–52, 104–5
Klondike (town), 99
Kloochman Creek, 18
Kment, Joanne, source for naming of Hood River, 109
Knight, Mary Brown, source for "well-traveled casket" tale, 64–65
Knight, Tanis (folklore collector), 52, 64–65

Knights of the Golden Circle, 36
Knox, Carol (folklore collector), 45
Kolace, made by Czechs, 113
Koontz, Echo (settler), 132
Koontz, Mr. and Mrs. J. H. (settlers), 132
Krautronza, recipe for, 63
Kusan Indians, 19
Kwolh Butte (The Aunt), 117
Kyle, Ellen (folklorist), 55

L

La Grande (city), 137–38
La Pine (Lapine) (town), 112–13
Labor Day Round-Up, at Lakeview, 158
Lake County, 5, 98, 105–6, 148; Hart Mountain, 154–55; Lakeview, 9, 145, 158–59; Paisley, 125, 160–61
Lake Oswego (city), 5, 51–52
Lakeview (city), 5, 9, 145, 158–59
Lamb, Charity (murderess), 4
Lane, Joe (gov.), 4, 36
Lane County, 5, 40–41, 43–46, 50, 61; Belknap Springs, 100–101; Eugene, 5, 36, 37, 46–48; Finn Rock, 48–49; Mapleton, 24–25; Noti, 53–54; Oakridge, 54–55; Pleasant Hill, 56–57; Springfield, 33, 36, 65–66
Language(s): Basque, 155–56; French, 60; role in the Neahkahnie Treasure legend, 23; Spanish, 23, 159–60. *See also* Chinook Jargon; Jargon
Lansing, Molly (Creswell resident), recipe, 63
Lapwai Indian Reservation, 136, 137
Larson, Karen (folklore collector), 46
"Last Needle, The," story of, 52, 163
Latigo Creek, 148
Lauener, Janet D., source for Scottish folk beliefs, 125–26
Laughton, Charles, 74, 75
Lauris, Priscilla Hake (actress), 74
Lavendure, Joseph (French trapper), 104
Law and justice, 33, 36; in Central Oregon, 98, 113; hangings, 92, 93; in Northeastern Oregon, 139–40; in Southeastern Oregon, 151, 160, 164
Lebanon (city), 52
Lee, Daniel (preacher), 35
Lee, Jason (preacher), 4, 33, 35
Lee, Robert E., 100
Lee's Encampment, original name for Meacham, 138
Legislature, provisional (Oregon), 35–36
Legislature, state (California), Northern California ignored by, 72
Legislature, state (Oregon), 61, 72
Lemati (former name for Cottage Grove), 43
Lemish Butte, 100
Lemurians, Table Rock as landing place for, 81
Lewis, Meriwether, 11–12, 13. *See also* Lewis and Clark expedition
Lewis, Pat (folklore collector), 120–21
Lewis and Clark expedition, 11–12, 13, 15, 18, 30; salt cairn, 5, 12, 30
Lewis and Clark River, 13
Lewiston, Idaho, cemeteries with unmarked gravesites, 130
Licktieg, Mary J. (folklore collector), 17
Lighthouses, 11, 14–15, 32
Lillis, Sally (folklore collector), 107
Lincoln, Abraham, 4, 36, 71
Lincoln (town), 85
Lincoln City, 12

Lincoln County, 13, 20–21, 28, 30–31, 32; Depoe Bay, 12, 19–20; Newport, 5, 12, 26–28
Lindsey, Peter (folklore collector), 16, 21, 30
Link (Yulalona) River, 111
Link River Bridge, 1881 incident at, 111
Linkville, former name for Klamath Falls, 111
Linn County, 41–43, 49–50, 52, 64–65, 67–68; Albany, 9, 33, 36, 37–38; Santiam Pass, 116–17
Little Boy, original name for town of Sonny, 100
Little Brother Mountain, 117
Little Elk, original name for Eddyville, 20
"Little Sally Walker" (counting-out game), 59
Liver-regulator, of a trail cook, 161
Llano (landmark), 148
Llewellyn, Diane, source for Oregon foodways, 62
"Llorona" ("weeping woman") stories, 8, 60, 88–89
Loc Mun (Chinese vegetable dealer), 124
Lockley, Fred, *Conversations with Pioneer Women*, 46, 163–64
Log truck drivers, legends about, 51, 54–55, 163
Logg, F. (farmer), 86
Loggan, Harry, source for story on Harney play within a play, 154
Loggan, Kate (folklore collector), 154
"Logger and Splinter-Picker Talk" (Davis), 69
Loggers and logging, 68; initiation, 54, 163; jargon, 69; jokes, 9, 16; legends, 49–50, 51, 54–55, 61, 65–66, 75–76, 79, 93–94; spotted owl issue, 9, 72, 77; "timber beasts" nickname, 49–50, 65. *See also* Timber communities
"Logger's Sweetheart, The" (song), 66
Logtown, 85–87
"Logtown Rose, The" (song), 86–87
London, Jack, 93
Lonergan, Lori (folklore collector), 87, 91
Lonerock (town), 99
Long, Reub (storyteller), 98, 105, 106
Long, Tex (ranch foreman), 150–51
Long Tom River, 37
Lord, Tracy (folklore collector), 85
Loring, David (railroad site engineer), 71
Lost Cabin Mine, 103
Lost treasure. *See* Treasure legends
Lost (Blue Bucket) Wagon Train of 1845, 97, 123, 128, 146, 157–58, 163
Louse (Grouse) Creek, 71–72
Lovejoy, A. L. (settler), 57
Low, Joann (folklore collector), 56
Lowe, D. J. (judge), 90–91
Lowe, Helen Myers, source for Joab Powell story, 64
Lower Deschutes (Wyam) Indians, 95
Lower Town, original name for Canyon City, 128
Lucier, Etienne (trapper), 35, 37
Lumtum (Chinook Jargon for rum or whiskey), as source for place-names, 18, 37, 99
Lumtum Butte, in Deschutes County, 18, 99
Lung-On (owner of Kam Wah Chung Co.), 135
Lynchings, 92

M

"McAlder homestead" story, 92–93
McArthur, Lewis A., x, 13, 18–19, 26, 52; on beavers, 95, 97; on Clarno's settlement, 95. See also *Oregon Geographic Names*

McCarl, Bob (folklorist), 114–15
McCarroll, Bonnie (cowgirl), 139
McClay, Joe, on Redmond jail escapes, 98
McCloud, Calif., 18
McCorkle, Chuck (Canyon City resident), 128
McCornack, George (storyteller), 49
McDole, Jim (folklore collector), 125
McGowan, George (settler), 149
McKay, Charlie (ranch hand), 128
McKay, Douglas (U.S. Interior secretary), 41
McKee, John and Maryum (settlers), and the yellow Logtown rose, 86–87
McKenney, Eva, source for domestic folk beliefs, 47–48
McKenzie River, 40, 48
McKinney, Matilda (settler), 64
McKinnon, Andrew (settler), 37
McLagan, Elizabeth (historian), 59
McLeod, Archibald F. (Hudson's Bay Co. agent), 18
McLoughlin, John (doctor and Hudson's Bay Co. agent), 23, 33, 55
McNeal, William H. (historian), 103
McTavish, Donald (settler), 4
Madras (town), 100
Magic: contagious and homeopathic, 111–12; Hispanic rites, 60–61; in the "McAlder homestead" story, 92–93
Maiden Gulch, 125
Maiden Peak, 117
Malheur County, 9, 145, 146, 148, 155–58, 161–62
Malheur Forest, 141–42
Malheur Lake, 108, 153
Malheur National Wildlife Refuge, 147
Malheur River, 146, 157
Malin (town), 8, 113
Mal ojo (evil eye), belief in, 60–61
Mammoths, role in Elephant Rock legends, 28, 127
"Man with the Hook" story: Cupid's Knoll version, 53; merged with "Ben Gun" legend, 15
Mann Lake, 159–60
Mann Ranch, 159, 161
Manzanita (town), 23–24
Mapleton (city), 24–25
Marginal distribution, effect on Basque folk customs and beliefs, 156
Marhoffer, Jacob (Waldo brewer), 87
Marion County, 38–39, 67, 68; Salem, 8, 36, 37, 61–63
Marple, Perry B. (settler), 19
Marriage: among Russian Old Believers, 68; Native American tradition of marriage trees, 103. *See also* Weddings
Marx, early name of Neskowin, 26
Mary's River, 39
Mathers, Michael, *Sheepherders: Men Alone*, 110
Matlock, Leslie, and Willow Creek flood, 108
Matsutake (wood mushrooms), 110
Matthieu, F. X. (trapper), 35
Maupin, Howard (rancher), 97, 99
Maupin (town), 5, 99
Mazama Indians, 117
Meacham, Alfred B. (settler), 43, 138
Meacham, Harvey (settler), 138
Meacham (station), 138
Meander land, created by French's irrigation project, 153
Meares, John (naval capt.), 11, 13, 14–15

Medford (city), 5, 72, 85
Medicine. *See* Remedies and cures, folk
Medicine Rock, 12
Meek, Joe (trapper), 35–36
Meek, Steven (guide), 97, 146
Memaloose Island, 9, 18, 100
Mendenhall, Manerva, notebooks on folk medicine, 132–33
Meriwether (place-name), 13
Merlin (town), 5, 71
Mermaids, Newport legend, 27–28
Meteorites, 51–52, 81, 90
Methodist missionaries, 33, 35, 117
Mexicans, 60–61, 88–89
Miller, Henry (cattle baron), 149
Miller, Hulda, story of "The Last Needle," 52
Miller, Joaquin, 3, 78
Miller, Linda Lorene (folklorist), 8, 147–48, 151, 153–54
Mills, Randall V., 18, 44. *See also* Randall V. Mills Archives of Northwest Folklore
Milton (town), 125
Milton-Freewater (town), 125
Miners and mining. *See* Gold
"Miss Mary Mack" (clapping game), 59
Missionaries, 33, 35, 117, 123–24
Missouri, pioneers from, 12
Mitchell, Richard, on fishing lore, 40
Mittendorf, Tom (folklore collector), 118–19
Miyo Iwakoshi, first Japanese settler, 37
Mochi (rice cakes), role in Japanese-Americans customs, 110
Modoc Indians, 5, 43, 95, 138
Modrell, Rusty, "Oregon Folks" performance, 7
Money, Beaver Money, 4, 55
Monmouth (city), 52–53
Monmouth University, 52
Monroe (town), 36, 37
Monster legends, 9, 12, 38, 127, 142–43; on origins of the tribes, 137
Moonshine, 63, 130. *See also* Whiskey
Moore, Theresa (folklore collector), 15
Moorhouse, Lee (major), 139
Mormon Bason (settlement), 124
Morris, A. F. (railroader), 78
Morrow County, 5, 99, 108–9, 134–35
Morton, Lornel Tweedy (editor), 138
Mosier, J. H. (settler), 113
Mosier (town), 113–14
Mosier Inn, 113
Mosquitoes, size on Hart Mountain, 155
Mt. Adams, 105
Mt. Angel, 37
Mt. Defiance, 100
Mt. Hood, 5, 97, 105, 116
Mt. Hood Highway, 63
Mt. Hood Railroad, 6
Mt. Jefferson, ix, 95
Mt. Mazama, 18; creation of Crater Lake, 95, 103
Mt. Multnomah, 117
Mt. Scott, 29
Mt. St. Helens, 105
Mt. Thielsen, 72
Mt. Vernon (town), 99
Mountain sheep, 99
Mountaineers, jargon, 116–17
Mountains, 5. *See also* individual mountains and ranges
Mucking Contest, Sumpter Valley Days Celebration, 140
Mules, Hathaway Jones stories about, 80–81

Mulino, Jim (settler), 130
Mullin, Susan, "Oregon's Huckleberry Finn," 48
Multnomah County, 37, 41; Portland, 5, 6, 36, 57–60
Multnomah Falls, 6, 37
Multnomah Indians, 104–5
Multnomah River, 97
Munra, Katherine L. "Grandma" (restaurant proprietor), 138
Murder Creek, 37
Murderer's Creek, 99
Murders, 4, 98
Music: Czech tradition, 113. *See also* Songs
Mutton Mountains, 99
Myrick, Timothy, memorialization in "Springfield Mountain," 41–42
Myrtle Creek (city), 77, 87
Myrtle Point (city), 25
Myrtle (California laurel) trees, 25, 87

N

Napoleon, former name for Kerby, 71, 84
Nash, Jack, source for card game story, 134
Nash, Tom (folklore collector), 40, 74, 77
Native Americans (Indians), ix, 4, 53, 138; attacks on settlers, 36, 39; Baker City location as "safe ground" for, 126; in Central Oregon, 95, 97, 99; Chinese as competition for mine laborer jobs, 124; on the Coast, 11, 22, 31; Crater Lake as mystery for, 103; cultural validity of legends, 163; The Dalles important for, 104; etiological legends. *See* Etiological legends; folk remedies, 17, 46; Forbidden Ground at Gold Hill, 81, 82; the horse acquired by, 128, 136; indifference to Christian missionaries, 33, 35; and Murilla Greenstreet Hobson, 67; myth-time, 9; and the Neahkahnie Treasure legend, 22, 23–24; as place-name source. *See* Place-names; in Southeastern Oregon, 145–46; on the *Tomonos* rock, 51–52; Warm Springs Reservation, 120–21; wives and children of trappers as, 33. *See also* Chinook Jargon; Coyote legends; individual tribes
Natural bridge, Bridge of the Gods as, 104
Naughty Girl Meadow, alternate name for Whorehouse Meadow, 162
Navigational blunders, Coast sites commemorating, 13
Neahkahnie Mountain, 11, 23. *See also* Neahkahnie Treasure legend
Neahkahnie Treasure legend, 22, 23–24
Ne-ahk-stow, Indian name for Hammond, 21
Ne-co-tat, Indian name for Seaside, 30
Nehalem Indians, 11, 22, 23–24
Nehalem River, 12
Nehalem Valley, 17
Neotsu (Devil's Lake), 12, 13
Neskowin (town), 5, 26
Netarts Spit, 13
New Albany, former name of Albany, 37
Newman, Ethan (postmaster), 23
Newport (city), 5, 12, 26–28
Nez Perce Indians, 117–18, 124, 136–37, 142–43; legend on origin of tribe, 137, 163
Ng, Wendy (folklore collector), 109–10
Nichols, Jim, source for Riddle Hotel information, 91

Nicknames: African-American attitude toward, 59; for Oregon, 3
Nissei (second-generation Japanese Americans), 8, 109–10
No Shirt (Walla Walla chief), 139
Nofog (town), 37
Norman, Jack, source for Shedd information, 65
North Canyonville, original name for Canyonville, 77
North Sister Mountain, 117
Northeastern Oregon, ix, 8, 9, 122–43, *map* 122; geography and history, 122–25; local place-names and folklore, 124–43
Northern spotted owl. *See* Spotted owl
Northwest Passage, 11
Norway (town), 13
Norwood, Will (storyteller), 61
Noti (town), 53–54, 163, 164
Nurse, George (settler), 111

O

O. R. and N. Railroad, 124, 138
Oakridge (city), 54–55
Oberg, John (Methodist minister), 83–84
O'Brien, John (settler), 87
O'Brien (town), 87–88
Ochoco (town), 146
Ochoco Creek, 146
Ochoco Mountains, 5, 123
O'Dell, Michael (folklore collector), 26–27, 29
Oestreich, Melissa (folklore collector), 126–27
Ogden, Peter Skene (mountain man), 95
Ol' Paul, The Mighty Logger (Tunney), 107
Olallie Butte, 18
Old Believers, ix, 9, 68
Old Maid's Canyon, 125
Old Man, The, in ''Three Sisters'' legend, 117–18
''Old Mr. Fox'' (song), 89–90
''Old One Hundred'' (hymn), as melody for ''Springfield Mountain,'' 41
Old Oregon Trail. *See* Oregon Trail
''Old S'' (Snake River Highway), 134
Old women (chuck wagon or trail cooks), 147–48, 149–50, 161
Olex (town), 100
Oliver, Ed (homesteader), 153
Olson, Victor (storyteller), 30
Olympic Committee, U.S., Monmouth's application to, 52–53
On (ascribed family obligation), for Japanese Americans, 110
Oregano (marjoram), as Oregon name source, 3
Oregon Caves, 77–78
Oregon City, 5, 36, 55–56
Oregon Coast, ix, 10–32, *map* 10; geography and history, 10–13; local place-names and folklore, 12–32. *See also* Southern Oregon
Oregon Desert, The (Long), 106
Oregon Farmer, The, pantry cures, 113
Oregon Folklore (Jones), 110
''Oregon Folks'' (song), 7
Oregon Geographic Names (McArthur), x, 19, 41, 60. *See also* McArthur, Lewis A.
''Oregon Girls'' (song), 39
Oregon Iron and Steel Company, 51–52
Oregon Oddities, 36, 107–8
Oregon Shakespeare Festival, 74–75
Oregon State Archives, 61
Oregon State Library, 61
Oregon Territory, 11, 12, 35, 64; legislature, 4; relations with State of Jefferson, 73

Oregon Trail, 9, 33, 64–65, 123, 126, 138; ''Goldilocks'' story, 87; Meek's ''shortcut'' south of, 97; migration from Missouri over, 97; young girl's grave marker, 5
Oregon Trunk Railway, 102
Oregon Vortex, 81–82
Oregon's Ghosts and Monsters (Helm), 38
Orient (town), 37
Orjun River (China), as Oregon name source, 3
Ortega, Primo. *See* Tebo
Oswego, former name of Lake Oswego, 51
Ott, original name of Myrtle Point, 25
Otter Crest (town), 28
Outsiders, 9; Indian legends told to, 120–21; insiders' jokes about, 103, 126–27, 158; for Russian Old Believers, 68
Oviatt, Frank (postmaster), 100
Owl(s): role in ''Siletz Whistleman'' legend, 31; spotted owls, 9, 72, 77; symbolism of feathers, 129
''Owl Man'' legend, from Siletz, 30–31, 163
Ox breakers, 61
Ox-driven wagons, 61

P

P brand, used by the P Ranch, 153
P Ranch (Pete French's ranch), 147–48, 151, 152–53
Pacific Coast. *See* Oregon Coast
Pacific Fur Company, 15
Packwood, William (settler), 139
Page, Sarah (postmaster), 26
Paisley (town), 5, 125, 160–61
Paiute Indians, 120, 145–46
Paradise (town), 125
Parker, Mrs. and Mrs. Charles (settlers), 100
Parrent, William ''Tip'' (settler), 127
Parson, Miss Frankie, proposal for Contention name change, 100
Pass of the Siskiyou, 18
Pasties, recipe for, 133–34
Patton, Shirley (actress), 75
Paul Bunyan Comes West (Stevens), 107
Paul Bunyan stories, as ''fakelore'' and folklore, 107–8
Paulina, Chief (Teanamad), 95, 97, 99
Paulina (town), 98, 99
Pelota (jai alai), as Basque tradition, 9, 155, 156
Pencil sharper, invention, 37
Pendleton, George Hunt (politician), 138
Pendleton (city), 138–39
Pendleton Roundup, 139
Perrington, Elmer (merchant), 151
''Pesky Servant, The'' (song), 42
Pettinger, Sadie, Hathaway Jones recollections, 79
Pettygrove, Francis (settler), 57
Phantom Ship, eruption in surface of Crater Lake, 103
Phillips, Bonnie and Roy (folklore collectors), 67
Phillips, Cheryl Lynn (folklore collector), 32
Phoenix (city), 88–89; *la llorona* stories gathered in, 8, 88–89
Picnics, at ice caves, 105–6
Pierce, Walter M. (gov.), 109
Pig farming, outsider/insider joke about, 9, 103
Pilot Rock (city), 5
Pine (town), 134
Pine Valley, 134

Pinedale Asembly Center, Hood River Japanese Americans at, 109
Pioneers/settlers, ix, 4, 9, 25; in Northeastern Oregon, 123–25; on the Oregon Coast, 12, 14–15; in Southeastern Oregon, 146–47; in Southern Oregon, 71–73; in the Willamette Valley, 33, 34–36; women's drudgery, 46–47, 163–64. *See also* individual counties
Pistol River, 89–90
Pitney, Clarence A. (settler), 50
Place-names, ix-x
_____ in Central Oregon, 98–119
_____ on the Coast, 12–32
_____ Native American sources, 3, 37, 53, 100; on the Coast, 12, 13, 18–19, 22, 23, 26, 30, 31, 32
_____ in Northeastern Oregon, 124–43
_____ in Southeastern Oregon, 145, 146, 148–62
_____ in Southern Oregon, 71–72, 74–93
_____ in the Willamette Valley, 36–69
Pleasant Hill (town), 56–57
Poker Creek, former name for Auburn, 123
Poker game(s), 123, 134, 148
Poker Jim (horseman), 139
Poker Jim Ridge, 148
Polk, James K., 36
Polk County, 36, 52–53, 60–61
Pond, Amos (Walla Walla representative), 139
Poorman's Creek, 85–86
Port, Lee (ranger), 86
Port Orford (city), 71, 72, 73, 90–91
Porter (prospector), P brand, 153
Portland (city), 5, 6, 36, 57–60
Portland Beavers (baseball team), 8
''Portland Hunter'' story, 126–27
Potatoes, grown by Czechs, 113
Potter, John (miner), 123
Powder River, 123, 139
Powell, Joab (preacher), 4, 64
Powell, John (miner), 141
Prayers: role in exorcism of the ''evil eye,'' 60–61; at the state legislature, 4, 64
Pregnancy, folk beliefs on, 45, 47, 53, 67, 82, 156
Price, Sarah, ''The Housewife's Lament,'' 46–47, 164
Princeton (town), 161
Prine, Barney (settler), 97
Prineville (city), 97
Prohibition, effect on Erickson's Bar, 58
Promise (town), 125
Property tax legislation, 61
Proposal Rock legend, 26
Prospect (town), as part of State of Jefferson, 72
Prostitutes, 58–59, 130, 140, 162
Proverbs: Basque, 156; of Reub Long, 106
Providence Church, in Scio, 64
Provisional government, 35–36
Psychic events, Gold Hill known for, 81–83
Public Accomodations law of 1953, 59
Pudding River (Riviere au Boudain), 37
Puncheon floors, 13–14
Putnam, Rex (educator), experience in Redmond, 114

Q

Quick Sand River, original name for Sandy River, 63
Quilling, on Native American clothing, 136

R

Raccoon, in Umatilla tale, 137–38
Rail Creek Ranch, 101
Railroads and railroad workers, 50, 91, 93, 99, 124, 138; Great Rail Race, 100, 101–2; jargon, 102
Rain, 58–59, 83, 95; role in Willamette Valley folklore, 39–40, 43, 45; song about, 24–25; sparsity in Southeastern Oregon, 145
Rajnus, Ellen, source for Czech recipes, 8, 113
Ralston, Jeremiah (pioneer), 52
Rametes, Fern (La Pine resident), source for foodways, 112
Ranchers. *See* Cattle and cattle ranching; Sheep and sheep ranching
Randall V. Mills Archives of Northwest Folklore, x, 8
"Rattlesnake Mountain" (song), 42–43
Rattlesnakes, 148, 151–52, 160; bites, 42–43, 132
Rattray family (ranchers), legend about, 106–7
Rave, Emilie Hulda Wilhelmina (Hartwhich) (pioneer), recipe, 63
Rawlins, Billy (Sumpter saloonkeeper), 124
"Realfoot" legends, 85
Recipes. *See* Foodways
Red Ledge Mine, 130
Redding, Calif., 73
Redmond, Mr. and Mrs. Frank (educators), 114
Redmond (city), 98, 114–16
Reed, Alfred W. (settler), 28
Reedsport (city), 28–29
Regional identity, 8–9; defined, ix
Religion, 39, 64, 83–84, Bethelite commune, 38–39; Hispanic mix of Catholic and folk rituals, 60–61; missionaries, 33, 35, 117, 123–24
Remedies and cures, folk, 8, 16–17, 132–33, 161, 162; Central Oregon, 110–12, 113; Willamette Valley, 45, 53–54
Renfro, Al (storyteller), 8, 25, 76–77, 92–93
Resort community, Sunriver, 118
Richmond (town), 100
Rickreall (town), 60–61
Riddle, Claude A., on venison barbecues in Riddle, 91
Riddle, William H. (settler), 91
Riddle (city), 91
Riddle Hotel, gambling in, 91
Rifles, *kalarup* guns, 49
Rituals: among the Spanish-speaking, 60–61; of the Russian Old Believers, 68
Riviere au Boudain (Pudding River), 37
Riviere aux Coquins, 71. *See also* Rogue River
Road hog, toll charge for, 50
Roaring Springs Ranch, 147
Robbins, Abner (merchant), 151
Roberts Air Field, smokejumpers, 114–15
Robinson, J. T. (Wonder merchant), 71
Robison, Old John (trail boss), 147
"Rocky Mountain Boys" (aging trappers), 33
"Rodent State, The" (Oregon nickname), 3
Rodeos, 139, 158
Rogue River (and city), 5, 71, 72, 92
Rogue (Rogue River) Indians, 36, 71, 72
"Rollin', Rollin', Cross the Bar" (song), 19
"Roll On, Columbia" (Guthrie), 41
Ronde Landing, original name for Irrigon, 134
Roosevelt, Teddy, 139
Roosevelt Military Highway, 12
Rose, Aaron (tavernkeeper), 92

Roseburg (Roseburgh) (city), 8, 71, 77, 92–93; as part of State of Jefferson, 72, 73
Rowley, Dick (guide and caretaker at the Oregon Caves), 78
Rube's Ridge (landmark), 119
Rubio, Beatrice (folklore collector), 128–29
Rum, "lum" or "lumtum" as Chinook Jargon for, 18, 37, 99
Russian Old Believers, ix, 9, 68

S

Sacajawea, 12
Sagebrush, 145, 153
Sagebrush Belt, Steens vegetation belt, 147
Saginaw (town), 61
Sahale (Great Spirit), role in the Bridge of the Gods legend, 104–5
Sailors. *See* Seamen
Sailor's Diggings, 71, 87–88, 93
Sailor's Diggings Beer, 87
Salem (city), 8, 36, 37, 61–63
Salish (Flathead) Indians, 30, 31, 137
Salmon, 21, 31–32
Saloons, 58, 124, 150, 160–61
Salt: Lewis and Clark's cairn, 5, 12, 30; price, 72, 88
Salt Springs, original name for Belknap Springs, 101
Samples, Joe (Halfway-area resident), 134
Sam's Sporting Goods Store, in Medford, 85
San Francisco Xavier (ship), 11. *See also* Neahkahnie Treasure legend
Sandals, sagebrush, found in cave near Fort Rock, 105
Sandy (city), 63–64
Sandy River, 63
Sanns, Randall (brewer), 87
Sansei (third-generation Japanese Americans), 109–10
Santiam Pass (landmark), 116–17
Santiam Wagon Road, early automobile at toll station, 50
Sasquatch, 9, 100
Sassafras tea, 53
Satan's Backbone (chamber of the Oregon Caves), 77
Sauerkraut, as staple and tonic, 16, 17
Sausage, made by Czechs, 113
Scantigrease, original name for Springfield, 65
Scapegoats, Chinese used as, 139–40
Scaredman Creek, 72
Schilling, Bruce (logger), Bruces Bones Creek named for, 13
Schwartz, Jack (lecturer), 81
Scio (town), 64–65
Scofield, Twilo (folklorist), 49–50, 137–38; foodways collected by, 8, 62; songs collected by, 14, 39
Scots, in Northeastern Oregon, 125–26
Scott, Levi (settler), 29
Scott, T. F. (preacher), 123
Scottsburg (town), 5, 29–30
Sea Gull (ship), 90
Seafood: fishing and harvesting, 32; Native American recipes, 22, 31, 91
Seamen: folk beliefs, 28–29; as gold miners, 87; jargon, 20; shanghaiing, 17; theatre customs influenced by, 74. *See also* Fishermen and fishing
Seaside (city), 30; Lewis and Clark's salt cairn, 5, 12, 30
Seaton, original name for Mapleton, 24

Secession
_____ from Oregon, Southern Oregon's efforts: prestatehood, 73; 1940s, 73–74
_____ from the U.S., support for during Civil War era, 36
Separation Creek, 117
Settlers. *See* Pioneers/settlers
Shakespeare Festival, at Ashland, 74–75
Shaman, "Siletz Whistleman" legend concerning, 31
Shedd, Frank (farmer and builder), 65
Shedd (town), 65
Sheep and sheep ranching, 145, 155; conflict with cattle ranchers, 98, 99, 110; customs and beliefs, 110–11; shearing, 130
Sheepherders: Men Alone (Mathers), 110
Shellfish. *See* Seafood
Sherman, Margot, source for domestic folk beliefs, 47–48
Sherman, William Tecumseh, 100
Sherman County, 95, 99, 100
Shipwrecks, 11, 13, 22, 26
Shirttail Gulch, 125
Shoshone Indians, 3
Shumate, Joan Cadwell, source for domestic folk beliefs, 47–48
Side hill gougers, 155
Signs, almanac, in folk beliefs, 45
Siletz (city), 30–31
Siletz Indians, 5, 19, 28; "Whistleman" legend, 30–31, 163
Silica (station), 99
Silver Lake (and town), 98, 161
Silver mining, 131
Simms, Walter "Honest Hank" (miner), 130–32
Sioux Indians, 39
Siskiyou Mountains, 18, 85
Sisters (town), 100, 117–18
Siuslaw River, 8, 24
Six-Bit House, at Wolf Creek, 93
Sixes River, 90
Skinner, Eugene F. and Mary Cook (settlers), 46
Skinner's Mudhole, early name for Eugene, 46
Skinnerville, early name for Eugene, 46
Skirving, Sandy (folklorist), 26
Skookum John and Sally (Noti Native Americans), 53
Skookumhouse Butte, 18
Skookums (evil spirits), 12, 100, 103–4, 127
Skull Hollow, creation of, 97
Slab Creek, early name of Neskowin, 26
Slavery issue, 36
Slip-Go-Down (dessert), 31
Smallpox, effect on Native Americans, 36, 128
Smith, C. B. (settler), 161
Smith, E. O. (doctor), 37
Smith, Fern M., source for Oregon foodways, 62
Smith, Karin (folklorist), 47–48, 60, 125–26
Smith, Mary Ann (settler), 4
Smith, Norm (state legislator), 61
Smith, Pat (searcher for the Neahkahnie Treasure), 24
Smith, Virgil (journalist), 23–24
Smokejumpers, 114–16
Snake Indians, 95, 125, 136, 145–46
Snake River, 146
Snake River Highway ("Old S"), 134
Snakes, folklore about, 41–43, 68, 151–52. *See also* Rattlesnakes
Snoose-burner, 69

Snout Creek, name source, 13
Snow, 101, 133, 140
Soap, recipe for, 112
Songs: "Alsea Girls," 13–14; "Beulah Land" parodies, 39–40, 101, 105; "The Frozen Logger" and "The Logger's Sweetheart," 65–66; "The Girl with the Striped Stockings," 58–59; "The Housewife's Lament," 46–47; hymns, 39, 41; "Judge Martin Duffy," 139–40; "The Logtown Rose," 86–87; "Old Mr. Fox," 89–90; "Oregon Folks," 7; "Rollin', Rollin', Cross the Bar," 19; "Roll On, Columbia," 41; "Springfield Mountain" and variants, 41–43; "The Strawberry Roan," 119–20; "Wake Up, It's Rainin'," 24–25
Sonny (town), 100
Sourdough, 147–48, 150, 157
Southeastern Oregon, ix, 8, 9, *map* 144; geography and history, 144–48; local place-names and folklore, 148–62. *See also* Southern Oregon
Southern Oregon, ix, *map* 70; geography and history, 71–74; local place-names and folklore, 71–72, 74–94. *See also* Oregon Coast; Southeastern Oregon
Southern Oregon State College, State of Jefferson Folklore Archives, x, 8
Southern Pacific Railroad, 91, 93
Space travel, and Gold Hill, 81, 82
Spangler, Ida, cures used by, 111–12
Spanish (language): buckaroo jargon source, 159–60; place-name source, 23
Spanish Charlie Basin, 164
Spanish explorers, 3, 11, 23
Spanish-speaking people (Hispanics), 8–9, 60–61, 88–89, 148
Sparta (town), 124, 139–40
Splintercat Creek, 37
Spotted owl, 9, 72, 77
Springfield (city), 33, 36, 65–66
"Springfield Mountain" (song), variants, 41–43
"Squeeze box" accordion, "Old Mr. Fox" accompanied by, 89–90
Stafford, Kim, "Wake Up, It's Raining," 24–25
Stage shows: at Erickson's Bar, 58; at Rawlins's saloon, 124
Stannard (state legislator), 61
Starvation Creek, 109
State of Jefferson, ix, 72, 73–74
State of Jefferson Folklore Archives, x, 8
"State with a Heart, The" (Oregon nickname), 3
Statehood, Oregon, Southern Oregon objections to, 72–73
Steel, William Gladstone (judge), ix–x, 3, 103
Steelheads (steelies), catching, 8
Steel Points, "Place Names" edition, ix–x
Steens Mountain, 5, 146–47, 148
Steirwald family (ranchers), legend about, 106–7
Stenger, Peter (settler), 149
Stephens, James B. (settler), 55
Stevens, Isaac Ingalls (Washington Territory gov.), 15
Stevens, James (author), 65–66, 107
Stevens, Tom (gambler), 150–51
Stevenson, Chester (author), 158
Sties (styes), folk cures for, 17, 111
Stingerville, possible name for Burns, 149
Stinkingwater Pass, 146

Stitz, Mrs., story of location of the Blue Bucket Mine, 157–58
Stokes, former name for Irrigon, 134
Stratification, social, in town of Gilchrist, 107
Strawberry Festival, in Lebanon, 52
Strawberry Range, 123
"Strawberry Roan, The" (song), 119–20
Striped stockings, as professional badge, 58–59
Strudl, Czech recipe for, 113
Stumbo, Harry (logger), 75
Stumptown, early name for Portland, 57
Styes (sties), folk cures for, 17, 111
Sublimity (city), 67
Sublimity College, 67
Sucker Lake, early name for Lake Oswego, 51
Sumpter (town), 8, 123, 124, 140–41
Sumpter Valley Days Celebration, 140
Sundown laws, 36
Sunriver (planned resort community), 118–19
"Sunset State, The" (Oregon nickname), 3
Suplee (town), 119–20
Swamp Land Act, 153
Sweathouse (sweat lodge) stories, 117–18, 120–21, 137
Swedes, 8, 47–48, 54
Sweet Home (city), 67–68
Swiss, 37, 44
Swisshome (town), 37
Switzerland of America, Wallowa Mountains known as, 142
Sylvia (fish story), 40–41

T

Table Rock, south of Gold Hill, 81
Tabler, Mamie (Foster resident), recipes, 62
Tabler, Wayne (folklore collector), 42
Tackett, Harry (folklore collector), 40–41, 143
Tahmahnawis (Bridge of the Gods), ix, 104–5
Taih (Upper Deschutes) Indians, 95
Tailholt, original name for city of Rogue River, 92
Takelma Indians, Takilma named for, 93
Takilma (town), 87, 93
Talapus (trickster-god). *See* Coyote legends
Talapus Butte, 100
Tall Tales from the Rogue River: The Yarns of Hathaway Jones (Beckham), 79
Tammany Hall (Antelope city hall), 97
"Tarheads," nickname for transplanted Californians, 124
Taylor, Sally Blisset (Seaside resident), 30
Taylor, Zachary, 4
Teanamad (Chief Paulina), 95, 97, 99
Tebo (Primo Ortega) (storyteller), 40, 151, 153–54
Tekilma Indians, 81
Telford, Harry (buckaroo), 8, 147–48, 151, 153–54, 160–61, 162
Temperance Creek, 125
Ten O'Clock Church, 37
Tenino Indians, 95, 120
Terrebone (town), 100
"Thanatopsis" (Bryant), use of Oregon name, 3
Theatre: folk beliefs and customs, 74–75; Oregon Shakespeare Festival, 74–75
The Dalles (city), 9, 97, 100, 104–5
"Them." *See* Outsiders
Thief Valley, 125
Third son, role in folktales, 76–77
Thirty-two Point Creek, 1257

Thomas, Edward Harper, *Chinook: A History and Dictionary*, 18
Thomas, Eleazar (preacher), 43
Thompson, Arthur (author), 23
Thompson, J. G. "Whispering" (mule skinner), 138
Three Sisters Mountains, 95, 107, 116, 117–18
Thunderers (Klamath deities), Lemish Butte named for, 100
Tichenor, Sarah Ellen, Ellensburg named for, 79
Tichenor, William (explorer), 72, 79
Tichenor's Humbug (Humbug Mountain), 72
Ticking spider legend, 48
Tillamook (city), 12, 31–32
Tillamook Bay, 31
Tillamook County, 5, 12, 16, 22, 23–24, 26; Idiot Creek, 13, 164
"Timber beasts," 49–50, 65
Timber communities, 61, 65, 75–76, 107. *See also* Loggers and logging
Tlat-skani, source of Clatskanie, 17
TNT Creek, 37
Tobacco, chewing, town of Top named for brand of, 125
Toelken, Barre (folklorist), 8, 9, 14, 19, 128
Toemannah ("Whistleman") legend, 30–31, 163
Toketee Falls, 18
Toll station, and early automobile, 50
Tom Dick and Harry Mountain, 37
Tommyknockers, legends of, 44, 140–41
Tomonos rock (Willamette Meteorite), legend of, 51–52
Top (town), 125
Tot Mountain (The Uncle), 117
Tourist, legend about "Huck Finn" and, 49
Trade center, The Dalles as for Native Americans in precontact period, 104
Trade language, Chinook Jargon used as, 17–18
Tradeable commodities, use instead of money, 55
Trail (chuck wagon) cooks (old women), 147–48, 149–50, 161
Treasure legends, 37, 88; in Coast region, 12, 22, 23–24. *See also* Blue Bucket Mine
Trelawney of the Wells (Pinero), 74
Trevitt, Vic (settler), buried on Memaloose Island, 100
Trickster-god. *See* Coyote legends
Truck-stop story, 84–85
Tualatin Plains, 33
Tubal (grandson of Noah), tale of the Basque language and, 155–56
Tule Lake region, Bohemian Czech settlers in, 113
Tunney, Virginia, *Ol' Paul, The Mighty Logger*, 107
Tupper, Alva (sheep thief), 98
Turner, Mary (actress), 74
Twickenham, suggested name for Contention, 100
Tygh Indians, 95

U

Uhlman, John (La Pine dairy owner), 112
"Ultimate Test, The" (loggers' joke), 16
Umapine (Cayuse chief), 139
Umatilla County, 125–26, 132–33, 138–39, 146; Elephant Rock, 28, 127; Native American reservation, 128–29
Umatilla Indians, 120, 128–29, 137–38

Umatilla River, Cayuse legend of Elephant Rock, 127
Umpqua River, 29, 72, 76, 92
Uncle, The (Tot Mountain), 117
Undermining the Great Depression (film), 83
Underworld, spirits of (Native American), role in creation of Crater Lake, 103–4
Union (city), 141
Union County, 123, 125, 137–38, 141
Union Creek (town), 71
Union Pacific Railroad, 101–2
United Brethren Church, Sublimity College, 67
Unity (town), 141–42
University of Oregon, 36; Randall V. Mills Archives of Northwest Folklore, x, 8
Upper Deschutes (Taih) Indians, 95
Upper McKenzie Valley, snow in, 101
Upper Town, original name for John Day City, 128, 135
Urban folk belief tales, "Man with the Hook" as example, 15, 53
"Us." *See* Insiders
Utopia (town), 125

V

Vale (city), 146, 161–62
Valen, John (miner), 88
"Valentine State, The" (Oregon nickname), 3
Vancouver, George (explorer), 11, 90
Vandevert, Claude (Bend resident), on first train into Bend, 102
Vaqueros. See Buckaroos
Variation (folklore process), 9
_____ examples: fish as pet or friend, 40–41, 153; in folk songs, 39–40, 41–43, 101, 105; "Man with the Hook," 19, 53; Nealıkahnie Treasure legend, 22, 23–24
Vegetation belts, on Steens Mountain, 147
Venator Canyon, 145
Venereal disease, medicine for, 162
Venison barbecue, at Riddle, 91, 163
Vernon, Buffalo (buckaroo), 139
Vincent, Joe (actor), 74
Virtue Flat (town), 125
Vitamin C, sauerkraut as source, 16, 17
Volcanoes, 105–6, 117, 155
Voltage (way station), 148

W

Wake Butte, 18
"Wake Up, It's Raining" (song), 24–25
Walapi Indians, 95, 97
Waldo (town), 71, 72, 87
Walker, Charlene (folklore collector), 48–49
Walla Walla Indians, 95, 128–29, 139, 146
Wallowa County, 41, 125, 136–37, 142–43
Wallowa Lake, 142–43; monster, 9, 142–43
Wallowa Mountains, 123, 124, 130, 142, 145
Walter, LaDessa, Fort Rock parody on "Beulah Land," 105
Wampus (forest demon), 100
Wampus (town), 100
Warabe (Bracken ferns), 110
Warm Springs, original name for Bingham Springs, 127

Warm Springs Indians, 95
Warm Springs Native American Territory, 120–21
Warner Mountain, former name of Hart Mountain, 154
Warts, folk cures for, 45, 47, 68, 112, 126
Wasco County, 4, 5, 99, 113–14; The Dalles, 9, 97, 100, 104–5
Wasco Indians, 5, 95, 120
Wascopam (trading post), early name for The Dalles, 104
Washington County, 37
Wasil family, source for Basque proverbs, 156
Wasson, George, source for "Old Mr. Fox," 89
Watts, Alex (Civil War–era Republican), 71
Weather, 95, 146, 148; folk beliefs about, 45, 47; snow, 101, 133, 140. *See also* Rain
Weberg, Bill (rancher), 119
"Webfoot Land" (song), 39–40
"Webfooters" (nickname), ix, 73, 124
Weddings: Chinese customs, 135–36; Russian Old Believers traditions, 68; Scottish folk beliefs, 125–26; showers, 45
"Weeping woman" ("Llorona") stories, 8, 60, 88–89
Wegelin, Tina (folklore collector), 61
West, Oswald (gov.), 114, 130
Westby, Betty (journalist), 38
Western Archers (bow-hunting group), 158
Western Folklore, "Llorona" legends published in, 89
Western Oregon State College, 52, 53
Wharf region of Portland, 57
Wheeler County, 100, 146
Whimple, Adam (murderer), 4
Whiskey, 38–39, 124, 140, 143; "lum" or "lumtum" as Chinook Jargon for, 18, 37, 99; moonshine, 63, 130
Whiskey Creek(s), 37; Grant County, 128; Tillamook County, 13; Wallowa County, 143
Whiskey Gulch, 128
"Whistle punk," in loggers' jargon, 69, 163
"Whistleman" (*Toemannah*) legend, 30–31
Whistling backstage, injunction against, 74
White Bird Creek, 136
Whitehorse Ranch, 147, 148
Whitman mission, Indian attack on, 36
Whorehouse Meadow, 162
Wife, The (mountain), 117
Wilder, Laura (Elmira farm wife), recollections, 46, 54, 67
Wildlife refuges, 147, 154–55
Willamette, original name for Oregon City, 55
Willamette Meteorite (*Tomonos* rock), legend of, 51–52
Willamette River, 5, 33, 36, 37; Coast Fork, 43; 1860s flood, 57
Willamette University, 35
Willamette Valley, ix, 9, 33–69, *map* 34; geography and history, 33–37, 97; local place-names and folklore, 36–69
Williams, Gladys (Medford resident), source for Logtown Rose material, 86
Willow Creek, Heppner flood, 108–9
Willow Creek (town), original name for Madras, 100

Wilson, Constance (rancher), 148
Wilson, Fred (judge), 114
Wilson, Mardi (folklore collector), 151–52, 159–60
Wilson, William A., "Folklore and History," 163
Wind, 90–91, 148, 161
"Windies," told by Hathaway Jones, 79–81
Windstorms, in the High Desert, 98
Windy (deserted outpost), 145
Wingville (town), 125, 141
Winnemucca, Sarah (Paiute princess), 145–46
Winnemucca, Nev., 146
Winship brothers (unsuccessful settlers), 4
Winslow, Walker (miner), 130–32
Winthrop, Wash., smokejumpers from, 115
Wirfs, Ralph, version of "Alsea Girls" collected from, 14
Wishram (town), Great Rail Race to Bend from, 101–2
Witches, 45–46, 60
Wives, advertisements for, 46
Wizard Island, eruption in surface of Crater Lake, 103
Wizzensnifters, 141–42
Wolf, in Coyote story, 121
Wolf Creek (town), 93–94
Wolf Creek Tavern, 6, 93
Wolf in the tail (cattle ailment), 162
Wolf meetings, 35
Wonder (town), 71
Wood, Mrs. John C., source for "Last Needle" story, 52
Woodall, Woody (Sumpter resident), 140
Woodburn (town), 68
Wool stompin', 130
Woolley, Betty Ann (folklore collector), 43
World War II, 15–16, 109
Woronitz, Henry (actor), 74
WPA Federal Writers Project, x
Wright, Ben (Indian agent), 71
Wright, Milton (educator), 67
Wright, Ruth, verse added to "Webfoot Land," 39–40
Wyam (Lower Deschutes) Indians, 95

Y

Yakima Indian Reservation, 146
Yakima Indians, joke on cattle ranchers, 134–35
Yakonan Indians, 13, 32
Yaquina Bay (town), 32
Yaquina Bay Indians, 32
Yellow Logtown Rose, 86–87
Yoncalla (town), 69
York (slave), 15
Young, Cal (settler), 53
Young, Ewing (settler), 35
Young, Fred (Sumpter resident), 140
Yreka (town), 73
Yulalona (Link) River, 111

Z

Zucchini, stories about, 9, 43
Z-X Ranch, 160